£27.99

The Origins of Globalization

Routledge International Studies in Business History

SERIES EDITORS: RAY STOKES AND MATTHIAS KIPPING

The Origins of Globalization

By Karl Moore and David Lewis

Routledge
Taylor & Francis Group
New York   London

First published 2009
by Routledge
270 Madison Ave, New York, NY 10016

Simultaneously published in the UK
by Routledge
2 Park Square, Milton Park, Abingdon, Oxon OX14 4RN

Reprinted in 2009

Routledge is an imprint of the Taylor & Francis Group, an informa business

Typeset in Sabon by IBT Global.
Printed and bound in the United States of America on acid-free paper by IBT Global.

Library of Congress Cataloging in Publication Data
Moore, Karl, 1955–
    The origins of globalization / by Karl Moore and David Lewis.
        p. cm. — (Routledge international studies in business history)
    Includes bibliographical references and index.
    1. Globalization—History. 2. Economic history. 3. Capitalism—History.
    4. Commerce—History I. Lewis, David, 1949- II. Title.
HF1359.M668 2009
337—dc22
                                2008039672

ISBN10: 0-415-77720-8 (hbk)
ISBN10: 0-415-80598-8 (pbk)
ISBN10: 0-203-88097-8 (ebk)

ISBN13: 978-0-415-77720-9 (hbk)
ISBN13: 978-0-415-80598-8 (pbk)
ISBN13: 978-0-203-88097-5 (ebk)

Contents

Acknowledgments

We would like to thank the many scholars in both management and history whose comments and insights have helped greatly improve our thinking. Special thanks go to Karl's colleagues at McGill, particularly: Henry Mintzberg, Nancy Adler, Kristen Oliver, Karen Borden, and Antonia Maioni. A very special thanks goes to our Style Editor and very good friend and colleague, Los Angeles journalist Neil Earle. As an award-winning writer, author and adjunct history professor, he not only smoothed out the flow of the book to make it more readable but his many many textual additions coming from his own reservoir of knowledge made the text more enjoyable and relevant. This book is also his in part. At Karl's other academic home, the Said Business School at Oxford, we are grateful for the help and insights of Alan Rugman, Richard Whittington, and Colin Mayer.

We owe much also to those scholars who hosted Karl during discussions at Dartmouth College, All Souls in Oxford, the Judge Institute at Cambridge University, LBS, IMD, The University of Tokyo, Keio University, the University of Southern California, Warwick University, Erasmus University, ENPC in Paris, HEC Paris and HEC Montreal, Claremont College, the University of British Columbia, Queen's University, and University College, London. Production of this book has been a long process and testing our concepts with audiences at such outstanding universities has been extraordinary helpful.

Other noteworthy individuals along the way who helped inform our analysis include John Dunning of Reading University, Peter Buckley at Leeds University, George Yip Dean at RSM, John Stopford and Julian Birkinshaw at LBS, Robin Osborne in Greek History at Cambridge, Vijay Govindarajan and Richard D'Aveni at Tuck School of Business, Dartmouth University, Geoffrey Jones in business history at Harvard, and Bruce Mazlish in history at MIT. Although we are appreciative of this learned collaboration, we are responsible for our conclusions and interpretations.

Preface

Our first book in this series, *Birth of the Multinational* (1999), received the expected mix of critical reactions for so sweeping a subject. International business scholars were, in general, quite favorable. The *Journal of International Business Studies*—the leading international business journal—and the *Journal of Economic Literature*[1] were supportive. Among professional historians, however, the reaction was more critical.[2] Dr. Hans Georg Niemeyer of the University of Hamburg wrote in the *Journal of World History*:

> [T]he reviewer is convinced that the book is quite interesting reading. The authors, K. Moore, a successful university teacher with twelve years of practical experience in marketing management, and D. Lewis, a historian with special interest in the development of the idea of a United Europe, obviously themselves were fascinated by and even enthusiastic about their subject. To some degree, they succeed in conveying to their reader this positive approach to a subject matter that is nonetheless more intricate than its treatment tries to make believe. This book stimulates debate about an issue that is indeed worthwhile. The reviewer, who confined his remarks to the field where he feels best competent, may be taken as a witness of this stimulus.[3]

The present volume is a complete update of *Birth of the Multinational*, rewritten with these fair criticisms in view. In general, two key criticisms of our first edition needed to be met. The first charge was that we missed including some relevant literature; the second was that we tended to overstate our case at times. We thank our critics for their appraisal, and also draw encouragement from Mira Wilkins in the *Journal of Economic Literature* and David Ricks in the *Journal of International Business Studies*. This edition strives to adjust our arguments accordingly.

The subject of "primitivism" needs addressing at the outset. This is the idea that the economic experiences of ancient societies have very limited and narrow applications for today's highly technological situation. Primitivism remains the primary model for understanding the ancient world. It originated with the writings of Karl Polanyi (1886–1964). Polanyi, a post-Marxist of the socialist camp, challenged the extreme free market economics of the so-called Austrian School of Ludwig von Mises. Von Mises asserted that the open, competitive market was the natural order of society. Polanyi took the other tack and insisted that markets, as we know them, were unknown in antiquity. By the middle of the twentieth century, most scholars felt Polanyi was wrong. Evidence for workable markets dependent upon complicated market forces exist as far back as ancient Sumer around 3500 BC.

We have concluded that mixed economies have been a constant across history even allowing for wide variations in their actual operation. This could be called the "adjusted Polanyi" view. We maintain that there is clear evidence that ancient Egypt, Minoan Crete, and China, for example, incorporated state-run palace economies along with flourishing local markets. China later developed a system of family entrepreneurs, and the early Greeks opted for free-booting entrepreneurship with some degree of government regulation. Assyria, Babylon, Phoenicia, and Carthage all throve on the "crown corporation" model while making allowances for energetic private traders. The diversified Roman economy, meanwhile, encouraged a mix of entrepreneurship, large private partnerships and some state-sponsored firms. Outlining this thesis is our brief in the pages that follow.

Some of our readers will be familiar with and subscribe to the updated argument for primitivism set down by Sir Moses Finley in the 1970s and 1980s. Finley, a Marxist and pupil of Polanyi, recognized that business enterprise and markets did exist in antiquity. He insisted, however, that any parallels between ancient and modern business were a fabrication. The ancient world was just too different, he argued, from the modern system of expansive turbo-charged capitalism. Finley argued, quite cogently, that rapid innovations after the year 1800—large-scale industrialism, calculations of risk, burgeoning investment strategies, accelerated economic growth along with a systematized, scientific approach to management—these all rendered parallels with the ancient world invalid. Thus, he taught that "what is impossible is a return to the past, in any form: the cult of the past is an abuse of the past."[4]

In recent years, a new generation of scholars is attempting to modify the primitivist approach. The authors tend to be of that school. While admitting the soundness of many of Finley's researches, we contend that he underestimated those features of ancient economic life that did point to significant degrees of economic diversity and noteworthy leaps forward in technical progress which progress reverberated back on economic life. We set out to show this more fully in this revised edition. It must be admitted at the outset that we emphatically did not find evidence of an embryonic IBM in the sands of Mesopotamia nor the fully-fledged hyper-connected economy we see today. Pharaoh Tutankhamen was not Bill Gates, nor was the Assyrian Empire a precursor of the World Trade Organization. Today's world is starkly and dramatically different in many features. The embryonic strands of globalization that this book studies omit Australia and the Americas, for example, regions catalytic to the modern phenomenon of what is called globalization. No doubt, even the "hemispheric" incipiently globalized economy of the Roman Empire, as we have chosen to call it in Chapter 7, was quantitatively and qualitatively different from today.

Yet, even conceding the above, this very concept of what is meant by globalization cries out for definition. We need to step back and try to define the term. As has become apparent in recent years, this is more difficult than might appear at first blush, hence some of the competing definitions appear in bold type.

QUESTIONS OF DEFINITION

Some see globalization solely in economic and business terms. Harvard Business School's Rosabeth Moss Kanter has written, "The world is becoming a global shopping mall in which ideas and products are available everywhere at the same time."[5] Author and *New York Times* columnist, Thomas Friedman, the most well-known exponent of globalization, is a cheerleader. "The driving idea behind globalization is free-market capitalism—the more you let market forces rule and the more you open your economy to free trade and competition," says Friedman, "the more efficient and flourishing your economy will be." He adds: "Globalization means the spread of free-market capitalism to virtually every country in the world. Globalization also has its own set of economic rules—rules that revolve around opening, deregulating, and privatizing your economy. Unlike the Cold War system, globalization has its own dominant culture, which is why it tends to be homogenizing.[6] Alan Rugman and Richard Hodgetts, in a widely used International Business textbook, define globalization as, "The production and distribution of products and services of a homogeneous type and quality on a worldwide basis."[7] Michael Bordo, a Rutgers Economics professor, sees it as "the increasingly close international integration of markets for goods, services and factors of production, labor and capital."[8]

Yet another school of scholars and experts stress the social side of globalization—the dynamic interactions between societies and individuals. Lord Anthony Giddens, former Director of the London School of Economics, argues that "Globalization can . . . be defined as the intensification of worldwide social relations which link distant localities in such a way that local happenings are shaped by events occurring many miles away and vice versa."[9] Roland Robertson of The University of Aberdeen takes a more phenomenological and psycho-social approach: "Globalization does not simply refer to the objective process of increasing interconnectedness. It also refers to conscious and subjective matters, namely the scope and density of the consciousness of the world as a single place."[10]

Globalization's critics are just as cogent in their dissent. Martin Khor is the Director of the Third World Network (TWN) and editor of its monthly publication Third World Resurgence. The Third World Network (TWN) is an independent non-profit international network of organizations and individuals involved in issues relating to development, globalization, and the Third World. His definition is a challenging one: "Globalization is what we in the Third World have for several centuries called colonization." Ay, there's the rub. Many see what Thomas Friedman sees as a completely new phenomenon as the same old struggle of the haves and the have-nots, only with a technological veneer.

Jan Aart Scholte, Professor in Politics and International Studies at England's Warwick University and Co-Director of the ESRC/Warwick Centre for the Study of Globalisation and Regionalisation, sets forth, text-book like, at least five broad definitions. Here is "globalization" as found in a survey of the literature:

- **Globalization as internationalization.** Here globalization is viewed "as simply another adjective to describe cross-border relations between countries." It describes the growth in international exchange and interdependence. With growing flows of trade and capital investment, there is the possibility of moving beyond an international economy (where the primary entities are national economies) to a "stronger" version—the globalized economy. In this scenario, "distinct national economies are subsumed and rearticulated into the system by international processes and transactions."
- **Globalization as liberalization.** This broader view sees globalization as "a process of removing government-imposed restrictions on movements between countries in order to create an 'open,' 'borderless' world economy." Those who have argued, with some success, for the abolition of regulatory trade barriers and capital controls sometimes clothe their rhetoric in the mantle of "globalization."
- **Globalization as universalization.** In this use, "global" is used in the sense of being "worldwide" with globalization viewed as "the process of spreading various objects and experiences to people at all corners of the earth." A classic example of this would be the spread of computational technology, wide-access television, etc. As we hope to show, there are many resonances here with the Hellenistic Era of the ancient economy.
- **Globalization as westernization or modernization** (especially in its Americanized form). Here globalization is understood as a dynamic, "whereby the social structures of modernity (capitalism, rationalism, industrialism, bureaucratism, etc.) are spread the world over with the concomitant destruction of pre-existent cultures and local self-determination in the process." This is the dark side of the picture.
- **Globalization as deterritorialization** (or as the spread of supra-territoriality). Here globalization entails a "reconfiguration of geography,

so that social space is no longer wholly mapped in terms of territorial places, territorial distances and territorial borders."[11] By this measurement, the globalization agenda is a truly revolutionary occurrence, one worth close study and evaluation.

No matter how defined, globalization is one of the dominant themes of our times, ranking with global warming, the rise of terrorism, the exporting of democracy and the "clash of civilizations" thesis as keys to understanding the present world system.

Thomas Freidman, in *The Lexus and the Olive Tree*, was convinced: "Globalization is not a phenomenon. It is not just some passing trend. Today it is the overarching international system shaping the domestic politics and foreign relations of virtually every country, and we need to understand it as such."[12] We will give our overall synopsis of this judgment in Chapter 9.

SURFACE OR CORE?

For purposes of illustration, let's start with an apple. In this analogy, the forces of globalization, as its proponents would have it, would reach toward the center of the core. Today's average Western European often slips into comfortable jeans stitched in China or Thailand under an American brand name, sips coffee from Peru, and frequents Sushi bars while gyrating to American-based music. Meanwhile, Americans salute flags made in China and drive Camrys and Subarus that run on gas and oil from Alberta and Saudi Arabia. It is an incendiary issue of our times: manufacturing and, ever more increasingly, service jobs in Europe and North America are being outsourced to China and India.[13]

The ancient world was, admittedly, very very different. In Julius Caesar's day, any gestures toward globalization on today's scale were tentative and incipient. It was more like the analogy of an apple, using the skin and the core as paradigms. In the Rome of Caesar and Augustus, the fruits and experience of hemispheric trade were primarily enjoyed by the wealthy classes. The newly prospering patricians and absentee landowners were the affluent consumers of luxury silks from China passing through Iran. Rome's lower classes had little contact with peddlers from Arabia and Spain. Even Rome's military servicemen, sailors, and merchants tended to be the exceptions. While the world was Rome and Rome was the world in the imperial heyday, Britain and the Middle East were viewed as important but troublesome resource suppliers, if not backwaters. North Africa—the granary of the empire—was where the action was!

Still, history records that the Emperor Tiberius (17–38 AD) had to impose trading controls on the sale of silk in the capital city. Too much gold was leaving the imperial vaults. This matter of trade balances and foreign indebtedness has a very up-to-date ring to it, even in the age of globalization. Here is one reason for a closer analysis of the trading networks in Roman and pre-Roman times, which are a major theme of this book. The similarities are there, and they may repay careful study. Even the Bible, a very ancient source indeed, enters the picture. The seer John of Ephesus, in the book of Revelation, Chapter 18, envisioned a voracious and virtually all-embracing world economy expedited by "sea captains, ships and sailors" bringing "cargoes of gold, silver, precious stones . . . wood, bronze, iron and marble . . . cinnamon and spice, cattle and sheep, horses and carriages." Here is poetic evidence for the first hints of intensively documented realities—a world accustomed to resource seeking and market development, surprisingly wide-ranging contacts (think of the "Silk Road" from China to India to Rome), commercial extension southward into Africa, the breadbasket of the Empire, and even northward into the northern and western parts of Europe (the tin mines in Cornwall). As shown more fully in the following, the ancient world developed a surprisingly large number of Small and Medium Size Enterprises (SMEs),[14] which operated on a truly international scale.

Indeed, it is remarkable the extent to which ancient economies had perfected vast, intricate systems whereby production and distribution activities were located in foreign lands replete with multi-cultural workforces, tariff-reduction zones, interregional taxation issues (the "publicans and sinners" of the Gospels), avoidance of currency risk strategies and other phenomena that we consider part of our every day globalized economy.[15] Smaller enterprises to be sure, but small is not only beautiful; it appears to have tremendous staying power. The European Web site says, "Micro, small and medium-sized enterprises represent 99% of all enterprises in the EU and provide around 65 million jobs and contribute to entrepreneurship and innovation." In the ancient world, they would represent almost 100% of all business organizations but the story of their success as precedents for what today's globalizers see about them is a remarkable one indeed. We claim that this foundational motif represents part of the triumph of ancient business. The links are not tenuous, not at all.

Our strategy in this account is to begin with the most important concepts of international business theory. We realize the difficulty of using the term "international" in a world where the nation–state, as such, did not exist, but its application throughout will simplify our presentation significantly. Chapter 1 investigates the methodological tools now available for assessing the nature of evidence from the ancient world. Scholars of international business can, without great harm, skip the later section of the chapter which will, however, greatly interest the more historically minded. Once again, the French concept of *"la longue duree"* will be of value in leavening the argument. The late U.S. President Harry S. Truman was reported to have said, "There is nothing new except the history you haven't read yet." In this spirit we proceed.

1 Modern Theory and Ancient Practice
Is Globalization New?

"History is bunk!"

This forceful dictum, usually attributed to the automobile magnate Henry Ford, can be usefully set alongside President Abraham Lincoln's more elegant, "Fellow citizens, we cannot escape history!"

The authors of this volume, one of us a management professor the other a professional historian, unstintingly give the palm to Lincoln. We do so fully aware that since about 1980, a host of academics, management experts, and corporate executives have proclaimed the coming of a new and unprecedented economic age: that of a borderless global economy based upon information, instead of production.[1] Skilful theorists and big-picture thinkers have sketched out the ligaments of a world economy dominated by giant multinational enterprises working in tandem with networks of more nimble, smaller firms. Most of those who study this global onrush of capitalist techniques linked with evolving telecommunication systems are convinced that this is something new under the sun. The claim is made that today's economy is *altogether* new. The argument is advanced that history offers few lessons, few parallels to guide us in the age of the mobile phone and the Internet, when products and commodities change hands at the flick of a cursor. In this view, Henry Ford was right.

This book argues the contrary. From our discrete but related disciplines, we resist the notion, even in these helter-skelter times, of what historian Eric Hobsbawm referred to as a "permanent present lacking any organic relation to the public past."[2] Despite the admittedly vast differences in scale, technology, and complexity between ancient and modern business, we assert the opposite. As Winston Churchill told an interviewer upon revisiting Niagara Falls after a thirty-year interlude, "The principles remain the same." We advance the proposition that, to a surprising degree, quite a few of today's business forms and business cultures existed in ancient times. Globalization, multinational enterprises, commercial partnerships, foreign joint ventures, and embryonic forms of mass production all had their precursors or prototypes in the very remote past.

While we see the need to proceed with caution, it is not a quixotic venture to apply modern business models in a way that sheds light on trading practices extant in the ancient world, and vice versa. There are enormous payoffs in this kind of analysis. There are those today who agree with former U.S. President Bill Clinton (1993–2001) and his sometime colleague Allan Greenspan,[3] that, with the virtual collapse of Communism, the Anglo-American brand of regulated capitalism has "won," and that the rest of the world must inevitably move toward this model. The long-term history of ancient economies and recent events suggests this view is rather naïve, tending towards a hubris that might unconsciously excuse the worst features of globalization (the "why" of the book). Nemesis follows hubris. A survey of ancient business practices seems to demonstrate that not only are there a variety of ways to run a large-scale economy, but that there exists a full menu of options to measure the success of such systems.[4] We conclude that history shows that one size did not fit all, then or now. A healthy diversity was the rule, and not the exception.

Our thesis has significance for those presently enjoying the benefits of today's globalized networks, this world-historic development that cannot be measured in isolation from issues of culture, diplomacy, environmentalism, societal strains, and a tendency towards conflict. Back in 1993, James Fallows of *Atlantic* magazine addressed fears extant among American planners that Japan and East Asia were moving further and further away from the Anglo-American model of *laissez faire* capitalism. Fallows wrote before present near-hysteria in some quarters over China's emerging and controversial presence in the world economy, a rise tied to 12-hour work days, overcrowded work environments, runaway pollution, and fast turnarounds. China's dynamic surge, it is feared in some quarters, could eventually derail the world's economic locomotive, the United States. An overview of the world's economy's ancient roots can offer a steadying perspective on some of these trends. So the authors hope and believe. Indeed, one firm result of our research is to confirm that, almost as far back as we can go, the world economy has been a study in a rich and teeming mulitiplicity.

SAFE FOR DIVERSITY?

This book is a call for today's globalizers to "make the world safe for diversity." In fact, that is the present reality. Silicon Valley may still be the most productive place in the world for high tech innovations, but are Sony and Phillips all that far behind? Nations, say the Thomas Friedmans, are much less relevant today, but don't tell that to President Hugo Chavez of Venezuela, who appears successful not following the pure capitalist model. Or the present rulers of Russia, who seem to have adopted the "Frank Sinatra" model of development—"I'll do it my way!" Good old-fashioned nationalism may begin like Sleeping Beauty and end up looking the Bride of Frankenstein, but nations still have strategic roles to play, as the Burmese junta's reluctance to slip aid into Myanmar showed the world in May, 2008. The federal government of Canada's recent funding of almost $1 billion over five years for aerospace reemphasizes the point.

Although global gets the most press, it is *regionalism* that has seen the greatest growth these last twenty years. The European Community is a case in point, and it is often overlooked that the world's richest common market involves the flow of goods between Canada and the United States every day. Nations still matter, and borders matter even more—ask Mexican immigration officers or Canadian trade delegates worried about Congressional protectionists in the United States.

Trend-lines and glossy stock market graphics are well and good, but as the President of a South American country explained a few years back, "The economy of Chile is doing well; the people of Chile are not." Arguably, one size does not fit all. America's system of regulated capitalism is notorious for periodic dislocations and distortions, expansions and contractions, recessions and depressions, or what Ohio farmers colorfully label "the hog cycle." Globalization sometimes appears to some analysts as nothing but turbo-charged capitalism run amok. A quick scan of our Table of Contents shows how variegated has been even the world's experience with capitalist models—from temple capitalism in Egypt to maritime capitalism in Phoenicia to Roman family capitalism in the world's largest empire till that time.

In short, a historical perspective is invaluable in showing how multifaceted are the incarnations of the economic imperative. "The present," Richard White of the Organization of American Historians recently argued, "contains only a limited range of what human beings have done and can do." The river of history may flow and cut different channels, but it has an uncanny tendency to flow back upon itself. This book, the third in a series, attempts to stimulate reappraisals from both the global economy's cheerleaders and critics. Few have attempted such a macro-historical view of international business. We begin with the origins of economic activity in the cottages, temples, and city states of Sumer around 3500 BCE, and crest with the surprisingly far-flung trading networks of the Roman Caesars. Along the way, we investigate an Egyptian economy that bore some distinct resemblances to modern state socialism before lingering over Assyrian and Phoenician models that appear to foreshadow today's proto-multinationals, the first economies to adopt cross-border strategies. We then catch a glimpse of the Greeks attempting what can almost be called the first entrepreneurial culture. We examine the cross-cultural networks of ancient Persia bringing India and China into its orbit as a vital precursor to the Romans, whose merchants and traders created substantive cross-border conglomerates. The merchants of India becoming Eurasia's middlemen are well worth a glance, as are ancient Chinese thinkers debating the merits of state capitalism while rooting the nation in family-based initiatives at the urging of their own version of Adam Smith.

We noticed that one of the lacks in the literature on globalization was what the French call *la longe duree*. In *Empire: The Rise and Demise of the British World Order and the Lessons for Global Power,* Niall Ferguson makes the claim that the British Empire's legacy of racism and xenophobia was also matched by a sense of "the triumph of capitalism as the optimal form of economic organization," a process Ferguson labels "Anglobalization."[5] The British in their heyday thought that they, too, were unique. Indeed there is much "incipient globalization" in the British experience with empire. Thus, *la longue duree* can be a healthy corrective, as well as offering insight into how such key economic players as India and China functioned anciently. In this context, we should note that much good work has been done on the history and development of multinational corporations in modern times and their precursors in the Middle Ages.[6] Economists have tended to leave the field to historians when they probe economic activity in the ancient world.[7] Inspired by Professor John Dunning, we set out to test the fascinating proposition that multinational enterprises, or MNEs, have had their roots in ancient times. As Dunning once wrote:

> [E]arlier examples of embryonic MNEs can, most surely, be found in the colonizing activities of the Phoenicians and the Romans, and before that, in the more ancient civilizations.... *However, this sort of history...remains to be written.* (emphasis added)[8]

The questions that need addressing include: When did the first embryonic proto-multinationals arise? What about other forms of state and private enterprise and the development of what could be called business cultures? To answer these questions, we both brought our distinct private perspectives to bear. One of us has contributed to international business theory,[9] the other is a well-published historian.[10] This interdisciplinary approach gave us a useful starting place from which to analyze ancient economies through the lens of modern international business and management theory.

COMPETING VISIONS

Our major methodological tool in applying modern business theory to ancient business structures was the *Eclectic Paradigm* model provided by John Dunning. With this as a guide, we proposed that Ancient Assyria afforded the first example of functioning proto-multinationals. Later, we offer evidence that the Phoenicians applied a similar model to their own intercontinental enterprises, one that foreshadowed, in many ways, the rise of "the merchants of Venice" and the *keiretsu* networks (groups of businesses teamed with specific funding partners) of contemporary Japan. The Greeks, on the other hand, preferred a more "arm's length" approach in dealing with their customers. "Barbarians" was their preferred term for non-Hellenes even as they sparked the first free-market revolution after 800 BC. In Carthage, and later in Rome, as we shall see, more highly structured and far-reaching mercantile operations would survive and expand, sending traders deep into Africa and Asia. With Chinese silk reaching the Rome of Tiberius Caesar, diversity was, indeed, the order of the day.

In examining ancient Assyrian and other businesses through the prism of Dunning and his colleagues in modern management research, we have tried to exercise caution. We understand the strength of the case made by historians who share Karl Polanyi's view that the economic systems of antiquity were incomparably different from those of today, and that the sources we use to examine them are few and antique. Polanyi, a socialist, denied the existence of markets in Ancient Egypt and Mesopotamia, for example. He seemed to imply that ancient economic systems were static and conservative, that they did not change or evolve. However, in the one decade of the 1960s, the world's fund of knowledge doubled and it is now doubling every eighteen months. It was now possible to show, from abundant research, that comparable markets did exist and that ancient economic systems rose, adapted, evolved and broke new trails for men and women in the relentless pursuit of trade. Laws of supply and demand operated then as now. Human beings were animated by the pursuit of luxury items and pharmaceuticals, then as now.

Two examples suffice to make the overall point. The Greek geographer Eratosthenes (276–194 BCE) calculated the circumference of the earth to an amazingly accurate degree, showing that even then there was a sense of a world outside the daily haggling in the *agora*. The frescoes and paintings that adorn the ruins of Pompeii show fashionable Roman matrons enjoying clothing and hair styles that are echoed along Rodeo Drive today. Perfumes and cosmetics have long been an economic lure across history, as Shakespeare knew describing Cleopatra's fleet ready to charm the stern Romans:

> "Purple the sails, and so perfumed that
> The winds were love-sick with them."

Luxury items have been a lure across history. Their pursuit has enlivened the acquisitive urge that fired the dreams of Antony and Cleopatra, as well as the sea dogs of the first Elizabeth (1558–1603). Some things do not change.

We hope to demonstrate in this volume that modern models can be applied indirectly to help us understand the economic life of the ancient world. Applying this understanding can, in turn, be used to predict, and hopefully avoid, some of the excesses that globalization has already brought in its wake. More accurate and reliable models from the ancient past are useful, if not life-saving. Planners and policymakers able to deal from a position of precedents, home truths, and sober morals deal more with steadying facts, rather than guesswork. They can enlarge the field of background data to draw upon in today's corporate boardrooms. We are convinced: The similarities do exist; the parallels are there. What we do with them is up to us.[11]

Karl Polanyi, himself, was engaged for most of his life in an ongoing debate with the Austrian-born Ludwig von Mises (1881–1973). Mises, patron saint of modern libertarians, saw raw individualism and unfettered markets as the natural order of society. Governments or despots who interfered with the price mechanism of supply and demand were in violation of natural economic law. Thus, in this scenario, President Andrew Jackson killed the Bank of the United States and left his successor to inherit the recession. Ronald Reagan left deficits so big that his successor was forced to fatally (for him) raise taxes. Polanyi, in his efforts to challenge the libertarians, made the argument that socialism was the natural order of things. While he somewhat overargued his case, Polanyi nevertheless demonstrated along the way that all economies are mixed economies, an argument we will see demonstrated in this book. Archaeologist Barry Kemp echoed Polanyi and made this challenging statement:

> At the level of individual states the modern world contains no examples, nor has it ever, of an economic system based fully on market forces. Even for those politicians who desire it, it remains an unattainable goal.[12]

As we show in the following, ancient Egypt developed an effective state- and temple-run economy, as did Mesopotamia. Indeed, economies in these early millennia of recorded history, were, in general, very much run from the top down, but with some notable exceptions, making the case for diversity. It is not for nothing that the heavy, top-down Egyptian pyramid or Iraqi ziggurat came to symbolize these societies. Still, as we shall see, more-or-less free markets operated quite extensively on a local level almost in the shadow of the temple-state. Mesopotamia, in particular, launched an increasingly bold mixed-state enterprise (using the term "state" rather broadly) whereby private merchants were given substantial freedom to pursue profits. Archaic and Classical Greece and Rome perfected economies that encouraged entrepreneurship, but their extension and prosperity, as we document, were often tied to government contracts. Chapter 8 shows how the Indian sub-continent mixed both public and private sectors, while ancient China blended state monopolies and family businesses. In all this, one factor remained constant:

> "All macroeconomic systems represent a balance, a compromise, an uneasy truce between two forces: the urge of the state to provide itself with a secure base for its own existence and plans, and the fragmented pressure of private demand."[13]

The evidence seems clear: There has always been more than one way to do business. Management cultures were as diverse in antiquity as they are now.

Before turning the clock back to antiquity, we must clarify two important topics. First, we will explain the *Eclectic Paradigm*, Dunning's basic theory of how and why enterprises become multinationals. Then, we will present a needed overview of the discoveries in the field of archaeology of the last two hundred years, especially of the nineteenth century. It is this ongoing knowledge explosion—doubling now every eighteen months—that has provided the documentation for economic historians to research and write on ancient business economies with confidence and comprehension.

THE ECLECTIC PARADIGM

John Dunning is a leading authority on multinational enterprises and international business studies.[14] Based upon more than three decades of study, Dunning has created a model to explain how international business operates. This model, known as the *Eclectic Paradigm*, will serve as an important guideline to bring ancient business trends and practices into clearer focus.[15] This allows us to establish our thesis that much of we call "globalization" hearkens back to much earlier examples.

The *Eclectic Paradigm* outlines the advantages a firm might gain over its competition by going multinational. If a firm can gain enough of these advantages, it will tend to become an MNE. If not, the company will either trade at home or trade abroad without any permanent foreign establishment in place. Let's elaborate that principle. To understand the stakes involved in becoming a multinational, one must first understand the precise definition of an MNE. The standard definition is offered by the Organization for Economic Cooperation and Development (OECD) and the United Nations Center for Transnational Corporations (UNCTC). Both the OECD and UNCTC define a multinational as "an enterprise that engages in foreign direct investment (FDI) and owns or controls value-adding activities in more than one country".[16] *Foreign direct investment* refers to investment in resources, money, people, or time in other countries. This usually takes the form of setting up a *permanent business establishment* outside the firm's home borders. For example, Microsoft can engage in FDI by setting up an office in Britain or a factory in Ireland; Toyota by opening a plant in Brazil.

Today's MNEs also engage in *value-adding activities* outside their home countries. These are activities that increase the value of an item. The Microsoft plant in Ireland will turn disks into software; the Toyota plant will assemble cars, not just sell finished cars. Branches of MNEs may also act as distributors, such as Wal-Mart or Tesco, or provide product services, such as a Xerox service representative repairing copiers in Helsinki. As we will argue, these permanent foreign establishments and value-adding activities are a feature of antiquity though the terminology sometimes serves to cloak that fact.

Usually, an MNE will have top management in one country, while operating and managing permanent establishments in other countries. These "foreign" offshoots will produce, distribute or assemble finished goods and services in those countries. Money, personnel, and goods typically flow back and forth between offices under the same management. This is known as *internalization.*

There are obvious advantages to companies when the *Eclectic Paradigm* works smoothly. Three major advantages accruing to a multinational are *ownership, locational,* and *internalization advantages.* Let's discuss each in turn.

Ownership or *firm-specific* advantages are known as strategic competencies. These are the capabilities and assets that give a firm its competitive advantage and allow it to succeed in the marketplace.[17] Examples of *ownership* advantages include branding and managerial expertise, all of which brings discipline to a slow-moving industry segment. For example, there is Southwestern's dominant position in the low-cost carrier sector of the airline industry, Microsoft's economies of scale and scope, Intel's knowledge of semiconductor manufacturing, Benetton's subcontracting relationships combined with a powerful brand name, Apple's ability to combine technologies, and 3M's innovative capabilities.

There are a wide diversity of potential advantages that come into play when discussing strategic competencies. The most obvious include factors spinning off from the firm's size. The size of a company's footprint greatly affects the ability to maximize economies of scale or product diversification. Others might include the management of organizational expertise; highly recognizable brands (following "O.K.," "Coca Cola" is the second most well-known phrase in the world); the ability to acquire and upgrade resources, labor, or mature small-scale intensive technologies; product differentiation; marketing economies; and access to domestic markets. Then there are the grand intangibles, what an American President called "the vision thing"—the ability to foresee and take advantage of foreign production and marketing opportunities, as well as the ready availability of capital and financial expertise. Factor in also the security of access to natural resources, and the all-important flexibility to adapt to structural changes.[18]

As firms grow, they seek ever new ways to profit from their obvious, or sometimes not so obvious, built-in advantages, such as Canada's Bombardier, Inc. going from being solely a snow-mobile maker to being the largest train maker and third largest plane marker in the world based on their experience in manufacturing and their ability to cheaply buy up troubled manufacturing businesses and turn them around.[19] There is a dynamic process at work. Firms normally expand in their home countries, turning to foreign markets only when opportunities at home are exhausted or have become considerably less attractive.[20] Wal-Mart, for example, is the world's second largest firm by revenue, with over 1.8 million employees worldwide.[21] However, its most important customer base, by far, is its United States-based home market. Thus, it wasn't until some 40 years after its founding that Wal-Mart opened its first foreign operations, and even then to neighboring Mexico in 1991. Today, the increasingly competitive nature of the global economy is accelerating the expansion of firms outside their home countries. They hope that "over there," competition will be less intense while simultaneously reaping the advantage of positioning their people to glean more information about foreign competitors. This, in turn, allows the MNE to defend its turf more effectively in the all-important home market. As Chapter 5 shows, this is a tactic as old as the Phoenicians. Wal-Mart, for all its strength in its home market of the United States, has had problems duplicating its success overseas.[22] Success is often much more risky when a firm leaves its home market!

There are reasons for higher risk out of country. For one, multinationals investing in a foreign country may be at a disadvantage vis-à-vis native competitors more familiar with local culture, industry structure, and government regulations. Japanese letters and icons were an enormous challenge for U.S. computer giants, as one example. The multinational must also surmount its competitor's existing networks with close-at-hand, long-term customers, suppliers, regulators, and other key players. This is one reason Wal-Mart's entry into Japan is proceeding very slowly. Wal-Mart is learning that it takes time to navigate the very different approaches to retailing in Japan vis-a-vis the United States.[23] This means that factors of *ownership* or *firm-specific* advantages ought to be a *sine qua non* if a firm is to venture into foreign markets. The question will always be: Can it beat the native competition?

Locational or *country-specific* advantages have been popularized by Harvard's Michael Porter in *The Competitive Advantage of Nations*.[24] Porter studies the advantages a firm might gain from operating in a particular country. This includes American and Canadian firms moving activities to Mexico to take advantage of low wages[25] or German firms investing in the Czech Republic for the same reason. The beat goes on. Today there are French and Swedish businesses investing in the United Kingdom and Ireland where taxes are lower;[26] Japanese firms attracted to China and Thailand's lower labor costs; and European, Canadian, and Asian firms moving their research and development labs to California's Silicon Valley and, increasingly, to China and Bangalore.[27]

IMPERFECTIONS AND INTERNALIZATION

This raises another key issue in the search for competitive advantage. Economists call it the *national factor endowments* of a given country— Canada and snowmobiles, New Zealand and dairy products, for example.

Country X's potential advantages might include: input costs, i.e., low wages and inexpensive natural resources; the level of labor productivity; the size and character of its markets; transportation costs; and physical distance between best customers and the home country. Tariff barriers, taxation structures, risk factors, attitudes to FDI, and the structure of national competition within an industry in any given country are all important factors in the mix. *Market-seeking behavior* and *resource-seeking behavior* are other potent realities. An example of the first is the many firms currently setting up ventures in China and India in hot pursuit of plus two billion potential consumers; an example of the second includes oil companies setting up drilling operations in multiple countries in order to obtain the greatest amount of petroleum possible.

Internalization advantages are gained when a firm uses its *ownership* advantages within its own hierarchy instead of dealing at arm's length in the market, signing licensing agreements, or forming strategic alliances or any of the relationships shown in Figure 1.1.

Internalization advantages seek to replace imperfect or nonexistent outside markets with internal ones.[28] Firms can be the most efficient means of production when imperfect markets exist. Imperfect markets refer to the failings of markets, that is, when Adam Smith's invisible hand doesn't quite work as economic theory suggests. The most important imperfect market for a firm is the market for information, such as research and development knowledge (both technical and marketing), managerial experience, new production techniques, production differentiation, and market knowledge.

All of these dynamic processes can be viewed as *public goods* that can be applied by any person or organization to a specific problem without

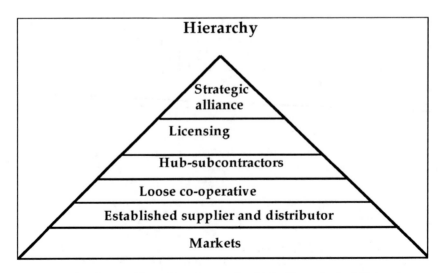

Figure 1.1 Markets to hierarchies. Source: David Faulkner, Oxford University.

destroying the ability to apply the knowledge to another use. The market cannot price a public good, so it is an imperfect market from the firm's point of view. They simply have to set the price that the traffic will allow and hope for the best. Company X may spend millions on a new technique for making computer chips, but if the technique is copied by competitors it could lose the potential to profit from the invention or even recover research costs. The firm will, therefore, use its internal market to monitor and control the use of knowledge in a way in which the wider market is unable to duplicate. The aggressive merchant princes of Carthage, whom we discuss in Chapter 5, would have understood this well. Internalizing a process sometimes ensures greater profit through control over employees, the process itself, and its use in the marketplace. The alternative is to try to sell the process in the market to outside competitors, but the problem here is *control*—what will the competitor do with the process? It might sell the process to other competitors at reduced price, benefiting the competition without earning full potential for Company X.

As Dunning's model shows, there are other examples of market imperfections that interfere with the economy's ability to self-regulate according to the pure classical model of supply and demand. Some of the most obvious are: government regulations, tax rates, local controls, tariffs, nonexistent futures markets, and missed connections between buyers' and sellers' knowledge of the value and quality of the product. (For example, many tariff barriers still exist between Canada and the United States, despite twenty-five years of free trade agreements.) All of these market imperfections distort price mechanisms and act as additional incentives for companies to use internal markets. In fact, as Dunning shows, many of these imperfections affect foreign firms more than national ones. Hence, *internalization* advantages are relevant for any firm who wants to remain competitive. They help explain why we see hierarchies in international business instead of the pure "free markets" of our commerce textbooks. The big question the Dunning model asks is: *Can we profit more in a foreign commerce by working through our own hierarchy in that country, or should we sell from our home base via foreign agents?*[29]

In this brief introduction, we have covered *FDI, MNEs, market* and *resource seeking, ownership advantages, location advantages*, and *internalization advantages*. These terms will recur in surprising ways as we study the history of international business.

UNCOVERING THE PAST OR HOW DO WE KNOW WHAT WE KNOW?

A brief overview of Dunning's prescription for modern multinationals to survive and thrive is an essential Step One. Step Two in this preliminary setting out is considering the evidence for our claim that ancient business offers lessons for today's global traders and competitors. An all-important task here is the question of *sources*: How reliable is the information we possess on economic activity in antiquity or antiquity in general?

Before 1800 AD, precise knowledge of how businesses worked and ran in the ancient world was sketchy, resting mainly on inferences from the Hebrew Bible and a few scattered classical writers. Economists such as Adam Smith (1732–1790) had begun to pinpoint the way supply and demand, division of labor, and external markets operated up to his own day—what historians call Early Modern times. The ancient Near East was known to us mainly through the lens of Greece and Rome, seedbed of our Western civilization. India was known only from a few religious texts, and China from her court historians and the tales of Marco Polo.

In the year 1800, it would have seemed a daunting task to reconstruct the gritty details of commercial life in the remote past. Where was the evidence? The once legendary cities of Assyria and Babylonia were buried under strange mysterious mounds called tells. Now and then, a Shelleyan "traveller from an antique land" would pass by them, sometimes to be told by Arab Bedouin that here was the site of a great city or the sacred mound where the Prophet Jonah preached.[30] Skepticism about ancient technologies and commercial strategies reigned. The Enlightenment was on; Europe was rising, the Near East seemingly mired in backwardness.

Yet, enough artifacts remained of the ancient world (Roman aqueducts, Greek and Persian temples) to allow the eventual decoding of its secrets once a few paradigms clicked into place. Peasants in Iraq and Egypt, out for the morning's plowing, would uncover tablets with bizarre wedge-shaped writing, unaware of what they were discovering. Enter the era of gifted amateur, the curious tinkerer, perhaps enshrined for us today in the fictional exploits of Indiana Jones. In the 1770s, one such explorer named Carsten Niebuhr, exploring the ruins of the ancient palace of King Darius at Behistun on the flat in Persian plain, made a sensational discovery. On a ledge known as the Behistun Rock, he found engraved strange characters, known as *cuneiform*, set in parallel columns alongside the more well-known Persian script. This was a sensational event in archaeology! The Behistun Rock allowed first Niebuhr and later Britain's Sir Henry Rawlinson to decipher the ancient language of Mesopotamia. By 1800, fully one-third of the cuneiform characters had been deciphered.[31] The Behistun Rock discovery was "the shot heard round the world," archaeologically speaking.

Enter Claudius James Rich, a collector of antiques and a superb linguist employed by the East India Company. Posted to Baghdad in 1808, Rich found he had more time off than he needed. He soon took an interest in local legends concerning the site of ancient Babylon. Rich visited the presumed site in 1811 and 1812, and wrote his *Memoir on the Ruins of Babylon* in 1813. This drew little attention. Next Rich began the hunt for Nineveh, once-proud capital of the Assyrian Empire. One site that drew his eye was a huge mound near present-day Mosul, just east of the

Tigris River. There sat a huge flat earthen bulge with steep sides, known locally as Kuyunjik. It was fourteen meters high, twelve kilometres long, and forty kilometres around, large enough to hide a city. The locals, however, objected to his digging there. Meanwhile, the resourceful Rich located the site of the earlier Assyrian capital of Ashur, beneath another mound named Qal'ah Shergat. Stretching along the shore of the almost ageless Euphrates River for three full kilometres, the six-meter-high walls of ancient Asshur, mixed with piles of brick and rubble, were still visible after 2,500 years.[32]

Rich, who died in 1821 trying to combat cholera in modern-day Iran, helped initiate the Romantic era in modern archaeology. Near Eastern archaeology might well have been the hobby of a few gifted eccentrics had not the spirit of the age nurtured widespread popular interest in the lands of the Bible. Victorian Britain crested along on a strong surge of Methodist and Evangelical piety, an *esprit* soon challenged by the followers of Charles Darwin and critical scholars in German universities. Leading sceptics questioned the historical accuracy of both Old and New Testaments. With this early round of culture war fiercely joined, it was natural that devout British Christians were keen to fund *and join* excavations to the Near East. The prize that glittered was the hope of confirming the literal truth of Scripture. The British Foreign Office, concerned because meddlesome Frenchmen were already penetrating the Near East, entered the fray. Official Britain underwrote archaeological expeditions as a pretext to establishing a British diplomatic presence in what is now Iraq and Iran. The *realkpolitik* behind all this was to protect the vital overland route to India and thus secure imperial trade and commerce.[33]

Following Rich's lead, the French diplomat, Paul-Emile Botta (1802–1870) also tried to dig on the site of Kuyunjik, but, lacking success, moved about twenty-three kilometres south to Khorsabad. In 1842, Botta was rewarded with the discovery of the imperial palace of Sargon II at yet another Assyrian capital, Dur-Sharrukin. Thinking he had found Nineveh, Botta published his findings in five huge volumes. "*Niniveh est retrouve*," he cabled excitedly back to Paris. He was wrong, but wrong in all the right ways. Interest in archaeology soared. Even the brilliant Englishman, Austen Henry Layard (1817–1894), made a similar mistake before ending up as Nineveh's discoverer. Using Rich's notes as a guide, Layard began digging down-river from Mosul, finding the royal palace at Nimrud, or Calah, which he also mistook for Nineveh. Here he unearthed the famous Black Obelisk of Shalmaneser III (which mentioned and depicted King Jehu of Israel) along with statues of huge winged bulls. These created a sensation back in Europe when they were shipped off to the British Museum. Between 1849 and 1851 Layard dug on the site of Kuyunjik and found ancient Nineveh at last. The ruins yielded the palace of the terrifying Sennacherib, nemesis of ancient Jerusalem. Found there were 24,000 tablets from the royal library of Ashurbanipal.

ARCHAEOLOGY'S HEROIC AGE

The heroic age of Near Eastern archaeology was launched! Sir Henry Creswicke Rawlinson was posted to Baghdad by the East India Company in 1843. By 1849, using the Persian language to decipher cuneiform documents in Babylonian and Elamite, Rawlinson had decoded those ancient scripts.[34] In the 1850s, long-buried Assyria, whose Semitic language was related to Babylonian and used the same script, was giving up her secrets. By 1855 Rawlinson had collected 15,000 clay tablets, many of which revealed a rich treasure trove of information about the religion, wars, literature, commerce, medicine, and daily life of a vanished world. Rich, Botta, Layard, and Rawlinson were almost inventing modern archaeology and, where archaeologists go, historians are never far behind.

In the meantime, Egypt, too, was coming more and more into the historical frame. The mysterious picture-writing known as hieroglyphics, found on the famous Rosetta Stone at the time of Napoleon's invasion of Egypt in 1798, was deciphered between 1818 and 1822 by the linguist Jean François Champollion. Another French scholar, Auguste Mariette, set up the first national antiquities service in the Near East. Between 1850 and his death in 1881, Mariette excavated at Memphis, Thebes, Sakkara, and other sites. The British excavator, Sir Flinders Petrie, built upon this work. Petrie was important not only for Egyptology, but for laying the foundation for the study of ancient history. Petrie came to Egypt in 1880. He was meticulous and methodical. He insisted that excavations be neat and orderly, every pot and artifact preserved and painstakingly examined. Archaeology was growing up, maturing. Petrie also discovered an archive of diplomatic letters in the city of Akhenaten on the site of El-Amarna. These letters mentioned Canaanite, Syrian, and Mesopotamian kings, along with Egyptian rulers. This allowed Petrie to begin to cross-date Egyptian history with other ancient Near Eastern empires.

This was an important breakthrough. Even today, Egyptian history is still the framework upon which the dating of antiquity is constructed, and this is crucial to our attempt to tell the story of ancient business in a fair amount of depth. A historian called Manetho, who lived in the third century BCE, compiled a history of Egypt's thirty-one dynasties. Its essential accuracy has been confirmed by the discovery of other king lists from the Egyptian monuments.

Petrie also innovated with *sequence dating*. As he dug on a site, he found that the artifacts were buried in layers. The oldest were on the bottom, the most recent on the top. Pottery and other buried objects changed with time, showing chronological development and sometimes regression. However, Petrie was confident that the seal or bracelet of an Egyptian ruler was a key to dating the other artifacts in the same strata.

Based upon Manetho, Petrie categorized Egyptian History with the framework shown in Table 1.1.

Table 1.1 Sir Flinders Petrie's Framework for Egyptian History

Predynastic	
Old Kingdom	Dynasties I–VI Unification of Egypt and Age of the Pyramid builders
First Intermediate Period	Dynasties VII–VIII Social unrest and political collapse
Middle Kingdom	Dynasties IX–XIII Revival and reunification
Second Intermediate Period	Dynasties XIV–XVII Domination by "Shepherd Kings"
New Kingdom	Dynasties XVIII–XXI Revival, world power, and decline
Persian rule and end of native Egyptian rule	

The nineteenth-century knowledge explosion continued unabated. While Petrie was digging in Egypt, Heinrich Schliemann was digging in the Aegean. Growing up in Mecklenburg, Germany, Schliemann was so intrigued by Homer's stories of Troy that he made it his lifelong quest to find both the fabled city and the graves of the Greek heroes who bought it down. Schliemann became a business man mainly to earn funds for his obsession; he taught himself both Greek and archaeology. Between 1870 and 1873, he uncovered the site of Troy near Hissarlik in northwest Turkey. Schliemann's genius idea was to read Homer very literally while many colleagues still dismissed *The Iliad* and *The Odyssey* as grand, but legendary, eyewash. Yet Schleimann found not one but *seven* Troys, an embarrassment of evidence. He then moved across the Aegean to mainland Greece, where he uncovered the shaft graves of what became known as the Mycenaean culture, ancestral to the later Greeks of Pericles and Socrates (see Chapter 6). When Petrie found Aegean pottery in Egyptian strata dating to Dynasty XII and Mycenaean pottery dating to Dynasty XVIII, he made it possible to correlate Greek history with the Egyptian. The pieces were falling in place.

INDIA AND EUROPE

The life and times of the ancient Near East were coming more and more into focus as archaeological data become fodder for historical research. Petrie's techniques were also applied from the 1880s onward in Mesopotamia and throughout the Near East as archaeological expeditions became more and more systematic and professional. The presence of a non-Semitic language on some of the tablets hinted that there had existed a whole civilization older than both Assyria and Babylonia. French archaeologist Jules

Oppert in 1869 labelled it "the *Sumerian*" after the land of Sumer, or "Shinar," mentioned in Genesis 11:2. Clay tablets being unearthed spoke in great detail of the daily life of Sumer and Akkad, including their economic transactions. In fact, much of the data uncovered spoke of contracts, bills of lading, commercial transactions—the stuff of daily life.

The Sumerians really came to life when Ernest de Sarzec began to excavate on the ancient site of Lagash between 1877 and 1900. By 1900, archaeology was becoming a full-fledged academic discipline, supported by major universities. Another 10,000 Assyrian and 69,000 Babylonian tablets were stored in the British Museum alone, rivalled only by the Louvre in Paris. By 1962, it was estimated that some 250,000 cuneiform tablets, many of them still unpublished, were stored in libraries and museums around the world.[35] American teams joined in, and began to unearth such sites as the Mesopotamian temple city of Nippur. Britain's Sir Leonard Woolley, working under the auspices of the British Museum, excavated the city of Ur in the 1920s and 1930s. Not only did he find the Royal Tombs, but he uncovered the commercial district of the most thriving business city of its time. One by one, the Sumerian cities of Eridu, Erech (Warka), Kish, and others were found. In Ur, Lagash, and Larsa, vast numbers of business records came to light.

The stream of archaeological discoveries would soon become a flood, stemmed only temporarily by two World Wars. Discoveries from 1890 to the time of World War I (1914–1918) uncovered several lost empires. Elam in southwestern Iran, the Hittite and other realms in Turkey, and the Minoan world of Crete were now established historic realities that fit into a growing, well-attested archaeological framework. In the 1920s, French archaeologists digging near Ras Shamra discovered the Canaanite Phoenicians of the biblical cities Tyre and Sidon. As we detail in the chapters that follow, post-World War II continued that trajectory with major discoveries in Ebla, Ugarit, and, more recently, in Southern Turkey.

But it was not just ancient Mesopotamia and Egypt—the lands of the Fertile Crescent—that were bursting upon the modern scene. In 1826, an alert British officer stationed at a small town in the Punjab called Harappa discovered the ruins of a vast ancient city. In the 1850s, the director of the Archaeological Survey of India, Alexander Cunningham, briefly dug on the site, looking for artefacts from the mid-first century BCE. The site was ignored for decades. Then, in the 1920s, fresh excavations began both at Harappa and some 570 kilometres to the south, on the site of Mohenjo-Daro. What the Archaeological Survey, now under John Marshall, found at both locations was a magnificent civilization much older than anything suspected in India before. These ancient cities of the Indus Valley were vast, neatly planned, and quite elaborate. Excavations by British and Indian archaeologists went on for decades, revealing a civilization of over 1,500 settlements spread out over almost 700,000 square kilometres of northern India and parts of Pakistan. It was twice the size of Egypt!

Harappan India, however, was silent, textually speaking. There were no written records except for a number of seals captioned in an unknown script. This made India unique. There were no triumphant inscriptions picturing conquest and war, and no evidence of rich elite burials. Were these first Indians peace-loving and egalitarian? The answer is still unfolding. What was clear was that the evidence from Harappa, together with the relics from Sumer and Mesopotamia, gave scholars the data to fit the Indus Valley civilization into their time frame.

One final Old World civilization needed to be recovered. In the 1920s, a Swedish expedition journeyed to the Yellow River Valley of China. There they found remains of the Yangshao Culture of the Late Stone Age. The Chinese, themselves, began to excavate the capital of their first dynasty, the Shang, at Anyang between 1928 and 1937. Politics intervened. Japan's invasion of China in 1931 and the civil war between Nationalist and Communist forces delayed further exploration, not resumed until the Peoples' Republic was established in 1949. What became clear was that Chinese civilization had developed quite separately from Mesopotamia and India, and needed independent dating from extensive court annals, radiocarbon dating, and other techniques. There were even records from Shang times carved into bone, which aided the dating process.

Finally, ancient Europe, itself, began to come into view. The Greeks and Romans of later times left behind extensive written records—Plato, Aristotle, Pliny, Cicero, Suetonius. Now what archaeologists call the material culture came into view. The presence of Greek pottery in Italy allowed archaeologists to date and examine the prehistory of the Roman Republic. Archaeologists studying Northern Europe, however, had no written records to go on. Meanwhile, Christian Thomsen of Denmark, writing in 1834, articulated a Three-Age scheme for organizing and dating ancient artifacts. History could be divided into a Stone Age, which was followed by a Bronze Age during which tools made of copper and tin became the most advanced technology. These ages he further subdivided. The latter part of the Stone Age was labelled the Chalcolithic, or Copper, Age. There was an Early Bronze Age, a Middle Bronze Age, and a Late Bronze Age. This was followed by an Iron Age in which iron tools and weapons began to spread, although never fully replacing bronze. The scheme is outlined in Table 1.2.

Table 1.2   Christian Thomsen's Three-Age Scheme of Archaeology

Historic Times of Classical Greece and Rome	
Iron Age	
Bronze Age	Late
	Middle
	Early
Stone Age	Chalcolithic (Copper)
	Neolithic (New)

In 1885, Edgar Montelius of Sweden and Paul Reinecke of Germany calibrated this overall scheme for European prehistory with the Greek and Trojan cross-dating of Schliemann. This was necessary because neither the early Celts nor the early Germanic peoples kept written records. The Late Bronze Age in Europe was called the Urnfield Culture, and the early Iron Age named the Hallstatt after a site in Austria. Later Celtic culture was called La Tène after a Swiss site. The common link was Italy. Italian arti-facts were found in the Celtic sites, and the same artifacts in Italy could be dated by Greek remains that could be tied to Egypt. Rome had a number of historians, but before Livy took to writing his *History*, the Italian boot was shrouded in darkness save for the mysterious Etruscans. Etruscan artifacts were fairly easy to find in densely populated Italy. The buried Roman city of Pompeii began to be excavated around 1800. More systematic archaeol-ogy came to Italy after 1850, as various Etruscan sites such as Populonia and Veii began to be unearthed. By the 1960s, the island of Pithekoussai and the eternal city of Rome itself were unearthed.

A WORKABLE CHRONOLOGY

The Three-Age scheme was important. It would come to be applied every-where as the alphabet of ancient history. That included Mesopotamia. Outside Egypt, however, it has proved harder to set reliable dates across antiquity. Archaeologists have found both a Sumerian and an Assyrian king list, for example. Large numbers of monarchs were listed, and even dates given, but scholars view these with caution. They strongly suspect the lists to be padded for political reasons: to establish either the great age of certain kingdoms or the legitimacy of certain rulers.

The king lists look something like the scheme in Table 1.3. However, there is a paucity of fixed dates for anything before around 900 BCE.

The year 1885 is another important date in the rise of a comprehensive ancient history, the backbone for our construction of economic life in ear-lier ages. In that year, the Tell-el-Amarna letters came to light, discovered in Egypt halfway between Memphis and Thebes. The discovery at Tell-el-Amarna contained much of the royal archives of the Pharoahs who lived about 1400 BCE. Written in Babylonian script, the Amarna Tablets once again linked the culture and economies of the Fertile Crescent. Some Kas-site and Middle Assyrian dynasties can be linked to the Dynasties XVIII and XIX of Egypt. Egyptian and Mesopotamian artifacts are often both found in Syria, source of the Amarna writings. All of this cross-referencing allowed historians to feel they had a handle on the ancient past. This was true—up to a point. Even with the help of radiocarbon dating, the further back one goes with ancient chronologies—it must be admitted—the greater the margin for error. Thus, any absolute dating scheme is heatedly debated among scholars. Early Egyptian dates are linked to a recorded observation

Table 1.3 The Dynasties of Ancient Sumer

Copper Age		Adapa and other Legendary Kings
Bronze Age	Early	Mesopotamian City–States: Dynasties I and II of Ur, Uruk, and I–II of Kish, plus Ashur, Awan, and Lagash Dominance by Empire of Ebla allied with Hamazi, then Kish II and IV Dominance by Kish, II and IV Dominance by Uruk III, then Dynasty of Akkad
	Middle	Gutian Period Sumerian Revival: Ur III, Lagash, Isin, Larsa; Old Assyrian Kingdom Dynasty I of Babylon, Mitanni
	Late	Kassite Babylonia Middle Assyria
Iron Age		Neo-Assyrian Empire Chaldean Empire

of the star Sirius; Babylonian dates to a recorded observation of a transit of the planet Venus in the reign of one Ammisaduga. This has caused scholars to champion "high," "middle," or "low" dating schemes for Egypt and Mesopotamia depending upon what date is used for an anchor point. The "middle" chronology is the most accepted in the academic world and we will generally use it in this volume, with the important caveat that lower dates are certainly possible.

The payoff in these last two centuries of digging, dating, and calibrating is that a historical chronology of the ancient past was becoming clearly established. Chronology is the backbone of history. By the early twentieth century, archaeologists from many different backgrounds were able to offer a remarkably in-depth outline of the past, based upon the sequenced dating of artefacts from Mesopotamian and Egypt (see Table 1.4).

The importance of all this can be readily summarized. In short, we know much more about the ancient world than we did at the beginning of the Industrial Revolution when such luminaries as Adam Smith, David Ricardo, and Robert Malthus pioneered modern economic theory. They proceeded without access to some important details of world history, including the elaborate supply networks along the Silk Road, the reasons for Hellenistic engineers to perfect a steam engine on the docks of Alexandria, the perfect acoustics in the large theatre at Ephesus, the advanced construction techniques that rendered virtually true the proverb that "all roads lead to Rome." Roman matrons may have appeared fully-adorned on the walls of Pompeii, but there was little understanding of the complicated trade routes that led spice merchants from China and Nubia to the heart of a trading empire that anticipated today's European Community.

Table 1.4   Sequenced Dating for the Bronze Age 3700–1200 BC

3700–3200 BC Copper Age	Predynastic Egypt, Ubaid and Uruk cultures in Sumer
3200–2100 BC Early Bronze Age	Egyptian Old Kingdom, Early Dynastic Sumer [Ur I–II, Kish I–II] followed by Ebla, Kish, Uruk III, and Akkad empires Early Harappan in India, Yangshao and Early Longshan in China [still in Stone Age]
2100–1500 BC Middle Bronze Age	Middle Kingdom in Egypt, followed by Second Intermediate Period, Neo-Sumerian revival in Ur III, Middle and Late Harappan in India, Late Longshan and Early Shang China
1500–1200 BC Late Bronze Age	Egyptian New Kingdom, Ugarit, Mycenae, Early Etruscan Villanovan in Italy, Urnfield in Northern Europe, Ganges culture in India, Late Shang China

In recent decades, knowledge acquisition has expanded exponentially. Technology, digital communications, and the institutionalization of knowledge available even on a laptop computer would have boggled the mind of Thutmosis III or Cicero. Access to such knowledge allows the possibility of the ever more accurate reconstruction of the remote past. "We cannot escape history." There are rich incentives to pursue historical analysis found even in the writings of that doyen of the economist's trade, Adam Smith himself. Chapter II in Book Three of Smith's pivotal *Wealth of Nations (1776)* begins with the state of agriculture after the fall of the Roman Empire, about where this book reaches its terminus.

This leads us to hope that the great Scotsman might, indeed, have endorsed our attempt to extend the canvas of economic history back to remote antiquity.

In this spirit, we proceed.

2 The Temple-Palace Conglomerate
Trade and Enterprise 3500–2000 BCE

PROTO-CAPITALISM AND THE DAWN OF COMMERCE

Trade. Commerce. Market specialization. Such pursuits are almost as old as humanity itself. We know that Stone Age villagers exchanged food, tools, and services with one another. Surplus of supply and the resultant bartering is a key to advancing economic activity. Human beings are creatures of needs and wants. Once Fisherman X could supply Farmer Y, the earliest economic network was born. Task specialization was encouraged by a natural process—one was a better fisherman, another, a better hunter.

Now think of some of the acronyms of our age. WTO. NAFTA. OECD. EC. HP. XML. Today's complicated tariff barriers, cross-border trade patterns, NAFTAs, WTOs, and multinational firms are phenomena of the newly globalized world. Primitive markets operated within the context of tribal communities. It was a much different world than today. Yet, tribalism itself appears far from dead. The hoary maxim "everything old is new again" tantalizes those who report on our modern "tribalized" communities going back to the writings of the University of Toronto's Marshall McLuhan who spoke, though somewhat differently, of "retribalized man." Three-time Pulitzer Prize-winner Thomas Friedman suggests that today's interconnected global economy makes the world "flat," as he puts it. This is his catch phrase for a world of intricate specialization along ever more complex social, as well as digitalized, networks. Benjamin Barber picks up on this and describes "the universal tribe of consumers defined by needs and wants that are ubiquitous, if not by nature than by the cunning of advertising."[1]

"SIX DEGREES OF KEVIN BACON"

In the 1960s, social psychologist Stanley Milgram published his pathbreaking experiments on the "small world," showing that every person in the United States could be connected to any total stranger by a remarkably short chain of "I-know-someone-who-knows-someone." The catch phrase, "six degrees of Kevin Bacon," echoes this, showing that (somewhat tongue-in-cheek) we can be related to a major celebrity by six people he and we both know. More serious research suggests that advances in transparent technology such as Google, and the Internet in general, and the nearly ubiquitous media have led to an unprecedented importance attached to the role of networks in understanding human culture.[2]

Today's networks, we are told, represent a quantum leap beyond interactions of the Late Stone Age. The accentuated geographic reach and clout thanks to communications technology and the rise of global virtualism cuts across kinship groups, villages, companies and even nations. The office-speak that said "Mary, get me Tokyo" has been largely replaced by text-messaging, laptops, and cell phones. Historian Kevin Reilly sums it up nicely: "[A]ll of human history can be understood as the story of increased interaction on a little planet."[3] Yet that history had a very specific beginning in place and time.

The first recorded stirrings of organized trading enterprise appear quite robustly in Mesopotamia, literally, The Land Between the Rivers, i.e., the two rivers, the Tigris and Euphrates. These rich, fertile, well-watered river valleys first achieved the status of a full-fledged civilization around 3500 BCE. Egypt, less urbanized, followed several centuries later. The Indus Valley was a third major culture to emerge around 2600 BCE. Far to the east, Shang China entered the urban age sometime near 1800 BCE. This chapter focuses on the economic origins of Mesopotamia.

THE RISE OF CITIES

The most likely founders of Mesopotamian civilization were the Ubaid and Tell Halaf peoples from the region of Azerbaijan, in northern Iran. As the Ubaidians wandered across the central highlands plateau, they left behind remains of pottery and copper tools and a luxury trade in obsidian. Marc Van De Mieroop records that houses were a feature of Halaf Culture that apparently spread from the Zagros Mountains to the east as far as the Mediterranean coast to the west. The usurping Ubaid Culture was notable for temples and an organized hierarchical structure.[4] For a time, they dwelt in the Persian/Arabian Gulf area, a memory preserved in the paradise legends of Dilmun. Around 3500 BCE, they settled in southern Iraq, where they became known as Sumerians.[5] Arid and dry, Southern Iraq before 3500 BCE was not an auspicious location for a great civilization until the climate began to improve.[6] Yet diversity was their saving grace. The new settlers fished, grew barley and wheat, and raised sheep, cattle, and donkeys. They and the Tell Halaf people of northern Iraq, practiced hunters, lived in mud brick huts and tilled the soil with primitive tools often made of stone or clay. Basic building materials were the mud bricks stuck together with pitch. This Copper Age economy was largely based on subsistence and barter within, and between, tribes led by patriarchs who often doubled as priests. At this time, there was little concentration of wealth, but this would soon change.[7]

Like most ancient cultures, Sumer was a society at the mercy of the elements. Windstorms, sandstorms, floods, and droughts were recurring disasters. This stirred the religious impulse. The gods needed appeasing, especially the spirits believed to control the forces of nature. Enlil, the storm god; Inanna, the goddess of fertility; and Enki, the god of prosperity, were responsible for good crops and had to be placated. Enlil was worshipped as "King of heaven and earth," the one who summoned forth plants and animals from the earth. Without his favor, sang the bards,

No cities would be built, no settlements founded . . .
In field and meadow, the rich grain would not flower.
The trees planted in the mountain forest would not yield their fruit.

This religious dynamic is a crucial force in the rise of ancient business. A powerful temple priesthood emerged as a natural development, because they were pivotal in the handling of the all-important sacrificial offerings. Herds had to be cared for and grain stored. Property values were highest in these sacred zones, where leather crafts and the skills of the butcher and the baker soon throve. Temples had to be maintained and their priests supported from the labor of others. The temples soon became the centre of the first two cities Unug (Uruk) and Eridu, the names perhaps recalling those of the Biblical patriarchs Enoch and Irad.[8]

Uruk first appeared around 3500 BCE, with a population of some 10,000 people, which would grow to 50,000 by 2900 BCE. The population of the whole area of Sumer itself would rise to 500,000 four centuries later. This demographic boost traced to flood control along the Tigris and Euphrates, opening new areas to settlement in the period after 3500 BCE and new jobs in engineering, bureaucracy, management, carpentry, etc. Sumer soon became the most densely populated region of the ancient Near East. As long as wise irrigation techniques were applied, the area could support more than one harvest per year.[9] This was a critical inflection point that provided the society with a sharp upturn in wealth, at least for certain classes. It also secured a ready supply of labor for the construction projects that still dot the landscape.

In this period, the mid-fourth millennium BCE, the Sumerian economy was dual—resting on both subsistence farming and temple tribute. Ancient houses excavated from this period in northern Iraq are filled with stone hoes and sickles. Further south, clay sickles, axes, and hammers were commonly found. The earliest elites were the tribal priests who collected tribute from the embryonic villages to support the temple cities such as Uruk and Eridu. As often happens, oppressive rates of tribute pushed less successful farmers off the land, into the growing towns where they would form a city mob, and pose a threat to public order.[10] Mesopotamia was often a violent society and keeping the peace further strengthened the influence and power of the king and the temple priesthood. The temple system thus became the mainspring for ordering and stimulating this first extended economy. Uruk and Eridu effectively pivoted what could be called the original "public sector."

A MIXED ECONOMY

As local trade and nearby markets gave way to more long-distance, larger-scale transactions up and down the Tigris–Euphrates water routes, the role of the literate priests and scribes increased all the more. The temples designed for religious and public ceremonies took on more and more of the banking functions of Mesopotamia. The decorated shrines of Eridu and Uruk, rising over the Sumerian plains, towered over the drab mud brick houses of those who built them. This is the old, old story of public works and monuments designed to create awe in the onlookers. Church and state—a fateful combination.

Inside the temples, excavators have found the earliest luxury goods, beads of lapis lazuli, clay seals for authorizing and regulating transactions for sacrificial offerings, those very clay seals that prefigured a catalytic Mesopotamian invention, *writing*. There was no coinage as yet, but already gold and silver were in use and accepted as standards of value, sometimes as ingots and rings, but always measured for weight. At Ur, Leonard Wooley found records of loans that had to be confirmed by writing (on clay tablets) and at rates set from 15% to 33% per annum. Copper, the oldest known metal adapted for human use, was found frequently as the basis for tools and weapons, and the temple was adorned with precious stones. These could not be found in Uruk or Eridu, or anywhere in Sumer, but had to be imported from outside.[11]

This emerging Sumerian economy, with ties to a wide geographic area, we have chosen to describe as a *temple-oriented economy* with few traces of Anglo-American-styled capitalism. *Merriam-Webster's Collegiate Dictionary* defines capitalism as:

> an economic system characterized by private or corporate ownership of capital goods, by investments that are determined by private decision, and by prices, production, and the distribution of goods that are determined mainly by competition in a free market.

Such a system certainly did not exist in 3500 BCE, or for another thousand years. On the local village level with its barter economy, however, perhaps a crude form of capitalism did function with the commanding heights of this primitive urban economy in priestly and, gradually, palace hands. The Sumerian temple-oriented economy, therefore, represented *a mixed economy* with the mix decidedly in favor of a public and tributary culture organized around the temple. Yet, even here, the urge and the need to branch out appeared at an extraordinarily early stage. By 3400–3200 BCE, the temple priests of Uruk had commandeered trading posts in Western Iran and on the strategic sites of Nineveh, Tell Brak, Samsat, and Carchemish at the important junctions of water and land routes. Carchemish commanded the main ford across the Euphrates River 100 kms above Aleppo and would occupy a position of importance almost like the Suez Canal would occupy later. It would never disappear from the ancient texts for long.

Busy temple agents traded textiles and grain in order to obtain copper, precious stones, and lumber from their hosts, who did the actual mining of the resources. Water routes were all-important. Even today, resourceful Iraqis fashion crescent-shaped canoes, or *mashufs*, from giant reeds along the Euphrates. But trading connections with Northern Persia, the Levant (the cedars of Lebanon), and the southern Caucasus made possible the first shipping routes in Mesopotamia. Uruk's trading posts with ties to the Levant and Iran represented the first halting steps toward the multinational enterprise. Here were operations internalized, managed from abroad, and set up as permanent establishments on foreign territory to seek out both resources and eventually markets. They were not, however, privately owned, managed for profit, or engaged in value-adding activities on foreign soil as are the true multinationals of our day. We could term them *proto-multinationals*, in that they pioneered approaches that would later be found in modern MNEs.[12]

The Uruk posts are the first recorded example of Dunning's *Eclectic Paradigm* in action. The managers of the Sumerian temple systems exemplified the principle of ownership advantages. This was through their in-depth knowledge of market prices and the hands-on control of valued commodities such as copper, precious stones, and lumber. The Uruk colonies could be likened to European settlements in Africa and Latin America in the 1500s. Sumer's trading outposts at the strategic trade junctures were more elaborate than simple impromptu barter and trade fairs. The documents reveal a "much more complex economic system" than that of the surrounding communities. Like Massachusetts Bay and Jamestown much later, these first pioneering probes were smaller, more dispersed, possessing "a simpler economic structure and a primarily agricultural orientation."[13]

In short, Uruk and Enlil positioned themselves to control the trading networks that had evolved across Syria, Iraq, and Iran. They deployed clear *locational advantages*. The site at Arslan Tepe commanded the passes of the Taurus near the copper mines of Tepecik. Sumerian agents posted near Godin, Sialk, Tell Iblis, and Tepe Yahya in Iran secured valuable copper supplies they shipped back home to be forged into tools and vessels for temples and households. Excavation attested to the presence of temple agents trans-shipping copper to the Eanna of Uruk and other shrines by donkey caravans managed by priestly agents along the supply chain. These *internalization advantages* made it easier to cover risks and absorb losses. Given the limited resources available in Sumer at the time, the temples could not have captured the vital copper market without evolving some form of *multinational* organization.[14]

The Sumerian economy was thriving from 3500–3200 BCE. Soon, other circumstances would come into play that would negate the operational dynamics of the *Eclectic Paradigm*. The Sumerian outposts, working like modern MNEs in developing countries today, tapped the mountain tribes to the north to work as commodity exporters. This exemplified *resource-seeking behavior*. But as the gap between the rich and poor widened, resentment against the Sumerians grew. This is the well-known tension between the center and the periphery, a form of which colonial Americans were forced to endure before 1776. The mountain tribes of Aratta/Urartu soon grew weary and wary of the hinterland–metropolitan arrangement. They adapted the Sumerians own tactics to regain control of their own trade and resources. The Sumerians themselves, as they imported more wood and copper, recognized these commodities had to be processed. This led to the existence of Sumerian middlemen who were needed to ship, store, and distribute the imported goods.[15]

Kish, Ur, Lagash, and other rising city states in Mesopotamia wanted access to their own trade routes. The canals along the Tigris–Euphrates and other constructions along the tributaries provided an interlocking web of water routes that would eventually "tend to strengthen local or regional units and impede the trend towards [Sumerian political] unification." This allowed the rise of multiple power centers.[16] Whichever tribal group gained access to the wood and copper of the North would gain a clear advantage.[17] The long, dark history of warfare among the city states began and soon intensified. Political authority in Sumer began to fragment as alliances took shape. The flat terrain along the rivers allowed access to fast-moving armies, as well as eager merchants. This shaped the region significantly. Eruptive, sometimes incessant, warfare meant that Mesopotamia remained politically fragmented for a much longer time than Egypt or early China.[18] Politics, often the handmaiden of economics, soon led to a period of transformation.

THE INDUSTRIAL REVOLUTION OF THE EARLY BRONZE AGE

Around 3200 BCE, Uruk and her sister cities entered what historians call the Jemdet Nasr period, which lasted until around 2900 BCE. Jemdet Nasr takes its name from a site not far from where Babylon would stand. There, metal was employed more creatively than before. In these three centuries, the Land of the Two Rivers went through an upheaval not unlike that of Western Europe in the early 1800s CE. Farming was transformed, cities grew, and commerce expanded. Craftsmen began to move from subsistence to specialization and from village to town and city. They began to make and sell ploughs, pottery, and other goods and tools. Peasants entered the towns to trade their food and cloth for luxury items, as well as staples. The production of goods began to concentrate in urban areas. This "necessitated a system of administered exchange," according to Professor Susan Pollock, "by which those goods could be moved from producer to consumer."[19]

The old patriarch–priest arrangement began to feel the strain. The growing city population, unable to grow its own food and expropriated by the temple–trading system, became more restless. Starvation loomed in some cities. The temples began to step on the accelerator, demanding more and more grain from the rural peasants who still worked the land. The peasants, not unlike many farm workers in modern Britain and America, could no longer afford to farm. Higher taxes made it harder for farmers to feed both themselves and the temples. The result would prove consistent across history. Many "voted with their feet" and moved to the growing towns. The surviving farmers had to depend more on the new urban markets as targets for their produce. Agriculture became more and more commercialized, dependent on the temple–priest system.[20]

Specialization arrived. The unemployed farmers of Uruk and its neighboring cities and towns would now have to support themselves by becoming artisans, traders, or employees. By 3200 BCE, population was shifting into the big cities in the south of Sumer to the detriment of the smaller cities of the plain. Uruk expanded to an area of 200 hectares. Farming suburbs sprang up around the big cities. The "new economy" put an ever-heavier strain on the Sumerian ecosystem, another constant across history. The frenetic dynamics of fewer and fewer feeding more and more pressured Sumerian peasants to force the ground. Shorter and shorter fallow periods and intensified irrigation to boost production became the rule. Result? Much of the land became salinized, and in the end, less productive. The growing of wheat, in particular, suffered, as whole Sumerian villages had to be abandoned.[21]

Arnold Toynbee once defined growth as a successful response to a challenge. As not infrequently happens, the time was ripe for a better idea. A search for increased efficiency in the production of basic staples goods among rival Sumerian towns accelerated the technological revolution we know as the Early Bronze Age.[22] Around 3100 BCE, Sumerian smiths discovered that if they mixed copper with tin in a furnace at 590–790°C, they could forge the newly created alloy (bronze) into fairly sturdy tools. In 2005, an impressive ancient tin mine was excavated at Deh Hosein in the eastern Zagros area of Iran. Anatolia was also an important supplier. The more tin one combined with copper, the sturdier the bronze. With less than 5% tin, it was very red; with up to 10%, it was golden yellow; when it reached 20%, it became pale yellow. The softer bronze was good for pouring and casting statues; the harder bronze was used to make both swords and ploughshares formerly made of clay.[23]

These technological innovations allowed archaeologists to stamp the name "Early Bronze Age" on this part of antiquity. Better bronze tools meant that peasants could now grow more food and create the needed surpluses to support others in more specialized occupations. Agriculture, itself, could now become a true *business,* opening the door for a more intensive urban–rural economy based on the profit motive. From their donkey-carts, Sumerian peasants could sell excess wheat to feed sculptors, carpenters, leather-workers, bricklayers, scribes—all the classes now able to earn a living in the city.[24]

Indeed, by 2900 BCE, Iraq, Syria, and southwestern Iran hosted dense clusters of concentrated farms and towns, as well as a dozen growing cities. Names such as Kish, Ur, Lagash, Umma, Awan, Hamazi, Shuruppak, and Ebla appear on the monuments.[25] Of the thousands of tablets from Mesopotamia dating back to the Uruk of 3200 BCE, there existed only a trickle of in-depth information before 2700 or 2600 BCE dealing with day-to-day affairs. Then Leonard Woolley's discoveries of the abundant archives at Ur were matched by a plethora of data coming from Shuruppak, Lagash, and Eblam. Real light was penetrating the darkness.[26] A rich array of tablets, seals and cylinders dating from 2500 BCE—most of them business records—opened up the world of Sumerian commerce, society, and politics.[27] (See Table 2.1)

The surging Sumerian economy after 3000 BCE still favored mixed enterprise wherein private subsistence methods meshed with the publically operated temple economies. The existence of markets with fluctuating prices is well-evidenced in the archaeological records. Even though coins were are still not in use as currency, precious metals, especially silver, were measured by weight and used as a method of exchange. Entering the third millennium BCE, economic life continued to thrive and diversity. As cuneiform translator Samuel Noah Kramer puts it, "Bureaucrats bustle about, their open palms following citizens even to the grave." Petty officials have to be paid off "with seven pitchers of beer and 420 loaves of bread."[28] Later, the introduction of coinage would definitely speed things along, but there was clearly a major "take-off phase" as society moved from the fourth to the third millennium BCE.

A clear sign of these new developments was the further concentration of wealth, not just in temples, this time, but in the palaces of regional governors and rulers. Some eventually trickled down to private hands as artisans, pottery makers, weavers, and traders felt the rising tide raising their boats. Previously, we described the Sumerian system as a temple economy. The temples were the first institutions in which wealth was concentrated and through which economic activity was supervised.[29] "Indeed," writes Peter Jay, "temples were the key to much of the economic life of Sumerian civilization."[30] Up until the 1960s, most writers followed the theories of Anton Deimel and Karl Polanyi, who saw a socialist state in which all land was owned by the temples. Then, in the 1960s, a collection of tablets from Lagash showed clearly that large tracts of rural territory were owned by family groups.[31]

Table 2.1 The Rise of Sumerian Capitalism

Copper Age (3800–3200 BCE)

Ubaid Period (before 3500 BCE)	Nomad ancestors of Sumerians migrate from northern Iran via Persian/Arabian Gulf.
Uruk Period (3500–3200 BCE): Dawn of temple capitalism	Unug or Uruk and Eridu founded. Sumerian trading colonies across Near East import copper. First economic records as picture writing becomes cuneiform.

Early Bronze Age I–III (3200–2250 BCE)

Early Bronze I (3200–2900 BCE): Jemdet Nasr Period	Coincides with Dynasties III and IV in Egypt. Bronze tools forged leading to urban revolution. Kish, Ur, Sippar, Nippur, Larsa, Shuruppak and other cities develop.
Early Bronze II (2900–2300 BCE): Beginning of Early Dynastic Period	First Age of the Grand City–States.
Early Dynastic I (2900–2700 BCE): Age of the God-Kings	Etana of Kish and other *lugal* ("big men") become hereditary God-Kings. Enmerkar trades with Aratta in Iran. Coincides with Dynasty V in Egypt.
Early Dynastic II (2700–2500 BCE): The Heroic Age	Gilgamesh briefly unites Uruk, Kish, and Ur. Palace emerges as rival economic center. Coincides with Dynasty VI in Egypt and Yang Shao in China.
Early Bronze III Early Dynastic III (2500–2300 BCE): The Age of Violence	Intense dynastic wars climax in Sumer and Asia Minor. Ebla archives and Royal Tombs of Ur. Coincides with Dynasties VII–VIII and end of Old Kingdom in Egypt.

Early Bronze IV (2250–2000 BCE): The First Capitalist Age

Early Bronze IVA (2250–2100 BCE): The Age of Empire	Akkadian Period. Lugalzagesi of Uruk and Sargon of Akkad erect first universal empire—basis of Nimrod story? Trading links to India forged. Some *Tamkāru* now private merchants. Coincides with Dynasties IX, X in Egypt.
Early Bronze IVB (2100–2000 BCE): The Golden Age of Sumerian Capitalism	Neo-Sumerian kingdom succeeds Akkadian rule. Coincides with Dynasty XI in Egypt. Ur becomes first documented true capitalist economy. Thriving commerce with India using Dilmun (Bahrain) as middleman.

Originally concentrated in the temples, the wealth of the new economy was spreading out, accumulating in powerful families who employed workers in farming, trade, and manufacturing. These households now owned large estates, flocks of animals, fields, orchards, grain silos, warehouses, and workshops. Many of those employed in harvest time or for construction projects were part of the extended clan.[32] The Book of Job in the Hebrew Bible, perhaps reflecting a much earlier era, documents a bias towards family-based mercantilism wherein one man could control vast holdings of sheep, cattle, and land. Job's 7,000 sheep and three hundred camels may not have been much of an exaggeration, preserving folk memories of wealthy independent operators going back to earliest days (Job 1:3).

Land—another great constant in history! Temple and family household businesses sought land ownership as a hedge against crop failure, war, and other calamities. This was an early step towards the further internalization of operations. In Lagash then, as in Los Angeles today, large units are "more resilient in the face of unfavorable conditions because they can pool resources, risks, and labor internally."[33] As well, they nurture the industrialization process by making it possible to produce the surpluses needed to develop what Pollock calls "newer riskier and costlier production strategies and technologies such as metallurgy."[34] Sophistication follows expansion.

Just as in Britain in the late 1780's, textile production also played a major part in the industrialization of Mesopotamia. Growing populations need to be clothed, as well as fed. Many of Sumer's influential households went into textile production. Cloth was easy to market and to ship in bulk by boat or donkey, and was always in demand. Production was outsourced on a large scale. Records show one household employing almost 6,000 weavers. Some large Sumerian households boasted a workable "factory" system. Women and children were the main employees. They were organized into work gangs sometimes numbering into the hundreds. Wool and flax was sheared, plucked, woven, washed, and finally sewn together into garments. Temple priests needed impressive robes and costumes, bowls for libations, and incense for offerings. Temple guards needed shields, spears, and leather footwear. To supply these sources of demand, private and public enterprise interlocked. Family households and factories would supply labor cloth to the temples or to other households that supplied them with grain, land, or pay wages in the form of food. Within and among these households a division of labor developed 5,000 years before the descriptions of Adam Smith.[35]

THE TEMPLE BOOM OF THE EARLY DYNASTIC; GILGAMESH

The best models archaeologists have formulated of the Sumerian temple economy arise from excavations of the structures in the Diyala region of east-central Iraq. The site of Khafajeh, or Kahafajah, is about 40 hectares in area. It presents a history of over a thousand years of Sumerian urban development, beginning around 3200 BCE. There were very few walled cities in Sumer at this time, but by the middle of the Early Dynastic Period most cities in Southern Iraq were walled. At first, temples were not directly involved in production; Khafajeh began with the small temple of the moon god Sin and the later Nintu Temple. By the first phase of Early Dynastic II, the time of Gilgamesh (2900–2700), the largest temple of all begins to rise at Khafajeh. Many important temples at this stage display an oval pattern, hence this structure bears the name of The Oval Temple of Khafajeh. A market place thrived between the temple and the city gate.

The Oval Temple sponsored the manufacturing of cloth and cooking wares. By 2500 BCE, as a steady stream of offerings of grain and animals poured into the temple priesthood, the region around the temple became a virtual "industrial zone" for clothing production, cooking, and trading. The buyers and the sellers were going at it with a zest and an élan that Jesus and his disciples might well have recognized. Spinning and sewing were segregated into different houses, done by different groups of people. During the Early Dynastic III period, the residences of the rulers move away from the temple. The outer wall of the temple becomes much thicker. As always, politics and economics interact. The period ends in an orgy of warfare with the temples being destroyed. Only the Oval Temple is subsequently rebuilt, in Early Dynastic IIIB, but then even this last temple is quickly abandoned. Then, at the end of the Early Dynastic Period, about 2300 BCE, political instability reared its ugly head. The record shows evidence of temples burned and plundered, with only Diyala's Oval Temple being rebuilt in a highly planned and walled quarter. It too, was soon abandoned.[36]

What was the working philosophy behind this Sumerian temple system? Growing evidence points to the conclusion that the temples, ziggurats, and walled cities were erected not by slaves, but by conscripts and hired laborers. Religious zeal was the predominant motive, as with Medieval Europe's cathedral builders. The temples were impressive engineering feats, mounted on platforms ten meters high, with their ziggurats (stepped towers) towering over the cities, visible for miles. It is small wonder that the story of the Tower of Babel traces to this region. Towering buildings sent a message that the temple hierarchy was a special class, and heaven willed it so. There was little of the modern Western separation of life into religious and worldly spheres. "Religion," Pollock summarizes nicely, "pervaded political and economic decisions." Here was a worldview that "saw the forces of nature and human and divine action as intimately bound up with each other."[37] In early Mesopotamia, trade followed the temple, not the flag.

Under this Bronze Age construction boom—what Marc Van De Mieroop calls "the Uruk expansion"—Sumerian theology began to change. Once society became more orderly, the gods seemed less needy of appeasing. Into this void stepped the city rulers, political strongmen aspiring to divine or semidivine status. "The kingly palaces were representative of kings who

wanted themselves to be seen as little gods," says historian George Gia-
mackus. Events could now be shaped by acts of human, as well as divine,
will. "The creation of the city implied a new form of social organization
in which tribal and kinship loyalties were replaced by political ones based
on common dependence on military machine headed by a king," writes
Hallo and Simpson.[38] In scenes reminiscent of *Star Wars: Episode Three*,
elected local rulers usurped power, became hereditary monarchs, and soon
equipped themselves with armies of swordsmen flourishing the efficient
new bronze weapons. These first kings, known as *lugal*, or "big men,"
began to build temples, canals, and other public works both to enhance
their prestige and to provide for the growing ranks of the urban unemployed. Thus, palace and temple worked together to sustain the market-
driven economy of the Early Bronze Age. By 2500 BCE, most Sumerians
lived in cities. Shuruppak, or Farah, reputed home of Ut-Napishtim, the
Sumerian Noah, grew in area from 40 hectares in 3000 BCE to between 70
and 100 hectares by 2300 BCE. Many cities now contained up to 30,000
people.[39] This was the urban revolution, one of the most important turning points in history.

Trade grew along with urbanization, but the full effect of the *Eclectic
Paradigm* was not always felt in Early Dynastic times. The mountain
tribes and peoples of the Gulf now formed their own kingdoms, and did
not want resident aliens from Sumer controlling their trade routes. In
Iran, these routes had already been taken over by Elamites to the east.
Thus, although Sumerian establishments could theoretically possess
ownership and *internalization advantages*, the refusal of the mountain
tribes to permit new colonies rendered *locational advantages* null and
void. The rising Sumerian *lugal* now had to secure supplies of wood, copper, and tin by imposing tribute on foreign chieftains, a process backed
by the threat of military force, which further consolidated the rule of the
strong man.

The ancient epic known as *Enmerkar and the Lord of Aratta* is full of
references to a commerce based on tribute. Enmerkar reigned in Uruk,
or Unug, around 2850 BCE. The city and its Eanna temple prospered
"before the commerce was practiced; before gold, silver, copper, tin,
blocks of lapis lazuli, and mountain stones were brought down together
from their mountains." Enmerkar demanded that the ruler of Aratta,
located in northern Iran or Armenia, supply him with gold, silver, and
precious stones. He warned that he might require them "at a current market rate."[40] The people of Aratta were to pack gold and precious stones in
leather sacks to be loaded on "donkeys of the mountains" for shipment
to Sumer. The Lord of Aratta was, in his heart, reluctant to submit to the
Sumerian, hoping that "he need not pour barley into sacks, nor have it
carted, nor have that barley carried into the settlements, nor place collec-
tors over the laborers."[41]

Nevertheless, Aratta was in need of Sumer's plenteous food supply. Emmerkar controlled the produce. The choice was obvious, if brutal: Submit to Uruk, then beneficent *lugal* Enmerkar would "have barley poured into carrying-nets . . . loaded on . . . jackasses at whose sides reserve donkeys have been placed . . . heaped up in a pile in the courtyard of Aratta."[42]

Enmerkar "opened his mighty storehouse, and firmly set his great . . . measure on the ground." The king "removed his old barley from the other barley . . . soaked the green malt all through with water" and "measured out . . . the barley for the granary." It was loaded on donkeys for Aratta. When it arrived in Aratta, palace officials measured it out, and "Aratta's hunger was sated."[43]

This scene of economic thuggery predates, by a thousand years, the Biblical story of Joseph and his brothers, who came to beg for grain from the new Egyptian overlord. The dominant role of the palace in supervising long distance trade is also confirmed in the famous *Epic of Gilgamesh,* dating from the first quarter of the third millennium BCE. Gilgamesh apparently lived some 200 years after Enmerkar. By this time, the kings, instead of merely living in harmony with the gods, were proclaiming themselves to be gods. Gilgamesh of Uruk was a feared and ruthless despot, engaged in a power struggle with Kish. Access to mines and forests was a prime motive:[44]

> He who saw everything to the ends of the land, Who all things experienced, considered all! . . . Two thirds of him is god, one-third of him is human. . . . The onslaught of his weapons verily has no equal. By the drum are aroused his companions."[45]

In this, perhaps the oldest literary composition in the world, there are the inevitable references to markets. Gilgamesh and Enkidu met for battle in a place called "Market-of-the-Land." Later in the tale, the goddess Ishtar "mounted the wall of ramparted Uruk" to curse both of them. "Riding through the market streets of Uruk . . . The people of Uruk are gathered to gaze upon them."[46] Gilgamesh journeys to the forests of Syria to obtain timber, and to the shores of Dilmun in search of pearls.[47] Gilgamesh, like Enmerkar, obtains his resources by marching out to capture them. He does not set up agents in Syria or in the Gulf. His reliance on war and plunder recalls the Axis powers of the 1930s and 1940s, ravaging China, invading Romania, coveting the Ukraine. These are other, sadder constants in history.

"THE BUSINESS OF EBLA WAS BUSINESS:"
A CAPITALIST CULTURE?

Until the 1970s of our era, it was assumed that the Early Bronze Age economy was built solely around the commerce of the Sumerian city–states.

Then, in 1975, a vast library of some 15,000 business documents was discovered on the site of Tell Mardikh in northwest Syria, most in classical Mesopotamian cuneiform. Archaeologists Giovanni Pettinato and Paolo Matthiae found the lost city of Ebla. Ebla was no mean city. From about 2600 to 2400 BCE, it was the capital of a magnificent trading empire. Archaeologist Paolo Matthiae's 1981 monograph, *Ebla: An Empire Rediscovered*, was not sensationalist, even though it sharply undermined the reigning idea that nation–states were unknown in ancient times. Before the archaeological finds first became published in 1975, the world knew nothing about this impressive economic powerhouse. Now we know it was the vibrant center of an Early Bronze Age regional economy that stretched from Sumer to Anatolia to Egypt.

Ebla's rather sudden rise to power was a product of her enormous prosperity and the *locational advantages* of her merchants. A helpful analogy to understand Ebla's significance is to think of them as the first Anglo-Americans, the Sumerians as the first Europeans, and the Old Kingdom of Egypt in the role of present-day Asians.

Archaeology confirms that although Egypt was the first recognizable nation, Ebla was the first recorded world power, a city capable of projecting itself far and wide. Excavators were astonished. The Ebla Tablets documented an international system "with Ebla the third pole alongside Egypt and Mesopotamia," one in which "Syria assumes the central role thanks to its marvellous geographical position."[48] The merchants of Ebla possessed immense locational advantages. The north–south and east–west commercial routes of the Fertile Crescent passed through Syria. Ebla controlled all of Syria and Palestine, even extending trade links out into the Mediterranean as far as Cyprus. Under Ebla's sway came the copper and tin mines of Asia Minor and northern Mesopotamia. One unearthed school text lists "17 countries in the hand of the king of Ebla."[49]

Interestingly, Ebla was a liberal empire, not unlike those of Britain or America. She ruled over seventeen other states while respecting their local traditions. The Eblaites had no standing army but used their enormous financial power to hire mercenaries. Ebla was a constitutional state. Her treaties with Mari, Ashur, and Hamazi refer not to the person of her king but to the "state of Ebla here presented." As in the United States, the Constitution was (theoretically) supreme. Eblaite treaties are very sophisticated. They show an understanding of business law, international taxation, and territorial jurisdictions. Any kingdom not respecting these rights would face a commercial boycott from Ebla and effectively face ruin. The first ruler of Ashur in Mesopotamia, Tudia, signed a treaty with Ebla knowing that the gods would punish his merchants if they acted in bad faith: "for the merchants who undertake a journey, water let there be none."

Ebla's religious and political culture stands out as unique and distinct from that of Egypt and even Sumer. Ebla offered the closest parallel to a separation of religion and state in the ancient Near East. Eblaites were certainly religious, with over 500 deities to worship. Chief were Dagon, god of Canaan; Sippish, the sun god; and Hadad, the Syrian storm god. Chemosh, Baal, and Moloch were also represented. There were also, however, independent prophets and a strong suggestion that there was one supreme God: "Lord of heaven and earth: the earth was not, you created it, the light of day was not, you created it, the morning light you had not [yet] made exist."[50]

Ebla traded in a world in which Egypt was ruled by the powerful Fifth and Sixth Dynasties. Neighboring Sumer finally achieved unity under the rulers of Kish, just south of the site of Babylon. Not unlike the British in India, the Eblaite kings tried to keep Sumer divided by concluding an alliance with the kingdom of Hamazi in Iran. The policy eventually failed, for around 2500 BCE the rulers of Kish overwhelmed Hamazi and, it would seem, Ebla herself.

According to Pettinato's researches, the Eblaites emerge as the first real capitalists of antiquity. Business was "their prime and all-embracing activity."[51] Copper from Cyprus and gold from Egypt poured into her coffers. The original source of Ebla's wealth was agriculture. She was not resource-poor like Sumer. Ebla was only forty miles from the oasis-city of Aleppo, an essential stop for traders and travellers such as the later Abram the Hebrew. Ebla's canals are mentioned in the Sumerian texts. Her well-watered and extensive farmlands could support 18,000,000 people—an astonishing number for that time. One thinks of the American Midwest and Great Plains, once the breadbasket of the world. Ebla was also rich in wine and olive oil, as well as flax. There were enough sheep and cattle to make her the Montana or Texas of the third millennium. The king, alone, owned 1,300 oxen and 80,000 sheep.[52]

Ebla's agricultural prosperity laid the groundwork for an even greater achievement in textiles. As in modern Britain and America, the woollen industry seems to have led the way. The government-established textile mills fostered the production of fabrics in huge quantities. Tell Mardikh tablet 75.G.2068 mentions "2,447 fabrics; 30 . . . fabrics of second quality; 227 . . . fabrics of top quality and multicolored; 61 multicolored . . . fabrics present in the opening mill." Another document, Tell Mardikh 75.G.2065, speaks of "5,891 fabrics; 69 . . . fabrics of second quality; 480 fabrics of top quality and multicolored; 2,334 . . . fabrics, multicolored, present." Ebla exported these in enormous quantities. One tablet alone, TM 75.G.2070, lists 16,000 fabrics.[53] Even though ancient figures must be viewed critically the numbers are impressive.

As might be expected, Ebla was also a manufacturer and exporter of bronze goods such as swords, luxury items, and tools. The tablets mention potters, sculptors, carpenters, smiths, textile workers, perfumers, bakers, and millers. Ebla operated on a gold and silver standard, and possessed huge quantities of both. One tablet record mentions 1,740 minas (870 kg) of gold. King Ebrium spent 8,389 minas (4,300 kg) during three years of his reign.[54] A mina was about £120, so 1,740 minas would be £208,800 and 8,389 minas about £1,006,680.

Ebla, itself, adhered to a mixed economy, one with strong temple involvement but still more open to private enterprise than either Egypt or Sumer. Everyone, even the king, paid taxes, and everyone, it seemed, received government subsidies. While busy bureaucrats regulated and planned on a large scale, Eblaite merchants nurtured a thriving private sector as well. "The great novelty of Ebla," according to Professor Pettinato, "lies precisely in the fact that in it coexist, in a perfect symbiosis, the public and private economy."[55] He finds "little doubt that free enterprise had ample space in which to operate, above all in commerce, the chief activity of the Eblaites." Alongside the state merchants, called a *kas*, operated the *lukas*, who were "certainly private merchants, not less active or affluent than the official representatives of the state." The private sector of the Eblaite economy, strong in trade and real estate, was dominated by the great families of Ebla.[56] Britain in her Victorian heyday was very much run by a few hundred landed classes, an oligarchy.

These great families traded within what Pettinato is bold enough to call history's first common market. Not unlike the British global economy in the nineteenth century, goods were traded across the Bronze Age world by royal overseers, as well as private merchants. Commerce was priced in terms of gold and silver. Five bars of silver were pegged at a fixed and stable exchange rate to one bar of gold. Ebla was a very different kind of empire from those that would ultimately defeat and replace it. It was "a markedly economic–commercial empire, not a political–military complex."[57] Although much trade still revolved around barter, the presence of an international gold and silver standard represents a major step towards a money economy. Silver was traded for various goods. One tablet mentions "10 minas and 45 Dilmunite shekels of silver barter for 2 minas and 9 Dilmunite shekels of gold."[58] Sometimes silver was openly used as money:

> 10 Dilmunite shekels of silver price of 10 (measures) of inferior linen, 16 Dilmunite shekels of silver price of 3 excellent materials from the part of Gulla of Mari; 15 Dilmunite shekels of silver price of rams of the city Mari; 20 Dilmunite shekels of silver price of bitumen.[59]

Domestically, the state controlled production, set quotas, and stockpiled crops. Ebla's silver and gold was in demand everywhere, allowing her to trade freely with anyone. Eblaite merchants coordinated the flow of goods from Egypt, Cyprus, Sumer, and Elam.[60] Here was a city standing at the vital crossroads of the ancient Fertile Crescent. She was the envy of her neighbors and that envy, as we show in the following, was her fatal undoing.

OLD KINGDOM EGYPT: HIDDEN MARKETS
IN A "SOCIALIST" THEOCRACY

"Man fears time but even time fears the pyramids." To turn to Egypt is to enter a world so seemingly familiar yet so vastly different from ours. Even today, names such as Tutankhamen, Marc Antony and Cleopatra, Gamal Abdul Nasser, and Anwar el-Sadat are forces with which to conjure. The Hebrew Bible praises "the wisdom of Egypt." For, although the first urban civilization was Sumerian, the world's oldest coherent nation–state emerged in the valley of the Nile. From the start, Egyptians were aware of being a distinct and united people. Egypt's Old Kingdom was much more prosperous even than Sumer. The long, life-giving Nile was predictable and benevolent, unlike the twisting and turbulent Euphrates. Very early on, Egypt became the granary of the world. Egyptian business culture was shaped by the fact that virtually everyone depended upon Father Nile. The great river became the organizing principle around which Egypt was administered, grain was stored and shipped, and land was drained and irrigated. The need to irrigate farmland and manage flooding encouraged the rapid growth of a strong, unified Egyptian state. This is the point, argues historian Paul Johnson, at which "Egyptian history diverged from that of the other alluvial valley-plains, the Tigris–Euphrates and the Indus, which cradled the earliest civilizations."[61]

Egypt's evolution towards a unified, coherent statehood spared her the constant wars of Mesopotamia. She thus bypassed the city–state phase, the impetus for trade and commerce in Sumer. Egyptian life was greatly centralized. It produced the most intensely religious culture of antiquity. Virtually all art, science, literature, and, we shall see, commerce revolved around the quest for immortality. Temples, especially tombs, were Egypt's growth industry *par excellence*. As local villages merged into the *nomes* or regions of the centralized Egyptian state, local gods merged into each another's pantheons. Memphis became the first capital. Ptah, depicted at a forge as a smith, became Egypt's first national god, offering a strong clue to the importance of basic industrial technique along the Nile. The Nile Valley, in places only ten miles wide, is protected from invasion on both sides by barren cliffs and desert sands. Consolidated under Pharaoh Menes around 3200 BCE, Egypt was well on the way to becoming a unified state and entered the Copper Age with her population rapidly expanding.

Large-scale economic activity in the fourth millennium was generally dominated by the public sectors of temple and palace. In Egypt, though, the royal palace was particularly powerful from earliest times. The first kings, soon known as *Pharaohs* ("the Great House"), managed the storage and distribution of grain, set up food depots, and monitored the level of the Nile. Egypt could afford this incipient form of socialism. Abundant grain supplies fed the peasants who were employed during part of the year on public works. Pharaoh portrayed himself as working in harmony with the gods to bring prosperity. From this, it was a short step to deification. As the Nile Delta and its rich farmland were developed through such inventions as the hoe and ploughshare, the royal food surpluses soon grew and, with them, so did the number of craftsmen and state employees.

During Dynasties I and II (roughly 3100–2686 BCE using Hallo and Simpson dates), the tombs of the Pharaohs grew in size and splendor, surrounded also by those of their officials and retainers. There is no evidence of the grisly human sacrifices Sir Leonard Woolley discovered in the Royal Tombs of Ur. King Djoser, founder of Dynasty III (2686–2613 BCE) pushed Egyptian rule south to the First Cataract of the Nile. Royal mining expeditions developed turquoise quarries and were sent into the Sinai, laying the basis for the later King Solomon's mines. Second in the kingdom to Djoser was the king's Vizier, or Chancellor, Imhotep, who conceived the idea of erecting entire buildings of stone. "The land was administered through central offices charged with granaries, assessments, taxes and disbursements of salaries."[62]

Above all things, Egyptian civilization was organized. The Step Pyramid erected by Imhotep appears to be the first planned architectural complex in the world. Pyramid mania soon swept Egypt. First Khufu (Dynasty IV—c. 2613–2494 BCE), then Khafre, and finally Menkaure erected gigantic tombs for themselves, which still stand at Gizeh. The Great Pyramid is still the most massive building on earth. These tombs were constructed by a nationwide effort of thousands of willing subjects who quarried the huge stones, floated them down the Nile, and rolled and lifted them into place. Salvation itself was a collectivist undertaking in the Old Kingdom. If Pharaoh attained immortality, his subjects would do so along with him. This belief helped inspire the Pyramid boom of Dynasties III and IV in which the Egyptian economic model fully took shape.[63]

Thus, Old Kingdom Egypt was both an intense theocracy *and* the closest parallel to a developed socialist state. There was little *visible* private sector. This is evidence, all by itself, against the one-size-fits-all economic model. The fact that "trade was a royal monopoly . . . was one respect in which Egypt differed decisively from the Mesopotamian city–states."[64] Sneferu of Dynasty IV sent royal expeditions into Nubia, Libya, and Syria. Sneferu sent forty ships, each about fifty meters long, to trade Egyptian grain for cedar wood from Byblos. Regrettably, there are no business texts to speak of from Old Kingdom Egypt. A picture from Dynasty V, though, is worth a thousand words. It shows a company of bearded, possibly Eblaite, Asiatic sailors from Syria arriving in Egypt. The old legend of Osiris, the Egyptian messiah, also sheds light on the timber trade between Egypt and the Levant. Trade went on big barges across the Mediterranean. The Levant includes modern Israel, Lebanon, and Syria. The Levantine trade would spread inland, the Eblaites and their Syrian successors becoming reliable customers for Egyptian products.

By the time of Dynasty V, the Pharaohs were sending royal expeditions to Africa. The Palermo Stone mentions a voyage to the land of Punt, located somewhere at the southern end of the Red Sea, perhaps Djibouti, Somalia, or Yemen. The Egyptian voyagers returned with ivory, ebony, and the resins of gum-trees. Similar expeditions were now sent down the Nile. Uni, an official of Dynasty VI, dug a series of canals around the First Cataract, just south of Aswan. Egyptian vessels could now sail up the Nile into Sudan, bringing Egyptian oil, honey, and clothing to exchange for Nubian ivory, ebony, and skins.[65]

THE PALACE MONOPOLY AND ITS DISCONTENTS

In Egypt, trade became a virtual monopoly of the palace. The royal granaries anchored the ability to trade elsewhere. The chief product the Old Kingdom craved was timber—wood for ships, building, and heating, so scarce in the Nile Valley. The most accessible supply of cedar, cypress, and pine was to be found in the land of Syria, in what would be known as Phoenicia. Very early did the Pharaohs send their crown merchants to the port of Byblos, where artifacts from both Predynastic times and Dynasty II (around 3200 BCE) confirm their presence.

Egypt would take a different road to economic development from that of Ebla or Sumer. Only the boldest Egyptian would admit to being a private merchant, as everyone seemingly worked in the public sector. According to Egyptologist Barry Kemp, "We will find no self-made men of manufacture, no merchants or moneylenders, or makers of other people's tombs."[66] Yet a closer look at Egypt indicates that, under the surface of what historian Paul Johnson calls a "totalitarian theocracy," individual Egyptians were more aware of the imperatives of successful trade than is usually thought. The administrative side of the Egyptian economy is well documented. The state and the temples owned the granaries and other key sectors and used its power, Joseph-like, to dispense grain to support the population in hard times. The Egyptian public sector has been likened to a Marxist-style command economy, without an egalitarian ideology. Its world-view was remote from materialism, dialectic or otherwise. Size and scale were powerful factors. Given the sheer size of the state, the Pharaohs were simply unable and unwilling to micromanage every aspect of the Egyptian economy from Thebes or elsewhere. Also, the numerous temples, shrines, tombs and other religious administrations each collected their own revenues and paid their own wages.[67] The Edict of Horemheb from the New Kingdom (commonly dated c. 1333–1303) gives the flavor of the whole. Royal decrees were invoked to deal with specific cases of improprieties in the collection of revenue. Egyptian tax-collecting agencies each seemed to have their own taxation powers and operated on a case-by-case basis. Egyptian temples and shrines all subscribed to the religious philosophy of the Pharaonic state, which, in turn, delegated many short-term functions to them. Old shrines lost patrons to new ones.[68] Egypt was polytheistic, and many deities were popular. No doubt, the popularity of some would grow and others decline among the populace depending upon their functions and needs.

In short, the revenue system of ancient Egypt was a tangle of conflicting jurisdictions. Sometimes Pharaoh, himself, had to make a decree awarding land and income to a specific temple, as well as fining and punishing the agents of another temple that sought to expand its source of revenue— "carpetbagging." Decrees were made noting that any agent interfering with royal ships bearing grain from Nubia to the Pharaoh's palace would be severely punished. The Egyptian system in one sense resembled modern totalitarian states. Jurisdictions and responsibilities overlapped. From the Delta to the Fourth Cataract, it was a challenge to run things systematically, although these very problems helped speed the promotion of some things we take for granted, writing being number one. The Egyptian alphabet, with its twenty-four signs, may have been in existence as early as 3500BCE. These innovations helped the palace to respond to the growing complaints and petitions of bickering bodies and agencies.[69] The Pharaoh in the Joseph story who seems harassed and unable to "get a grip" may have been a reflection of Egypt's massive administrative overload.

As noted, private demand and small-scale private enterprises did exist in a somewhat socialist, but very totalitarian, Egypt. Even in Predynastic times, individuals amassed goods in their own personal tombs, for example. In the Old Kingdom up to Dynasty VI, the tombs of local leaders were surrounded by those of lesser folk. After the Old Kingdom collapsed, around 2040 BCE during Dynasties VII and VIII, graves between Herakleopolis and Thebes were no longer clustered but spread out, indicating a taste for individual choice and preference.[70] Egypt was always more complex than Shelley's Ozymandias Ode might leave us to believe.

GREAT POWER STRUGGLES

By way of a quick summary overview, if the Egyptian model represented one pole of the Bronze Age spectrum (the Quasi-Socialist), the Ebla model held down the other (Quasi-Corporatist). In between the two lay the Sumerian model, the "third way" of a temple-led economy (see Table 2.2).

By 2600 BCE, a viable and growing trading system had emerged in the Eastern Mediterranean, with Ebla in the center, Egypt and the Aegean in the west, Anatolia in the north, and Sumer and the Gulf and Indus Valley in the east (see Chapter 3). Although Sumer and Ebla were the most urbanized, with the former boasting half a million inhabitants, cities were beginning to pop up throughout this extensive trading region, centers such as Memphis in Egypt and Harappa in the Indus Valley. The core of the Early

Table 2.2 Models of Temple/Palace Economy in Early Bronze Age

Egyptian "Quasi-Socialist"	Mesopotamian "Quasi-Corporatist"	Eblaite "Quasi-Entrepreneuria l"
• Strong palace • Diverse temples with strong management role	• Competing palaces • Diverse temples with strong management role	• Strong palace, subject to rule of law • Diverse temples with lesser management role
Minimal private management	Minimal, then emerging private management	Strongest private management

Bronze and Middle Bronze system, though, would remain Mesopotamia. A struggle for control over that system would soon develop, which would last for several centuries. The outcome would make the Sumerian model dominant for some 1,500 years.

Conflict between Ebla and Sumer was almost inevitable. Ebla, rich in wheat, barley, cattle, silver, gold, and textiles, dominated Syria, northern Mesopotamia, and part of Anatolia. Meanwhile, hegemony in Mesopotamia had passed to the city of Kish. Kish, near the southern Euphrates, held the position of "first among equals," a title bestowed by the priests of Nippur. It conferred the right to arbitrate disputes among the other Sumerian city–states. Kish was challenged not only by Ebla, but also by proud Uruk, already ancient by those standards. The warrior king Eannatum of Lagash also contended for power. The Early Dynastic age ended in a series of savage wars when Eannatum conquered Umma, Uruk, Ur, Elam, and even distant Mari, only to be resisted by an alliance led by Kish and Akshak.[71]

These climactic wars of the Early Bronze Age were both good and bad for business, as wars tend to be. "The dogs of war" constricted trade, raised taxes, ran up deficits, and destroyed people and property. On the other hand, the "military Keynesianism" perfected later by Carthage and Rome and rampant in our own time, had its precursor in this conflict between Kish and Ebla. War is the ultimate test of the state. As such, it can be a significant accelerator of technological growth, encouraging almost frantic research and organization. These military clashes up and down the Euphrates/Northern Levant axis stimulated state-subsidized contracts. This further accelerated the growth of the palace economy. Demand for specialized goods was voracious. Chariot-makers, weapon-smiths, makers of uniforms, donkey drivers, textile and garment makers, carpenters, bricklayers, leather craftsmen, herdsmen, shopkeepers, and the farmers who fed them all were the men of the hour. The cry for rapidly finished goods also meant the search for raw materials. Overland–overwater trade skyrocketed. The Ebla–Sumer standoff produced one of the first demand economies of which we have record. Eannatum and his rivals needed plenty of copper and tin to melt into chariots, battle-axes, swords, spears, daggers, shields, and arrows. Sumer was resource-poor in regard to metals, lumber, and precious stones. Her warring kings could only get them by trading more intensively to the four corners or launching aggressive imperial wars.[72] Enter history's first fighting CEO.

SARGON'S TRADING EMPIRE; EARLY BRONZE AGE COLLAPSE

During the final phase of the Early Bronze Age, both political and commercial leadership of Sumer passed from Syria back to Mesopotamia. Sometime between 2400 and 2200 BCE, the aggressive Lugalzagesi of Uruk subjugated the Land of the Two Rivers. He, in turn, was deposed by the ambitious Semite *Sharrukenu*, or Sargon, "the Legitimate King." Ruling from the new city of Akkad, near the present-day Iraqi heartland between Baghdad and Babylon, Sargon's conquests became legendary, the model for imperial conquerors to follow.

Sargon, "King of Battle," (c. 2300–2230 BCE), soon overran all of modern-day Iraq and most of Iran and Syria. The mighty state he set up displaced Ebla and went on to pivot a trading economy stretching from Cyprus to the Indian Ocean. Trade went by sea as well as overland. The pattern was not new: Sargon stepped into the shoes of the commercial empires and networks that had now existed for centuries. But, like the later Napoleon Bonaparte, Sargon's energetic acquisitiveness and lust for expansion injected new life into old networks. Sumerian textiles were traded for copper, tin, and precious stones in greater bulk than ever before. Mythological writings connected with the god Enki show Mesopotamian traders, both private and public, now journeying far west, as well as to the east. In the legends, Enki's craft sails along the Tigris and Euphrates from Ur in the south to Ashur in the north.[73] A coherent land and sea empire at last!

Marc Van De Mieroop mentions records of "far-flung forays for the procurement of rare goods, hard stone, wood or silver. . . . Ships from overseas areas, such as Meluhha (the Indus Valley) are said to have moored in Akkad's harbor."[74] The Enki stories tease with the mention of these far-flung and mysterious locations: Dilmun (Tilmun), Makan (Magan), and, most important, Meluhha. In *Enki and Ninhursag*, the god is said to bless Dilmun as the destination of the wares of eight different realms.[75] It must have been important. Giovanni Pettinato, epigrapher at the Ebla site, identified Dilmun as the island of Bahrain, "famous in antiquity as the source of heavy metals."[76] The land Meluhha would send Enki "tempting, precious carnelian," rare wood, and large boats; the land of Makan (Onan) brought "mighty copper" and other precious stones. The texts sing the glories of empire: "May the wide sea bring you its abundance; The city—its dwellings are good dwellings, Dilmun—its dwellings are good dwellings."[77] Another legend, *Enki and the World Order*, more philosophical, again alluded to seaborne trade conducted by boats from Dilmun and Makan sailing far out into the Persian/Arabian Gulf: "The lands of Magan and Dilmun looked up at me, Enki, moored the *Dilmun*-boat to the ground, loaded the Magan-boat sky high; The *magilum*-boat of Meluhha transports gold and silver, brings them to Nippur for Enlil, the king of all the lands."[78]

Even 4500 years later, it is hard to miss the zest and enthusiasm for foreign trade and travel and for the spoils of commerce suffusing these texts. It is vaguely familiar. It is the language of empire, of an expansive and all-inclusive kind that the English writer Joseph Addison used in 1711 in his admiring reports on London's royal exchange. It recalls, too, the exhilarating American tribute to 1800s expansion, "Westward the Course of Empire Takes its Way!" If Enki's texts do not reflect globalization, they, nevertheless, attest to latitudinal and longitudinal expansion! Sargon's own records tell of the boats of Dilmun, Makan, and Meluhha moored at the wharves of Akkad. Other texts speak of links between the economy of Mesopotamia and India, thus cementing a regional trade that already extended from Egypt in the west to the Indus Valley in the east. The site of Rasal Junayz on the southeastern tip of Arabia was a staging point in this trade (see Chapter 3). Westward—and eastward—spread the course of the Akkadian empire.

The prosperity and power of Sargon's Empire rested upon hard silver currency that Sargon's merchants obtained from the mines of Burushattum (Purushkanda) in southeastern Turkey, ancient Anatolia. A monument found in Iraq shows Akkadian soldiers capturing prisoners with hairstyles, short daggers, and drinking vessels that are unmistakably Anatolian. Sargon did not *occupy* Anatolia, but obtained its silver by controlling the mountain passes and sending in royal traders to purchase it—yet another example of *locational advantage*.[79]

Having plundered the imperial seat of Ebla and its immense reserves of high-quality gold and silver, the kings of Akkad presided over the most far-flung economy of the Bronze Age. Goods, loans and commodities were priced in terms of silver, which was traded in the form of ingots. Grain, cattle, pigs, or donkeys served as currency where silver was not obtainable.[80] The need for a common currency was becoming more and more obvious.

Sargon's trade, still dominated by temple and palace, was nevertheless more and more in the hands of a rising class of private merchants. These were known as *damgara* in Sumer and Akkad, and *tamkārum* (plural *tamkāru*) in Babylonia and Assyria. In the beginning, *damgara* were employed by temples and palaces, trading on their behalf. By Sargon's time, some of them were rich enough to trade their own silver in private deals for personal profit. This was true only for trade within Mesopotamia. Long distance trade with Egypt or India was too expensive and risky for any but royal or temple merchants. Archaeologist Benjamin Forster found "no evidence" that the Akkadian *damgara* "played any significant role in the acquisition of products foreign to Mesopotamia" or was "anyone other than a businessman who sought profits for clients, including the state, in Mesopotamian markets with mostly Mesopotamian goods."[81]

Still, a growing number of *damgara* built their personal fortunes during what some call "the Akkadian Century" of power and prosperity. They became creditors, moneylenders, and independent agents who acted on their own. Their private business records were far less formal and bureaucratic than those of the temple. Specialization thrived. Ur-Sara of Umma raised state livestock; his contemporary Ginunu traded in grain and silver; Sunitum in barley. Even women such as Ana-é dealt in real estate, metals, and grain. It must not be forgotten that in these interactions with the palace, they worked as private contractors, not civil servants.[82]

The influence of this Akkadian Century lingered. The language became a lingua franca. It is taught and studied in our universities today. But, after hubris, nemesis; after expansion, contraction. The great empires of the Early Bronze Age seem to have collapsed due to ecological,[83] rather than political, disasters. The Old Kingdom of Egypt, seemingly secure and invincible, fell apart from within, in a manner not unlike the Soviet Union. This collapse took place around 2350 BCE, when the monsoons of the Indian Ocean shifted. The waters of the Nile, the source of Egypt's seemingly eternal prosperity, seemed to all but dry up. Egypt was smitten with scorching desert winds and dust storms. An inscription of the Sixth Dynasty shows emaciated, starving peasants. The totalitarian theocracy crumbled in revolution, replaced by the anarchy of the Seventh and Eighth Dynasties. The *monarchs* or governors reasserted their power. Every prince for himself seemed the order of the day, with each ruler driving out hungry foreigners. The Papyrus Ipuwer laments this terrible time of economic collapse:[84]

> The fruitful water of Nile is flooding,
> The fields are not cultivated,
> Robbers and tramps wander about and
> Foreign people invade the country from everywhere.
> Diseases rage and women are barren.
> All social order has ceased,
> Taxes are not paid and
> Temples and palaces are being insulted.
> Those who once were veiled by splendid garments, are now ragged,[85]

The Empire of Akkad lasted for over a century before it, too, was weakened from within by ecological problems. This was around 2100 BCE. If Egypt's collapse recalled the USSR, the fall of Akkad conjures up Rome. Several sites have been excavated in northern Iraq and eastern Syria, notably at the site of Tell Leilan. The sites tell a similar story. A layer of mud brick representing a flourishing settlement of the Sargonid Empire is followed by a layer of volcanic ash, and then some eight inches (or twenty centimetres) of dust. Deserts spread in the wheat fields of what would eventually be Assyria, and many northern Mesopotamian communities became ghost towns.[86] People flocked southward to the Sumerian plain, and some, such as the fair-haired Gutians, came as invaders, setting up a barbarian dynasty that ruled Mesopotamia for almost a century much as the Goths later ruled Rome.[87]

Eventually, the Gutians would be expelled by a revived Sumerian power under Ur-Nammu and his successor, Shulgi. Although the turmoil at the end of the Early Bronze Age was tragic for the people involved, Mesopotamia, although down, was by no means *out*. A new age was about to begin, one in which private enterprise, in the person of the *tamkārum*, would become far more important than in the past. The groundwork for effective business management, involving firms that looked even more like today's multinationals, would be laid in what is called the Middle Bronze Age. That story awaits our next chapter.

3 The Golden Age of Temple Capitalism
Mesopotamia and India 2250–2000 BCE

In his magisterial *Story of Civilization*, historian Will Durant was bold enough to outline four essential elements that anchor a healthy civilization. He listed them as

- economic security,
- political organization and stability (the rule of law),
- a common body of moral traditions, and
- the pursuit of knowledge and the arts.

Our survey of the economic life of the ancient world has already listed the acquisitive instinct so prominently. "Culture suggests agriculture," Durant added, for the simple reason that, without a reliable and sustainable supply of food and water, humankind is subject to "the precarious fortunes of the chase."[1] But if culture suggests agriculture, civilization suggests the city, from the Latin, *civitas*. Chapters 1 and 2 discussed studied three important cities—Uruk, Memphis, and Ebla—each rising to prominence as pivots of a distinct civilization. We have seen that Sargon's Akkadian Empire had proved immensely beneficial to the rising merchant class of Mesopotamia, perhaps copying the pattern that had made Ebla mighty still. The collapse of the Akkadian *uber*-state sometime after 2300 BCE fragmented the economy of the Fertile Crescent, but this would not ring in the end of economic and political advances.

Far from it.

"Progress is real if discontinuous," wrote the respected Gordon Childe in *What Happened in History*. "No trough ever declines to the low level of the preceding one; each crest out-tops its last precursor". During the next phase of development in Mesopotamia, the Middle Bronze Age (2100–1600 BCE), two distinct centers of power arose. These were a Sumerian-dominated region along the eastern Euphrates, balanced by a Semitic-controlled western sphere with trade ties dating back well before Sargon. Thus, both continuity and change worked in tandem as the Near Eastern world moved from the Early to Middle Bronze. Still, even with many cultural constants remaining from Sargon's era, population densities in strategic centers such as Egypt, Palestine, and Anatolia were lower. The disintegration of the Akkadian Empire had proved a massive setback for trade, commerce, and cultivation. Nevertheless, economic innovation and development proceeded apace, the story of this chapter.

BOOM AND BUST AT UR: 2100–2000 BCE

Within a century or two of the Early Bronze collapse, the eastern-bound trade of the Persian Gulf region, into which emptied the Tigris and Euphrates Rivers, witnessed a staggering revival. A succession of miniempires led by Ur, Isin-Larsa and, most spectacularly, that of Babylon under Hammurabi, adapted and improved the Sargonic model of palace/temple expansion. The source material for this unfolding is rich and abundant. From 1923 to 1929, a joint British–American expedition under Sir Leonard Wooley uncovered the Royal Library of Ur, the most extensive and detailed of any before Ebla. "Virtually no period of ancient Near Eastern history presents the historian with such an abundance and variety of documentation," testifies Marc Van De Mieroop.[2] The commercial records of the neo-Sumerian kingdom of Ur from the Middle Bronze Age were opened for study. Historians could construct the most detailed picture yet of Near Eastern business practices. The scale of these transactions was truly impressive. In fact, the picture emerging was astonishing, especially when the Indus Valley culture was factored into the equation. Although Early Bronze patterns of trade persisted, they manifested themselves in ways that can only be described as revolutionary. History repeats, somewhat, but never exactly in the same way.

Around 2093 BCE, a ruler named Shulgi ascended the throne of Ur in what is today Southern Iraq. The result was that "the Mesopotamian economy began to flourish as never before."[3] Temple building and refurnishing expanded even as Shulgi simultaneously built a defensive wall at the narrow waist of the Tigris–Euphrates to guard against attacks from the west. If Sargon was a prototype for Napoleon, perhaps Shulgi was ancient Sumeria's Alfred the Great for his sterling efforts to bring order out of near-chaos. Historians place him in what is called the Ur III dynastic state. This ostensibly devout ruler saw to it that the royal cattle pens that serviced the great temples of Nippur and Uruk were a top priority. Texts uncovered from Ur-Numma included large numbers of letter–orders reflecting a sophisticated banking system backed by disbursements in kind from royal storage centers. Ur III was not a totalitarian state. Labor had to be recruited for vast irrigation projects that guaranteed the food supply. Hence the rise of literacy to make possible the vast bureaucracy needed to supervise these ongoing public works and repairs. Archives retrieved from nearby Lagash revealed an elaborate judicial system in operation.[4]

Meanwhile, the functions of government and business had greatly expanded. Grain from Gursu undergirded a secure food supply, and neighboring Umma provided wood, reeds, and leather. This was supplemented by copper, tin, and luxuries from Northern India and Afghanistan. Ebla had showed the way. As the flow of goods intensified along what is now the Persian Gulf, the increasing role of ready money slowly began to infiltrate an economy where barter was still the preferred method of exchange. Much of the produce shipped eastward—fish, textiles, barley, and wheat—was classified by the palace of Ur-Nammu as exchangeable goods. These were assigned a fixed value in terms of silver. In contrast to these fixed prices, which both in Ur and the successor regimes of Assyria and Babylon pegged to silver, the prices of many other items—such as copper, tin, lumber, spices, wines, and cattle—fluctuated greatly according to their markets.[5] It would seem reasonable that businesspeople would take advantage of theses prices fluctuations to enrich themselves.

More and more, the traditional temple-based economy was developing into a temple/palace economy. In some cities, priests alone would rule; in others the *lugal* ruled from their palaces. Shulgi himself instituted an elaborate schedule of monthly obligations levied on all the major Akkadian and Sumerian provinces. The purpose was to provide for the priestly families and the sacrifices at the Nippur temples. This idea would never go way. It showed the pivotal role of temples in driving economic expansion. The merchants, however, now increasingly operated on their own as international trade began to pass into the hands of the self-employed, rather than crown merchants. By 2000 BCE, as trade increased and trading patterns grew more complex, the concept of private enterprise grew in significance across Mesopotamia. According to Peter Jay, "private enterprise had taken over much of the trade that was previously the preserve of the state."[6]

Why did self-supporting private enterprise flourish more in the Neo-Sumerian than in the Akkadian environment? The answer involves history's first recorded instance of outsourcing. Under Sargon's vast empire, the state was richer and more powerful and better able to finance long-distance ventures all the way to India. The kingdom of Shulgi was smaller and the Ur state simply could not afford such ventures. Private merchants, operating on a smaller scale and using Dilmun–Bahrein as a base and Gulf traders as middlemen could. This might be described as a case of *government*, rather than market, failure.

This move towards a limited form of privatization would accelerate later in the Old Babylonian period around 1800 to 1600 BCE. As an illustration, the Dilmun-boats that traversed the Gulf in the days of Ur-Nammu (2100 BCE) weighed some 90,000 litres. Three centuries later, the vessels of Hammurabi's time rarely weighed more than 12,000 litres. The use of smaller boats suggested that voyages to the east were now not only safer and more regular, but also self-funded in the absence of royal subsidies or temple tithes.

It is noteworthy that in the Ur III period, the Mesopotamian ships reached only to Magan Oman, and in Old Babylonian times no further than Dilmun. By contrast, the rulers of pre-Sargonic Lagas and of Akkad recorded direct trade with all these areas, including Meluhha (ancient Pakistan). This absence of official records may reflect conditions in the Gulf, but it may also have to do with a shift within Mesopotamia from publicly supported ventures to private enterprise. The zealous penmanship of the court recorders were not as busy, hence records on the clay tablets were more scarce. The tendency of bureaucracies to leave records is another constant in history. All this, however, implies a reduced capital investment from the priestly and palace official and a move from official state control.[7]

Around 2000 BCE, as the Ur III dynasty gave way to the less powerful kingdoms of Isin and Larsa, these new kings possessed neither the capital nor the personnel to renew state-sponsored international commerce on the scale of Sargon and his immediate heirs. Given that Sumer and its ascendant heir, Babylon, needed to trade or die, it is not surprising that something akin to our own 1990s trend of renewed *privatization* took place. That is, the merchant community, itself, stepped forward to fill the vacuum created by the public sector.[8] Supervision of international trade devolved upon a new commercial institution, known as the *Kārum*, a term best translated as "harbor," reflecting its mercantile origins. The *Kārum* had their origin in the communities of traders living alongside the docks of large Sumerian cities near the Euphrates, cities such as Ur, Umma, and Lagash. These cities depended greatly on Gulf commerce. As in medieval Europe, these informal associations of *dam-gàr* gradually grouped themselves into guild-like associations to help share the risk. They were soon granted a semiofficial status by the local *lugal*. By the time of Hammurabi, those the Babylonians called *kāru* were recognized organizations headed by a chief merchant, or *Orwakil Tamkāru*. This magnate was granted administrative authority by the crown to conduct and regulate commerce. The merchant adventurers of Tudor England and the later proprietary colonies in America offer a close parallel.

Kāru in various cities were empowered to exercise the commercial, legal, and administrative duties that the public sector could no longer afford to sustain. Both Newfoundland, Britain's earliest overseas possession, and later India, under the East India Company, developed in this way. A reduced palace presence led to the rise of the private merchant class. As the rulers of Ur III struggled to impose secure military government over the Mosul plain and the troublesome Zagros Mountain area, the merchant traders stepped into the breach. This was paralleled by the various officials of the first British Empire reporting to the London-based Board of Trade as much as to Whitehall. Trade often went along with and even ahead of the flag. In Mesopotamia, the donkey caravans and Dilmun-boats continued to carry the copper, tin, wheat and textiles that had journeyed in and out of the two rivers for generations[9]

GOLDEN AGE AT UR

This was Ur's finest hour. At Ur, Woolley found remains of a prosperous neighborhood in the heart of the city. Among the little houses with their narrow walls were the shops and wharves of the business district. As in Ebla, many business records were buried among the clay tablets. The Ur texts, the best Sumerian business archives to have survived, are generally dated from the time of Rim-Sin (1822–1763 BCE) of Larsa, who preceded the illustrious Hammurabi of Babylon fame.

Not unlike Samuel Pepys' Diaries recording the habits and foibles of the great and near-great in Restoration London, the Ur archives shine a spotlight on several Sumerian businesspeople. First was the banker, Dumuzi-Gamil, who formed an investment partnership with one Shumi-Abiya. Around 1769 BCE, they borrowed 500 grams of silver from Shumi-Abum. This was a five-year loan at a 3.8% rate of interest. Dumuzi promised to return some 300 grams on his share of 250 grams after five years. Shumi-Abum then sold his loan to other merchants who subsequently collected from Dumuzi. Sumerians lent money to Dumuzi and Shumi-Abiya at low interest, which the latter then put to work. The capital borrowed from Shumi-Abum was invested in bakeries. These shipped bread to the chief temple at Ur, as well as to the palace and nearby Larsa. Dumuzi was shrewd. He borrowed money on his future income and made short-term loans of silver to fisherman at exorbitant rates of interest of 20%. This did not endear him to his debtors.[10] The "invisible hand" was quite visible at Ur.

The priests of the Temple of Nannar had a more favorable view of Dumuzi, for his long-term borrowings of silver from the temple treasury were, in turn, loaned out to clients to help stimulate the money supply. J. P. Morgan's periodic interventions to prevent panics on the New York Stock Exchange in pre-World War I America come to mind. According to Professor William N. Goetzmann, "while the ancient Babylonian temples were a long way from being federal reserve banks, they may have performed some of the same functions."[11] Will Durant shrewdly reported the ups and down of ancient money matters:

> A system of credit existed by which goods, gold or silver might be borrowed, interest to be paid in the same material as the loan, and at rates ranging from 15 to 33% per annum. Since the stability of a society may be partly measured by inverse relation with the rate of interest, we may suspect that Sumerian business, like ours, lived in an atmosphere of economic and political uncertainty and doubt.

The search for workable instruments of fiscal security and workable firewalls has not altered greatly across the centuries.

Although Ur did not have a formal stock exchange, its citizens were well-accustomed to speculating on future profits. Sumer, in its waning days, had a thriving market in bonds whereby a promissory note was as good as silver. It is important to remember that business law in ancient Sumer, Assyria, and Babylonia was, in some ways, close to a Milton Friedman or Margaret Thatcher ideal. Property rights were absolute and inviolable. Creditors had life and death power over debtors. Only the ancient Israelites, as we will see later on, had a legal code that stressed the rights of debtors (although it was rarely enforced). Across the ancient Near East, debtors were often forced to sell themselves and their families into slavery, and lawsuits brought judgements whose results could last for decades. The palace itself had a vested interested in promoting indebtedness because it made their subjects work harder and produce more—the very visible hand of state power. The loan contracts that Dumuzi offered to his customers may have been good for Ur's business classes, but they were horrendous for peasants and artisans, who were then taxed for the benefit of temple lands. He became a very rich man on the debts of others.[12]

In the same district as Dumuzi lived Ea-Nasir, who ran a thriving import–export business in the Gulf. He organized and financed trading expeditions from Ur to Dilmun and back. The Dilmunites of Bahrein, as we have seen, prospered as middlemen linking the Sumerian and Indus Valley markets. The Dilmun trade was big business for Ea-Nasir. On one occasion, he assembled fifty investors, along with their goods and silver, to sail to Dilmun. They and their trading partners brought back copper, spices, and valuable stones. These Persian Gulf operatives were pioneering some of history's earliest limited partnerships and joint ventures. According to Professor Goetzmann, this was not unlike the financial partnerships that back modern oil drilling and real estate activities. The investors each reaped profits, often enormous, in proportion to the value of their investments. Ea-Nasir, of course, won the lion's share. The partners were not liable for anything beyond their original investment.[13]

The Ur tablets include many records from Ea-Nasir's clients, whose written agreements breathe the transactional style that is still recognizable:

> Minas of silver, 5 g of sesame oil, 30 garments, for an expedition to Tilmun to buy copper there, as capital for a partnership Lu-Mešlamtal and Nigsisanabsa have borrowed from Ur-Ninmar. At the safe return of the expedition, he (the creditor) will not recognize commercial losses. They (the debtors) have mutually agreed to satisfy Ur-Ninmar with 4 minas of copper for each shekel (of silver) as a just price (?); this they have sworn conjointly by the King. Before Sin-ili, Sin-asarid, Sin-mutabbil, Sin-[ ]su, [ma]gir; seals of the witnesses. In the month *Addaru*, 12th day, of the year he built the wall of Zarbilum (Rim-Sin 28).[14]

Another tablet suggests Ea-Nasir had agents in Dilmun: No one investor could muster the capital to finance an expedition that far down the Gulf. These early "shareholders" pooled their money. The royal palace often added its own resources as well, just as Elizabeth I was wont to join in with the nautical adventures of Raleigh and Hawkins (1558–1603). The temple at Nannar in Ur had been financing these expeditions since Sargon's Akkadian heyday. Small, private investors got involved as well. Ea-Nasir, in one sense, managed *the first mutual fund*. Ur had a population of perhaps 15,000 to 20,000 people, and it is possible that hundreds of smiths, farmers, shopkeepers, even laborers committed a few shekels each to Ea-Nasir on the expectation of big earnings in copper.[15]

Here, already, was the classic economic "bubble." It went the way of all its imitators. Ea-Nasir's investors were wiped out in the Great Crash of 1788 BCE. The long-term cause was, of course, "irrational exuberance," people buying and borrowing on profits they did not yet have. Government mismanagement was the immediate trigger. Having favored creditors for years, the *lugal* Rim-Sin of Larsa suddenly declared all loans null and void. Imagine if the Commission of the European Union or the United States Congress did this today! Dumuzi, Ea-Nasir, and others were instantly wiped out. The mere threat of future state edicts effectively squelched the extension of long-term loans. Interest rates for short-term loans skyrocketed. Proud Ur was ruined financially, and capital fled to Larsa. Economic weakness tempted aggressors. The vultures were already waiting in the wings. Sumer, itself, would soon be engulfed by the Amorites of Babylon led by Hammurabi, who had already conquered Assyria to the north.[16] This is a ruler and a people we will hear a lot more about in Chapter 4.

THE INDUS CIVILIZATION

In *Empire*, his exciting retelling of the British Empire as the precursor to an early form of globalization, Niall Ferguson recapitulates the stunning fact that when seventeenth-century Britons moved into the India trade, they, the "advanced" Europeans, had "little to offer Indians that they did not make themselves." Calico, silk, and cotton from the sub-continent were the mechanisms that would soon transform the trade of Mother England, herself.[17] Likewise, Sumer and Akkad, economic leaders of the second and third millennia BCE, when building an interlocking trading system that included Egypt and the Minoans to the west, were only too glad to include the Indus Valley in their networks. That impressive civilization to the east had been strikingly self-originating! The rediscovery of the Indus Valley civilization or, as some call it, the Harappan culture, was one of the twentieth century's great archaeological triumphs. The 1,000-mile-long Indus Valley is located in today's Pakistan, and includes the two strategic regions of the Sind and the Punjab. The excavation of Harappa (named after the god *Hara*, or *Shiva*) was begun in earnest by Sir John Marshall and D. R. Sahni in 1921. The digging of Mohenjo-Daro, six hundred kilometres to the southwest, began in 1922. There the expedition uncovered hundreds of solidly-built brick houses and shops, rising sometimes to several stories, along both wide streets and narrow lanes.

The surprise came in Marshall's article in *The Illustrated London News* of January 7, 1928: "Even at Ur, the houses are by no means equal in point of construction to those of Mohenjo-Daro." Indeed, the excavation unearthed the material remains of a civilization that far surpassed that of Mesopotamia and Egypt in size and scale. Its 500,000 square miles formed a gigantic triangle with sides a thousand miles long. Its base lay in the Arabian Sea as far south as Bombay; its apex reached far up the Indus River system and perhaps to the Ganges. Its cities and villages covered 1,500 kilometres from north to south, stretching from the south-eastern corner of Iran to as far as the Aral Sea in Russia. Arising in tandem with Mesopotamian, the Indus accomplishment was still unique to itself. We have virtually no written records from this period, except for large numbers of small, square steatite seals written in a yet undeciphered script. Nonetheless, the material remains of Harappan civilization excite wonder and admiration.

Dating the rise of the Indus civilization proved a challenge, given the absence of written records. Some overlap between Indian and Sumerian artifacts provided the barest clues, nothing conclusive. A consistent pattern of radiocarbon dates, however, strongly indicates that the rise of the Indus cities began around 2600 BCE. The cities, therefore, reached their peak sometime between 2300 and 1700 BCE.[18]

This indigenous culture along the Indus laid the foundation for modern India and Pakistan. A comparison of the black-and-red pottery found on the site of villages such as Rana Ghundai, with similar vessels in the lower strata of Harappa, showed that the large cities arose later than the surrounding villages. The first excavations suggested a rather egalitarian society, but later findings by Sir R. E. Mortimer-Wheeler and others after 1946, quickly changed this picture. The Indus cities had well-fortified citadels for the ruler and the temple hierarchy. A uniform pattern prevailed, such that the layout of the streets, the plan of the houses, and even the bricks were essentially the same. The evidence of extensive planning at Mohenjo-Daro, Harappa, and their sister cities, suggest, in the words of Indian historian A. L. Basham, "a single centralized state rather than a number of free communities."[19]

The urbanization phase in the Indus Valley coincided with that of the Akkadian and neo-Sumerian kingdoms. Although the Indus Valley civilization was distinct, it still bore all the features of a highly organized, autocratic state. The ten or more layers of strata of the cities revealed a society that was nowhere near as dynamic or as innovative as its trading partners to the west. From 2500 to 1700 BCE, the street plans of the cities remained the same, as did the script on the seals. The picture is one of an "unparalleled continuity" of government, a conservative society "theocratic in character."[20] Other researchers maintain that "it remains uncertain whether authority lay with a priestly or a commercial oligarchy."[21]

The Harappan Culture bears the imprint of three major cultural traditions across time. These were: the Indus proper in Pakistan and India, the Baluchistan tradition in Pakistan, and the Helmand in Afghanistan. Each of these has been divided into eras and/or phases, as shown in Table 3.1.

The Indus Valley region was linked by common trading, cultural, social, religious, and political ties dating back to the Neolithic Era. Cultural transformation became more rapid in the Copper and Bronze Ages. The Regionalization Era coincided with the Early Dynastic phases of Sumerian civilization.[22]

Just before 2600 BCE, the Indus entered a period of clearly defined integration. Trade networks began to expand towards the south, suggesting new alliances, internalization, and resource-seeking behavior. A shift in trade from black to brown chert[23] suggests a changed view of trade based on notions of ethnic identity.[24] At its peak, the Harappan represented a vast cultural and linguistic community with standard weights and measures. Painted pottery symbols, seal motifs, and figurines were similar from Central Asia to the Rann of Kutch. The cultural trajectory describes a civiliza-

Table 3.1 Chronology of the Indus Valley Civilization and its Sumerian Links

Early Subsistence Era: Trade, ceramics, and specialized crafts arise in separate regions.

Regionalization Era (*Late Stone and Copper Age*): Indus Valley civilization united, Early Harappan phase, rise of Harappa and Mohenjo-Daro. Trading contact with Early Dynastic Sumer.

Indus Valley	Baluchistan	Helmand
Balakot Phase	Kachi Phase	Mundigak Phase
Amri Phase	Kili Gul Muhammad	Helmand Phase
Hakra Phase	Phase	
Kot Diji Phase	Sheri Gan Tarakai Phase	
	Kechi Beg Phase	
	Nal Phase	

Integration Era I (*Early Bronze: Middle Harappan Phase: 2600–2200*): Indus Civilization reaches peak. Direct trade with Akkad. Dilmun flourishes.

Indus Valley	Baluchistan	Helmand
Harappan Phase	Kulli Phase	Shahr-I-Sokhta Phase

Integration Era II (*Middle Bronze: Middle Harappan Phase: 2200–1900 BCE*): Indus cities trade with Ur, Larsa through Gulf middlemen. Decline through ecological crisis, flooding, salinization

Indus Valley	Baluchistan	Helmand
Harappan Phase	Periano Phase	Shahr-I-Sokhta Phase

Localization Era: Fragmentation of Indus Civilization after 1900 BCE.

Indus	Baluchistan	Helmand
Punjab Phase	Bampur Phase	Seistan Phase
Jhukar Phase	Pirak Phase	
Rangpur Phase		

tion affected by decisions made by a centralized authority for a period of over five centuries.[25]

Nothing like the Royal Tombs of Ur have been found in Harappan India, nor centralized temple or palace complexes. There is, however, evidence of elite economic structures at Mohenjo-Daro and Harappa. An impressive bath complex at Mohenjo-Daro would have done credit to the later Romans, with adjoining rooms for robing and disrobing and a pool some forty feet long and eight feet deep. These seem to have been used for priestly or purification purposes, but it confirmed the existence of a powerful ruling class in a city supporting 20,000 people. Mohenjo-Daro offered elaborate drainage systems and public baths, as well as differentiated residential dwellings. This suggests that trade in the Indus Valley area, as well as political alliances, was based upon kinship ties. At the top, merchants and priests may have competed for control. The largest cities across the region were probably city–states with a fair amount of autonomy, but integrated with others through trade. It seems that no one social group could retain complete control. In one city, traders ruled; in another, priests; in another, herdsmen. All shared common tastes in art, common languages, and beliefs.[26] Undoubtedly, this was one of the ancient world's premier civilizations, yet still fairly unknown in the Western world.

"THE SHIPS OF MELUHHA"

Commerce in India at this early stage is poorly documented, but archaeology offers substantial evidence of the impressive infrastructure that once supported trading ties to Sumer. The port of Lothal on the Gulf of Gambay in the Arabian Sea boasted an enclosed brick shipping dock over seven hundred feet long. A sluice gate capable of loading ships at high and low tide is clearly evident. This commitment to ocean-going trade was spurred by the produce of the rich hinterland, gold and copper from the interior, and the all-important timber from the Himalayas—a prized commodity along the flatlands of Mesopotamia.[27] There is, thus, every indication that, as in Sumer, private merchants were an essential part of the Harappan economy, but not much evidence on how business was organized. Most earned their living through agriculture, not industry. The Indus Valley countryside was, even at this early time, crisscrossed with irrigation channels used by independent farmers growing rice, peas, dates, sesame, and grain. Village peasants depended on the plowing capacity of their water buffaloes and white *zebu* cattle, which slept in the front of their shacks. Life in the Indus Valley was filled with the irruptions of drought and flood, the rotating "wheels" of poverty and prosperity, plenty and famine, perhaps inspiring the teaching on life's vicissitudes found in later Brahamist philosophy.[28]

The Indus–Mesopotamian trading connections have been cited in the Ur tablets, as mentioned in Chapter 2. That connection was primarily by sea, as evidenced by the distribution of Indus artifacts in many Persian Gulf sites. The location of the ports of Sutkagen-dor and Sotka-koh near today's Iranian border show how important westerly connections by sea were for Harappan culture. We have little direct evidence of the type of vessels used. The longest voyages were probably made by timber-built boats, although boats made from reeds are depicted on a Mohenjo-Daro seal. These boats would have been much cheaper to make and could be quite seaworthy. Rowboats, on the other hand, were better adapted for the rivers and short voyages, and their bigger crews incurred more costs. The Meluhha ships that sailed to Sumer no doubt had sails, as did both the flat- and round-bottomed vessels from Mesopotamia. The clay models of ship remains found at Lothal show they were narrower, flatter, and swifter than their Sumerian counterparts. The Lothal ships had a sharp stem and stern, and a mast with a square sail. They could sail with the wind, but had to rely on rowers when sailing into the wind. The ships of the Bronze Age were fastened together with either metal couplings or wooden pegs, instead of traditional iron nails. How much could these ships carry? Comparisons with modern Arabian vessels suggest Harappan or Dilmun-boats were ten meters in length, and could carry about seventy or eighty tons.[29] No doubt many "mute, inglorious Sinbads" made these journeys, whose tales may yet appear once other sites have been unearthed.

"MIDDLE CLASS PROSPERITY?"

Harappa[30] in the Punjab was, itself, a city of some 35,000 people. Its fifty-six kilometres of circumference was surrounded by a brick wall approximately fifteen metres thick. A citadel on the western side of the city rose about sixteen metres above the ground. North of the citadel, several large granaries were found along the banks of the Ravi River. These granaries, laid out in two rows of six warehouses each, were ventilated, ideal for storing grain sent down the Indus, possibly from Sumer.[31] Within the walls of Harappa were also found the living quarters for artisans and laborers. The streets of the city were well-planned, nicely laid-out in rectangles. The houses—a hallmark of this culture—although not necessarily of equal size, were fairly uniform in style, and the finest system of sewage in early antiquity drained the bathrooms. In some ways, the urban Indian masses of the Early and Middle Bronze Age lived better than some of their descendants in modern times. Sir Mortimer Wheeler was reported to have described city life at this period in the Indus as reflecting "middle-class prosperity with municipal controls."[32] The rectangular city blocks appear to have been segregated by occupation. Public wells, barracks, and rows of shops adorned the street in history's first example of urban planning.[33]

In some ways, Harappan India anticipated the consumer societies of the future. Red-and-black wheel-made pottery appears at all of the Indus sites, decorated with animal and geometric motifs. Then, as now, Indians expressed a preference for disposable drinking cups. Clay vessels were used once, then thrown away. The Harappan cities were home to craftsmen working in stone and bronze, sculpting figurines of dancing girls. One such figurine displays the likeness of a noble-looking bearded figure dressed in a robe, who may have been one of the city's first priest-kings. Indus Valley craftsmen also created the little square seals that they sold to merchants. Soapstone seals, usually about an inch square, were used to identify bales of cotton or bags of grain. Here is the earliest version of corporate branding. According to Stanley Wolpert of UCLA, the exquisite likenesses of tigers, Brahma bulls, elephants, and other Indian animals were "probably made for merchants who used them to 'brand' their wares," along with inscriptions in a as yet untranslated language.[34] These were India's first business documents, written in some four hundred pictographic characters, some of them quite possibly bearing the names of merchants using the seal. One seal, for example, found near Mohenjo-Daro, showed a yogi with a horned dress surrounded by a tiger, elephant, rhinoceros, water buffalo, and deer. It is possible that this seal may have represented the mighty hunter and destroyer Shiva, who was venerated as a fertility god, a tamer of beasts, and a planter of seed.[35]

SECURITY OF SUPPLY: BRONZE AGE TRADE ROUTES

The propensity towards branding gives testimony to the lively and sophisticated streams of commerce flowing along the northern ports of the Arabian Sea: granaries, warehouses, docks, and trans-shipping. The merchants of Lothal and its rich hinterland would have understood the rough dictum ascribed to Sir Walter Raleigh: "He who controls the seas of the world controls the trade of the world; he who controls the trade, controls the world." This is a political–economic principle fact whose importance will be underscored over and over in the chapters that follow.

By the 1990s of our own era, some seventy Harappan cultural sites had been excavated. They stretched into northern India and from the southeastern corner of Iran to the Himalayas to the Rann of Kutch (south of the Indus) and the borders of Gujarat. Harappan outposts in the southwest near the Makran coastal routes, such as Sutkagen Dor, offer evidence that the merchants of the Indus Valley comprised the enigmatic "land of Meluhha," with which the kings of Sumer and the Sargonid rulers of Akkad carried on a most profitable long-range trade. These regions today correspond to the coastal region of the Indian state of Gujarat and the Indus Valley and coastal regions of Pakistan and the Pakistani state of Sindh. The robust sea trade along the ports lining the 1,000 kilometres of passage from Lothal to the Gulf was well ahead of its time. In our time, the Iranians are at work building a naval base at the port of Okamar as we write. In the Bronze Age, the huge granaries at the mouth of the Indus stored wares destined for the eager markets of Sumer and Akkad, a prefiguring of mighty New Orleans before Katrina. Strategic port cities are yet another constant in world trade, as the importance of Rotterdam, Hong Kong, and Singapore attest.

In 1932, Wolpert and other researchers concluded from seals found among the remains of Ur that "merchants from Harappa and Mohenjo-daro were trading with their Sumerian counterparts between 2300 and 2000 BCE."[36] As well as vital grain exports, the merchants of the Indus traded in finished industrial products, notably cotton cloth (the earliest found anywhere) that was spun and woven in the numerous cities. This, as noted, would be an Indian staple for centuries. The bulk of the trade that sailed westward on Sumerian boats or jogged across Iran on donkey caravans was in luxury goods—beads, jewelry, necklaces, ceramic figurines, precious stones, ivory, and aromatic woods. Archaeologist Sir John Marshall reported that the exotic bangles and ear-ornaments moving along the Indus coastal routes "might have come out of a Bond Street jeweler's of today rather than from a (sic) house of 5,000 years ago".[37] While goods flowed west, imported silver, tin, and other metals flowed south into Mohenjo-daro from what is now Afghanistan and from the Kerman region of modern-day Iran, especially from the chlorite center of Tepe Yahya. This region was famed also for turquoise, mother-of-pearl, and lapis lazuli. Anatolian obsidian has been found in its remains, just as a pottery shard from there has turned up in Mesopotamia, attesting, once again, to a far-reaching trade in precious metals.[38]

As Harappan and Sumerian boats could only sail with the wind, or row against it, awareness of seasonal winds and tides became an important factor in the timing of trade between ports.[39] At some point, they began using the winds of the mighty monsoons that blew from the southwest. The monsoon hits southern India earlier than it does the Gulf of Kutch and Sind at or near the mouth of the Indus. Thus, ships from these areas could sail well into June, but those based further south had to be in port by May. Ships could leave Sind in late August. Those based further south had to wait until October. The ports along the coast of Makran, in modern Pakistan, were free from the monsoon.[40]

The Meluhha-ships sailing from Sind or Lothal to Akkad or Ur would typically leave India in February or March to set out on their return in May. Those leaving Sumer in May might dock in Dilmun until September. They would then set out for India and return using the light northeast monsoon that blew in mid-November. Many ships were "makran-ships," Makran sailing between Sumer and the coast of Makran. Those 1000 kilometres were fairly sheltered from the southwest monsoon. After the Akkadian Empire collapsed, trade had constricted. Voyages were between Sumer and Makran, and eventually fell back on the Sumer–Dilmun passage. When they returned to Ur from Dilmun (Bahrein), however, the flow of goods from the Indus was unabated, being transhipped from the Indus Valley to the Makran coast. Security of supply was greatly aided by those lighter vessels hugging the shoreline of Baluchistan and the Arabian Sea. Both the Dilmunites and the merchants of Mohenjo-Daro operated smaller subsidiary way-stations along the shore to protect this commerce.[41] One can see at work here the attempts to mitigate the vagaries of wind and tide, the timeless motivations that later led to Lloyd's of London and the first insurance companies. The sea can be a capricious and sometimes cruel partner, fathering plays such as *The Tempest* and songs such as *The Wreck of the Edmund Fitzgerald*. The seaman's exploits from the Makran to the Gulf have yet to be fully unearthed.

Indeed, the costs and risks involved in shipping goods between India and Sumer in the third millennium BCE necessitated large-scale bulk shipments to make the risk return attractive. According to Indian scholar Shareen Ratnagar, "consignments of cargos between India and Mesopotamia were possibly made but once a year" and the shipments may have often faced delay and loss of crew and goods.[42]

Goods were also shipped overland from the mines of Tepe Yahya in Kerman (under Elamite control), and from the cities of the Indus by donkey caravan, all in an effort to reach the monsoon-free ports of the Makran. Steady drivers could make up to thirty kilometres a day for periods of up to ten days. Two-wheeled oxen-driven carts were in use all over India by this time, carrying much fewer wares than the thousand kilograms per unit they manage today. Why? Ancient axles were made of wood, not iron. It is interesting that the city planners in Mohenjo-Daro and Harappa had built the ox-carts into their plans. There, the streets were broad and well-maintained, as against the narrow streets of Mesopotamia, which were better suited for donkeys.[43] Commerce, then as now, pre-empted city planning. In fact, the Indus Valley's two-wheeled carts provide one of our oldest examples of two-wheeled vehicles.

The genius of Harappan and Mohenjo-Daro's economic and cultural achievement was the relative ease with which goods could move up and down the Indus and its tributaries. "Punjab" literally means "land of the five rivers," and in the ancient world water was almost everything. As in Sumer, "the prosperity of the Indus civilization depended on constant and intensive cultivation of the rich river valley."[44] This agricultural imperative was, once again, the hinge development for all the specialized feats that followed. A close examination of the city records of both Mohenjo-Daro and Harappa shows that ships carrying grain and other goods could dock near the city entrance, allowing them to be taken on foot quite quickly to warehouses or to the central business district. In ancient prefiguring of America's "mighty Mississippi," it was possible to sail the Indus and its tributaries on heavy wooden boats from the Arabian Sea clear up into Kashmir.[45]

MULTI-LEVELLED MANAGEMENT IN THE INDUS

As noted, although no vast archives of business tablets exist for the Bronze Age cities of the Indus, the hard-to-decipher seals do allow some conclusions to be drawn about the style of business organization employed. Mohenjo-Daro, Harappa, and Lothal sites turned up hundreds of square seals inscribed with animal figures for use as trademarks. Those from Lothal are attached to jars, baskets, or other containers. Those found at the other two cities are straight-forward *message documents* unaccompanied by goods. Communication, then as now, is the lifeblood of trade. In addition to serving as brand names, the function of the seals was to convey "the identity of the sender of a certain piece of merchandise, or the authority allocated by an individual or state department to a particular agent who carried the seal impression."[46] This confirms that Mohenjo-Daro and Harappa were true administrative and redistributive centers. Lothal was a transportation center, strategically located between the major Indus cities and the cities of Gujarat, a relationship roughly equivalent to New York vis-à-vis Chicago in the late nineteenth century. According to Professor Ratnagar, Lothal was both a transit center and a place where opening, checking, repacking, and sorting took place. Harappan seals have been found in Sumer, suggesting the presence of merchant representatives in Mesopotamia and Elam. These company troubleshooters "had come abroad to see the dispatch of goods to India." They helped ensure that Harappan's goods were "sent under contract or commercial partnership to Mesopotamia."[47] A large number of seals have also been found at Failaka in the heart of the Persian Gulf, which functioned as yet another center where Indus traders met their Sumerian counterparts.[48]

This prompts the question by way of summary: *What kind of economic system was used to manage operation in the Indus Valley Civilization?* Until very recently, scholars have maintained that the Harappan culture lacked an organized state structure. The Indus was clearly different from the easily recognizable unitary Egyptian state, and there are no records of Akkadian-like autocratic *lugals* directing things along the Indus. The very size of the trading area—500,000 square miles—might militate against the easy rise of a Sargon or a Napoleon without the modern tools of intimidation. Excavators have revealed three distinct archaeological traditions that argue for evidence of multi-levelled or power-sharing arrangements by Indus Valley managers.

The abundance of message seals, metals, precious stones, and warehouses in Harappa and Mohenjo-Daro, together with the size of the cities themselves, points to a striking individualism in action, in addition to the complex system that redistributed goods from central locations. Does this mean that all trade was administered by a strong, centralized government overseeing the economy with a scheme of fixed prices? Was the flow of goods regulated without recourse to bargaining or flexible market mechanisms? The evidence is not completely clear, but there are factors which would seem to militate against such a conclusion. True, a twentieth-century style totalitarian dictatorship could monitor even Mohenjo-Doro's well-developed overseas and overland trade routes. But there is no Shulgi or Imhotep in the archaeological records. "We do not even know if there were hereditary kings," writes John McKay.[49] As at Ur, the earliest foreign trade was in the hands of the palace and temple. By the time of the Larsa period, we find individuals going on their own expeditions and paying import tithes to the temple. In this development, the palace preferred to tax private trade to the Gulf rather than fully initiate it, yet remaining an active participant—the mercantile model favored by such later ruler/promoters as Philip of Spain and Elizabeth I of England (1558–1603).[50]

The evidence from the Indus Valley on how this rich, hemispheric trade was organized is scanty. True, the all-important silver exchanges were concentrated in the two major cities. Yet some few seals contain inscriptions that bear the name of an appointed dispatcher or state agent.[51] The very broad distribution of seals from the Indus strongly suggests that much westward trade was managed by merchants acting under state control, but who were given much latitude. Imported containers and shipments of silver are found almost entirely at Mohenjo-Daro and Harappa, instead of being concentrated in the seaports, as the seals attest. Dr. Shareen Ratnagar, the ranking expert on Indus trade relations, asks the question: "Could they have been seals of a Harappan authority which had dealings with its own agents stationed abroad?"[52]

The Sutkagen-dor forward settlement along the Makran in the westward reaches of today's Pakistan seems to have been "deliberately established by the Harappan administration." Furthermore its involvement in the sea trade "was not simply a local phenomenon."[53] Although most of this trade was probably between state administrations, private merchants may well have been involved as active players. These merchants would have needed the authority to send shipments quickly. Artifacts found in Bahrein (Dilmun) suggest that the trade between Sutkagen-dor and Sumer included, *but was not confined to*, independent peddlers. Once again, the large number of weights and seals from the Indus Valley scattered throughout the Gulf are indirect evidence for this multi-layered style of management. This led Ratanagar to conclude that the trade between India and Sumer via the Gulf was managed by mercantile hierarchies of the *dam-gara* (trade association) pattern. It was "a contractual trade with a scheduled and predetermined movement of merchandise, of the Assyrian type." This meant trade was "partly under state control and partly in the hands of professional merchants, subject to price-regulating market conditions."[54]

In conclusion, we can say that before the Indus Valley civilization collapsed soon after 1900 BCE from a malevolent mix of forces—earthquakes, irregular rainfall patterns, floods, salinization from over-done irrigation projects, and Aryan invasions[55]—there seemed to have been a precarious, but workable, compromise between private merchants acting as state agents, and these same agents given considerable latitude. This is more the model we have seen in some parts of Asia today.

But it is Professor Ratanagar's reference to the Assyrians that points up the significance of the Indus Valley in terms of the dynamic forward movement of ancient business. The Sumerians had perfected the art of the mercantile economy with both state and temple involved, perhaps pushing it as far as it could go, given the distances involved. By the Middle Bronze Age, the center may have been impeding the periphery. Administrative "drag" seems to have overpowered the privatizing forces of "lift." The very obscurity of the Harappan civilization's style of business management for its far-flung trade into the Sumerian gulf ports offers a lesson in the obvious. The old system of intensive palace–temple oversight was proving unwieldy. The old order was changing. The size and scope of commercial contacts extending from Mohenjo-Daro to Memphis called for more flexible models of economic adjustment. The Assyrians, as Professor Ratanagar indicated, would be the leading agents in propelling Bronze Age commerce to the next level. It is to that fascinating story we now turn.

4 Assyria and Babylon
Previewing the Multinational in The Middle Bronze Age (2000–1500 BCE)

> Quinquireme of Nineveh from distant Ophir,
> Rowing home to haven in sunny Palestine,
> With a cargo of ivory,
> And apes and peacocks,
> Sandalwood, cedarwood and sweet white wine.

As best can be ascertained, the poet John Masefield did not study at the London School of Economics. Yet his elegant word picture of ancient Assyria is one not well-known to most. Assyria the Warrior is a figure well-researched; Assyria the innovative Merchant Prince is the theme of this chapter.

Vying for the title of Assyrian Revisionist-in-Chief today is Professor H. W. F. Saggs and her protégés among the Assyrian-American community who edit *Zinda* magazine. They insist that the stereotype of Assyrians as ruthless barbarians is unfair and one-sided. Assyria saw herself as the defender of civilization from Arameans, Elamites, Medes, Scythians, and Moschians, who could be just as fierce and cruel, say these scholars. Even Assyrian soldiers generally behaved correctly unless provoked into terror by determined resistance, goes the argument. Truth be told, there is much to this claim. Across 1400 years of civilization, the Assyrians were an extremely progressive force in technology and philosophy. The first thousand years of Assyrian history does point to a people preferring to expand by peaceful trade and investment.[1] Only when this failed did Assyria unleash the dogs of war.[2] This chapter touches on this story, drawing a picture of an even larger and more significant reality: Assyria and Babylon as the essential precursors of multinational enterprise, always allowing for the fact that the term "nation" had a slightly different meaning than it does today.

THE ASSYRIAN KĀRUM: PERMANENT CROSS-BORDER ESTABLISHMENTS

Assyria as a people first took shape as the Old Assyrian Kingdom of the Middle Bronze Age. This was about 2000 to 1750 BCE. We know virtually nothing of Old Assyria from remains in the original site at the city of Ashur, but there are extensive records from Assyrian merchants and traders who planted trading colonies in Turkey, source of both the Tigris and Euphrates Rivers. The biggest market was Kanesh located near the dead center of modern Turkey near the modern city of Kayseri beyond the Taurus Mountains. This is hundreds of miles from their headquarters region in present-day Iraq, along the upper reaches of the Tigris River. The story of Old Assyria does seem to favor Mammon more than Mars. "Located on the Tigris in the very south of Assyria, Ashur was the central point of a network that traded tin from the east, textiles from Babylonia, and silver and gold from Aantolia," summarizes Marc Van De Mieroop. "The system is known to us from the discovery of more than 20,000 tablets left by Assyrian merchants in a colony at the edge of the central Anatolian city of Kanesh, some 1000 kilometers from Ashur."[3] Long before groups of Assyrian soldiers marched to terrorize the ancient world in the first millennium BCE, families of Assyrian merchants peacefully founded commercial colonies in Babylonia, Aram, and Anatolia. The details and transactions they recorded were inscribed on voluminous records, allowing us to analyze, with a fair amount of precision, their business culture, its style, and ongoing operations. The texts show ancient Assyrian colonists creating the first multinational firms or *proto-multinationals* in recorded history. The evidence for this claim is more fascinating than simply reprising the more familiar picture of the Assyrian military machine.

The first Assyrians took their name from their god, Ashur. Their first city was named in his honor, south of modern Mosul on a narrow strip of land west of the Tigris. On the flat inland plain, the Assyrians possessed few resources and no ports, and no defensible borders. The Assyrian very early, felt surrounded by powerful and hostile neighbors who threatened to strangle them. Assyrian pastureland was suited for sheep-raising, but the soil "yielded hardly enough agricultural products to support its population."[4] This meant that Assyria was very early on in a *resource-seeking* mode: expand or die. "The Assyrians looked beyond the narrow borders of their own land in order to supplant their own resources by trading with other countries."[5]

Up until the time of the Great Crash at Ur in 1788 BCE, Assyria was tied to Sumer economically and culturally. Around 2000 BCE, however, Puzur-Ashur had declared independence and made Assyria a power in its own right. In contrast to the palm trees, swamps, and irrigated deltas of Babylonia, the northern plains occupied by the settlements of Ashur and Nineveh and Erbil were temperate in climate, rolling and green as they shaded off to the hills in the east and the wheat-fields of Gozan in the west.[6] Assyria inherited the Semitic language of Akkad and the religious and social structure of the Sumerians, just as the Japanese absorbed the Confucian culture of China.[7] Kings such as Ilushuma (1962–1942 BCE), and Erishum (1941–1902 BCE) governed not as despots, but in accord with an oligarchical council of elders.

These overseers were responsible to the ancestral god Ashur.[8] Erishum entrusted functions to groups of *kāru* of private merchants. Very early on, the kings of Assur left domestic and international commerce almost entirely in the hands of what could be called the private sector, perfecting "in modern terms . . . the first experiment of free enterprise on a large scale."⁹ Just how large we shall see. The public sector of palace and temple continued to exist along with these *kārum*, or private associations of merchants willing to accept the risks and reap the profits of long-distance ventures.¹⁰

Assyria's food, textiles, copper, and tin depended on a brisk import trade. Erishum and his successors were not like Sargon, strong enough to wage a war of conquest in the grand manner. How did his elders and merchants solve the problem? They copied the old technique of the permanent foreign establishment that had been pioneered by the temples and palaces of the Copper Age, those at Uruk in particular. They then adapted it to the vigorous prosecution of *private* business investments.¹¹ The first step was to petition the princes of Anatolia and elsewhere for the legal right to set up Assyrian *kāru* in their countries. This gave Assyrian merchants access to the tin and copper mines on their own doorstep. One of the first *kārum* was established at Nuzi, along the Lower Zab, a tributary of the Tigris. A second *kārum* was founded further south in the Akkadian city of Sippar. This arrangement ensured that the precious trade in clothing and foodstuffs remained as much as possible in Assyrian hands.¹²

These *kāru* became the first cross-border private business establishments we have on record. Most were planted in the old Eblaite economic sphere near the abundant forests and mines of Syria and Anatolia to the northwest. It was easier and more profitable not to have to ship copper or tin from the Gulf via Sumer but to obtain it from the rich mines of Burushattum. This was near the Taurus Mountains in Cilicia, a region in the northeast elbow of the Mediterannean in modern Turkey. Just after 1950 BCE, then, a score of Assyrian *kāru* were operating along caravan routes leading from Syria to Kanesh in the heart of Turkey—a risky thousand kilometre trek from Ashur.¹³

Evidence for this long-range resource-seeking behavior surfaced in 1925 when a Czech scholar named Bedich Hrozny began digging near the Turkish city of Kültepe. Within a week of digging in a large terrace on the site of what was the city of Kanesh, he uncovered a mass of clay tablets. When Hrozny's findings were published in 1926 and 1927, they astounded scholars. The Kanesh tablets were records of contracts, partnerships, profits, orders, bills of lading, and other transactions from the business district of a prosperous trading city. They were written, however, not in the language of the natives, but in an old dialect of Assyrian. A significant section of the city, it was clear, was populated not by Hittites, but by merchants and their colleagues from the time of Erishum and Ikunum in what was called "the Assyrian quarter."¹⁴

Two decades of in-depth excavations in Kanesh under the leadership of Turkish archaeologist Tahsin Özgüç, after 1948, confirmed the message lying in the more than 10,000 tablets. For two centuries, Kanesh had been the home of a large and permanent community of Assyrian businesspeople. Similar Assyrian tablets found at other Turkish sites, notably Böghazkoy and Alaça Hüyük, confirmed the presence of other resident merchant colonies.¹⁵

The tablets also allowed archaeologists to reconstruct the history of the Old Assyrian kingdom of the second millennium BCE. This was a major breakthrough. Until then, "virtually nothing is known about Ashur and the rest of North Mesopotamia in the Ur III period, beyond the names of a few local rulers."[16] This trading regime held sway from about 2000 or 1900 BCE until it was overthrown by Hammurabi a couple of centuries later. The Middle Assyrian kingdom of 1600–1100 BCE was to leave few records or verifiable dates, likely because it played an insignificant role alongside more powerful states such as Kassite Babylonia and the Kingdom of Mitanni. Much later, the Assyrian pattern of military plunder would emerge during the Neo-Assyrian Empire of the Iron Age Period. This is told in the *Eponym Chronicle* after 911 BCE, and is securely dated by reference to the solar eclipse of 763 BCE.[17]

THE KANESH CONNECTION

The Kanesh discoveries had widened scholars appreciation for Assyria the Merchant. The last Old Assyrian ruler, Shamshi-Adad I (1813–1781 BCE), was overthrown by Hammurabi, traditionally fixed to about 1792–1750 BCE. By a reference to certain movements of the planet Venus in the reign of one of his successors, Ammisaduga, possibly in 1702 BCE, historians can date the Old Assyrian kings mentioned in the Kanseh tablets. This locates approximate dates for the Assyrian business colonies.[18] Özgüç uncovered four successive layers of occupation at Kanesh, each of which was assigned a Roman numeral by his archaeologists. The oldest, Level IV, lay on the bottom of the others and represented the first evidence of organized human occupation on the site. The artifacts found in both Level IV and Level III indicated that during the third millennium BCE, Kanesh and much of Anatolia experienced growing populations, increasing commerce, the evolution of a culture foreshadowing the later Hittites, and brutal rounds of warfare.

By comparing the styles of pottery, tools, weapons, and the other material remains found in these bottom levels, Özgüç and his team were able to date Levels IV and III to the Early Bronze Age, which in Mesopotamia coincided with the Early Dynastic, Akkadian, and Ur III periods. All of this preceded the foundation of an independent Old Assyrian kingdom. The significant breakthrough here was that, even in this early period, the Turkish archaeology team discovered evidence of commercial links between the eastern and central parts of Anatolia and the plains of Syria, northern Mesopotamia and the Sumerian cities of southern Mesopotamia. Affinities in the art and engineering style of bronze spearheads and other remains at Kanesh existed with remainders found south of the Taurus Mountains which separated Asia Minor from Syria and Mesopotamia. Özgüç determined that the region of Kanesh played an important part in world commerce around 2000 BCE, long before Assyria the Warrior appeared on the scene.[19]

Level II contained the most important discoveries for business historians and Assyriologists. Here, where Hrozny had unearthed the cache of tablets,

Özgüç found a well-planned Anatolian city with a considerable business district. Further digging showed that Kanesh II was neatly split into various quarters, divided by streets wide enough for carts. The city center contained large workshops, foundries, other businesses, and even restaurants. Özgüç's team also found over a hundred windowless brick houses, into which both sunlight and fresh air entered via open roofs and doors. In the northern and central parts of Kanesh, such homes were occupied by a self-contained community of Assyrians. Within the ruins of their closely-bunched six- to eight-room homes were well-preserved numbers of business tablets, filed in vases in special rooms. Living in one part of their homes, it was clear that the Assyrian traders maintained their offices in another, indicating a determination to establish long-term colonies. Women were important for the textile trade as central members of the workforce. The condition of these Old Assyrian texts from Level II was very good—either having been baked in the fireplace, or left unopened in their envelopes. The clear evidence of fire indicated that the city and its colony had been suddenly attacked and largely destroyed by an unknown invader. Level IC, just above Level II, showed little evidence of settlement.[20]

Then, Level IB showed evidence that the city had rebounded, and the Assyrian presence along with it. Kanesh IB was even bigger and more crowded than Kanesh II, its buildings rising upon the burnt rubble of Level II. Brick houses gave way to sturdy stone dwellings. This urban revival perished in fire. When the final level, Kanesh IA, was reached, all traces of the Assyrians were gone, and the culture of the emerging Hittite Empire became dominant.[21] (See Table 4.1 for a graphic representation of the various levels.)

Table 4.1 The Rise and Fall of Assyrian Business in Kanesh

Kanesh Level IA: Hittite buildings, *kārum* site deserted as destruction of Kārum Kanesh ends all traces of Assyrian presence when Hammurabi defeats Assyria 1781 BCE.

Kanesh Level IB: stone buildings and return of Assyrian *kārum*.
Shamshi-Adad I: 1813–1781 BCE.
Hammurabi reigns in Babylon: 1792–1750 BCE.
Larsa supreme in Sumer, Ur enjoys boom and bust economy.

Kanesh Level IC: Destruction of *kārum* followed by no Assyrian presence.
Naram-Sin 1819–1815 BCE.
Erishum II 1814–1813 BCE.

Kanesh Level II: Extensive Assyrian occupation on Level II of *kārum* site shows thriving Assyrian trade for 60 to 80 years.
Erishum I 1942–1902 BCE. Shu-Laban settles in Kanseh.
Ikunum 1900 BCE. House of Ashur-Imitti thrives, Imdilum and Pushu-ken managers in Kanesh.
Sargon I. Pushu-Ken corresponds with King Sargon.
Puzur-Ashur II.
Commerce flourishes in Larsa.

Levels III, IV coincides with Ur III dynasty. No evidence of Assyrian occupation.[22]

MARKET-SEEKING BEHAVIOR

The records of the Kanesh tablets and from other sites show that the Assyrians had built upon and extended the old trading networks of Uruk and Ebla. A string of Assyrian *kāru* and lesser trading posts stretched from northern Iraq to the southern shore of the Black Sea. *Kārum* Kanesh was the most important.[23] Van De Mieroop estimates that in one forty-year period, 100,000 textiles and 100 tons of tin were imported across the Taurus Mountains. Zalpa and Nihrija occupied the bend of the Euphrates in the vicinity of Haran. Ursu (on the site of Ebla), Hahhum, Hurama, and Durhumit followed the Euphrates upstream to where it met the upper reaches of the Halys. On the Turkish side of the Taurus Mountains lay Burushattum and Wahsusana in the vicinity of Lake Tuz and its precious silver mines. *Kārum* Hattusas lay in the future capital of the Hittite empire. Between them were half a dozen lesser trading stations.[24]

It is important to recognize that these settlements, just as the Uruk settlements 1,500 years earlier, were commercial, not military, establishments. They were planted there with the full consent of the princes of Aram and Anatolia. The Assyrians came as customers, not conquerors. They were subject to residential taxation by the fully-sovereign native princes. Military imperialism was a Sargonic and Akkadian trait, but only an Old Assyrian practice for a brief period under Shamshi-Adad I. Old Assyrian expansion was mainly along economic lines. It was also codified, and to some extent regulated, by sophisticated international marketing arrangements governing permanent establishments in foreign lands.

Assyria's great priority was opening up the rich treasure-bearing regions of Anatolia, both as a market for her own exports and as a permanent area of commercial exploitation and settlement. The Dutch, French, and British experiences in India immediately come to mind, as names such as the East India Companies enliven the story of world commerce. Vigorous and explicit market-seeking behavior underscores the Old Assyrian accomplishment in economic history. No other Mesopotamian power had yet succeeded in systematically knitting together a vast trading "empire" in a foreign area without recourse to war.[25] Territorial commerce was given a mighty boost.

The resident Assyrian merchants in Kanesh lived in Anatolian-style houses and adopted many Anatolian ways. Sometimes they married natives, but by and large they remained Assyrians. They spoke Assyrian, sacrificed to Ashur and Ishtar, and governed themselves by Assyrian, not Anatolian, law. While treating Hittites and other Anatolians respectfully, most Assyrians tended to look down upon the culture of their hosts.[26] They were there to make money, not to "go native." Even though women's complaints about absent husbands do enter the records, the prime directive was clear—promote the firms and trading interests of Assyria.[27]

The Anatolian *kāru* guaranteed the survival of the resource-poor, enemy-surrounded Assyrian heartland. This Old Assyrian economy was one of "commerce without an extensive productive branch."[28] With little in the way of their own productive industry, resources, or food, the merchants of Assyria became middlemen between Sumer and Babylon, especially in securing the valuable mining deposits of the Anatolian Plateau.[29] The leading *kāru* in Assur set up a *kārum* at Sippar in the land of Akkad, through which they purchased vast quantities of fabric and clothing from Larsa and Babylon for resale to thousands of Anatolian buyers. Babylonian and Sumerian traders could sell their wares in Ashur, but were forbidden to maintain a permanent establishment on Assyrian soil. This was more a result of Assyrian xenophobia than protectionism. But like nineteenth century America, they prospered behind their "Assyria First" policy. The Assyrian firms then shipped grain and textiles from Sumer *along their own privately-owned networks* to Kanesh and other *kāru* and *wabartum* (trading posts) in Syria and Asia Minor.[30]

The best-known of these networks was operated by the House of Ashur-Imitti, which might well have been the top import-export firm in all of Assyria. Its story is told intermittently within the Kanesh tablets, and well worth the reading. It evidences some of the trials and tribulations of early proto-multinationals.

THE HOUSE OF ASHUR-IMITTI: MULTINATIONAL TRIALS

The House of Ashur-Imitti flourished during the reigns of Erishum, Ikunum, Sargon I, and Puzur-Ashur of Assyria, sometime approximately between 1950 and 1850 BCE (Kanesh Level II).[31] Ashur-Imitti, who lived in the city of Ashur, was the brother of Shu-Laban, one of the business pioneers of the *kārum* in Kanesh. Family ties played a very important role in the subsidiary trading networks out of Kanesh. Shu-Laban managed the Kanesh operation on behalf of his brother, Ashur-Imitti, who was effectively Chief Executive Officer, although such a title was unknown in 1900 BCE. Shu-Laban eventually retired to Ashur, but not before he trained his son, Imdilum, to take over as branch manager, suggesting that even subordinate positions in Assyrian management were hereditary. Imdilum in Kanesh was then entrusted with supervising all operations in Anatolia. His two sons, Puzur-Ishtar and Amur-Ili, aided him, as did his daughter, Ishtar-Bashti. Ishtar-Bashti—not untypical in this era—received orders from her father and passed them on to her brothers.[32]

Imdilum was not the only branch manager. His cousin, Amur-Ishtar, supervised the firm's office in Durhumit in Syria on the Upper Euphrates. Imdilum's employees, Addu, Idi-Adad, Usanum, and Uzua led the donkey caravans that shipped Assyrian and Anatolian goods to Amur-Ishtar. Amur-Ishtar then sold the goods to obtain copper and then sold some of the copper to obtain the precious silver—functioning like the dollar or the euro—sometimes from the mines of Burushattum.[33]

With a silver loan from Imdilum to cover their expenses, Addu and his fellow caravan drivers played an indispensable role in the far-flung operations.

They saddled their donkeys with sealed packages of Sumerian textiles consigned to them by Shu-Ishtar, Ennanum, and Puppuranum in the head office at Ashur. The bills of lading were written on clay in cuneiform, and the seals were not to be broken until the caravans reached Kanesh. The journey could be perilous. Donkeys went out in groups of less than twenty, often with only two or three at a time. At Durhumit, Amur-Ishtar would take some of the consigned textiles and trade them for copper. Addu would pick up some of the copper for Kanesh. Other copper would be traded for silver or taken by Uzua back to Shu-Ishtar or Ennanum in Ashur. Bad weather, wild animals, brigands, and the loss of donkeys accentuated the element of risk, made worse by the taxes and consignment duties paid in Assyria and other principalities the caravan traversed.[34]

Finally, Addu reached Kanesh, where the goods were unpackaged. Imdilum then consigned Idi-Adad to report to Pushu-Ken and take some of the textiles to Halys. He consigned Usanum to load up his donkeys with silver or copper from the mines of Burushattum and return to Durhumit and Ashur. Alternatively, the metals could be taken to other posts of Asia Minor under Kanesh jurisdiction. Most of the donkeys were also sold. The profit margins either way were close to a hundred percent. This return on Assyrian tin and the even greater margins for Babylonian textiles and garments, compensated for the hazards, expenses, and taxation encountered on the journey.[35]

The Kanesh tablets describe many of the operations of Imdilum and the firm he served. In one instance, Imdilum writes to Puzur-Ashur, letting him know his tin is at Hahhum, in the establishment of Idi-Ashur. Imdilum's records show him all too often dealing with dishonest customers. Imdilum warns Puzur-Ashur to give no credit to the son of Zigaya, for he will regret it later.[36] Amur-Ishtar in Durhumit writes to Imdilum: "I will trade your copper for that of better quality and bring it with my own copper to Purushaddum [Burushattum]."[37] Imdilum, from Kanesh, replies, telling him to sell his donkey carts and bring all the copper to Purushaddum. The two talents of copper shipped by Idnaya, however, are to be his. Imdilum will, meanwhile, make his way to Purushaddum, telling his cousin to give his copper to his agent Tishmurna. Shipments of goods were often quite large. Imdilum's letter to Amur-Ishtar mentions eighty talents of white wool and thirty of red wool.[38]

In another letter, Imdilum enumerates the goods his donkey driver, Amur-Ili, will take to Burushattum. Much of it is in silver:

- 17 minas to Eannum-Bellum
- 10 minas to Enlil-Bani
- 30 minas to Usur-sa-Ashur
- 25.5 minas to Idi-Ashur
- 5 minas to Ashur-Sululi
- 13 minas to Usur-sha-Ishtar
- 7 minas to Ishtar-Pilah
- Other payments [39]

Ancient currency fluctuated, but not as much as today. The mina, one of the lowest denominations of wealth, was the base of the well-known Near Eastern shekel. Pettinato estimates 60 minas to a shekel as fairly standard in this period, and 3000 shekels to the talent appeared to be the old Eblaite reckoning.[40] Imdilum's letter also mentions textiles that Ashur-Tab and Eannum-Belu have deposited with the *kārum* in Burushattum. These two appear to have been Imdilum's *tamkārum* agents there. Imdilum gives orders to "make payment to all my *tamkārum* and Amur-Ili will not have to tarry there."[41] The top donkey driver, however, sometimes had an interest in his own profit, to the detriment of Imdilum. On one occasion, Imdilum sent Amur-Ili to Burushattum. Amur-Ili, instead, was rumored to have gone, on his own initiative, to Wahshushanna to sell Imdilum's goods there:

"I have learned that Amur-Ili has proposed to sell my tin and my textiles for copper in Wahshushana. You are my brothers [ensure?] that Amur-Ili would not go to Wahshushana. [Make sure] that he would have to send all my merchandise to Burushattum, in order to sell them [according to] my accounting."[42]

Ashur-Nada was much harder to deal with, and Imdilum quickly became frustrated with writing to him. It seems that, once, Ashur-Taklaku was about to go to the Assyrian *kārum* in Burushattum and accuse Ashur-Nada of embezzling significant quantities of money and merchandise.[43] Imdilum also had trouble with Eannum-Ashur of Kanesh, likely another customer. Cuneiform "e-mails" were flying thick and fast from Ashur. Imdilum lobbied incessantly for repayment of the thirty minas of silver, plus interest, Eannum-Ashur had borrowed. Eannum-Ashur would not pay up and kept hedging, making Imdilum furious. Eannum-Ashur not only slandered his creditor, but also kept promising that one of his employees would repay Imdilum. Eannum-Ashur, however, never paid, and Imdilum was ready to invoke the wrath of Ashur and Ishtar—the tribal founder and the tribal goddess—against his debtor. He threatened that either Eannum-Ashur send the money via Idi-Adad, or Imdilum himself would pay him a most unpleasant visit.[44]

The finances of the House of Ashur-Imitti were centrally managed from Ashur. Imdilum writes to Ashur-Imitti and his own agents in the capital, asking them to apply twenty minas of silver to his account to cover customs duties and shipping taxes. Pushu-Ken, our first *proto-multinational* CEO, was to ship the money. On another occasion, Imdilum asks also that silver for these taxes be applied not only to his own account, but also to that of Pilah-Ishtar, who was to send silver ingots stamped with his name.[45] Sometimes, Imdilum had difficulties dealing with his own head office, and was not afraid to file a complaint with his CEO. As an example, someone in Ashur once delayed the caravans of Puzur-Ashur, Alahum and Amur-Ili. Imdilum quotes from one of his previous letters to headquarters:

All my merchandise, whether that transported by Amur-Ili . . . Puzur-Ashur . . . [or] Alahum, must quickly come to Nab-Suen at Kanesh, in order that he can trade it for silver.[46]

There seems little doubt that Orlin is right when he summarizes that the House of Ashur-Imitti "fashioned a highly-organized commercial enter-prise, an international import–export business in the fullest sense."[47] Do we have here history's first recorded multinational enterprise? By a strict OECD definition, perhaps not. The Assyrian establishments abroad did not engage in production. If we apply a broader definition, however, that of *proto-multinational*, and focus on the fact that these were privately-owned companies operating permanent branch offices under their control, then we can more confidently answer in the affirmative. The traders and merchants of Old Assyria took giant steps towards pioneering the multinational form we see about us today.

SUMER TO BABYLON: REVIVAL UNDER HAMMURABI

The Assyrian colonies dried up quickly when the great conqueror Ham-murabi of Babylon struck at the home base of the Old Assyrian kingdom in 1781 BCE. The great Assyrian innovation of the *tamkārum*, nevertheless, would endure for centuries throughout the Near Eastern world. Chapter 5 shows the Phoenicians pushing it to extensive heights. Even half a century before Ashur fell, we catch a glimpse of the wandering tribal merchant and their interactions with diverse political and ethnic groups in the career of one prominent *tamkārum*, Abramu of Haran or, as he is more well-known, Abram the Hebrew. The patriarchal narratives in Genesis preserve lively and colorful accounts of an emigrant trader wandering across the whole Fertile Crescent. Some time around, or soon after, 1900 BCE, the narrative mentions Abramu gathering his family and his dependents, several hundred of them, in Haran and then journeying into Canaan and Egypt. Unlike other *tamkāru*, he had no permanent establishment, but was quite wealthy in livestock, gold, and silver. His nephew, Lot, also a *tamkārum*, took up residence in the Canaanite city of Sodom, where he apparently exercised a civic and judicial function. This was relatively common, as it appears that *tamkāru* may have had their own military detachments, as did the Dutch and British East India Companies in modern times.

According to the account in Genesis 14, the cities of Abramu's new homeland rebelled against the tribute imposed upon them by their over-lords back in Mesopotamia. Amrpahel, king of Shinar, is the biblical ren-dering of "Sumer," Shinar. Arioch, or *Eriaku*, King of Ellasar appears to have been—once his name is rendered into Akkadian—none other than Warad-Sin of Larsa. Larsa dominated Sumer at this time. The invaders from the north took hostages and levied a vast amount of shoes and textiles as tribute. In response, Abramu armed some of his corporate household and routed the invaders.

As the story continues, Yahweh, Abramu's God, is about to destroy Sodom, but Abramu, so proficient at bargaining, *haggles* with his Creator. God initially offers to spare Sodom if he can find fifty righteous people. But Abramu continues to deal. Like any good Assyrian *tamkārum*, he haggles Yahweh down to forty, then thirty, then twenty, and finally ten. But . . . there are not ten righteous people in Sodom.[48] There was only one—Lot, Abramu's nephew. Later, after the death of his wife, Abramu, now called Abraham, bargains with Hittite merchants who recognize his *tamkārum* status: "Hear us, my lord: thou art a mighty prince among us."[49] The patriarchal narratives support the secular evidence in the cuneiform texts that preserve memories of a fairly sophisticated economy throughout the Near East. Barter and haggling were—and are—essential tactics, but outright legal purchases of land for bullion also appear in the records. That, and a surprising mobility, fits the picture of a world on the verge of one of its peaks of power and influence, the imperial age ushered in by Hammurabi (traditionally 1792–1750). History records Hammurabi taking the strategic city of Mari on the Middle Euphrates. Mari was the gateway to the Mediterranean, and Abramu would have passed through here on his way to Palestine.

Hammurabi's rapid rise led to the first Assyrian kingdom being overthrown by the new Amorite dynasty of Babylon. The word "Amorite" simply means "Westerner," and their founders were semi-nomads from Syria. As noted, the Assyrian outpost at Kanesh vanished from the historical record at this time. Quickly overrunning Sumer, the Babylonian armies absorbed Assyria as well. Enough records have survived from the Old Babylonian kingdom, mostly clay tablets from the ruins of Sippar, to show that the business and trading practices of Hammurabi and his successors closely resembled those of the Sumerians who preceded them. Babylonian *tamkāru* continued to control the caravan routes across Iran to Afghanistan and to sail the Arabian Gulf to Dilmun, Arabia, east Africa, and the Indus Valley.[50]

Under Hammurabi and his successors, Babylonian trade remained a joint venture involving the crown and its connections with private merchants. Each contributed 50% of the capital. Relations between king and nobility, including *tamkāru*, remained on a feudal basis in which nobles and merchants received land grants in return for military and other forms of homage, not unlike those in medieval times and even down to the reign of the first Elizabeth (1558–1603). Profits from royal herds and lands contracted out to *tamkāru* were subject to crown royalties. As in Sumer and Assyria, palace and temple worked together to control prices, facing the same difficulties that prices and income policies have encountered in more recent times, namely, black markets and wealth's weak relationship to true market value.[51]

Following the death of Hammurabi[52] (1750 BCE by the Middle Chronology), the Babylonian Empire began to shrink. Parts of Sumer became, once again, independent while Assyria fell under sway of the new kingdom of Mitanni to its northwest. For the remainder of the millennium, Babylon, itself, was under the rule of a foreign dynasty.[53]

Old Babylonian records, however, show forth the wealth and splendor of Hammurabi's Empire. Clay tablets from the ruins of Sippar show that the trading practices of Hammurabi's merchants were not markedly different from those of the Assyrians. The great hemispheric economy of Sargon that had once drawn the Gulf region into its orbit would flourish only briefly, however, as the brilliant Harappan civilization of the Indus Valley also collapsed. Cloves indigenous to the Spice Islands of the Moluccas have been found in Babylon, indicating that some of the probes made by Babylonian merchants and *tamkāru* may have been more extensive than was formerly thought. It is Hammurabi's Code, however, carved onto a six-foot diorite stela now in the Louvre Museum in Paris, which gives us an insight into the trade and commerce of this Middle Bronze Age powerhouse.

BUSINESS ETHICS IN STONE

The laws of Hammurabi are the most extensive known from the ancient Near East. Many of them relate to business operations, some of them quite detailed. An example might help illuminate the system. Suppose a *tamkārum* named Kaspam-Marduk makes a loan. Grain and silver were loaned by merchants at rates of 20 or even 33% interest. A borrower's goods were to be accepted as collateral. If Kaspam-Marduk formed a partnership or joint venture with another merchant, the risk was equal. "If a man gives silver to a trading agent for investment in a partnership venture, before the god they shall equally divide the profit or loss."[54]

The ethical functioning of business agents was also covered on the stela. Imagine that Kaspam-Marduk, living in Babylon, entrusted Bel-Samallum to be his agent. He would send Bel on a business trip to Mari and give him silver in the form of ingots, on which Bel must calculate interest of 20%. "If a merchant gives silver to a trading agent for conducting business transactions and sends him off on a business trip," the agent was required to calculate the total interest "on as much silver as he took, and he shall satisfy his merchant."[55] If Bel did not make any profit, he would have to remit to Kaspam double the amount of silver he took. If the agent suffered a loss on an investment journey, he had to restore the principal to Kaspam.[56]

The Hammurabi Code recognized other risks. If Kaspam's goods were seized by Amorite brigands, Bel had to go to the temple to declare an oath before the god, Marduk,[57] and he would be released. Agents needed to keep sealed receipts on grain, wool, oil, or any other commodity for local transactions and to return to the merchant the silver for each transaction. If Bel failed to collect a receipt, any silver he earned would not be included in the final accounting. If Bel took the silver and then denied Kaspam's claim,

Kaspam could take the agent to court before the temple and demand three-fold restitution. Likewise, Bel could also press a claim against the merchant if the merchant denied ever receiving the silver. In this case, Kaspar would have to compensate Bel sixfold.[58]

Laws sometimes multiply when people are enjoying a measure of freedom and prosperity. Legal systems, with their conservative tendencies, are much in evidence when there is something to conserve. The archaeological testimony to the longevity of the Sumerian–Assyrian–Babylonian *tankāurm* could be celebrated as an expanding economy's inherent bias toward delegation, privatization, and a measure of entrepreneurial capitalism. This tendency could be seen as inevitable, had not the ancient world thrown up other competing models as a testament to diversity. This is borne out in the palace–priestly economy of Middle Kingdom Egypt, to which we once more turn.

'PALACE SOCIALISM': EGYPT AND THE AEGEAN 2000–1500 BCE

Babylon's calamity was Egypt's opportunity.[59] In the period when first the Old Assyrian and then the Old Babylonian kingdoms dominated Mesopotamia, the kings of Thebes, led by Mentuhotep II, reunited Egypt.[60] This was around 2040 BCE. This effectively inaugurated the period designated as Middle Kingdom Egypt. The Middle Kingdom period comprised the Eleventh, Twelfth, Thirteenth, and Fourteenth Dynasties, and coincided with the Middle Bronze Age. Many of the cultural features of the Old Kingdom were revived, but with significant differences. There were no massive pyramids being built, and there was evidence that the Pharaoh was forced into some power-sharing arrangements that led to his being viewed as somewhat less divine.[61]

The Egyptian economic model remained essentially what it had been under the Old Kingdom. Palaces, as well as the many opulent temples and shrines, continued to sit at the center of a largely public sector economy. Literature from the period, notably the *Story of Sinuhe*,[62] set in the time of the Twelfth Dynasty and recorded around 1800 BCE, illuminated the nature of Egypt's temple–palace economy. Sinuhe was an Egyptian royal official who absconded from Egypt and absconded to Syria/Palestine to become famous. His title in exile was Judge and District Overseer of the Domains of the Sovereign in the Lands of the Asiatics. In short, Sinhue clawed his way to the top by dint of the organizing ability to tackle large-scale projects he saw all about him growing up in Egypt. He finally returned, forlorn and homesick, to be buried according to the rites of Egypt rather than being buried, Semite like, on the lone prairie. The story concludes with the obligatory accolades to the all-beneficent Pharaoh. Yet the subtext of this tale—"Egyptians succeed by really trying"—evokes some of the success literature of our day, a genre that takes its inspiration from *The Autobiography of Benjamin Franklin* in the American colonies. Franklin, poor boy from Boston, sweeps Philadelphia off its feet. *The Story of Sinhue*, with its muted bow to rugged individualism, was equally revered in Egypt, becoming a required school text much later in Egyptian history.

The Sinuhe story, with its tribute to individual initiative and drive, is paralleled by the much better known narrative of Joseph in the Book of Genesis. Although many scholars deny Joseph's existence as a historical figure and insist the story was penned in Palestine much later than its original setting, the picture presented is, once again, a fairly accurate reflection of the political economy of Egypt in the Middle Kingdom. Joseph and his brothers were shepherds in Palestine. Angry over Joseph's status as Jacob's heir, the brothers first plotted to murder the interloper before deciding to make a profit by selling him to Arabian traders. These traders operated the familiar camel caravans bearing gum, balsam, resin, and other goods across Canaan to Egypt. They also traded in slaves, which the seventeen-year-old Joseph now became. The traders brought Joseph to Egypt where he was purchased by Potiphar, who was a courtier of the palace.[63]

As the story unfolds, Joseph's management skills quickly enable him to become a household manager and even a prison capo after he was falsely accused of sexual harassment. Eventually, he is released from prison and, after showing the ability to impress the Pharaoh, was appointed vizier of all of Middle Kingdom Egypt, made responsible for the entire Egyptian economy. With a famine threatening, Vizier Joseph stored grain in Egypt's state granaries during the seven good years. He then distributed it to the Egyptian populace, and even to Egypt's Canaanite vassals, after their prosperity turned to famine. According to Genesis 47, however, the counter-cyclical policies of the palace may have prevented starvation, but at a price: the enserfing of the entire Egyptian peasantry. Free-holding peasants first traded their money, then their herds and flocks, and finally their land and freedom in return for grain. They became serfs on crown estates, and worked them subject to a 20% tax. Only those lands owned by the temple priests remained exempt.[64]

In spite of these rhetorically embedded salutes to individual enterprise, the business cultures of the Near East, which dominated trade during the second millennium BCE, were clearly running along internalized "top-down" models of management. With the exception of Assyria, both Egyptian and Mesopotamian god-kings, merchant princes, and temple priests were prominently involved as sponsors of and regulators of the economic suzerains who sent out the Dilmun boats and enriched the coffers of Memphis and Ugarit. Yet, for every action there can be a strong counter-reaction. The first seeds of an alternative business model, one based upon small, independent enterprises, were beginning to take shape in the Aegean. Working in a much freer and less urbanized world, the traders of Greece forged history's first free-market economy, bypassing the internationalization advantages of the *Eclectic Paradigm*.

It is one of history's most exciting sagas. Freewheeling Greek entrepreneurs, built along the lines of Jason and the Argonauts and Homer's "cunning Odysseus," traded around the Mediterranean largely independent of hierarchies or internalized operations. Visionary independent traders from the Greek ports and along the Levant in the Eastern Mediterranean helped launch the first truly entrepreneurial business cultures. It would reach its full maturity in Periclean Athens of the fifth century BCE, with flourishing overseas trade, private banks, and relatively free capital markets. Here, despite its largely agrarian nature, was an economic system whose outlines resemble the North Atlantic consumer and shareholder cultures of our own day, an innovation more fully described in Chapter 6. Its origins, however, can be seen in the Middle Bronze Age.

In the beginning, the peoples of the Aegean operated with a regimented palace economy not unlike that found in the Near East. The luxury-loving Minoans on the island of Crete were anything but entrepreneurial.[65] If anything, they resembled the more "socialist" and highly centralized Egyptians to their south. The palace[66] authorities in Knossos set quotas, arranged specialized production, and even dictated patterns of consumption. These are not the markers of a market economy. Foreign trade with Egypt, Cyprus, and Syria in foodstuffs, olive oil, wine, and bronze goods[67] was under the purview of the palace–temple hierarchy. Thomas R. Martin declares that the Minoan state "operated as a monopoly through the palace system . . . with little role for independent merchants and traders."[68]

Minoan civilization suddenly vanished from history in the mid- to late-second millennium BCE in one of humanity's most mysterious catastrophes. It was replaced by the unmistakably Greek Mycenaean civilization on the fringes of the European continent to its north. The Mycenaeans were discovered in modern times by Heinrich Schliemann, who represents one of the truly romantic figures in archaeology.[69] After uncovering the seven layers of Troy in modern Turkey, Schliemann began digging near Corinth in the hopes of uncovering the home of the Greek warriors of the *Iliad*. Find them he did. The Mycenaeans he uncovered were genuinely Hellenic (from "Hellas," the Greek name for themselves), forged weapons of bronze (Homer's "bronze-clad Greeks"), and traded back and forth with Egypt, the Levant, and the rest of the Near East. The first recognizable Greek finds, called Middle Helladic, dated from the time of Old Assyria and Babylonia. The full development of this first culture came in the Late Helladic at the end of the Bronze Age. This was the same time that a merchant named Sinaranu,[70] whose story we pick up in Chapter 5, made his fruitful voyages from wealthy Ugarit to Crete.

Mycenaean Greece was composed of a number of tribal kingdoms, each based around a palace-oriented economy. In spite of the stifling restrictions of this system, the rural, localized world of Mycenaean Greece laid a foundation upon which yeomanry-style agriculture could prosper. Out of this, a system of free-spirited, independent enterprise could gradually emerge, aided immensely by Greece's truncated and jagged geography, which militated against territorial empires as in Egypt and Mesopotamia or crowded Crete. Thus, tribal kings had little surplus capital, cities were small by Near Eastern standards, and no overweening centralized power dominated in temple or state.

Greece seemed made to nourish sturdy individualism. Although geography is not destiny, the mountainous countryside, with few connecting roads, abetted an isolated population sprinkled along numerous peninsulas and hundreds of tiny islands. All of this further ensured religion, economy, and politics would be isolated and localized to a degree unknown in the Near East.[71] The warrior spirit throve, as *The Iliad* later documented. Late Helladic tribal kings and nobles fought one another in chariots wearing heavy bronze armor, wielding bronze swords produced by local craftsmen.[72] The shipbuilding and seafaring skills of the Bronze Age were advanced enough to permit Mycenaean traders to sail to Egypt, Anatolia, and Syria, just as they encouraged Ugaritic, Hattian, and Egyptian traders to trade wares along the Aegean. The markets of the Aegean and the Near East could not help but interact along those "wine-dark seas." Ships and vessels were never much farther than forty miles from land or from sight of the hauntingly beautiful islands (such as Mykonos) that are still a traveller's delight.

What is surprising is the Greek's extraordinary reach. Early Mycenaeans traded with Sardinia and Spain. Their distinctive pottery has been found in the Bay of Naples, and at a number of sites in south-eastern Sicily and on the heel of the Italian boot.[73] Even in this early stage, it appears that Minoan control of the eastern Mediterranean, under whose beneficent aegis Greek islanders plied their wares, diverted free spirited mainland traders to explore more westerly locations. The full flowering of the Greek mainland's palace civilization in the Late Helladic coincided with evidence of Mycenaean artifacts in Crete, the Dodecanese, Egypt, Cyprus, Anatolia, and the Levant. More will be said on this in Chapter 6.[74] Suffice it to say that the seeds of that individualistic "white-hot" quality of innovation that we think of as distinctively Greek were already nurtured by the Mycenaeans. The patterns nurtured in their Heroic Age came to later fruition, the story of Chapter 6.

SHANG CHINA (1500–1050 BCE): SETTING THE MOULD

"Let China sleep," Napoleon Bonaparte is supposed to have said, "for when she wakens she will shake the world." Pundits and politicians in our own time are afraid that that shaking has begun among 20% of the world's population. A *Time* magazine cover of January 22, 2007 proclaims "Dawn of a new Dynasty," ominously superimposed upon a bright yellow Communist star rising over the Great Wall. The breathless subtitle reads, "With the U.S. tied down in Iraq, a new superpower has arrived. Here's how to deal with it." Earlier, the more sober *Atlantic* magazine led with the title "How to Fight China." Something about the size of the world's largest population has always engendered superlatives of the kind archaeologists and historians evince when contemplating the long tableaux of China's well-preserved dynasties. But generalizations need rounding out with facts. That fact is that while Old Kingdom Pharaohs erected their pyramids and the *damgara* of Ebla and Sumer flourished at the dawn of the Bronze Age, the peasants of the *Huang He*, or Yellow River, remained in a Stone Age economy.

Who were these founders of China? The Yangshao people (fourth and early third millennium BCE) lived in small villages, fought with bows and arrows, grew millet, and made only a few primitive pots and silk cloth for their own needs. Their successors, the Longshan people (late third and early second millennium BCE) were somewhat more advanced, but still lagged behind their Akkadian and Indus Valley contemporaries. A trail of their black pottery identifies settlements enclosed with walls and spread along the Yellow River, with scattered outlying towns as far away as Manchuria, the Yangzi, and the southern regions of the Vietnamese. These town dwellers raised cattle and sheep and began to learn the art of chariot-making and working in bronze.[75]

Dating the very earliest Chinese civilization is, thus, much more difficult than with Fertile Crescent cultures. No Sumerian or Egyptian-style artifacts have yet appeared in Chinese archaeology to effectively link its chronology to early Mesopotamia. Specialists such as Kwang-Chih Chang[76] and Gina Barnes have had to rely on eclipse records in the ancient Chinese annals and the results of radiocarbon dating. From these, they were able to tentatively reconstruct the foundations of Oriental civilization (see Table 4.2).

The Longshan culture of the Yellow River was but one of a series of late Stone-Age cultures that developed in northern China around 3500–2000 BCE. These were extant when Sumer had entered the Early Bronze Age. The Longshan included the Hongshan people in Manchuria, the Dawenkou on the coast, and the Liangzhu in the Shanghai Delta. All of these cultures demonstrated a trend toward specialization and social differentiation.

Table 4.2 The Origins of Chinese Civilization

Late Neolithic Yangshao: millet, red painted pottery, weaving.	Legendary ruler Fuxi. Contemporary with Egyptian Old Kingdom, Ebla and Early Dynastic Sumer.
Late Neolithic: Longshan and other cultures: Hongshan, Dawenkoo, Liangzhu. First metalworking and pentatonic music scale. Probable Chinese tribal kingdoms.	Legendary rulers Yao and Shun. Xia Dynasty 2100–1600 BCE? Contemporary with Neo-Sumerian Ur, Larsa, Old Assyria, Harappa.
Mainland Bronze Age: Shang dynasty. China unified under Emperor Tang: Anyang and Zhengzhou cultures. State industries cast bronze artifacts.	Shang Dynasty, contemporary with Babylonian and Middle Egyptian kingdoms.

The first temples and palaces appeared then, as well. The Liangzhu were proficient in sophisticated jade work and ceramics. Other developments in the Longshan culture, described by Professor Gina Barnes, were more ominous. Burials of headless and footless bodies with weapons, and the coming of walled settlements testify to an increase in social conflict. Building walls required collective efforts, and, as in Sumer, chieftains emerged to build palaces and become kings. Human sacrifice of prisoners was instituted as a means of social control.[77]

China entered the Bronze Age in earnest shortly after 2000 BCE. The rise of metalworking coincided with the political consolidation of the Chinese kingdom. The first rulers were the legendary Yellow Emperor Huangdi, said to have reigned around 2600 BCE. Later come the wise Emperor Yao, and his heir Yu Shun. The Xia dynasty, once deemed mythical, is now confirmed to have been real. The power of the Xia was eventually challenged by the usurper Tang, founder of the Shang dynasty sometime before 1700 BCE.

Most of what is known about Shang China comes from excavations begun in 1928 and continuing to 1937 on the site of Anyang. Anyang was north of the Yellow River about 500 kilometres from Beijing. Here peasants had been digging up bones cut with notches. Expeditions uncovered about some 100,000 of these bones, which comprise the most ancient Chinese records carved on bone and tortoise shells. Some 1,000 have been translated, confirming details about the Shang Dynasty and some thirty rulers written in about 100 BCE by the famous historian Sima Qian. The characters on the bones proved to be direct ancestors of the modern Chinese script. The Shang records are courtier's reports, not commercial documents, and reveal that the early Chinese economy was a state-run command operation. Thus Mao Zedong, founder of modern Communist China, had a socialist tradition hearkening back millennia on which to build.

Then, as now, flooding on the Yellow or the other great river, the Yangzi, was a matter of life or death. The all-important crops had to be saved. The Shang organized their realm around towns settled by *zu*, or kinship groups. Smaller *zu* were combined into larger ones, ruled from a central town, subject to supervision by yet larger towns that served as clan capitals. All were subject to the *wang* (king) in Anyang. This kinship structure, in which the king was patriarch of all, controlled economic and political life. Land in Bronze Age China was owned not by private farmers, but by the king himself, who spoke of "my lands" or "our lands." A maxim from the succeeding Zhou Dynasty intones, "Everywhere under Heaven is no land that is not the king's."[78] The strong bonds of family life, so evident among Chinese even today, was strengthened by an approach that Westerners would call extremely conservative, if not authoritarian. Yet a new generation of historians and researchers have questioned the stereotype that in the East old ways change slowly. They have supplemented the traditional Confucian narrative of China's past with a storyline where religion and ritual play a more important role. The Confucian thesis of statecraft, hereditary succession, writing, and technology tied to flood-control as the mainspring of Chinese history is yielding to this more complex account.[79]

"THE CENTRAL COUNTRY"

This surprisingly strong religious ethos may account for some of the most characteristic Shang legacies—the lavish underground tombs, the abundant evidence of high refinement in the art of bronze, the precision of the ancient lunar calendar so vital for calculating agriculture across its varying seasons.[80] The Egyptian–Mesopotamian imperatives of rivers and resources thus played its part in China's early development, as well. Under the Shang, new land was cleared and sown on the king's orders in June and December of every year. Trees were stripped of their bark and burned away where they were impediments to raising food. Plows were made of wood and other implements—axes and spades—of stone. This slash-and-burn farming was carried out not by rural entrepreneurs but by collective farming teams supervised by Shang officials. A recent Chinese writer named Zhang Zhenglang describes these farmers as having a very lowly position. There was very little title to the land. Peasant farmers were instead bound to "agricultural collectives, controlled by the rulers." This meant that "lives and possessions were controlled by the king and the nobles, being in essence their tools and possessions."[81]

Even more than authoritarianism, it is the collectivist principle that seems to be evident across Shang culture. Kinship and lineage were the basis for occupational units not only for wheat and the raising of livestock, but in the trades as well. These *zu* had their own crests, with distinctive titles such as "pottery," "flag," "cooking pot," "wine vessels," "cordage," "horse plume," "fence," etc. There seems little doubt that stone-, wood-, and leather-workers had their own imposed associations as well. Grating as this early "soviet" trait may seem to Western ears, this bias toward the extended collective and the common good of the kinship group has helped give Chinese society a remarkable stability across four millennia.

In some ways, the great Shang technological achievement reacts back on aspects of both religious and economic life. These are the prolific bronze remains of the Shang Period. "Lady Hao" has become a minor celebrity in recent popular texts dealing with China. She was one of the many wives of the powerful emperor Wu Ding (c. 1250 BCE). Her underground tomb is the only Shang tomb not to have been robbed before being excavated, and the remains were truly noteworthy. Archaeologists uncovered four hundred and sixty bronze objects, which included two hundred ritual vessels, more than one hundred and thirty weapons, twenty-three bells, twenty-seven knives, four mirrors, four tiger heads, nearly seven hundred and fifty jade objects, seventy stone sculptors, nearly five hundred bronze hairpins, more than twenty bronze arrowheads, and three ivory carvings. The nearly 6,900 cowry shells lead to speculation that this was a form of currency. Inscribed bones near her tomb show she was a formidable figure at one time, leading 13,000 troops into battle.[82] The five hundred bronze hairpins at Lady Hao's tomb recalls Adam Smith's parable of the "trifling manufacture" of a pin. Without specialized labor, he noted, it would take all of one day to make a pin. China early evidenced the ability to produce skilled work.

Shang bronze-working seems to have been very centralized, with two major workshops situated at Anyang. One of these was an earthen house where clay molds were found. The large molds tell a very important story. As much as China seemed to lag behind the West, its first engineers had already developed a radically different approach to metalworking. Instead of forging tools, vessels, and implements piece by piece, the Chinese king's smiths in their earthen workshop poured superheated molten copper and tin into these elaborate, even decorated, molds and created cast products of great beauty and quality.[83]

This raises an important point in business history. It was once thought that bronze workers from the Mediterranean must have been the source of the Shang achievement. However, "various much more primitive bronzes, greatly inferior both in alloy ands casting techniques have now been discovered in Shang cities earlier than Anyang."[84] This suggests evidence of indigenous development from a slower beginning. Thus, although Shang China leaves behind no records of diligent Ea-Nasirs or complaining Imdilums, an important technological achievement in bronze would anticipate some of the main lines of China's economic contribution to world business in later periods. Bronze-working could have arisen indigenously, given the copper and tin deposits found in the Shensi and Shansi Mountain (Shaanxi) areas further west. R. Huang, in his respected *China: A Macro History*, lends support to the now regnant theory that Shang bronze and metal casting was self-originating.

Not surprisingly, then, with this specialist art as a backdrop, an early form of capitalism would, indeed, spring up in China. This was under the Zhou, who would rule from 1027–256 BCE, although in two separate spheres. It would arise in a China in which either the state or the kin group would be the fount of trust and authority, while temples or other forms of private and voluntary associations would decline in importance. But the Shang influence lives on in the Chinese ability to envision and produce on a scale that is truly epic. The old scholar's maxim about "one million Chinese with teaspoons building the Great Wall" has relevance. Chinese town planners today still build along the foursquare designs of the Great City Shang with their rulers at the center of all. From this sense of themselves comes China's name for itself, down to today—*Chung-kuo*, "the Central Country."

The Middle Bronze Age ended a little later in China than along the Fertile Crescent. By then, about 1500 BCE, neither Assyria nor Babylonia nor

Egypt was able to dominate the Near East as they had once done. "The Late Bronze Age was characterized by a constantly shifting balance of power among a half-dozen major states, each ruled by a different ethnic element."[85] Trading links with India were all but broken as the Indus Valley civilization receded, largely a victim of climate change, environmental collapse, and outside invaders.[86] Environmental problems sorely bedevil China even today, some would say especially today. Economic colossi sometimes stand on feet of clay.

At this stage, trading links to China, isolated in its Shang collectivism, lay far in the future. For the ancient Near East, however, a new era lay ahead. A great historic shift was in the making. The locus of international trade and business would steadily begin to move from Mesopotamia to the eastern shores of the Mediterranean, to the Semitic peoples we know as the Hittites, Syrians, Hebrews, Cypriots, Minoans, and Canaanites. That last group, later called Phoenicians, would raise seaborne commerce into a fine art and slowly, but inexorably, bring Europe into the emerging hemispheric economy.

5 Maritime Capitalism at High Tide
Trade and Investment Under the Phoenicians, 1500–500 BCE

The Phoenicians!

Who has not heard of their sea-faring exploits; their fabled voyages to Cornwall in search of tin; their swift, bronze-prowed ships that may have carried some of them to the New World? The Phoenician achievement was made possible by a constellation of economic and political factors that vindicate the theory that diversity rules.

It happened like this: During the Late Bronze Age (c.1500–1200 BCE), no single great empire dominated the world. What historian Marc Van De Mieroop calls "the Club of the Great Powers" had emerged. The Indus Valley culture was virtually submerged under natural calamities and Aryan invasions. Shang China remained isolated. Assyria had not yet totally recovered from Hammurabi's hammer blows. Mesopotamia was dominated, but not terrorized, by a series of Iranian rulers called Kassites,[1] who considered themselves the heirs of once-great Babylon. This political backdrop was important for the Phoenician expansion, but more important economic factors were mightily at work.

THE LATE BRONZE EQUILIBRIUM AND THE MOBILE TAMKĀRUM

The conquering Kassites were to rule Babylonia longer than any other dynasty. Kurigalzu I and his successors set out to rebuild trade ties in the Persian Gulf. Crown-sponsored commercial establishments were planted on the rich metal-producing island of Bahrein (ancient Dilmun) to the south. Another trading center, at Dur-Kurigalzu near today's Baghdad, controlled the mountain passes to the horse-breeding regions of Iran in the east.

Babylonia was part of that stable Late Bronze balance of power (1500–1200, Middle Chronology), essential for the great Phoenician expansion. Other national groupings grasped the chance to "make money, not war." By now this included not just powerful Egypt, but also Elam to the southeast of Babylon, the Hatti of southern Anatolia, the Mitanni and the Moschi and Tiberani of Asia Minor, and the Mycenean Greeks, as well as assorted city–states in Syria/Palestine. The Middle Assyrian Kingdom was perhaps best positioned of all to enjoy this era of relative stability. The Assyrian *tamkārum* was everywhere, his trading activities circumscribed by well-defined treaties and rules. These were usually written in Akkadian, the new common language of the ancient Near East. Literacy had taken hold. In many palaces and chancelleries of the Fertile Crescent, a newly recruited class of court and temple scribes and thinkers preserved and transcribed the ancient religious epics; discussed the theology of suffering, injustice, and morals; and helped codify state law. The documents from mid- to late second millennium BCE reflect both the abuses of state capitalism and attempts to regulate it. Like Hammurabi's Code, the legislation of the Late Bronze Age bored in on market stability and protecting property. This statute of the Hatti in Anatolia protected *tamkāru* trading in foreign lands:

> If anyone kills a merchant (in a foreign land), he shall pay 4,000 shekels of silver. He shall look to his house for it. If it is in the lands of Luwiya or Pala, he shall pay the 4,000 shekels of silver and also replace his goods. If it is in the land of Hatti, he shall also bring the merchant himself for burial.[2]

Paralleling Mesopotamian models of a mixed economy, the Hatti admitted the right to private ownership and transactions in real estate, but combined them with obligations for public service—the last imposed by the king. Priests and households of weavers living in several key towns were exempt, as were bowmen, carpenters, and others involved in the royal chariot industry.[3] Restraints on production were minimized. Coppersmiths were expected to participate in "ice procurement, construction of fortresses and royal roads, [and] harvesting vineyards."[4] Theft of livestock appeared to be common, along with pilfering of the royal granaries. The penalty for stealing a plow had once been death, but it was commuted to a fine, suggesting plows were more abundant, but still more valuable than wagons.[5] These specifics of a sophisticated economy were protected by state decree:

> If anyone offers a house, a village, a garden or a pasture for sale and another goes and obstructs (?) the sale, and makes a sale of his own instead, as a fine for his offense he shall pay 40 shekels of silver, and buy [the . . .] at the original prices.[6]

The royal writ, however, still regulated wages and prices. There was no equal pay for equal work. A man hiring himself out "for wages, to bind sheaves, load them on wagons, deposit them in barns, and clear the threshing floors" was to be paid 1,500 liters of barley for three months' work. A woman was to be paid only six hundred.[7]

Other prices were fixed in shekels (whereby one shekel of silver equalled eight grams) as follows: plow: twelve, sheep: one, horse: twenty, garment: twelve, fine garment: thirty, wheat (one hundred and fifty liters): one, vineyard: forty for 3,600 square meters.[8]

The laws of the Middle Assyrian Kingdom were somewhat harsher, but they were still recognizably geared to a regulated market economy. An individual wanting to buy a field or house had to make a public proclamation three times within one month in the city of Ashur. The proclamation stated: "I intend to purchase the field or house, within the common irrigated area of this city, belonging to so-and-so, son of so-and so."[9]

Plaintiffs who wished to contest the purchase were required to bring their tablets before the royal officials. All land deals were to be witnessed by the city scribe, herald, mayor, and three noblemen of Ashur.[10] These were remarkably sophisticated arrangements 1,500 years before the birth of Christ.

BYBLOS: CRADLE OF PHOENICIAN CAPITALISM

The Late Bronze Age state system, so conducive to the growth of international trade, especially benefited the city–states of Syria and Palestine. Here was a region well suited by climate, location, and background to serve as the middlemen of the ancient world. Indeed, the first historical reference to Greater Syria is in the Egyptian annals recording expeditions in search of cedar pine and cypress in the fourth millennium BCE. Sumer, as already mentioned, imported cedars from Lebanon and gold and silver from north of today's Antioch.[11] The term "Phoenician" is a generalized Greek term applied to the peoples living on the Syrian and Lebanese coast of the Mediterranean, the Levant. It traced from the Greek word for "purple," attributed to the shellfish out of which the coastal people made purple die. The purple robe was a sign of dignity all across the Near East, showing how early and pervasive had the merchants of the Levant developed as suppliers and manufacturers in one of the first luxury trades. The individualistic Phoenicians, however, preferred to name themselves after their cities—they were Tyrians, Byblites, or Sidonians. Levantine cities back in the Copper Age had traded woven textiles with Sumer. Byblos itself was a valuable trans-shipper and supplier between Old Kingdom Egypt and early Dynastic Sumer. Beginning with Dynasty II and continuing with Dynasty III, royal Egyptian merchants sailed to Byblos to obtain timber, metal, and luxury items. The mythical tales of their gods Isis and Osiris allude to a permanent Egyptian presence in Byblos as early as 2600 BCE.[12]

Byblos, between today's Beirut and Tripoli, lay in the Eblaite trading sphere, as did Ashdod, Jaffa, Akko, Sidon, Beirut, Alalakh, Megiddo, Lachish, Homs, and Hama. Byblos seems to have been the chief entrepot for gold shipments coming from Egypt and Africa on the way to Ebla. From

Ebla, the Byblites traded crude metals, textiles, livestock, and food products in return for linen and finished metal objects. The Byblites and Eblaites were on a more equal footing, after the king of Byblos married an Eblaite princess. The social unrest that likely toppled the Old Kingdom Egypt had its effect on Byblos, bringing the first Levantine trading economy to an end[13] (about 2400–2300 BCE). The *Papyrus Ipuwer* notes:

> "WHY REALLY, they who built the pyramids have become farmers. They who were in the ship of the god are charged with forced labor. No one really sails north to Byblos today. What shall we do for cedar for our mummies? Priests were buried with their produce and nobles were embalmed with the oil thereof as far away as Keftiu [Crete], but they come no longer. Gold is lacking. . . . How important it now seems when the oasis people come carrying their festival provisions. . . ."[14]

Yet Middle Bronze Age Byblos retained its role as the leading trading city in Syria/Palestine, resting as it did at the intersection of the Syrian/Mesopotamian and Canaanite/Egyptian trading spheres. Its highly developed economy and need for advanced forms of literacy gave us the Greek word for "books," showing up in "Bible," taken from the name Byblos itself. For the keen merchants of Byblos, their locational advantage between the Middle Kingdom of Egypt and the kingdoms of Aram, Mari, and Old Assyria was a given as ancient texts reveal. The story of Sinuhe, a royal Egyptian trader of the Middle Kingdom, mentions the importance of Byblos: "One foreign country gave me to another. I set off for Byblos and approached Qedem and spent a year and a half there."[15] Byblites continued to trade with Egypt well into the time of the New Kingdom. Thutmose III (traditionally dated 1490–1436 BCE) invaded Lebanon for the timber that his agents gathered yearly at Byblos for shipment to Egypt. One inscription on the tomb of his Chief Treasurer, Sen-Nefer declares:

> I brought away timbers of 60 cubits [30 metres] in their length. . . . They were sharper than the beard of grain, the middle thereof as thick. . . . I brought them down from the high-land of God's Land. They reached as far as the forest-preserve. . . . I sailed on the Great Green Sea with a favourable breeze, landing in Egypt.[16]

The Royal Egyptian accounts show state enterprise still driving the Nile's foreign trade. Akhenaten's (traditionally dated 1363–1347) diplomatic archive unearthed at El Amarna shows the importance of Byblos. He also mentions Tyre, Sidon, and Berytus (Beirut) as flourishing commercial cities free to govern themselves under Egyptian suzerainty. Ugarit, Hazor, and Kadesh are also mentioned, reflecting, says scholar Glen Markoe, "a complex and vigorous intra-regional network of economic exchange."[17] Ugarit, Tyre and Sidon were becoming important as Late Bronze Age prosperity continued though

Byblos still held pre-eminence. The Byblite King, Rib-Addi, wrote to Akhenaten noting both the existing wealth of Ugarit (to the north) and the rising
prosperity of Tyre. Tyre, initially founded in the Early Bronze Age, appears
to have vanished in the Middle Bronze to be re-founded in the Late Bronze
along with sister-city Sidon. Thus even the correspondence of the Pharaohs
highlight the importance of the Syro-Phoenician region to the eastern Mediterranean economy, especially the carrying trade. Thutmose III, for example,
began importing copper from Cyprus, but the Amarna records show the
inevitable involvement of the Phoenician cities in the copper trade. Deposits
of the metal have been found in Lebanon.[18]

Amenhotep III (traditionally dated 1402–1363 BCE) began to import
Levantine metals in bulk. Amenhotep moved his capital to Memphis and
set forth on a temple- and city-building boom. This spurred the demand for
Phoenician timber, from which the Egyptian state industries could fashion boats, roofs, columns, altars, doors, and shrines. Egyptian–Phoenician
trade expanded further under Ramesses II of the Nineteenth Dynasty (traditionally dated 1303–1200 BCE). In an Abydos Inscription, Ramesses
mentions the seagoing vessels of the royal temple. Archaeologists have
shown a Phoenician presence in the form of Ugaritic *amphorae* (jugs) in the
Egyptian cities of Pithon and Ramesses in the eastern Nile Delta. The presence there of Phoenician shrines to their gods Baal and Astarte evidence
that the Phoenicians were busy sending trading colonies to the Delta.[19]

"WESTWARD HO!"

South lay Egypt, to the west was Cyprus. Phoenician merchant seamen had
early probed into the Mediterranean. Cyprus was destined to play a key
role in the growing Late Bronze economy. Its very name meant "copper."
In the days of Ramesses II, the mining of copper began to boom. A smelter
at Enkomi on the east coast, was matched by a south coast refinery. The
valuable ore was melted down into ingots and carried to both the Levant
and the Aegean in sailing ships much like the two discovered off Cape
Gelidonia and Ulu Burun in Turkey. According to Markoe, "the thirteenth
century, in fact, marked Cyprus' emerging role in Central Mediterranean
trade with Sicily and Sardinia."[20]

Cyprus, strategically located and often visible from the Levantine
shore, was the first port of call for Phoenician ships sailing onto the Great
Sea. The population remained essentially Greek until Phoenician colonists
arrived after 1200 BCE. Both the Aegean and Mediterranean Seas thus
became incorporated into a Phoenician trading sphere. Phoenician sailors
were already charting the coastline of Sardinia and even Spain (Tarshish), but leaving no permanent presence. The scanty records at Byblos
testify to the managed nature of trade. The crown controlled most industry, and Phoenician crews typically carried agents of the prince who were

given extraterritorial guarantees in foreign ports. As both the consumer and commodity markets became more complex and as Phoenician agents sailed further and further from home, the germs of a somewhat free-wheeling maritime capitalism took shape. With no great power threatening its back, Phoenicia was free to probe westwards.[21]

The journey of the Egyptian royal trader Wen-Amon to Byblos reveals the hierarchical and feudal nature of the enterprises at the mainspring of this maritime expansion. The ruling King of Byblos, Zakar-Baal, describes shipping in both Byblos and Sidon as state-sponsored:

> Perhaps there are not twenty ships in my harbor that trade [hubur] with Ne-su-Ba-neb-Ded? As regards this Sidon . . . the other [place] through which you passed, are there not fifty more ships in it, that trade with Werket El, and are dependent on his house?[22]

Yet Wen-Amon negotiates directly with the King, making the title "merchant princes" much more than a metaphor in ancient Phoenicia. He asks the Byblite ruler to sell him timber as his father and grandfather had done. Zakar-Baal, more than willing to do so, naturally demanded something in return: "In truth, when my people fulfilled this charge, the Pharaoh . . . sent six ships loaded with Egyptian merchandise and unloaded them in my storehouses." This being the Late Bronze era and Byblos no longer a vassal of Egypt and her god Amon, Zakar-Baal arrogantly made it clear that the Byblite timber industry was under his royal jurisdiction. "If I shout to Lebanon, the heavens open and the logs lie at rest [on] the seashore!"[23] This was the kind of rhetorical outburst that both Elizabeth I and Phillip of Spain might have made, both of them monarchs in a heroic era of maritime expansion, and both of them uncommonly watchful over their investments. As Wen-Amon desired, three hundred lumberjacks under royal supervision then felled the trees, but the Egyptian was most unlucky—a fleet of eleven pirate ships rapidly descended upon the Phoenician port. Summoning his assembly, Zakar-Baal plotted to betray the Egyptian to them, but the latter, escaping in a ship manned by a royal crew, sought refuge with a Cypriot princess.[24] Egypt, Cyprus, Byblos— the triangular trade of the 1700s in our era was nothing new.

Why did Byblos feel confident enough to buck the Egyptians? One reason was it had a strong ally in the King of Ugarit just up the coast. It is time to study this powerful Ugaritic hub and maritime entrepot more closely.

UGARIT: MARITIME METROPOLIS

Ugarit, located about one kilometre from the seacoast, ruled a principality in maritime Syria. Although never a large city, its strategic location near the great trade route to the Euphrates and Tigris made it both a rival and part-ner of both Byblos and the more well-known city of Tyre. When the armies of Hatti defeated the forces of Ramesses II, Ugarit was drawn into the Anatolian orbit. The world was almost blissfully unaware of this thriving commercial and cultural center until 1929, when French archaeologists under Claude F. A. Schaeffer uncovered the site named Ras Shamra in western Syria. Ugarit appears to have been quite cosmopolitan with many official buildings, temples, and libraries. These buildings housed the valuable cuneiform tablets that confirm contacts with Mycenaean Greece. Excavators discovered rows of two-story houses, business quarters, temples of Baal and Dagon, and, most important, the ruins of the huge royal palace of Ras Shamra. Written in a language akin to Akkadian, Eblaite, and Hebrew, the clay tablets of Ugarit brought the world of the Canaanites alive.[25]

Ugarit's records, written on clay, survived when other Phoenician records, written on papyrus, did not. Archaeologists in Sidon, Tyre, and Beirut face a problem with excavating in urban areas. Artifacts buried beneath apartments and office towers and not under desert mounds are harder to get at.[26] Most archaeological evidence for Phoenician settlement has come from its overseas colonies, rather then the Levantine homeland itself. Given the shortage of texts from first-millennium sites, the Ras Shamra-Ugarit tablets were a gold mine—the only usable body of Phoenician documents.[27] The Amarna tablets from Egypt describe Ugarit as being splendidly wealthy. "See, there is no mayor's residence that can compare with that at Tyre. It is like the residence at Ugarit. Extraordinarily large are the riches there."[28]

Most Phoenicians in the Ugarit hinterland were independent farmers until the usual cycles of monopoly and consolidation forced many into dependent labor. With a dense urban population, access to timber reserves and a people obviously skilled in the development of architecture, Ugarit exploited its comparative advantage in shipbuilding, manufacturing, and seaborne trade. Well-outfitted fleets built from the forests of Lebanon sailed between Egypt, Cyprus, Canaan, and the Cilician coast. Grain grown in Egypt or Babylonia was traded to Cyprus and the Hittites of Asia Minor in exchange for copper, silver, gold, and tin processed in Phoenician workshops, which were then shipped by caravan and river boat to Babylon, Sippar, Ashur, and beyond. Kassite horses were sold to Egypt; Egyptian ivory sent to Mesopotamia, Elam, and Hatti with much of the financial transactions fattening the coffers at Ugarit. Into Ugarit's port sailed metals from Cilicia and Cyprus. The copper and other valuable ores were then distributed to guilds of merchants and traders by the harbormaster. The cycle then completed itself as profits and royalties paid to the crown were then reinvested in the construction of even more seagoing vessels. This created the nucleus of the rich carrying trade for which Phoenicia was famous. Mammon, not Mars, spurred a vast interconnected trading regime, one where Ugarit and her sister cities playing a pivotal role.[29]

In Ugarit and the other coastal cities, guilds of highly-skilled craftsmen—most of them self-employed—smelted and shaped copper and tin or worked with the gold and ivory from Egypt to fashion finished products.

Royal factories harvested the dye of the murex shellfish, creating the purple robes and stimulating a garment industry from where more than a thousand items of apparel went to every *bazaar* of the ancient world.[30] The specialized knowledge involved was a jealously guarded state secret. Today we would label this *product specialization*—a national competitive advantage revolving around an industrial cluster in the purple dye industry.[31] But the gist was there 1,400 years before Christ.

As in Mesopotamia, the *tamkāru* of Phoenicia were divided into two categories. First were the *tamkāru sha mandatti*, who paid taxes on their operations. The *mandatti* were also *bnsh mlk*, or "royal dependents." Their livelihood depended upon diplomatic treaties and trade agreements the King of Ugarit signed with his partners. This meant that much of the profit returned to the crown. The second category, *tamkāru sha shepe* ["of his feet," i.e., personal], on the other hand, were the personal traders of the king, as is witnessed by a letter from the King of Amqi to the Vizier of Ugarit: "And customs duties have not been taken from him. Yet [?] give the duties of the tamkar of his feet . . . from ever the duties were not taken from the tamkar of his feet."[32]

A tablet from the time of King Amistamru illuminates the feudal-like role of the *tamkāru*:

> From the present day, Amistamru, son of Niqmepa [King of Ugarit], took the houses and fields of Abutenu and gave it to Abdihaqab, son of Shapidanu and his sons forever. And the service of the *tamkār*ship he shall perform. Further: [till?] the service of the *tamkār*ship is performed by Abdihaqab, nobody shall take away (these lands) from Abdihaqab and from his sons and grandsons forever. The seal of the great King. Iluramu, the scribe.[33]

Here is a case of land and property rights accruing to commerce, not agriculture, a considerable advance on Medieval Europe. In addition, *tamkāru* also obtained grain, oil, and other products from the royal stores. The *tamkāru sha mandatti* acted in the interest of the crown. They traded on behalf of the king and obtained land during their period of service. They not only possessed their own property holdings but also traded with their own goods in their own private transactions. For this, they had to pay an income tax on their profits.[34]

The Ugarit texts describe an economic system of managed seaborne trade.[35] This prototype would continue into the period of Phoenician overseas expansion under the kings of Byblos and Tyre. The system found in Phoenicia is, in some ways, suggestive of some medieval and modern models. "We find here," says Professor Michael Heltzer of Haifa University, "something similar to a royal monopoly of foreign trade: mutual regulation by political agreements between neighboring countries and states concerning their trade."[36]

Thus, trading networks in Ugarit were in the hands of *tamkāru* who sometimes served as royal commercial agents and sometimes managed their own business affairs. These *tamkāru* were given land by the Prince of Ugarit in return for the military service as archers and other services called *tamkārutu*. Major trade relations between Ugarit, the Hittite Empire, and its vassal in Carchemish (a city on the main ford of the Euphrates) were governed by treaties and decrees of the Hittite kings. According to these agreements, royal *tamkāru* of Ugarit traded in Carchemish, and the royal *tamkāru* of Carchemish traded in Ugarit. Both were protected by a reciprocity agreement punishing anyone who killed a *tamkārum*. If the killer could not be found, the populace of the territory where the murder took place was fined a large sum of silver.[37]

Royal *tamkāru* were not always popular. They were foreigners and they had money. Prince Niqmepa of Ugarit complained to the Hittite King Hattusilis III that the *tamkārum* of Ura, a Hittite seaport, had overstayed his welcome. Hattusilis then decreed that the royal merchant would have to leave:

> The seal of the Tabarna Hattusili, the great King, King of Hatti: to Niqmepa say: According to what you have said before me "that the son of Ura, the *tamkārs* are very heavy upon the land of thy slave." and the Sun (Hittite king) the great King has the treaty of the sons of Ura in summer in Ugarit in their *tamkār*-operations . . . act and in the days of winter from Ugarit they shall go out to their country.[38]

Tamkāru enjoyed vast powers. They could seize goods in another country to pay debts, even arresting family members, as well as the debtors themselves. Only land, which returned to the Ugaritic crown, could not be seized. Ura was the chief port through which Ugarit traded with the Hittites. A Ras Shamra text, 20.213, records the Hittite king ordering the King of Ugarit to ship him two hundred *kur* (five hundred tons) of grain via Ura. Of course, Ugarit did much business with Byblos. The *tamkāru* Abihili carried goods to Byblos. Ras Shamra, 18.025, mentions five hundred and forty shekels of silver pledged for the King of Byblos. The texts also mention trade with Egypt. The Princes of Ushnatu and Ugarit signed a treaty for a joint venture to the south. Marc Van De Mieroop mentions that there were moves towards trade regulation and trade embargoes among this "club of the Great Powers." Then as now, all was not well, as even royal *tamkāru* could be crooked. Baaliya, likely from Ugarit, was sent to Egypt and gave over one of the people he took with him to the Egyptians, embezzling his property (RS 18.025). In RS 34.158, the King of Ushnatu writes to the Vizier of Ugarit complaining of this incident.[39] Trade and diplomacy were clearly linked in this era of territorial states jockeying for advantage, although usually peacefully.

SINARANU: MERCHANT EXTRAORDINAIRE

A number of the Ras Shamra texts mention Ugaritic trade with both Cyprus and the Aegean. Horses were traded from Ugarit and sold to the King of Cyprus. The Greek staple, olive oil, was also traded, and Cypriot, as well as Phoenician *tamkāru*, were mentioned. Trade with Crete was in the hands of the *tamkārum* Sinaranu, son of Siginu. Sinaranu lived in Ugarit in the time of Ammishtamru II, son of Niqmepa, whose reign is usually dated to some time after 1250 BCE. King Niqmepa had, in the last years of his reign, awarded the estate of his father, Siginu, to Sinaranu: "the house, field and everything else that Siginu, son of Milkiahu (has), to Sinaranu, son of Siginu, he gave."[40] None of Sinaranu's brothers had any share. This land was given to Signinu and to Sinaranu for services to the king as a merchant. Sinaranu's mercantile status was considered official. When the land of one *Shumiyanu* was awarded by the king to the scribe Yasiranu, Yasiranu had to pay one hundred and fifteen shekels of gold, not to the king, but to Sinaranu. Sinaranu acted as a royal agent, a *tamkār sha shepi*, or personal commercial agent of the king. He bought property from the king, in one case for over 1,000 shekels, and received a number of other properties the king had appropriated, each for four hundred shekels of silver. If the silver shekel stood at sixty cents and the gold at about one dollar in today's terms, these were substantial sums. The lands acquired by Sinaranu for 4,100 shekels (about forty kilograms of silver) became his own property, making him the richest man in Ugarit.[41]

During the reign of the Ugaritic King Niqmepa, the cuneiform tablets recorded the story of Sinaranu, who, like Abdihaqab, received title, horses, and fields from the crown on the condition that he serve as a *bnsh mlk* or royal *tamkārum*. As a crown real estate agent, Sinaranu earned far more capital in the form of silver and land than any other merchant in Ugarit. Nonetheless, Sinaranu also had his private shipping fleet, which worked the markets of Crete and the Aegean under Niqmepa's royal protection.[42] Under a special franchise, any cargo imported from Sinaranu's shipping firm would go directly to the king and not to the royal inspector or harbormaster, as in the case of self-employed merchants. Much of Sinaranu's activity was devoted wholly to his ruler. And why not? Another function of royal *tamkārum* was that of taxman. Having to provide Niqmepa with a certain share of taxes, which the king had to pass on to his own Hittite overlord, Sinaranu delegated many of his company duties to his own vassals.[43]

The crown granted Sinaranu other privileges. He was exempted from receiving foreign merchants sojourning in Ugarit, performing messenger services, or offering hospitality to travellers. His official status was that of "friend of the king," a royal councillor upon whom the king relied for advice and other purposes.[44] In all of this, the almost irrational Phoenician fear of industrial espionage may have been a factor.

What does modern research tell us of Sinaranu's trading voyages? Professor Michael Heltzer of Haifa University cites a text from the Ugarit archives that describes this royal *tamkārum's* journeys to the Aegean:

> From the present day Ammishtamru, son of Niqmepa, King of Ugarit, exempts Sinaranu, son of Siginu. As the sun is clear pure, he is clear. His grain, his beer, his olive-oil to the palace he shall not deliver. His ship is exempt when it arrives from Crete. Then his presents to the king he has to bring. And the herald must not approach to his ship. For the king his lord-Sinaranu is busy. He and his house are for the eunuchs. May Ba'al, lord of mount Hazi obliterate anyone who obliterates these words. In the future is everything to the sons and grandsons of Sinaranu forever.[45]

"The favor of the King"—from the book of Proverbs to the Rothschilds and Rockefellers, and down to Bechtel and Haliburton, the theme endures in business history.

TO THE SEA IN SHIPS

Phoenician *tamkāru* traded as members of mercantile guilds, where every member was responsible for any royal personal or financial property. Overseas commerce in Ugarit, Byblos, Sidon, and Tyre was dominated by an assembly of private and royal merchant princes. The Phoenicians were astute enough to formalize these maritime ventures because the hazards of sea travel were known well before the time of Jonah, the ill-starred Hebrew voyager. To help insure against risks in the overseas trade, merchants organized the contract of *tapputu* or comradeship. This was an early form of joint venture. A guild or group of individual merchants would pool their assets either in Ugarit or in another nearby Phoenician principality such as Usnatu, Byblos, or even Tyre. They would then trade in Egypt, Greece, Mesopotamia, or Anatolia more securely. In one such arrangement, four merchants from the village of Apsuna combined their resources, including 1,000 shekels (8,000 grams) of silver, which they would trade in Egypt for gold that they could resell to their Hittite and Mesopotamian customers at a much higher price. Activities like this on a much larger scale appear in the royal archives of Ugarit, not only supervised by the crown, but often with the king a direct participant.[46]

One expedition sponsored by the ruler of Byblos included some five hundred and forty shekels of silver, fifty of which were carried in the king's own personal vessel.[47] Joint ventures such as these saw the crown investing in a variety of trading and shipping ventures known as *hubur*.[48] Harbormasters such as Ugarit's Abiramu and his superior, the *sakinu*, or vizier, played an important managerial role in Phoenician business. Strategic industries such as lumber and shipping were under strict state control.[49] The Ugaritic monarchy and the Sinaranus and Abdihaqabs in its employ, commanded the fleets trading with Cyprus, Egypt, and Cilicia. Loading up grain from the mainland and shipping to Cyprus was a common occurrence. Given what Linder describes as the "special position of Ugarit as supplier and agent for this essential commodity" the royal grain enterprise fit the dictates of the *Eclectic Paradigm*. The endeavor benefited from the organizational and internalization advantages which accrued to being "monopolized by the king and shipped by his fleet".[50]

Thus, Phoenician *tamkāru* traded by land and by sea. Some journeyed eastward to Carchemish, others south to the Phoenician stronghold of Kadesh. Most of these *tamkāru* were overseen by the *sakinu* (vizier), the *makisu* (customs official), and the *akil kari* ("overseer of the quay"). Heltzer speaks of "a bureaucratic apparatus overseeing trade activities in this kingdom [likely Carchemish]."[51] Overland trade proceeded, as it had for almost two hundred years, by donkey caravan.

Commodity prices and currency exchanges were regulated and denominated in terms of silver. Wheat was sold at ninety liters a shekel; olive oil was priced at twenty-two liters per shekel. Wine, figs, raisins, cheese, and honey were also commercial goods. An ox was worth ten shekels; a sheep, one; a horse as much as three hundred. Textiles and garments were also carefully assessed for value.[52] A number of tablets from the royal palace of Ugarit talk about market sales and prices. One mentions six hundred shekels of silver in the account of Ybnn. Another relates that "on the day of the new moon," Belmedr and BnHlp, a man of the village, bought gold for four hundred shekels of silver. A large document lists goods sold to consumers on behalf of the royal store. An accounting list of those in the bronze-smith trade mentions delivery of copper to the coppersmiths for reworking instead of for public sale. A letter from Amurru to Ugarit mentions a commercial timber deal. The overseer of the quay, Rashapabu, records paying silver to four dozen sellers of artifacts and goods. Most of the customers were from the hinterland and sold their wares for one-half to two shekels apiece. In another transaction, Rashapabu received a hundred shekels of silver for a shipment of purple wool.[53]

Craftsmen involved in diversified branches of production became *bnsh mlk*, or royal merchants. They were given rations and raw materials from the palace, in return for performing their duties, occasionally without compensation. There is no doubt that pottery and textiles were made at home in Phoenicia and that small private markets worked as well here as they did under palace–temple aegis in other parts of the ancient Near East. The vital staples of flax and wool made for a thriving domestic industry and some weavers were promoted to the status of royal merchants. Wool dyed in purple at the shoreline was outsourced to fullers to create a range of apparel, some custom-made with deft needlework. Bigger and more strategic operations such as shipbuilding, chariot-making, lumbering, and building construction needed more infrastructure and organization, and so tended to be state-run. Some parts of the production—breastplates, bows, and arrows—were outsourced to craftsmen. "The manufacture of military equipment and weapons was important to the economy, which was fully controlled by the palace authorities," says Heltzer, "and run by the *bns mlk* system, although individual work was possible."[54]

Copper, so vital to Phoenicia's craft and manufacturing industries, was imported from Cyprus through another monopoly of royal *tamkāru* who then distributed the copper to others in the harbor at Ugarit—"if you want it, here it is." It is likely that copper, shipped in large quantities in the royal and private fleets of Ugarit, served to stimulate the growth of the huge merchant fleet. We also know these cunning traders of the Levant persuaded the natives of Spain to part with silver in exchange for olive oil. In the words of one historian, the *tamkāru* were the shrewdest of the shrewd. In effect, they "stole from the weak, cheated the stupid, and were honest with the rest." Olive oil was so precious in the Middle East that it was considered a royal monopoly as much as copper—both supervised by the harbormaster. Given all this, how important was business news or the latest data on market conditions? One of the legends about the Phoenicians is that, rather than betray the best trade routes, they would run their ships aground if competitors followed too closely and could expect to be compensated for this daring deed by the royal treasury.

As we might expect, foreign merchants, known as *ubru* in the Phoenician tongue, found themselves strictly regulated by the harbor master. Aramean, Hittites, Egyptians, and Mesopotamians dispatched their own merchant/ambassadors into Phoenician cities, where the practice of extraterritoriality still held. The regulations imposed by the local harbormaster, however, presented them with a primitive version of what would today be described as *de facto* tariff barriers. *Ubru* were forbidden to leave the foreign business quarter district of the host city, were barred from the residence of native traders, or to conduct business in a Phoenician city without strict supervision from the local harbor master.[55] They took no chances on even the intimation of industrial espionage.

WATER-ROADS OF EMPIRE

In all of this, mighty Ugarit and her sister cities were pioneering a system of *naval* or *maritime capitalism*, whereby the navy and its typical activities reinforced and often led the way for the merchant adventurers. Sponsored by the palace and implemented by a refinement of the old Assyrian *tamkārum* methodology, the trade and commerce of the Levant steadily increased. There are more than a few overtones here of the accelerated forms of market dominance that would look very familiar to medieval Italians (Venice), early modern Portugese, Spanish, and Dutch. The joint-stock companies of seventeenth- and eighteenth-century Britain and post-1867

Japan would follow in their wake.[56] Popular historians are now enunciating what many textbooks fail to stress: the linkage between sea-power and commerce, a theme Sir Walter Raleigh had drummed away at to his Virgin Queen. The sea lanes were—and are—the true roads of empire. The author of *To Rule The Waves: How the British Navy Shaped the Modern World* reported that "the sea remains the cornerstone of today's global system" in that 95% of trade that crosses international boundaries is waterborne.[57] The obvious is not always evident.

As well, historians of ancient economies tended to neatly compartmentalize the style of operation as either state-run or privately-run. This view is being altered. Specialists such as Maria Eugenia Aubet of Spain's Universitat Pompeu Fabra recognize that the boundaries between the two were much more fluid. Palace, temple, and private operations were often intertwined. There was, of course, always a strong element of royal direction, or at least underwriting, of many of these operations. As a general rule, the further the overseas trade the stronger, the royal writ ran. The kings of Byblos and Ugarit were clearly in charge, as were Philip of Spain and his nemesis Elizabeth I. This is a good corrective of the tendency to overgeneralize or to see patterns where patterns are not there. One swallow does not make a summer. Phoenicians did not, according to Heltzer, have companies organized vertically or horizontally in ways we would recognize. They did not possess the vast bureaucracies on the order of Japan's twenty-first-century trade ministries. Overseas trade took place on a much smaller scale, generally confined to luxury goods.[58] But, the basic principles ran on remarkably similar lines. The parallels with later naval capitalisms are there. In ancient Phoenicia, commerce flowed along hierarchical structures but allowed a surprising amount of scope for private initiatives and entrepreneurship. We have noted how *tamkāru* such as Sinaranu and Abdihaqab served both as royal vassals and, at the same time, as feudal overlords of lesser merchants or *bidaluma*. The lesser merchants collected royal taxes, skimming off a profit and sending the rest to the *tamkāru*. Like the small Japanese firms of the 1980s and even 1990s, these were bound by long-term allegiances to larger clients. Although the lines of authority were clearly drawn, the principle of delegation was well understood. Some *bidaluma* were assigned whole towns to rebuild and resettle, notarizing deeds on the part of the crown, and playing an active part in public affairs.[59] Walter Raleigh, founder of Roanoke, would have understood.

Then there was the practical feature of those doing business in great waters needing to guard against risk. As might be expected, Phoenician *tamkāru* maintained strong ties with their princely navies. Pirates and storms ensured that long-distance trade could be a perilous venture. Vast fleets of round galleons and elongated Viking-style warships sometimes numbered a hundred ships or more, manned by professional sailors and artisans. These vast armadas were set up along feudal military lines.[60] In Phoenician maritime capitalism trade was sometimes very definitely war by other means. Capturing markets became as valuable as the ability to make battering rams and organize boarding parties. There was not a long step from peaceful trade to the full militarization of Phoenician commerce. According to archaeologist A. F. Rainey: "The reason for this association between business agents and the military is not hard to find. Mercantile enterprise . . . was a dangerous adventure."[61] *Tamkāru* were often murdered on their trading ventures. Trade, war, and diplomacy were inextricably linked. A whole body of treaty law came into existence to supervise the activities of competing merchants. *Tamkāru* were often obliged to serve in various diplomatic corps, going beyond the trade missions of today. The El Amarna archives speak of Babylonian merchants being sent on a state mission to Egypt. According to Rainey, "commercial, diplomatic and military activity went hand-in-hand."[62] The equation was simple: No navy, no economy. In 2002, historian Niall Ferguson asked if it were possible to have globalization without gunboats. The Phoenicians would have answered in the negative.[63]

TYRE'S FIRST CIRCUIT: THE AGE OF HIRAM

The indented coves and harbors of the Levant are a seaman's world. Ugarit's maritime capitalism reproduced itself in both Byblos and, especially, at Tyre and Sidon, whom even the prophet Ezekiel saluted as "seamen that had knowledge of the sea" (1 Kings 9:27). Tyre's harbor, carved out of rock on a small island, was an ideal sanctuary to shelter ships from storms and enemy vessels.[64] The scanty records from Tyre show a thriving managed trade, crown-sponsored commercial projects, and shipping crews in the king's employ empowered to travel far and wide. No doubt some variant of the Ugarit pattern of crown/vizier/harbormaster and a royally sponsored merchant prince–lesser prince commercial nexus thrived in Arvad, Byblos, Sidon, and Tyre. By the time of the United Monarchy in Israel, the princes of Phoenicia operated profitable shipping consortia called *hubur*. Israel's first three kings—Saul, David, and Solomon—acted as buffers between Tyre and raiders from Mesopotamia. The Biblically-attested alliance with Israel allowed Tyre's princes and merchants to launch a new era of robust commercial expansion. This multistaged expansion is best summarized in chart form (see Table 5.1).[65]

Table 5.1   History of Tyrian Commercial Expansion and Retreat

---

1000–900 BCE: First Circuit: Age of Hiram: Direct investment in and partnership with King Solomon to exploit Red Sea routes.

900–800 BCE: Second Circuit: Age of Ethbaal: Investment in Omride Israel, Syria and Anatolia to exploit Assyrian trade.

800–600 BCE: Third Circuit: Age of Pygmalion: Peak of Tyrian commercial network stretching from Spain to Babylon.

600–331 BCE: Tyre's Age of Decline: Partial conquest by Babylonia, absorption into Persian economic sphere, defeat by Greeks, independence of Carthage, final conquest by Alexander.

What realities lay behind this now legendary outburst of economic expansion? Sabatino Moscati believed it was the pressure of the Neo-Assyrian Empire threatening to gobble up Mesopotamia and the Euphrates Basin, which forced resilient Tyrians to look west. William Albright, the dean of Palestinian archaeologists in the middle twentieth century, thought that the trigger was purely internal—a Phoenician need for raw materials, security of supply. In the second edition of her important study on Phoenician commerce, Maria Eugenia Aubet argued for a multiplicity of factors. She asked: When did it become profitable for Tyre to mount huge, costly, and risky ventures of naval capitalism into far distant areas? For an answer, Aubet looked first at ecological factors. By the end of the Bronze Age, 1200–900 BCE, weather patterns changed, effecting a drying out of the Lebanese interior. The cities of the coastal strip still enjoyed a Mediterranean climate, but could not feed their growing populations. The anti-Lebanon mountain chain not only hampered agriculture but blocked expansion eastward. The encroaching desert gave the coup de grace to intensive cultivation. To feed herself, Tyre would have to turn to other lands and people groups. Just to her south lay the fertile plain of Esdraelon, populated by the northern tribes of Israel. In 1010 BCE, David's armies broke the power of the Philistines who had dominated the Levantine coast for centuries. Israel was both the new power and the breadbasket of the region. Ahiram I of Tyre, the famous "Hiram" of 1 Kings, offered David an alliance that was renewed under Solomon. Tyrian commercial settlements were set up in the Galilee and Carmel along the coast, evidenced by the remains of Phoenician jugs dug up in the tribal territories of Asher, Zebulun, Issachar, and northern Manasseh. Aubet dates these remains as early as David's time.[66]

The Solomonic alliance (971–931 BCE) was the cornerstone of Hiram's strategy, one dictated by population and food. Through it, Tyre gained access to Israel's winter wheat and olive oil. Solomon, in return, ceded twenty Israelite cities to Hiram as collateral.[67] With her food supply secure, the merchants and artisans of Tyre could flourish. Tyre was an urban centre populated with craftsmen who earned a good living producing luxury goods for Near Eastern elites. Ivory, gold, silver, copper, tin, bronze, glass, and rare woods poured into her port and along the great caravan routes. Tyre's industry was built on a secure supply of raw material. This intensified the process already extant in Phoenicia for centuries. As luxury items flowed out to Egypt, Israel, Babylonia, Hatti, Assyria, Elam, and elsewhere, bullion poured in. Control of overland and maritime markets was essential, making the Israelite alliance a mainstay. Joint enterprises were begun with King Solomon, through whose territory passed the great caravan routes linking the Euphrates, the Levant, and Arabia.

The Book of I Kings, based upon the court history of the Kingdom of Israel, records that Ahiram supplied Solomon with the timbers for the First Temple in Jerusalem. Solomon's request implied that the timber was supplied by Ahiram's crown merchants, and that Solomon supplied Tyre with wheat and oil:

> Now therefore command thou that they hew me cedar trees out of Lebanon . . . for thou knowest that [there is] not among us any that can skill to hew timber like unto the Sidonians. . . . And Hiram sent to Solomon, saying . . . My servants shall bring [them] down from Lebanon unto the sea: and I will convey them by sea in floats unto the place that thou shalt appoint me, and will cause them to be discharged there, and thou shalt receive [them]: and thou shalt accomplish my desire, in giving food for my household. So Hiram gave Solomon cedar trees and fir trees [according to] all his desire. And Solomon gave Hiram twenty thousand measures of wheat [for] food to his household, and twenty measures of pure oil: thus gave Solomon to Hiram year by year. [68]

Another Israel–Tyre joint venture was designed to counter the Egyptian monopoly over the Near Eastern metals trade. A joint fleet of Israelite and Tyrian ships was strategically placed at Ezion-Geber (Eilat) at the mouth of the Gulf of Aqaba. This bold move helped neutralize the Egyptian presence along the Sinai border. Nearby, in Israelite-controlled Edom, lay a complex of copper-smelting furnaces, originally investigated by archaeologist Nelson Glueck, which remarkably anticipated the Bessemer system in more modern times. Solomon and Hiram's combined fleets imported gold, silver, ivory and precious stones from Arabia, Somalia, and, perhaps, India. These revenues allowed Hiram to reinvest in capital warehouses, ships, and wharves. Metals and imported goods flowed up the "King's Way" east of the Jordan and across the Negev.[69] In short, for this corner of the Levant, business was never so good.

TYRE'S SECOND CIRCUIT: THE AGE OF ETHBAAL

After Solomon's death (c. 930 BCE), a tax revolt tore ten of the twelve tribes away from the ruling house in Jerusalem to form a separate nation. This was a new nation, the House of Israel, under the dynasties of such well-attested biblical figures as Jeroboam I, Baasha, and Omri. Jeroboam's new ally, Shisak of Egypt, invaded and plundered the surviving House of Judah in Jerusalem. The Arameans, desert tribes to the east of Judah, revived and began to close the King's Way. Without allies, the Kings of Judah could not reopen the Red Sea trade. Fortuitously, a new dynasty seized power in Tyre, led by the Baal priest Itobaal I, the Biblical Ethbaal (891–59 BCE). Ethbaal modified Hiram's strategy, merging Tyre and Sidon into a single *uru*, or Phoenician state. He then solidified his ties to the grain-rich nation of Israel by marrying his daughter, the notorious Jezebel, High Priestess of Astarte, to Ahab. Ahab was a scion of the well-known Omride dynasty in Samaria, Israel's capital.[70]

Trade revived. Guilds of Phoenician merchants and craftsmen settled in Samaria, Hazor, and Megiddo, the key cities of Israel. Tyrian ivory products and other examples of conspicuous consumption became status symbols for Israel's elites. The rush for profits brought out the prophets. Outspoken dissenters such as Amos and Elijah denounced the growing economic inequalities resulting from the crass commercialization of Israel's life.[71]

Archaeology has corroborated that new second wave of prosperity for the upper classes in the Kingdom of Israel. Tyre's merchants, dwelling along Israel's seacoast close to its grain and wine growing hubs, bought and shipped Israel's produce north to Tyre while selling Ethbaal's manufactured goods and Cypriot copper to the Hebrews. Copper was needed to supply the bronze lavers and altars at both Samaria and Jerusalem. Archaeologists uncovered white-painted containers from Cyprus buried alongside vases from Tyre. Cypriot pottery appeared in Israel, and Tyrian pottery was found in Palestine and Cyprus. What do these artifacts mean? They indicate trade between Tyre in Lebanon, the Northern Kingdom of Israel ruled by the House of Omri, and Ahab and the island of Cyprus. What, however, was the nature of that trade? Who supervised it? Was it done by independent merchants? A more intriguing possibility is that goods were manufactured in Tyre and then shipped in the vessels of Tyrian merchants to various Tyrian establishments in Israel and/or Cyprus for resale there. Tyrian merchants may also have shipped grain from Israel to Lebanon and/or Cyprus and copper from Cyprus to Tyre, Sidon, or Israel. On the other hand, the copper, pottery and other goods may have been carried by Cypriot merchants in their own ships.[72]

In Tyre, as in most of the ancient Near East, religion and economics were intricately joined. As at Ur and Uruk, Ashur and Ebla, when business prospered, merchants and craftsmen thanked the gods. Ras Shamra texts praise the Baal Hayyin, patron of Phoenician metalworkers, for example: "Hayyin would go up to the bellows . . . To melt silver, to beat out gold. He'd melt silver by the thousands [of shekels], Gold he'd melt by the myriads."[73] This patron deity of craftsmen, also known as Kapthor, was worshipped in the palaces of Baal across the Levant and out into the Aegean:

"There now, be off on thy way . . . to Kaphtor, the throne that he sits on, Hikpat the land of his portion. From a thousand fields, ten thousand acres, at Kotha[r']s feet bow and fall down, prostrate thee and do him honor. And say unto Kothar-wa-Khasis, Repeat unto Hayyin of the Handicrafts: Message of Pui[ssant Baal, Word of the Powerful Hero]."[74]

Fear of the gods enforced honesty in business, for they were held to bless and establish commerce via the temple priesthoods. This was the supreme example of the marriage of commerce and religion. But the results were surprisingly effective. Morris Silver insists imposed religious standards for merchants not only "lowered their costs of cohesion (joint action)" but also "facilitated monopolistic business practices (i.e., restricting production to raise prices and profits)."[75] Every guild celebrated its own patron god or goddess. Patent laws began with the control of economically valuable inside formation by priests who considered it sacred to the gods who were its source:

> The magical/holy component associated with new technologies served (like modern patent laws) to reserve them and their economic gains for the innovator and, thereby, encouraged profit-seeking individuals to invest in intellectual capital and consequently to benefit society at large.[76]

Priests at the temples and shrines of the various *baalim*, at ports in major cities located along trade routes at the borders of Phoenician territory, drew up and enforced contracts. Priests acted as notaries, and temples doubled as banks and warehouses. What Phoenician would dare to default on a loan to the priests of Baal-Melqart, the storm god, who could not only withhold financial prosperity, but also bring rain that threatened his crop?[77]

The shrines of Baal-Melqart and Astarte were integral to Ethbaal's plans to greatly expand Tyre's trade. Religion aided social cohesion. It made customers and suppliers more accountable and pliable. What could be more binding than a contract sealed by the storm god who could sink your ships? This was the later Protestant Ethic with a vengeance! Or, to alter the analogy, a preview of the often unfortunate church–state alliances of medieval Europe still extant in parts of Latin America even today. Americans who print "In God We Trust" on their currency should not be overly surprised. Tyrian metal-working shops in Cyprus have been found directly adjacent a nearby temple whose walls were covered with graffiti depicting ships. In Cyprus and at Ugarit, Phoenician temples incorporated anchor motifs into the temple walls, as well as at Byblos and cities on the shores of the Red Sea. The god Kapthor gave his name to the island of Crete. Well-organized and tax-exempt, temples enjoyed a competitive advantage over private firms that allowed them to increase their share of asset ownership along with income. The temples were a prime source of available capital. Tyrian guilds would sponsor trading voyages to faraway cities and erect shrines giving heavenly sanction and earthly direction to their overseas investments and partnerships.[78]

The worship of Baal spread across the Eastern Mediterranean. This gave additional impetus for organizational and internalization advantages already possessed by the trading networks based in Tyre. Religion lubricated the external market. Religious syncretism represented "a positive incentive for individuals or communities to reduce transaction costs by investing in the creation of common gods."[79] When Tyrian managers passed on Baal-Melqart's secrets for shipbuilding or bronze and iron work to distant markets, the recipients were obligated to add Melqart to their pantheon. Mention of the god of Tyre in places under Tyre's sway often signified the impact of a new technology.[80] The Tyrian cult of Baal-Melqart ("King of the City") was a product of the city's new riches and power. Created under Hiram, Melqart, the god of storms, was also the protector of prosperity and the dye industry. Here was a regal deity with an adorned hat and battle axe. He was said to rule in feudal fashion over the lesser *baals* of mountains, forests, and springs. Soon he would become Patron of Westerly Navigation, with temples in Samaria, Syria, Cyprus, Malta, Carthage, Sicily, and Spain added to his domain.[81]

Indeed it was the structural dynamic of Tyre's temple hierarchy with its wide-ranging coherence of belief and practice that testifies to the parallels with the multinational networks of the future. For example, Phoenician and Sumerian deities often boasted "branch temples in several cities."[82] Local sanctuaries reported to bigger centers. This meant that financial transactions and the transfer of capital and goods within similar temple network systems were a strong incentive towards market cohesion. If Tyrian long-distance trade was internalized, as these authors believe it was, who did the internalizing? Did the Melqart network, with a head temple in Tyre, and branch temples elsewhere give Tyrian traders the key advantages of internalization? Did agents employed by the royal palace or under contract from the royal place provide the internalization? As Clifford says,

> In explaining financial connections among cults or administrative controls of one cult by another or the sharing of temples or the merger of cults or temple complexes, the economist would of course be inclined to stress explanations in terms of efficient organization or the exercise by mother cults of quality controls over franchiser cults or economies of scale or scope. Standard explanations stress battles over supremacy and cultic imperialism or mere "friendly connections" between sites worshipping the same deity.[83]

Religion, dealing as it does with ultimate concerns, can be a source of strong social bonding, of catching potential customers in a more receptive mood. Amongst the church-goers of Colonial America, for example, the church door was often a source of news and informal updates, as well as back-country gossip. It was common for well-off planters to admire each other's horses and get updates on how planting and harvesting were being done or to size up each other's slaves. This was more common than discussing the merits of the parson's sermon. Capitalism is very much a system dependent upon such grand intangibles as trust and good information. As Gordon Childe noted, in the ancient world, temple worshippers had strong emotive ties to bind them by paying homage in the temple of Melkart or Marduk:

> The cult of the gods was, in fact, designed to secure not what we call holiness, purity and the peace of God, but good harvests, rain in due season, victory in war, success in love and business, children, wealth, health, and an indefinitely long life. Immortality was conceived . . . as essentially a prolongation of earthly life. That is why the noble dead have to be provided continually with food, drink and other offerings, supplies of which were to be secured by the perpetual dedication of . . . chantry priests.[84]

By the Late Bronze Age, the link between religion and economics in Phoenicia was almost complete. Under Ethbaal, Tyrian crown traders in the ninth century BCE planted temples at Myrandrios in Cilicia, near Carchemish along the Euphrates, and near Aleppo in Syria. Where Mammon led, Baal was not far behind:

> Thanks to a network of factorships and trading posts in place in the Gulf of Alexandretta and the coastal region of Cyprus, Tyre was able to secure a monopoly of the trade in metals and slaves in Cilicia, the Taurus Mountains and the Euphrates and, at the same time, to control the sea routes to the Aegean.[85]

As noted, this second phase of Tyre's remarkable economic expansion was spurred by ominous rumblings from the East. The Assyrians were flexing their military muscles. This Neo-Assyrian revival began shortly before 900 BCE. Under Ashurnasirpal II (883–859 BCE) and Shalmaneser III (859–824 BCE, traditional dates), the Assyrian war machine stormed westward, seeking a way out of the economic stranglehold imposed upon Nineveh by the Mitanni and her oppressive neighbors. The Assyrian armies did not come to stay, just yet, but did exact heavy tribute.[86] For example, Ashurnasirpal II received from Tyre, Sidon, and Byblos payment in the form of "gold, silver, tin, copper, copper containers, linen garments with multicolored trimmings . . . ebony, boxwood, [and] ivory from walrus tusk."[87] His predecessor, Shalmaneser III, collected tribute "on ships from the inhabitants of Tyre and Sidon."[88] Shadows were falling across Tyre's mercantile empire.

The Phoenician goods described in Assyria's exhaustive annals are choice luxuries, accessible through Tyre's contacts with Syria and Cilicia in the northeast corner of the Levant. Just as Assyria seemed to be roaring back to greatness, shortly before 800 BCE, the capital region stumbled, held back by weak leadership and an alliance between her old enemies. This cut Tyre off from Assyria and from the caravan routes. The biblical Book of Kings showed how this affected Syria and Palestine. The powerful Aramean kingdom of Hazael, located in Damascus, scourge of Israel, made a supreme effort to control the trade routes into Arabia. With Assyria temporarily neutralized, new outlets could be explored and developed. This brief breathing space set the stage for the third and most far-reaching era of Phoenician expansion.

TYRE'S THIRD CIRCUIT: THE AGE OF PYGMALION

In 831 BCE, Pumayyaton, or Pygmalion, ascended the Tyrian throne. Pygmalion is credited with inaugurating the great overseas expansion for which the city is now famous. Pygmalion shrewdly bet on the Assyrian relationship as worth developing even with the temporary eclipse of Nineveh. The Assyrian Shalmaneser III was succeeded in 810 BCE by Adad-Nirari III. Adad-Nirari no longer wanted luxury goods, but bulk shipments of silver, iron, and copper for his war policy of defensive aggression. With Israel perhaps coming under Assyrian sway, Pygmalion needed to find large quantities of food and raw materials outside the Levant. Here the Dunning Paradigm kicks in with a vengeance. By the ninth century, Tyre's merchants possessed the expertise, institutions, the location, and the networks to undertake a new series of long-distance commercial ventures. They now had a motive.

Pygmalion stepped up copper production. New factories were set up on the island of Cyprus outside Kition in the late ninth century BCE. Five other settlements, scattered across the island soon followed. Evidence of metalworking suggests the presence of craft guilds processing copper goods on "Copper Island." Guilds of metalworkers were first mentioned in the Ugaritic texts as royal dependents. Led by an elder, guild members served at the king's pleasure. The guilds were hereditary, with their members often receiving royal fiefs in the Phoenician manner. By this time, many of the guilds were composed of some individual smiths who were self-employed, no longer royal dependents. Nevertheless, evidence of royal oversight, feudal loyalties, partnerships, supervision, and financing of these Cypro-Phoenician enterprises by the temple-priests of Kition suggest that craftsmen dispersed abroad still participated in an internalized, managed trade.[89]

Pygmalion stepped up overseas colonization with three major settlements, conscious branch plants from Tyre. The first was in Carthage in North Africa, in 814 BCE. The name of the city, *Qart-Hardasht*, or "New Town" was identical to the name given to Kition. According to tradition, Carthage was founded by Elissa, sister of Pygmalion. The purposes for founding Carthage and the supporting African colonies of Hadrumeto and Utica were both as a food source and as an outlet for surplus population fleeing the escalating wars in Mesopotamia.[90] Sardinia was next. The Minoans and Mycenaens were already trading here in the Bronze Age. The Cypriot influences on the island suggest that Sardinia was settled from Kition on the basis of its own profitability, and not as an aftermath of the Cadiz plantation in Spain. The city of Cagliari in southern Sardinia attracted the original Tyrian settlement, which then expanded in the late eighth century BCE to Nora and Bithia. Bithia, on the southwest coast, became a distribution center for Tyrian goods from Spain, Carthage, Ischia, and Phoenicia itself. Sulcis was founded after 750 BCE and may well have included Cypriots in its settlement. Not only Tyrians, but also Greeks from Euboea, traded here (see Chapter 6).[91]

The next strategic settlement in Pygmalion's plan was in Spain, on the site of Cadiz (anciently called Gadir or Gades). Phoenicians had traded in the central and western Mediterranean for at least a century. Their agents knew of Spain's resources of silver and tin but the distances militated against permanent colonies. The Greek poet Homer depicted Phoenicians as independent traders buying and selling small volumes of goods in the Aegean. Was the same true of those who now, after 820 BCE, began to permanently settle in the central and western isles and coastlands of the Great Sea? Or was this trade more organized?[92] Melqart's priests and other ambitious traders knew that the Huelva region of south-western Spain had immense potential. The geographer Strabo wrote that a temple oracle inspired two failed Tyrian expeditions to Spain, but the third voyage founded a Melqart temple on the site of Cadiz.[93]

The giant Cadiz temple, controlled by a few aristocratic families, copied its Tyrian homeland and effectively linked both ends of the Mediterranean. This expansion into the Western Mediterranean marks a significant moment in history as the spotlight of history begins to slowly shift from exclusive focus on the ancient Near East to the more remote corners of the Great Sea. In Cadiz, Kition, and in Tyre itself, the temple hierarchy recorded transactions and enforced contracts and consistent exchange rates by controlling weights and measures.[94] Where the Phoenicians went, the Greeks were not far behind. Tyrians and Euboean Greeks jointly founded the settlement of Pithekoussai on Ischia, off the coast of modern Naples around 775 BCE. Two or three decades later, colonists from Corinth and other Greek cities began a mass movement to southern Italy and Sicily. The Tyrians responded by establishing permanent settlements in Malta, at Motya in Sicily, and at Sulcis in Sardinia.

The pace of westward expansion accelerated when Tiglath-Pileser III (745–726 BCE) seized the throne of Nineveh. This strong ruler rapidly reversed a half-century of Assyrian decline and set the ancient Near East on a dramatic new path. By 732 BCE, Tiglath's armies had overrun all of Aram (the present Syria and Lebanon) and much of Israel. Shalmaneser V (726–722 BCE) and Sargon II (721–705 BCE) completed the conquest of northern Israel. Tyre, though, as a banking and commercial center, was a goose laying golden eggs. Assyria shrewdly allowed Tyrian independence to guarantee profitable enterprises. The new reality of living in a world under Assyrian sway would shape the trading/investment strategy of Pygmalion's successors. Phoenician tribute money and trade contacts helped fill Nineveh's coffers.[95] A letter from an Assyrian governor to Tiglath-Pileser dated from 738–734 BCE mentions Tyre as a tool of economic warfare: "He has allowed the people of Sidon to fell wood [of the Lebanese mountains] and to work with it *but not to sell it* to the Israelites or the Egyptians."[96]

Assyria needed ever-larger quantities of silver and hard metals to finance and equip her large armies. The Bronze Age had already yielded to the Iron Age. Technology mattered even more. Only Tyre had the means to access hard minerals and guarantee safe delivery. Once Tyre was pre-empted from supplying Egypt, the rock city was more vital to Assyria as a supplier and financier than as an Assyrian province. Functioning as a sort of island Switzerland, Tyre saw not just a chance for surviving the Assyrian deluge but for profit on a scale large enough to secure the westward expansion of mercantile activity.[97] This unofficial Tyrian–Assyrian Entente would help effect one of the great axial shifts in the world's history—the eventual transfer of civilization from the Near East to the Western Mediterranean. The hinge was ready to turn.

THE FIRST MNE—AND THEN SOME

In the 700s BCE, the rock city of Tyre, by dint of her commercial zeal, her flexible trading tactics and skilled seamen, lay at the locus of Near Eastern, Mediterranean, and North African trade routes. Command of the sea allowed princes, royal agents, temple priests, and growing guilds of independent merchants to found factories and trading posts in distant lands. Support from both temple and palace, feudal loyalties, and family connections combined to internalize and stabilize far flung operations beyond Italy and into the Western Mediterranean.[98] Tyre's skilled shippers, guilds, temple hierarchy, and information networks updating both knowledge of maritime conditions and the ability to conduct "value added" activities overseas made the Phoenician Empire the closest incarnation yet to appear of John Dunning's *Eclectic Paradigm*. Dunning's *Eclectic Paradigm* turns on three factors explained in Chapter 1, namely Ownership, Locational, and Internalization Advantages.

Ownership: The knowledge of markets, opportunities, and techniques of manufacturing, for example of the famous purple dye, were jealously guarded secrets that were central to the success of not only the Phoenician nation but also to individual firms and their owners. The network of Phoenician colonies and outposts provided invaluable market insight that guided the actions of Phoenician businesspeople.

Locational: Grouped along the Eastern Mediterranean coast like an accessible ladder of sister-cities, the merchants and craftsmen of Tyre, Sidon, Byblos, and Ugarit were fortunately placed at the terminus of major overland trade routes going south to prosperous Egypt and west to the open Mediterranean. It was a natural advantage, just as the British Isles would benefit from being at the junction of Europe and North America, or Dubai would benefit from being the major transportation hub between Europe and Asia's new dynamic markets.

Internalization: This is the advantage gained by keeping operations under a similar and readily-agreed upon chain of management. In the case of the Phoenicians, expansion as far as Spain was simplified by a network of cultural assumptions that flowed like an electric current from the Levant to Cadiz and back again. As we have shown, Phoenician religion greatly strengthened this dynamic. The development of a far-flung, elaborate, internalized trading network resting on intercontinental seaborne trade was summarized by Maria Eugenia Aubet as a "solid and solvent organization" of shippers. Tyre's navies dominated the trade routes. All this was reinforced and underwritten by a temple–palace consortium with the managerial experience to transport both heavy metals and finished goods across the sea lanes in sufficient bulk to absorb potential losses:

> The expansion to the west and the founding of the colonies in southern Spain could only be undertaken by Tyre when she was sure of attaining her objectives: guaranteed silver ore and plentiful food resources, and the certainty of real economic rewards.[99]

Tyre's record of overseas expansion speaks for itself and can be summarized in chart form; see Table 5.2.

T. Judice Gamitó agrees with Aubet that Tyre's operations were intensively internalized. Overseas settlements were closely linked to family-based companies in Phoenicia. Far-flung operations were privately-owned, with their own fleets, and run by merchant-princes with high political and social status at a time where royal and family ties were very important.[101] British archaeologist Richard Harrison sheds even more light in his description of Tyrian family-based structure and the internalization advantages that resulted. The phrase "multinational enterprise" springs readily to mind. What else can we call a network of specialist production centers stretching from the Levant to the Pillar of Hercules with consistent exchange rates and a form of vertical integration? Shipping in the hands of Tyrian family firms headquartered in Lebanon possessed most of the advantages we associate with multinational enterprises today.

Table 5.2 History of Tyrian Colonization[100]

Before 800 BCE: Kition, Carthage, and Cadiz. Other settlements in Cyprus. Cagliari in Sardina founded from Cyprus.

800–750 BCE: Tyrian presence alongside Greeks in Ischia. Possible settlements in Crete and Rhodes, Memphis in Egypt, and Utica in Africa.

750–700 BCE: Major Greek colonization of Sicily and Southern Italy begins around this time. Motya in northwest Sicily; Sulcis, Nora, and Bithia in Sardinia; Tyrian settlement on Mediterranean shore of Spain.

700–600 BCE: Tyrians then expand into central and northern Sardina to Olbia and Mt. Sirai.

Merchant princes could stimulate demand and reap huge profits from their permanent establishments in Spain and elsewhere. The vertical integration of these firms permitted them to absorb the enormous costs and uncalculated risks of trans-Mediterranean bulk commerce.[102]

Cadiz (Gades) was the milch-cow for Tyre's vast new empire. Even into Roman times, it remained a prime shipbuilding center. The famed "ships of Tarshish" constructed there were approximately seventy-five feet/twenty-five meters long, rounded, with large square sails and ample room for passengers and crew. Warships with square sails boasted up to sixty oars and battering rams. Smaller ships were used by fishermen. Once in Spain, Tyrian colonists pursued further locational advantages, spreading inland up the Guadalquivir and along the Rio Tinto. In 750 BCE, another strip of colonies was planted along the Mediterranean shore of Andalusia, beginning in 750 BCE. The dig site at Toscanos yielded evidence of a massive stone warehouse, citadel, stone houses, and slag remains. Toscanos possessed its own metal and purple dye industries allowing it to trade and rework materials and goods from Tyre, the Greek world, and inland Spain. Colonies in the Málaga region were self-sufficient in farming, cattle-raising, and production of purple-dyed garments. Red Slip pottery and metal goods were made locally in eastern Spain, and these were traded with Africa, the Iberian interior, and even the tin mines of Britain.[103]

Harrison believes that gravesite remains confirm that the local Tyrian managers were "probably from important trading families who headed the firms that were based in Tyre and Sidon."[104] This is ownership advantage many leagues from home base. The seventh-century graves of Phoenician Spain, their styles copied by Iberians eager to embrace Phoenician customs and gods, reveal "an aristocracy" installed in the Phoenician settlements of the West.[105] The Tyrian establishments in Iberia purchased tin imported by their native hosts from Britain, giving rise to the legend of ships reaching Cornwall. Pottery finds also linked these establishments with Tyrian settlements in Algeria and Morocco, notably Lixus and the Isle of Mogador. These two posts, with the Algerian sites, granted overland access to the gold trade of Guinea and other points in sub-Saharan Africa.[106]

Nor was the boot of Italy exempt from this commercial onslaught. Tyre's Italian operations served as natural way-stations to and from Spain. A Phoenician tomb in Malta yielded a horde of Spanish silver. Sulcis and Motya, according to Professor F. Barreca, were "ports of call on the routes of Phoenician ships coming into the western Mediterranean in order to transport metal to sell in the marketplaces of the Near East."[107] Kition, on Cyprus, was the key way-station in the eastern Mediterranean. Egyptian and Assyrian artifacts and the first distinctive Phoenician Red Slipware found in Spain provided compelling evidence that goods passed through there. Russian archaeologist Yuri Tsirkin summarized that "parallels are found between the objects of Hispano-Phoenician and Cypriote arts." Spanish exports went to the Aegean via Kition, although direct

Helleno–Iberian trade also existed.[108] The place of Kition or Kittim as Tyre's Gateway to the West is confirmed in the writings of the Hebrew prophet Isaiah, who predicted that ships from Cadiz would one day learn of Tyre's destruction upon reaching Cyprus: "Howl, ye ships of Tarshish: for it [Tyre] is laid waste, so that there is . . . no entering in: from the land of Chittim it is revealed to them."[109]

Tyre's Assyrian connections intensified in the seventh century. In 705 BCE, Prince Luli attempted a revolt against the dreaded Sennacherib (705–681 BCE). He was replaced by the more tractable Ethbaal II. Another revolt led by Abdi-Mikulti of Sidon and Baal (Ba'alu) of Tyre broke out under Esarhaddon (680–669 BCE), who imposed harsh penalties. The Lebanese mainland was carved into three Assyrian provinces, and many Phoenicians were deported east. Esarhaddon also imposed a treaty upon Ba'alu, which strictly regulated Tyrian Near Eastern trade imposing an Assyrian governor in Tyre itself and listing the ports through which Ba'alu's merchants were permitted to trade. The treaty was ratified in the presence of the priests of the *baalim*. The document stipulated that these worthies were to put a hex on the Tyrian monarch by raising an evil wind against Ba'alu's ships, undoing their moorings and sinking them in the sea, if agreements were violated.[110]

So much for separation of church and state! Nineveh's kings, nonetheless, respected Phoenician business acumen, and entrusted their new vassals with much of the empire's long-distance trade. Assyrian annals tell, for example, of the Sidonian Hanunu (Hanno), chief supplier of the empire's dyed fabrics. Oubasti, exiled by Sennacherib in his youth, went on to exercise a powerful role as a chief porter in Nineveh in the reign of Esarhaddon.[111] An eastern network of Tyrian merchants in Cilicia, Aleppo, and Carchemish in Syria, and including Nineveh and Babylon, made sure that Tarshish (Spanish) silver and Levantine purple dye made it to the heart of the empire, never leaving the hands of the Phoenician merchants who procured them with the help of their relatives, partners, and/or subsidiaries.[112] This hemispheric trade—from the Atlantic to the Persian Gulf—set the style for other empires, other regimes, as the Club of Great Powers gave way to territorial empires.

A HINGE OF FATE

By the time Esarhaddon marched into Egypt in 673 BCE, the kings of Tyre had forged an economic investment empire that amounted to the world's first intercontinental enterprise. Including Phoenicia's trading partners, Tyre's maritime capitalism penetrated marketplaces stretching from Spain, the British Isles, and West Africa to Babylonia and the Arabian Gulf. Historians like to postulate that there is nothing inevitable in history. As noted, the shift of the center of world civilization from the ancient Near East to the Mediterranean lands adjacent to Europe did not happen by accident. The evidence presented in this chapter would seem to call for a readjustment of the role played by the Greeks in this world-historic shift of history's wheel. This reconstruction of the growth and extension of Tyre's business network recognizes a new multinational dimension to Phoenician trade which effectively moved the axis of trade and commerce away from the palaces of the Land of the Two Rivers to the Mediterranean littoral. "Westward the course of investment made its way." Yes, but the process was mediated and abetted by the Phoenician westward movement, which reached back east into the palaces and armories of the Neo-Assyrian Empire.[113]

This was a momentous historic achievement. So great, in fact, that it would take the pen of a superb poet to even begin to encompass it all. Fortunately, we have such a writer. "The prophets of Israel were so well-informed," exclaimed Paul Dion of the University of Toronto's Near Eastern Studies Department. A detailed, although slightly impressionistic, description of the Phoenician achievement, written half a century after its peak, has survived in the writings of the Jewish priest/prophet Ezekiel. His is the unique vantage point of a detention camp outside Babylon (Ezekiel 1:1). Ezekiel was a prophet against profits. No great admirer of Tyre's imperial pretensions, its materialistic commerce, and especially its religion with a propensity for infant sacrifice, Ezekiel set down the mighty trading mart as a bastion of greed fused with idolatry. He skilfully skewered Tyre's pride by using the analogy of one her own trading vessels, a tactic Longfellow would use centuries later in depicting the American Ship of State.[114]

Written about 588 BCE, the portrait of Tyre in Ezekiel 26 and 27 provided a detailed description of the city's enormous clout. "Situated at the entry of the sea . . . a merchant for many isles," Tyre was described as a vessel of fir, cedar, and oak from Lebanon, Syria, and Israelite Bashan. The ship–nation was decorated with linen from Egypt and ivory and purple from Cyprus and the central Mediterranean. Ezekiel's list of commodities "reads like a cargo manifest" says Old Testament scholar Christopher Wright. Ezekiel 27:12–24 cites the wares of the Phoenician empire: vessels of bronze, horses, steeds, mules, ivory tusks and ebony, fine linen, corals, rubies, wheat, honey, oil and balm, iron and saddles, lambs and rams, precious stones and multicolored apparel. The prophet/reporter alludes to the multiethnic crews manning her stays, with Sidonians and men of Arvad working the oars and the elders of Byblos specializing in ship construction. Ezekiel doesn't miss much—he details the *mkrm* of Tyre serving as the chief officers, helmsmen, and pilots (verse 8). The army, meanwhile, was cosmopolitan in spades, being manned by mercenaries from as far away as Persia, Lydia, and North Africa. Noticeably, the insightful poet assigned the partnership with Spain a special role in Tyrian prosperity:

Tarshish was thy merchant by reason of the multitude of all kinds of riches: with silver, iron, tin, and lead, they traded in thy fairs. . . . The ships of Tarshish did sing of thee in thy market: and thou wast replenished, and made very glorious in the midst of the seas. . . . When thy wares went forth out of the seas, thou filledst many people; thou didst enrich the kings of the earth with the multitude of thy riches and of thy merchandise.[115]

Ezekiel's description of Tyre's Spanish trade confirms the vastness of the Phoenician cultural achievement.[116] Moving in his mind's eye from west to east, Ezekiel's prophetic lament takes in Greeks, Anatolians, Arameans, Israelites, Arabians, East Africans, and finally Assyrians—all of them good Tyrian customers and consumers. The text indicates Tyre's suppliers from the products carried: timber from the Levant, linen from Egypt and North Africa, copper from the Aegean and Anatolia, wheat and iron from Israel and Aram, ivory from East Africa, and rich apparel from Mesopotamia. A close reading of Ezekiel 26–28 also implied that much of Tyre's trading and investment was now in private hands. The Hebrew word for "merchants," most often used in those chapters, was derived from *rokel*, "broker, merchant, or trader." The Tyrian *sahar rokelim*, most often mentioned by Ezekiel, were private *tamkāru*, in contrast to the *sohare yammelek* or *sohare yadek* of II Chr.1:16 or Ezek.27:21, who were royal *tamkāru*. Nevertheless, even the major *rokelim* were deeply involved with royal and temple agents.[117]

Like any good prophet, Ezekiel foresaw Tyre's doom. The great empire had flourished under its Neo-Assyrian patron but made it fatally dependent on Assyria's tacit support. By 622 BCE, the overextended, depopulated Assyrian colossus began to stagger and, within twenty years, collapsed under the pressures of holding down such an assortment of peoples. The Medes and a newly resurgent Babylonia under Nebuchadnezzar II administered the coup de grace in 612 BCE. Tyre, itself, would be besieged and taken by this very Nebuchadnezzar. After this, its vast commercial empire began to splinter and fragment.

Christopher Wright, a historian as well as a biblical scholar, adds a fascinating postscript to the tale of Phoenician maritime capitalism and its surprising prosperity and sophistication. "If Ezekiel were bringing his prophetic challenge into the world of the early twenty-first century," asks Wright, "what would be the equivalent of his Tyre?" We quote his answer to establish the newness of the old in business history rather than support any metaphysical conclusions. "It is more likely," concludes Wright, "that it would be a transnational corporation, or brand name, than any single nation state. For the fact is that in the globalized economic world of hypermodernity, real power has shifted from national political communities to transnational economic giants." Not all would agree with this analysis, but it is telling that it is economic superpowers vying for "total global saturation" that draws the attention of even a theologian when ancient economics are discussed. Wright reminds his readers that of the world's one hundred largest economies, fifty-one are corporations. General Motors is bigger than Denmark and Toyota bigger than Norway. The Time-Warner and AOL merger has produced a corporation larger in economic weight than several European countries.[118]

Whatever the merits of Wright's linking of prophets and profits, a significant moment in economic history had been reached. Although Tyre's economic hold was broken, the island city's resourceful merchants had already extended the boundaries of world trade to the central Mediterranean. Assyria nemesis—the Babylonian Empire of Nebuchadnezzar (626–539 BCE)—was the last such that would arise out of the Mesopotamian heartland. The hinge of fate had turned. Finally exhausted from its internal conflicts and weakened by the centripetal forces unloosed in the Late Bronze Age, Mesopotamia slipped from the center of world trade and as its primary source of foreign direct investment or banker of last resort. Tyre, too, was in decline but Carthage lived on as its zestful offspring, challenged more and more by the already extensive seaborne commerce of the Greek city states. The enterprising Greeks, building on Tyre's achievement, were now coming more and more into their own. Under the Greeks, the center of finance and culture would shift even more to the westward with consequences still with us to this day. Chapter 6 tells that story.

6 Entrepreneurs of the Aegean
The Greek Free-Market Revolution, 825–480 BCE

In an insightful study titled *The Origin and Goal of History*, philosopher Karl Jaspers advanced the concept of "the Axial Period" in world history.

Jaspers reviewed the years 800–200 BCE, and was impressed with the number of revolutionary thinkers who emerged in the 500 or more years before Christ, men who reoriented human thought in new directions: The Buddha, Plato, Zoroaster, Confucius, Jeremiah in Jerusalem. Here were founding sages with new ideas whose fresh intellectual recastings renewed the ancient world's bloodstream.[1]

Jaspers was not without his detractors. Yet the phrase "Axial Period" possesses a rhetorical zest. Chapter 5 of our study advanced the thesis that the Phoenician civilization spreading from Tyre and Sidon, in the Levant, to Spain, in the Western Mediterranean, helped set civilization along a new gradient. This chapter shows how the people who built best on this innovative approach to overseas commerce were the Greeks of the Aegean basin. Bold Hellenic Greek traders and merchants effectively shadowed the crown-sponsored merchants of Tyre across the Mediterranean world. In the process the adaptable, acquisitive Greeks—building on some of the peculiar characteristics of their geography and culture—developed and perfected a new business model very much akin to independent free enterprise.

The Greeks, we shall show, were the first to create a genuine "free market" system, although markets and entrepreneurs had existed as far back as ancient Sumer. A key background factor here is Moses Finley's reminder that the economy of the ancient world was overwhelmingly subsistence-based and agrarian. Any "modern" capitalist features we cover in this book are thus present in embryonic form, but they are there just the same. The creative, synthesizing Greeks of the first millennium BCE were to finally abandon the hierarchical temple–palace economy dating back to Uruk and Ur. In its place, they laid out the dimensions of the most market-oriented system the ancient world had yet seen.[2] This chapter shows how it happened.

GREEK INDIVIDUALISM AND THE
FIRST FREE-MARKET CULTURE

Sumer is flat; Greece is mountainous. Egypt is alluvial; Greece is alpine. The Indus Valley is undulating; Greece is hemmed in by the sea. The Greeks lived on a spiky collection of islands and peninsulas that could support only a limited number of farmers. They were almost forced by geography to look outside their borders if they were to move beyond subsistence labor. The typical early European cultures of the Bronze Age, including the Greek, originally followed versions of the temple–palace economy found in Asia. Even then, however, the Greeks were making moves towards a more market-based economy, although possessing nothing yet comparable to the trans-national traders of Old Assyria. The Greek model would be an independent one, not an internalized one. Hellenic traders, sometimes non-Greek immigrants called *metics*, or even enterprising slaves seeking opportunity, bypassed larger forms of organization. They traded around the Mediterranean world, with the free-booting spirit of Jason and the Argonauts or of wily Odysseus pumping in their blood—temperamental opposites of the clannish crown merchants and conservative elites of Phoenicia. This sturdy culture of independent Greek traders extended and grew and reached full maturity in the Athens of the fifth and fourth centuries BCE. Along the way, they would develop major mining and military enterprises, high-risk overseas trading ventures, private household banking systems, and relatively free capital markets. If one looks beyond the trade in commodities, one detects the cutting edge driving the economy is a small, but vital, nonagricultural sector. It is this feature that points toward developments akin to today's Western, and especially Anglo-American, consumer capitalism.[3]

As noted, neither the Minoans of Crete nor the Greeks of Bronze Age Mycenae were entrepreneurial. The palace elites in Knossos and Mycenae told farmers what to grow and set quotas. The merchants trading with Egypt, Cyprus, and Syria in foodstuffs, olive oil, wine, and bronze goods were employed by the crown. The royal house "operated as a monopoly through the palace system . . . with little role for independent merchants and traders."[4] The Greek mainland in the Late Bronze Age was divided into a series of kingdoms centered on Mycenae. These included Tiryns, Pylos, Oilkos, Orchomenus, Thebes, and Athens. One site contained an artifact with the name Amenhotep III of Egypt, showing extensive trade ties early in Greek history. Many of these cities experienced a wave of destruction at the end of the Bronze Age (1200–1000?). The site of Mycenae reveals much about Greek culture before the market revolution. The royal palace, dominated by a *Megaron* or Great Hall, was in a state of continuous growth. On the wall of the *Megaron* was a frieze of warriors in chariots. Within its chambers were the delights of treasure hunters: debris of ivory, gold, copper, and precious stones used to make luxury items.[5]

The fortified palaces of the Minoan and Mycenaean periods developed during the long Bronze Age as populations grew and hived together. As in Mesopotamia, government played a strong role in such essentials as providing common storage facilities and redistribution for times of famine. The facilities at *Megaron* stored the common wealth of the community. Control of this surplus was obtained by a tribal patriarch who became the chief *basileus* (noble or king). Here lay the progenitors of men such as Homer's Agamemnon. Local craftsmen were usually in the employ of the central manager of the palace, who was known as a *wanax*. By pooling its resources, the Mycenaean community provided its subjects a hedge against famine for two to four years. Beehive shaped tombs called *tholoi*, constructed by a large workforce, indicate the community reach of rulers who retained a strong role in shaping the economy.[6]

Bronze Age *basilei* fought in chariots wearing heavy bronze armor and wielding bronze swords produced by local craftsmen.[7] They employed shipbuilders and palace traders who might have reached Sardinia and Spain. Their pottery has been found in the Bay of Naples, at a number of sites in southeastern Sicily, and on the heel of the Italian boot. Mycenaean traders seem to have focused on these more westerly locations. It was once thought that the Minoans dominated the eastern Mediterranean, an idea now rejected by historian Philip de Souza and others. Neither was piracy a major problem in the Bronze Age. The full flowering of the mainland palace civilization in the Late Helladic period coincided with evidence of Mycenaean artifacts in Crete, the Dodecanese, Egypt, Cyprus, Anatolia, and the Levant.[8]

Most historians once taught that the Aegean Bronze Age ended in a wave of destruction around 1200 BCE. Then followed a long "Dark Age" period that ended shortly before 800 BCE. There is evidence for some serious destruction and depopulation. In the 1960s, however, this assumption was challenged. Given the shortage of literary texts from this period, it is fruitless to debate these claims.[9] Our story picks up well into the Iron Age, beginning around 1000 BCE and deriving its name from the shift in technology at that period. The breakdown of international trade cut off much of the copper and tin supplies for Mesopotamia and led to extensive development of the more available iron ore in Anatolia and the Levant (see Table 6.1).

There is no discussing Greece without mentioning Homer. This great epic poet was an admirer of the old aristocratic warrior ethic. Writing about 700 BCE, he can be read as a voice against the changes associated with both the Iron Age transition and the emerging market economy. This is why *The Iliad* and *The Odyssey* both glorify the warrior culture of Mycenaean heroism—his two-part Book of Hellenic Virtues. Homer saw those virtues endangered by a new emerging economy of petty hustlers and swindlers. Traders, still a small minority, were corrupting the values of the youth, thought Homer, turning Greeks into contemptible, cold-blooded Phoenicians.[10] *The Odyssey* idealizes a land of self-sufficient communities led by strong-minded *basilei* (noble or king) such as the crafty Odysseus (Ulysses).

Table 6.1 Greece in the Bronze and Iron Ages to 480 BCE. (James, et al., 68–112)

Late Bronze:
Late Bronze I: Late Helladic I–II.
Late Bronze II: Late Helladic III A, B, and C, followed by destruction of cities in Eastern Mediterranean.
Greek Dark Age with 'Protogeometric' pottery follows according to most traditional histories.

Iron Age: Begins in Cyprus, spreads to rest of Aegean and Greece

"Geometric" Period (900?–700 BCE): Market Revolution begins with Euboean/Tyrian trading synergy, settlement of Ischia, Southern Italy, Black Sea. Time of Lelantine War; Homer laments rise of capitalism.

"Orientalizing" Period (700–600 BCE): Rise of the *polis* and oligarchies. Corinth and Miletus flourish. Hesiod teaches private work ethic and observes effect of supply and demand.

"Archaic" Period: (600–500 BCE): Iron weapons and Hoplites democratize war. Greeks colonize Western Mediterranean, rival Carthage. Tyrannies seize power in Corinth, Athens, elsewhere, promote coined money and development. Thales begins Greek "Enlightenment." Solon discusses social issues. Cleisthenes brings democracy to Athens.

Raising animals is still more important than growing of crops and the overseeing *basileus* still plays a large role in the redistribution of produce. Sturdy independence reigns. There is little surplus for trade and minimal market activity. Wealth, in the form of livestock and land, followed behind noble warrior status in Bronze Age Europe.[11]

Homer seems well enough acquainted with entrepreneurial practices, however. In his poem, the goddess Athena bargains and haggles for the best ship and recruits the best volunteers in Ithaca for her favorite, Odysseus.[12] Odysseus later visits the imaginary Ionian city of Phaiakia on the coast of Turkey, in which business, by now, is first among equals. *Basileus* Nausithos tells Odysseus his Phaiakians now "have no concern with the bow or the quiver," the weapons of Asiatics, "but it is all masts and the oar of ships and the balanced vessels . . . in which they delight in crossing over the gray sea." Ionians were now "expert beyond all others for driving a fast ship on the open sea." Homer's ideal hero and literary mouthpiece, Odysseus, is offended. Forced to mix with traders was bad enough, but later accusations against him as a rootless, greedy merchant unworthy of home, tribe, or honor was worse. Odysseus later faces the charge of going to sea as "master over mariners who are also men of business, a man who, careful of his cargo and grasping for profits, goes carefully on his way." Homer puts in Athena's mouth the lament that the values of the market are distorting the new generation: "few are the children who turn out to be the equals of their fathers, and the greater number are worse; few are better than their father is."[13]

HOMER'S "GEOMETRIC" GREECE: HELLAS AND PHOENICIA

Homer's Greece, then, was part of a world in the midst of a major economic and cultural upheaval. *The Odyssey* is full of contacts between the Hellenic and Near Eastern worlds as the two continued to react upon each other for centuries. ("Hellas" was the older term for Greece.) The new technological processes of iron spreading from Cyprus to the Levant and the Aegean, also impacted Mesopotamia. Iron weapons and tools were slowly starting to rewrite the rules of commerce and warfare. Iron swords and chariots had made Assyrian shock troops all but invincible. Plows, machetes, and hoes would eventually cut down Indian jungles and allow European and Iranian farmers to better subsist outside the great river valleys. Iron implements would make possible a more settled life in the Latin, Celtic, Indian, East Asian, African, and other areas, making new power centers in Europe possible.[14] It is true that "when paradigms shift we all go back to zero." Culture remains a strong force, however. Although economic influence was gradually shifting power from the Euphrates to the Mediterranean, the spread of iron tools and weapons in Greece "upheld continuously refined principles of individualism in all spheres of human life."[15]

Barely a century after the smithies of Cyprus began making iron knives, daggers, and swords, they were found in use throughout the Aegean, spreading to the Hallstatt Celts and the early Germans.[16] At the very end of the Bronze Age, Greeks began to migrate across the Aegean to Asia Minor to found new settlements along the coast of present-day Turkey, in what came to be known as Ionia. These colonies soon became very rich and were to eventually engage Greece in the wider affairs of Asia (as shown in Table 6.2):

Athens, inhabited since Neolithic and Early Bronze days, began to develop as an important settlement due to its geographic position in the middle of Greece, a marvellous fortress still called the Acropolis, accessible supplies of silver, and an ancient river. The Attic Peninsula seemed to have escaped the destruction of the Dark Ages, giving Athens a sense of cultural superiority it never lost. In the period traditionally called "Protogeometric," just before Homeric times, Athenians made the transition from bronze to bronze and iron (see Table 6.3):

Hellenes, after 900 BCE, quickly embarked upon their own search for new iron sources, a search that involved a growing interaction with the

Table 6.2   Traditional Basilei and Ionian Settlements at End of Bronze Age[17]

Androklos	Ephesus	Egertios	Aipytos
Neleus	Miletus	Chios	Priene
Andraimon	Colorphon	Tembrion	
Phocaea	Samos	Philogenes	

Table 6.3 Bronze and Iron Finds in Athens 900–800 BCE[18]

	Bronze	*Iron*
Shards	0	8
Spearheads	4	4
Daggers	0	2
Knives	0	4
Dresspins	13	47
Fibulae	9	12
Axes, tools, arrowheads	0	3

Cypriots and Tyrians. The island of Euboea, largest of the Greek islands after Crete and just east of Athens with a serviceable port at Lefkandi, became the strategic entry point for iron technology, gold, ivory, and other goods. It absorbed, too, the Phoenician knowledge of overseas markets. In return, Euboeans began selling pottery and drinking vessels to the Tyrian and Cypriot vessels that came calling.[19]

The pottery Sir Leonard Woolley found near the site of Al Mina in Syria tells the story of renewed Greek commerce. The oldest finds are Syro-Phoenician, but later Greek finds also appear.[20] The site at Al Mina was probably founded by Tyrians who wished to link the Aegean to Urartu and her neighbor Assyria. Euboean pottery is found in the early strata (see Table 6.4). The earliest pictorial depiction of a ship in Greece has been found at Lefkandi. In the oral tradition, Euboea was "famous for ships."[21]

The eastward trade from Euboea to the Levant was still in Phoenician hands.[22] Driven by the quest for iron products, Tyrian contacts, and the pioneering Euboean trade, the historic pattern of Greek commerce emerged.[23] Iron ingots from Italy flowed into Greece from fast, sharp-prowed ships— Tyrian and Greek. In Athens and Corinth, ever more proficient smiths hammered iron into hoes and plows. Euboean shippers showed Corinth and Athens the benefits of trans-shipping iron from Italy to Syria. The Al Mina region lay in the sphere of influence of Urartu, and was very much coveted

Table 6.4 Pottery at Al Mina

800 BCE: Euboean pottery appears

775 BCE: Tyrians and Euboeans from Lefkandi colonize Ischia, work iron in Etruria. Rome founded.

750 BCE: Growing amounts of Rhodian, Corinthian, and other pottery. Greeks settle Southern Italy and Sicily

700 BCE: Lelantine War. Euboean finds disappear.

by the Assyrians. Neither Sargon II nor Sennacherib destroyed Al Mina. It was simply too profitable. The trade moving in and out of Al Mina covered a wide variety of goods: from copper and iron to Babylonian and Tyrian textiles, and slaves.[24]

Looking west, Euboeans appeared in force on the island of Ischia or Pithekoussai ("Ape Island") off the Campanian shore of Italy. The story of Odysseus and the writings of Hesiod suggest early Greek trading patterns. Ithaca, home of Odysseus, the gateway to the Adriatic, was frequented by Euboeans sailing into the Central Mediterranean.[25] Tyrians and others accompanied them in "a large, prosperous and multinational community."[26] Euboeans, followed by Corinthians and other Greek cities, thus signed on as "junior partners" in that rich Phoenician stream of trans-Mediterranean commerce before actively seeking their own markets. The first Euboean pottery on Ischia dates from around 775 BCE, although Euboeans made contact with the Etruscans of Tuscany as early as 800 BCE. Ischia, on the western approach to Naples, was settled as a base for acquiring local iron, copper, and tin, and even some imported from the northern Celts. This is because the Etruscans thriving at that time seem to have had an economic organization not too different from that of Bronze Age Greece—scattered, energetic, and resource-driven. The Euboeans transmitted to them an improved knowledge of ironworking, and may have bartered with them in wine. The colony on Ischia would flourish until 700 BCE, when it would be overshadowed by the Euboean settlement at Cumae on the mainland. The Euboeans were on Ischia not to farm, but to refine iron ore.[27] The Greeks early evinced a sharp eye for where economic advantage lay.

Thus, Euboea's port of Lefkandi was near the pulsating heart of a trading regime covering most of Thessaly and the Aegean. Emigrant farmers from Lefkandi joined fellow Greeks to become iron-workers in Ischia, smelting the ore imported there from Elba. Their cross-border resource seeking is documented by Euboean artifacts, iron slag, bellows, and mouthpieces.[28] Euboeans settled in northern Italy, providing market demand that would stimulate the Etruscan, and eventually, the Roman Iron Age. David Ridgway saw the sudden appearance together in the eighth century BCE of Euboean vases and Etruscan iron-work as strong evidence of "Euboean interest in the metals of Etruria."[29] Mined on Elba by Etruscans and processed on Ischia by Euboeans, the ore of Italy inspired "market, or at least resource-seeking behavior on the part of the Euboeans" and fed their westward expansion.[30]

This Euboean settlement in Ischia was momentous. It accelerated the Iron Age in Italy and served to encourage the founding of a number of Greek farming colonies in Southern Italy. Rudimentary market research in the settlement of Ischia was definitely involved, as well as a shrewd aware-ness of the laws of supply and demand.[31]

Other finds allowed archaeologists to reconstruct an already impressive trading network joining Greeks, Tyrians, Egyptians, and others.[32] A trail of Egyptian amulets, pottery, and iron artifacts stretches from Syria, through

Cyprus and Euboea, ending in Ischia and Tuscany. In this network, Greeks appear as *private individuals and enterprises operating on a small scale*, not the organized state-supported firms of the Assyrian model. Menelaus, a merchant mentioned in *The Odyssey*, is a free trader, operating independently, buying cargo on a contractual basis, bringing the profits back to Greece along with iron ore and prestige items. There is no sign of an internalized hierarchy.[33] The tides of commerce blew differently in the Aegean. Menelaus is portrayed as an independent shipowner doing business across the eastern Mediterranean, even bringing Africa into the orbit:

> Much did I suffer and wandered much before bringing all this home in my ships when I came back in the eighth year. I wandered to Cyprus and Phoenicia, to the Egyptians, I reached the Aithiopians, Eremboi, Sidonians and Libya where the rams grow their horns quickly.[34]

Excavations at Lefkandi, at the center of this early Greek network, point to the beginning of a market revolution in Greece and the Aegean. Lefkandi was continuously occupied. The site was destroyed and abandoned at the end of the Bronze Age, but then rebuilt. Even in the Dark or "Protogeometric" Age, traces of goods imported across the Aegean from Egypt in Cypriot, Cretan, and Phoenician vessels appear. In the ninth century, around 875 to 825 BCE, the graves of Lefkandi are suddenly filled with Near Eastern luxuries. The settlement, however, begins to shrink after 825 BCE, as the rival cities of Chalcis and Eretria assume the leadership in Euboea.[35]

According to Professor David Tandy, the population of Attica and the Peloponnesus grew rapidly in the eighth century BCE. Farmers grew more wheat, feeding the new, slowly-growing Attic communities. The land was able to support more people, and the population of the Greek world began to rise slowly in the 700s BCE.[36] New communities began to dot the shores of the Attic peninsula: Eleusis, Palaia, Kokkina, Anaphlystos, Myrrhinous, and Marathon—all springing up near a coastline that was increasingly free from the dangers of piracy. Thucydides later described the rise of coastal cities "founded in more recent times, when navigation had at length become safer." These new centers were "beginning to have surplus resources . . . and the isthmuses were occupied and walled off with a view to commerce and to the protection of the several peoples against their neighbors."[37] He was no doubt thinking of Corinth and the surging cities of Ionia, as well as Attica. Excavations reveal an expansion of building activity and a higher density of sites around Athens, in Crete, and on the Peloponnesus. The gradual rise in population was linked to a renewed optimism for the future brought about by increased security, dependable food production and greater access to foreign markets and resources.[38]

Rising population seeking outlets and the increase in Greek navigation skills around 750 BCE helps explain the first great wave of Greek colonization. This out-migration came mostly from Corinth, Megara, Chalcis,

Eretria, Phocaea, and Miletus. The mechanics of this colonizing impetus was much more market-driven than temple- and palace-led. Adventurous Greeks, motivated by diminishing expectations back home, became, in a sense, "the Scotch–Irish of the Aegean," choosing to migrate to Italy, Sicily, and the Black Sea in search of individual betterment with little official coercion. Settlements were organized informally around a core value of shared self-interest as the quest for subsistence turned into ever more increasing specialization.[39] At this stage, Homeric and Archaic Greece was still very rural-based, with Corinth, the Euboean cities, and the towns of Ionia—Miletus, Smyrna, Phocaea—overshadowing the later powerhouses of Athens, Thebes and Sparta.[40] But the rising tide of commerce was raising all the boats. Wheat flowed into the Aegean from the new overseas colonies, inevitably spurring urbanization and encouraging metropolitan Greeks to become ever more organized and specialized. Even the farmers of the Peloponnesus, Attica, and Ionia emerged as rural entrepreneurs raising increasing quantities of wine, oranges, and the ubiquitous olives.[41] The market revolution was on!

MONEY, POLITICS, AND TYRANTS

During the eighth century, Lefkandi's inhabitants began to sort themselves out into conservative farmers and ranchers and an aggressive breed of ever more confident sailors and overseas traders. Some historians have seen a division along class lines, with the landed *basilei* pitted against the aggressive new traders, chafing under the restrictions of antique social structures. This social upheaval foreshadowed the governmental crises in seventh century Greek cities as the market revolution accelerated. Trade and colonization became more regularized and systematic as the busy docks and ports became the center of action. Dynamic new market forces began to rearrange Greek economics, society, and politics.[42] The Greece of the Golden Age was already present in embryo as tiles and woollens sailed from Corinth and olive oil, wine and fruit began to be gathered from the Peloponnese. Athenian shippers opened routes for vital wheat supplies to come from the Black Sea while a growing class of artisans prepared to sell the flourishing wares from its quarries, tanneries, and workshops—smelted zinc, refined silver, polished marble, leather goods, ceremonial pottery, lamps, and finished furniture. A consumer cornucopia was steadily emerging.

Two developments, in particular, sped the process. The first and most important, of course, was the spreading impact of the Iron Age Revolution. Iron had revolutionized warfare, which in turn revolutionized the development of the city–state. When the Greeks turned to the widespread use of iron, they were destined to change their tactics and their strategy of warfare. This technological shift effectively yanked control from the hands of the old warrior class, Homer's "lords of men," the Agamemnons and

Nestors who strutted before the walls of windy Troy. Mycenaean Greece had boasted cavalry and chariots, which only rich tribal chieftains could afford. The coming of iron was destined to favor the new master of the battlefield, the lightly-armed "hoplites," or foot-soldiers. Vases from the seventh century BCE depict massed ranks of hoplites, a defensive wall that heavily-armored aristocrats on horseback could no longer penetrate.[43] With their shields, hoplites no longer needed costly bronze body armor. The sheer press of numbers now counted. The individual soldier became more important as the "focus of battle was now as much on the weak as on the strong."[44]

Away from the battlefield, the iron revolution reached critical mass in the period called Iron Age II (900–600 BCE). Originally applied in full by the Anatolian Hittites, iron is one of the most common elements in the earth's crust. The application of this technology would work a revolution as consequential as the computer revolution of the 1980s, or anywhere a recognizably useful technique is first introduced. "Cheap iron democratized agriculture and industry and warfare too. Any peasant could afford an iron axe to clear fresh land for himself and iron ploughshares wherewith to break up stony ground. The common artisan could own a kit of metal tools that made him independent of the household of kings, gods or nobles."[45] Result? The Bronze Age kingdoms began to fragment, replaced with over 1,300 independent city–states. Independent farming and enterprise was free to flourish in what could be called a more "Jeffersonian" society. The farmer, with household and slaves, owned his plot, paid few taxes, grew his own food, and traded locally to supplement his income. Rather than serve ignominiously in the faceless ranks of Sargon or Shisak, the Corinthian and Milesian yeoman was more of a militia soldier along the lines of the American Minuteman or the modern Swiss. Every hoplite farmer could afford a bronze helmet and breastplate and an iron sword. Most of his wars were brief, and few died in skirmishes based upon land, and not ideology.[46]

No major wars are recorded in Greece between about 700 BCE and the invasion of Darius two centuries later. A lot of small wars did take place, but they were very brief, lasting maybe a day or two. These hoplite skirmishes between *poleis* were not fought over the issues of whether oligarchy or tyranny were the best forms of rule. Typically, two *poleis* would be unable to resolve a boundary dispute, and so both armies would line up on the battlefield and quickly fight it out.

The second innovation of the Iron Age had been long in coming, but was equally revolutionary in its effects. This was the perfecting of the use of metal coins as currency, an innovation attributed to the Lydian Kingdom in northwestern Asia Minor.[47] Soon after 600 BCE, the cities of Aegina, Athens, and Corinth began issuing small change in the form of copper or small silver coins. Gordon Childe details the impact of this seemingly small innovation:

> Now it had doubtless been a nuisance for the wholesaler to have to travel about with scales and weights, bars of metal and sacks of grain; for the small retailer it was a crippling handicap. A big landowner . . . may have grumbled at the bother of weighing out the silver and the sharp practices of the purchaser who tried adulterating his silver with lead. But how was the small landowner to pay for a new pot, an iron ploughshare, or a trinket for his wife?[48]

Small change led to a big change. The peasant farmer could convert his surplus into a portable medium of exchange that could be more easily exchanged for manufactured goods. The workman or artisan could accumulate his wages for capital investment or for purchasing the minute refinements made possible by spreading iron technology. True, the banes of usury, mortgages and debt, travelled in the wake of this convenience revolution, but the payoff in establishing the world's first consumer economy was immense. More important, the money men of Athens eventually turned this innovation into a reliable method of international exchange, which greatly expedited the triumph of Greek capitalism. The rise of Athens, however, was to be through the familiar, but brutal, path of war, another preoccupation of the 1,300 Greek city states.

Wars can be devastating in their effects and not at all an economic boon, a lesson our generation may be forced to learn all over again. One major war, the Lelantine, fought around 700 BCE between two cities on Euboea over possession of its rich plain, drew other Greek forces into the eddy. According to Thucydides, this savage conflict was the worst military engagement between the Trojan Wars and the Persian Wars of the 400s BCE. Military quagmires are nothing new. The Lelantine conflagration shattered the prosperity of the Euboean cities and helped shift commercial leadership to Corinth and later to Athens.[48] Corinth had early exploited her unique position on the well-sited isthmus between the Aegean and Western Seas. This helped her excel in shipbuilding and the carrying trade with the accompanying rise of manufacturing that her commercial clout encouraged. Corinthians vases and pottery travelled far and wide. The poet Pindar praised Corinth in the fifth century BCE for its political and economic influence: "I shall take knowledge of prosperous Corinth, portal of Isthmian Poseidon. . . . Within her walls dwelleth Law . . . Justice and Peace . . . those guardians of wealth for man."[49] Rich Corinthians founded colonies in Sicily, Corfu, and elsewhere, and the government collected tolls from a tramway that carried small ships across her isthmus. Corinthians also perfected the state-of-the-art warship of the Mediterranean world. Known as the *trireme*, this warship helped smash piracy and was to exercise a multiplier effect on the expansion of Mediterranean trade. Both the Carthaginians and the Romans adopted the main lines of this sleek vessel.[50]

Taken together, these revolutions in technology, economics, and warfare accompanied and effected a revolution in government. The numerous city–states that had replaced the old tribal kingdoms became known as the *poleis.* The Greek *polis* was the first community in history organized on the *civic* basis of a social contract. Its people were citizens, not subjects. They possessed inscribed citizenship rights and were subject to the encoded rule of abstract laws instead of the whims of semi-divine god-kings. Aristotle himself would later observe "the law-abiding *polis* . . . outranks senseless Nineveh."[51] Most *poleis* were collections of farming villages much smaller than an English county or an American township. Each contained a few thousand citizens. A fortified town in the center of the *polis* was built around its *agora, or* marketplace.[52]

This new *polis* was very different from the Near Eastern form of city–state extant in Uruk or Ur. Its cohesiveness was based upon a thriving sense of community. The writer Archilocus hoped that the *polis* would embody justice for all citizens. It was far less intrusive than the monarchies of Asia, making it ideally suited for the fructifying spirit of private enterprise that was spreading across Greece.[53] Nevertheless, as shown in the following, even the limited government of the *polis* set limits to what markets could and could not do.[54] Because the Greek achievement in government so affected and reflected the economic zeitgeist, it is worth our study. The dynamic interplay between politics and economics hardly ended with Solon of Athens.

The Greek economic surge of the seventh century produced a new style of government, tyranny. That word needs unpacking. Historians have seen the tyrants of the seventh century BC as reformers, capitalists, or opportunists, depending upon which city–state they ruled.[55] A tyranny is one-man rule, often nonhereditary, over a *polis.* The Cypselids at Corinth, the Orthagorids at Sicyon, and the Peisistratids at Athens became hereditary political dynasties much as the Bhuttos and Nehrus attempted in our time. Tyranny often rested upon military power hired by commercial elites to protect their interests. Aristotle linked tyranny to hoplite warfare, for "as the states grew and the wearers of heavy armor had become stronger, more persons came to have a part in the government."[56] Of course, war means the shedding of blood and those who give it prefer to have a choice in how, when and where if at all possible. Thus, Pheidon of Argos and Cleisthenes of Sicyon, early seventh-century tyrants, may well have been hoplite leaders who rose through the ranks.[57]

Were these tyrants early capitalists? The sober Thucydides drew a connection between the market revolution and the new politics:

> As the power of Hellas grew, and the acquisition of wealth became more an object, the revenues of the states increasing, tyrannies were by their means established almost everywhere, the old form of government being hereditary monarchy with definite prerogatives, and Hellas began to fit out fleets and apply herself more closely to the sea.[58]

Cypselus of Corinth and Peisistratus of Athens were outcast aristocrats, not gutter demagogues. As career politicians, they generated popular support and hired hoplites. They appeared to be much more tolerable than the kings

Table 6.5   Business Connections of Major Greek Tyrants: Seventh Century BCE[60]

Theagenes of Megara: trade
Polycrates of Samos: shipping, harbor, waterworks, metal, wool
Cypselus of Corinth: pottery
Peisistratus of Athens: silver mining

who had aspired to divine right.[59] More important, as men who had risen from the commons, they did not oppose the rise of the market but channelled it to their benefit. Many tyrants, like the English gentry of a much later time, became businessmen. They saw opportunity in the new age of sailing ships, trade, and iron, as Table 6.5 briefly outlines.[60]

ECONOMICS AS PHILOSOPHY: HESIOD

The epoch of the tyrants coincided with an attempt by the poet Hesiod to come to terms with the new economy that had so offended Homer. Without being conscious of it, Hesiod took the first steps toward fathering and rationalizing Greek economic and management thought. Hesiod's treatise, *The Works and Days*, hearkens back to Solomon and points ahead to John Calvin in its equating of hard work with prosperity and laziness with poverty. Hard work fed a family, whereas indolence brought shame and hunger and offended the gods, for charity was limited in Hesiod's Greece.[61] Hesiod saw the erupting market competition around him as a benevolent goddess compared to the evils of political competition, which led to warfare:

> She puts the shiftless man to work, for all his laziness. A man looks at his neighbor, who is rich: then he too wants work; for the rich man presses on with his plowing and planting and the ordering of his state.[62]

Competition feeds economic incentive: "so the neighbor envies the neighbor who presses on toward wealth. Such strife is a good friend to mortals."[63] Under market competition, "Then potter is potter's enemy, and craftsman is craftsman's rival; tramp is jealous of tramp, and singer of singer."[64]

Like Jefferson, Hesiod sensed the market revolution, but his work ethic was deeply agrarian. He realistically accepted the fact, however, that many a farmer working the stubborn Greek soil had to earn extra income by sailing abroad. The poet himself had been to Euboea. He counselled common sense for traders. Merchants should send goods in big ships for less risk and trade in volume for more profit. One ought to beach one's ship in the winter months and set sail in late June, July, or early August. Don't anger the gods Zeus or Poseidon. One needed to voyage quickly, for by September, Zeus would bring the wind and the rain.[65] In short, Hesiod was a reluctant capitalist. It was better to farm than to trade: "Do not adventure your entire livelihood in hollow ships. Leave the greater part ashore and make the lesser part cargo."[66] Losing one's life and goods on the open sea "and have all the freight go to nothing" was a serious risk.[67]

Hesiod's farmer–traders were independent yeomen. The centralized palace economy of Odysseus and the Aegean Bronze Age was gone. Hesiod's poetry moved beyond Homeric nostalgia to incubate a philosophy of history, one that would directly involve economics. In that sense, Hesiod's vision paralleled *Genesis* and the Babylonian epics. Zeus was portrayed not only as creator, but as a guarantor of justice. As such, he embodied stability, the handmaiden of trade. He punished those who bribed officials and acted greedily. Hesiod, unlike modern economists, including Karl Marx, did not trust that industrial technology would eventually eliminate poverty and create a leisure class. Rank consumerism appalled him. Thus, fair-minded Zeus hid technology from humanity on purpose, otherwise they would come to the point where they would cast aside both oars and oxen and do a year's work in a day. Work is a positive good. One of his most well-known adages is that "before the gates of excellence/the gods have placed sweat." The rebel Prometheus gave technology to humans anyway, thwarting the will of the gods just as "cunning Odysseus" attempted repeatedly. Hesiod considered the will of Zeus inscrutable. The divine Father had created the five eras of human history, destroyed four of them, and might eventually destroy the fifth. Hesiod's overview of history reveals a people, the Greeks, with a profound sense of self-awareness, of men participating in the flow of great events. Hesiod's exposition of the five ages of man makes him a pioneer political economist.

In the first, the Age of Gold, humans lived in an Eden-like world without hard work or pain. The next age was the Silver Age, where people began to ignore the deities, degenerate, and rob and murder one another. Then came the Bronze Age, the description of which fits very much the Sumerian Urban Revolution. People went from robbery to warfare, becoming arrogant and boastful, as in the time of Gilgamesh or Noah. They perfected bronze technology: "The weapons of these men were bronze, of bronze their houses, and they worked as bronze-smiths. There was not yet any black iron."[68] The fourth age was the Heroic, and corresponds to what we now call the Mycenaean. The world was now in the fifth, or Iron Age, a time of hard toil: "'For here now is the age of iron. Never by daytime will there be an end to hard work and pain, never in the night to weariness, when the gods will send anxieties to trouble us."[69]

Hesiod worried about the implications of spreading military technology:

"Right will be in the arm" in an Age of Force, where people lose all sense of right and wrong, dishonor parents, despise the honest, embrace the spirit of envy, and praise violence. This age, too would be punished by Zeus, who had 30,000 spirits watching mortals."[70]

A close reading of Hesiod reveals a veiled reaction to the market revolution and its effect upon an ever more materialistic Hellenic culture. Although the society remained overwhelmingly agrarian, the growth of population and the rise of markets was undermining the older value system. As farmland became scarce, the aristocrats used the common land for their herds, squeezing out the poorer farmer. Wheat farming, ignored in Homer, is prominent in Hesiod. Ownership of land became a political issue. Trade had the effect of privatizing social relations. Imported luxuries were seen as the property of *individuals*, not communities. Even state land was now was seen as the private possession of the *basileus*, and not held in trust for the community. The sense of *noblesse oblige* was passing, the new philosophy of the landowning aristocrat became "I've got mine, now you get yours." Status followed wealth, not skill in arms. The same aristocrats cleverly controlled the levers of power of the oligarchical *polis*. A farmer could now owe more than he owned and no longer rely upon the courts or the Odysseus-like *basileus* for economic help.

Hesiod feared that control in the city–state was passing to the highest bidder. The *polis* was thus becoming an object of distrust. It is in this context that Hesiod trumpeted his survival manual for rural workers. His message: life is becoming privatized and farmers needed to work hard for they could only depend upon themselves, their *oikos*, or family household, and, perhaps, their neighbors. Hesiod, if he was an actual individual, was probably a peasant from Boeotia. His maxims on trade were inspired by his first-hand grasp of the growing power of the market twenty or thirty miles distant, or on the huge island of Euboea, where a hard-pressed peasant could sell his surplus. As Britain experienced in the 1700s of our era, Hesiod's world included a growing number of landless people, some living by hunting and fishing, others becoming potters, weavers, tanners, and construction workers in the growing cities. For those unable to survive as independent farmers or tradesmen, there was little option save to take to the sea. Those with resources must fit out ships; those without them hire out as rowers.[71]

The appearance of both Homer and Hesiod's writings in the 700s points to another important development that would greatly speed the Greek market revolution. This was the transfer of the phonetic alphabet from the Levant to Greece and its quick adoption by the Hellenes. Greek writing begins as the script of Euboean traders, in which the verse of Homer and Hesiod is recorded.[72] A well-known sample appears in Ischia on a drinking vessel known as Nestor's cup, imported from Rhodes. On it is an inscription that could be seen as the first commercial advertisement. It reads: "Nestor had a most drink-worthy cup, but whoever drinks of mine will straightaway be smitten with desire of fair-crowned Aphrodite."[73] Aphrodite was the goddess of love. Thus, an alluring payoff seemingly awaited the purchaser.

Hesiod was a bit of a reactionary. His philosophy of history shows his reservations about what was happening around him. Although the new market economy had to be endured, it did not have to be enjoyed. It was, he felt, far from pleasing to Zeus. It seems that the early Greek *literati* were less enthused about commerce than the more mercantile Canaanites or Babylonians. The working class artisans of Corinth and Attica, meanwhile, were bullish advocates of consumer capitalism.[74] Inscriptions on pottery witness the early birth of *branding* even in Hesiod's time. Corinthian and later Athenian potters hawked their brand-names on the vessels they created. One vase said "Sophilos painted," another boasted "Exekias painted and made me," and one vase of Euthymides boasted of quality "as never (were those of) Euphronios."[75] By 700 BCE Corinth's skilled potters led the way in target marketing, citing specific customers stretching from Iberia to Scythia. Market competition had arrived as Corinthian potters produced attractive brands of vessel that "guaranteed . . . contents and marketed an image." Others were "challenged to produce even more persuasive packaging and even more attractive images," even for local markets.[76]

One can even trace the makers of different wares by logos as distinctive as Ford's or Mitsubishi's. Euboeans began this practice of labelling their work, soon followed by Corinth and Athens. Sophilos identified his work by parading the gods and goddesses of Athens around the mouth of his vases.[77] Although perhaps trivializing Zeus and Athena, his distinctive decorations exhibited "pride in the product and a desire to attract future orders." Their scale and elaboration "seem to justify the artist's self-promotion."[78] Others pursued the mass export market of Italy, with vessels of lower price and lesser artistic quality than those of Sophilos. Etruscans and Latins loved the racy "Tyrrhenian" pottery, adorned with the sex and violence of mythology, including *The Iliad*. Even works of art such as Homer were co-opted by the rampaging market.[79] The diverse regional styles gave way to a dominant Athenian style when Corinth declined after 550 BCE. Here is the first documented market shakeout.[80]

Situated strategically between Euboea and Corinth, Attica presented itself as the thriving center of a new era of Aegean commerce. The flood-tide of tyranny engulfing Corinth and other *poleis* came late to Athens, whose large size made it more difficult for any one man to seize power. A worthy named Cylon tried and failed around 630 BCE. The first wave of unbridled, runaway capitalism in the Greek cities had widened the gulf between rich and poor into a chasm. Impoverished farmers and tenants and small proprietors seethed against those Hesiod called "bribe-devouring judges." Even more significantly for the future of business, Athens and Attica had staked its future on the open sea. Gordon Childe records how she provided "the first example of a political unit risking dependence for the staff of life upon distant lands across the sea in order to concentrate on the production of goods for which the country and its inhabitants were peculiarly fitted".[81] The social pyramid's base was weakened. Sturdy independent producers were yielding to the frenetic explosion in overseas trade. As always, insecurity resulted. Panic spread more easily. The Athenian oligarchy of *archons*, now led by Draco, decreed harsh punishments, even death, for the pettiest of crimes, trying to slam down the lid on social discontent.

It didn't work. One former aristocrat turned entrepreneur stepped forward with a new proposal: reform instead of repression or revolution.[82] Where Hesiod warned that Zeus would punish the Hellenes for their greed and injustice, Solon of Athens (640–561 BCE?) harangued that the Greeks, especially the Athenians, would soon *destroy themselves*. Athens was an anomaly, a gigantic nation–*polis* the size of Luxembourg with 35,000 citizens crowded into the busy city and another 200,000 scattered across the other subdivisions of Attica. Major events of early Greek history, such as the Lelantine War and the mass migration overseas had bypassed Athens, but the social dislocations triggered by trade would not. The spotlight of history soon turned upon Solon's city.

SOLON: HEADLONG CAPITALISM AND SOCIAL DIVISIONS

Solon, like many reformers, was born of an aristocratic family. His father had dissipated the estate, so the son, according to Plutarch, "therefore applied himself to merchandise in his youth."[83]

Solon was untypical in an era where trade was becoming more respectable. The philosopher Thales; the physician Hippocrates; and Protis, founder of Massilia (Marseilles), were actively involved in trading. Solon himself, if one believes his poetry, was not acquisitive. He did not judge people by whether they were rich or poor, but by their character. The wave of tyranny sweeping the Greek world had so far been resisted in Athens with the defeat of the ambitious Cylon. Still, the economic and social conditions that might spawn a tyranny were far along advanced in Athens. Plutarch, like an ancient-day Kevin Phillips, recorded that "the disparity of fortune between the rich and the poor at that time also reached its height,"[84] that the Athenian populace begged for a tyrant, for "all the people were indebted to the rich."[85] Tenants were paying one-sixth of their earnings to landowners and selling themselves or their children into slavery, sometimes far away. Some fled Attica to escape their creditors. Politics in Athens began to polarize. On the left, the poor rallied around the "Hill" party to free debtors, divide the land, and change the propertied regime. On the right, the "Plain" party defended the privileges of creditor and property. A third party, the "Seaside," sought a compromise. So did Solon, the Franklin D. Roosevelt of his day, who promised both land reform and the security of debts. The political left supported him due to his honesty, the right because of his wealth.[86]

When Solon became *archon*, he is said to have banned debt enslavement, but may actually have just lessened the interest on debtors. He devalued the drachma by approximately one-third, a political and economic expedient that would have a long life across the centuries. Solon's moderate, middle-class reforms alienated the rich, "angry for their money," and the poor, disappointed "that the land was not divided, and . . . all men reduced to equality."[87] More important, Solon repealed the brutal laws of Draco, who punished both idleness and petty theft by death (hence our word "draconian"). As a successful *archon*, he was soon granted even vaster powers. He took a census of the wealth of Attica. The richest were those owning 500 measures of fruit, the next lower class owned 300, or a horse. The third class owned 200, and anyone poorer was classified as a *thete*, eligible for jury duty but not public office. Solon was the first politician to recognize that Athens, with her growing population, could not prosper on her Attic farmland alone. He therefore "brought trades into credit," promoting commerce and industry and ordered the ruling oligarchs to "examine how every man got his living, and chastise the idle."[88]

Solon, himself, took leave of his *archon*ship to enter into business as a travelling entrepreneur. If Plutarch is correct, he combined profit with education. He studied with the most learned priests in Egypt, constructed a city in Cyprus, and met the fabulously rich ruler of Lydia, named Croesus. Croesus was one of the first on record to vigorously push gold and silver coinage. Even the cosmopolitan Solon was able neither to heal the political divisions of Athens nor stop her slide into tyranny. The Hill party rallied around the ambitious Peisistratus, who became the first Athenian tyrant. Opposing him at first, Solon eventually supported and even advised the tyrant.[89] Neither Zeus nor Athena would destroy Athens, Solon kept preaching, the Athenians themselves would accomplish it, through simple greed. "But the citizens themselves . . . are bent on destruction of their great city, and money is the compulsive cause."[90] The leaders of Athens would provoke civil war and great suffering "for they do not know enough to restrain their greed and apportion orderly shares for all as if at a decorous feast."[91] (See Table 6.6.)

Table 6.6 The Rise of Athens

Monarchy: Before 700: Athens ruled by monarchs. Advent of hoplite tactics.

Conservative Oligarchy: 683 BCE: Athenian oligarchy of *archons*. 655–585: Age of Corinth and Tyrannies. 621: Draco becomes lead *archon* in Athens.

Reformist Oligarchy: 594: Solon becomes *archon* in Athens, cites abuses of unrestrained capitalism. 595: Earliest Greek coins in Aegina. 585: Thales predicts solar eclipse.

Tyranny: 561: Peisistratus becomes first Athenian tyrant. 546: Final tyranny of Peisistratus, Cyrus of Persia conquers Lydia. Xenophanes of Colorphon discusses economics. 539: Cyrus takes Babylon, founds Persian Empire. 528: Death of Peisistratus; son Hippias rules in Athens. 521: Darius becomes Persian Shah, begins to standardize Persian Empire.

Democracy and War: 510–508: Peisistratids overthrown; Cleisthenes reforms Athenian constitution. 499: Ionian Revolt vs. Persia. 494: Persians sack Miletus. 490: Darius invades Greece, defeated at Marathon. 486: Xerxes rules Persia; Athenian *archons* chosen by lot. 483: new silver discovered at Laurion; *Archon* Themistocles persuades Assembly to build large navy. 480: Xerxes invades Greece; Greek war with Carthage in Sicily; Persian fleet defeated at Salamis; Carthaginians defeated at Himera. 479: Persian army defeated at Plataea.

Solon's significance is the insight his career offers into how economics affects politics. One does not have to be a Marxist professor to see that the substructure and the superstructure are connected, although not absolutely and, certainly, not always. Not unlike a Kevin Phillips or a George Soros today, Solon became an innovative social reformer sensing the danger in unbridled market forces. Solon chided the gentry for "sparing the property neither of the public nor of the gods" and enacted strict bankruptcy laws. Slavery and exile for Hellenic debtors was banned and rescinded. Solon warned that greed and severe inequalities resulted "when great prosperity suddenly befalls those people who do not have an orderly mind."[92]

The monetary revolution, by-product of the Iron Age, also showed the cultural linkage between money and politics. King Croesus of Sardis first used iron tools to stamp his logo upon a coin made of gold mixed with silver.[93] Ionian traders in the Persian sphere adopted the Lydian idea of stamped coinage, which spread into the Aegean.[94] Coins now circulated in Miletus, Smyrna, and Ephesus around 600 BCE, and spread across the Aegean around 550—to Aegina, Corinth, and finally Athens, stimulating commerce as it did do.[95] By 500 BCE, most Greek *poleis* minted their own coinage to ensure control by the local agora. The new innovation soon took on political significance: currency stamped with a ruler's image, in effect, represented a declaration of economic sovereignty. The *polis* created the conditions for coined money to circulate and to spread, especially the silver Athenian *drachma*. Unlike in Lydia, the Greek *drachmas* were more easily convertible. They were also heralds of a genuine cash-based economy.[96]

Barter did not disappear, but haggling goatherds and olive-growers in the Hellenic countryside now quoted prices in *drachmas*. As already noted, the coming of a money society simplified commercial dealings across the board. Independent enterprises grew and spread even further when commercial risks were handled by cash contracts instead of barter. Both in the Aegean and in China, as shown in the following, the coming of iron and coined money permitted supply and demand principles to work on a much broader scale. Technology drove innovation and flexibility and innovation, once it starts, feeds the upward spiral of profits. Supply and demand thus became almost unwritten economic laws.[97] Coined money developed within the *polis* economy and then transformed it. Its rise was not championed by any one particular social group. Originally, the Greeks of Homer's time denominated goods in terms of cattle. Now coins were being issued by civic authorities and the elites who controlled them.[98]

RELIGION AND RISING CAPITALISM

This robust and wide-spread market revolution necessarily impacted Greek thought and religion. An important factor here is that the individualistic Hellenes lacked the powerful, centralized temple hierarchies of the Near

East. Most Greeks worshipped in small local shrines. Priests of Zeus had far less say in the workings of the market than those of Marduk, Melkart, or Ashur. Greek shrines did post on trade routes, serving *emporia* in key places such as Thermopylae and Delos.[99] Greek religion, itself, was often more "entrepreneurial" than in the Orient, with self-appointed roving prophets.[100] A people whose central oracle prescribed "Know Thyself" and "Nothing to Excess" were not easily given to mass exuberance.

Yet, in spite of the market revolution, most Greeks continued to maintain their fear of the gods and goddesses of Olympus, notably Zeus. Hesiod sought to invoke Zeus to enforce economic justice much as the Hebrew prophets invoked the God of Israel. A few Greeks, notably those engaged in foreign commerce, began to develop more unorthodox views. Most notable was Thales of Miletus (646–536 BCE). Seeking to corner the grain market, Thales traded both in Egypt, from whose priests he learned geometry. In Babylon, he studied the cycles of the heavenly bodies. Because he needed to know the best time to sail in terms of light and tides, he probed into astronomy. Borrowing from Babylon, he divided the year into 365 days. He successfully predicted the solar eclipse of 585 BCE and gained much prestige for the rising interest in Greek science and its practical, commercial benefits. Others, Anaximenes of Miletus, Xenophanes of Colorphon, and especially Heracleitus of Ephesus (535–475 BCE) also had contact with the non-Hellenic civilizations, as did the renowned Pythagoras. These contacts engendered a belief that the universe operated according to knowable natural laws set in motion by an unknown God, instead of the whims of the fractious Olympian dieties.[101] "All things were in chaos when Mind arose and made order," wrote Anaxagoras (500–428 BCE).

Xenophanes of Athens (430–354 BCE), visiting the Ethiopians and the Thracians, noted the tendency for humans to make gods in their own image. *They couldn't all be right.* There had to be one supreme God, he reasoned. Free markets and travelling savants were interacting with and reinforcing each other, thus encouraging even freer minds, minds that would begin to question the economic, as well as the natural, order. Xenophanes despised the "useless luxuries out of Lydia" and her "odious tyranny." The gods did not do much to enrich man, said Xenophanes, but "man seeks, and in time invents what might be better."[102]

If the deities operated more by a distant natural law than by direct supernatural intervention, then was it possible that their influence on the private transactions of everyday life might be, in the minds of many traders, more distant as well? The Greek's "free market" in ideas undergirded and stimulated the possibility of a free market in economics: "Once the theology was taken out of causal thinking, it became plain that ideas were quite simply competing with one another on their own merits."[103]

Questioning the writ of Olympus in human affairs helped lead some Athenians to questioning the writ of oligarchs and tyrants, as we've already seen. Solon already foreshadowed a new kind of *archon*, the well-born social reformer as democrat. But although the Greek bent toward freedom of thought and experimentation was making possible the Greek commercial eruption overseas, the territories of the ancient Near East had come under the control of a more benevolent yet still absolutist state, the Persian Empire. The Persians had come to exercise sway over the outlying regions of Asia Minor and the rich Ionian cities of Ephesus, Miletus, and Sardis. After half a century, the Persian experiment in cross-cultural management through heavy taxation was beginning to fray. The Ionian Greeks staged a revolt. This led the Persian Darius I to send in his armies and the ships of Tyre to suppress the uprising in 494 BCE. The sudden loss to Athens of these rich Ionian markets triggered a political revolution in Attica. The ruling *archons* who had briefly replaced the Peisistratid tyrants were now succeeded by the democrat Cleisthenes. Cleisthenes completed the work of Solon and dethroned the ruling oligarchs, replacing them with a system in which every free man had the right to vote. Athenian democracy had been born, but under a swiftly falling Persian shadow.[104]

The dramatic clash between the Persian Empire and the rising Hellenic merchant traders of Greece was a clash of economic, as well as political, systems. Cyrus the Great, Persia's founder, had earlier mocked the individualist spirit that abetted Greek capitalism with disdain: "I have never yet been afraid of men who have a special meeting place in the center of their city, where they swear this and that and cheat each other."[105] By the 490s BCE, Darius and his successor, Xerxes I, saw the Hellenes, and especially the Athenians, as a threat to Persian sovereignty. The stage was set for one of history's most decisive conflicts—monetary and military.

PERSIA: PIONEER IN CROSS-CULTURAL MANAGEMENT

"The Athenians. Who are they?" Darius is supposed to have uttered hearing of Greek forces aiding Ionia. He would soon get to know them better at Marathon and Salamis. Greek history did not take place in a vacuum. The Persian Empire to the east was one of history's monumental achievements. In accommodating varied races and religions, it represented a partial break with the Mesopotamian tradition. Its founders were Iranians from the mountains surrounding the Land of the Two Rivers in the area today called Fars. Persia's rise was even more sudden than that of Babylon. Around 650 BCE Cyrus, leader of *Parsua*, united the Iranians of the plateau by conquering the Medes. Next, the Great King marched northwest, bringing most of resource-rich Anatolia under his rule.

Finally, Cyrus took the "impregnable" fortress of Babylon, not by storming its thick walls but by using his engineering skills to divert the Euphrates, allowing his army to enter the unprotected part of the city (see Table 6.7). Babylon supposedly fell in one night in 539 BCE. Cyrus then expanded his rule into Central Asia. The Persian Empire was larger and

Table 6.7 Chronology of the Persian Empire

Cyrus II: 559–530 BCE
547: Cyrus conquers Lydia
539: Cyrus conquers Babylon

Cambyses II: 529–522 BCE
Persia conquers Egypt

Darius I: 522–486 BCE: Persia's greatest Shah, conquers part of India.
522–21: Darius seizes throne from Bardiya
520 on: Darius begins to standardize gold and silver coinage, tax system, royal
road system. Houses of Egibi and Iranu. Prices begin to rise sharply.
513–12: Darius attacks Thrace and Macedonia
490: Greek victory at Marathon

Xerxes: 486–465 BCE
480: Salamis: Greek navy crushes Persian and Tyrian fleets.

Final Persian rulers, mostly weak and ineffective: Artaxerxes I: 465–423 BCE

House of Murashu
Xerxes II: 424 BCE, Darius II: 423–405 BCE, Artaxerxes II: 404–359 BCE,
Artaxerxes III: 358–338, Arses: 337–335 BCE, Darius III: 335–330 BCE

Greco–Macedonian conquest of Alexander

more diverse than any yet seen, stretching from the borders of Europe to those of India.[106]

Assyria and Babylon tended to rule with an iron fist, provoking conquered peoples into revolt. The Persian rulers knew that such methods fail in the long term. Terrorism, persecution, and intolerance are bad for business *and* for ruling an empire much vaster than any that had gone before. The Achaemenids—Persian's ruling house—tried a new approach. They pioneered giant steps in the art of cross-cultural management and even government paternalism. The Iranian shahs adopted the administrative techniques of Assyria and Babylonia, but applied them in a spirit of tolerance, rather than terror. Not only were Cyrus and Darius accepting of different cultures and religions, they actively promoted them. Their governing philosophy was imperial unity, not uniformity.[107] An excellent case history was their dealings with the Jewish captives in Babylon. The Hebrew scriptures record Cyrus' proclamation on behalf of the Jews in 538 BCE after his capture of Babylon:

> Thus saith Cyrus king of Persia, The LORD God of heaven hath given me all the kingdoms of the earth; and he hath charged me to build him an house at Jerusalem, which is in Judah.[108]

Cyrus permitted the Jews to return and appointed Jewish governors such as Nehemiah and Zerubbabel. Persia's new Jewish subjects were admonished to contribute to the restoration. The rebuilding of the temple was to be funded by the Persian state, a pragmatic, as well as paternalistic, move to secure reliable access to strike at Egypt, should she cause trouble. Cyrus instructed his treasurer, Mithredath, to restore to the returning Jews almost 5,500 gold and silver items Nebuchadnezzar had taken from Solomon's temple.[109] Construction on the temple was soon halted by opposition from Samaritans and others, but was resumed by order of Darius to his satraps, Tatnai and Shethar-boznai. They were to aid the Jews in any way possible and severely punish anyone who sought to interfere with their work.

> I made a decree . . . that of the king's goods, even of the tribute beyond the river, forthwith expenses be given unto these men, that they be not hindered. And that which they have need of . . . let it be given them day by day without fail . . . I Darius have made a decree; let it be done with speed.[110]

Following Cyrus came a period of upheaval under Cambyses, who projected Persian power into Egypt. The empire plunged into a period of civil war, during which Darayavaush, or the afore-mentioned Darius, seized the throne. Darius I, "The Great" (522–486 BCE), embarked upon a political, economic, and even religious revolution, seen by some as the real beginning of the Persian Empire. Darius was a disciple of a new religion named after Zoroaster. Traditionally, the Medes and Persians were polytheists who worshipped Mithra, the sun god; the fire god, and other deities. Zoroaster, who lived in north-western Iran, claimed a vision from Ahuramazda, The Wise Lord, the only true God. All the other gods were divas, or demons, under the rule of Satan, whom Zoroaster called Ahriman. The new religion taught a final judgement after death, very much tied to living well in this life. Meeting much opposition, Zoroaster fled to eastern Persia, where he was befriended by the ruler Hystapses, whom he converted. The young Darius became his disciple. Zoroastrianism became the state religion, and Darius continued the Cyrus policy of tolerant management and paternalistic oversight.[111]

Toleration always had its limits and the Persian experiment in cross-cultural management had to be often modified, although never fully rescinded. Babylon revolted early in Darius's reign and Babylonian national pride, based upon worship of Marduk, had to be brutally suppressed. Samaritan and Arabian hostility to the Jewish restoration forced a temporary halt to the rebuilding of the temple in Jerusalem. Commerce continued in Judea under the post-Exilic governors, who were forced to take action against fraudulent practices. The biblical books of Ezra and Nehemiah show a system of taxation getting out of hand. Debt-ridden Jewish peasants were forced to mortgage homes, fields, and even children to the landed aristocracy and public officials of Persia just to purchase grain. These officials were charging exorbitant interest rates to their countrymen. Nehemiah forced the Jewish elite to cease such practices, doubtless endemic to such a widespread empire. One of the banes in Judea was clearly the onerous

Persian tax system. This taxed wealth, real or assumed, instead of actual earnings. The practice was driving many into destitution: "There were also those that said, 'We have borrowed money for the king's tribute, and that upon our lands and vineyards.'"[112]

Darius took action. He standardized the infrastructure of his domain into twenty *satrapies* stretching from Egypt and Asia Minor to the borders of India. More trustworthy Iranians were inserted into local administrations and the tax system was reformed. Subjects would be taxed upon earnings at a flat rate of 20%, not upon assumed wealth. A reading of Herodotus and other ancient sources shows the amount of tax paid by each satrapy in the empire. India was the richest, followed by Babylonia, Egypt, and Media. India paid about three hundred and sixty talents or 330,000 pounds of gold dust. Babylonia paid around 1,000 silver talents, Egypt seven hundred, and Media four hundred and fifty.[113]

Darius also attempted to expand the boundaries of the empire. His invasion of Scythia, the modern Ukraine, ended in failure. He was more successful in India, where he added a rich slice of territory west of the Indus, which became the satrapy of Hindush. The Persian realm now included Jewish freedmen; Ionian entrepreneurs; Indian *Vaishyas* (traders); Babylonian, Anatolian, and Elamite *tamkāru*; and Phoenician royal traders. It was a compendium of ancient business cultures.[114] The biblical book of Esther was not exaggerating with its rich narrative of a sprawling imperial system of 127 provinces.

The control of imperial territory posed problems in an empire far exceeding that of the Akkadian, Assyrian, or Babylonian realms. Greek writers were fascinated by the extent of the Persian domains and the means by which the Persian kings held it together. Chief among these were the military roads adapted and expanded from the Assyrians and Babylonians. The most important was the King's Road that stretched some 13,500 stadia or 1,677 miles from Susa to Ephesus. It took three months to make the journey. These highways were wide dirt roads, well maintained and marked, that could be used by both traders and military chariots. Keeping these roads in usable condition required, according to French historian Pierre Briant, "a sizeable, specialized administration."[115] Roads and bridges were maintained by satraps and sometimes by the army. Such an engineering feat required active and energetic cross-cultural cooperation. When Darius and Xerxes invaded Europe, for example, they bridged the Bosporus with cable cords from Phoenicia and Egypt. Generally, the major roads were very safe for travellers. The Royal Road from Sardis to Susa never left inhabited territory.[116]

To accomplish these extensive public works, Persian kings used internal passports and standardized procedures to control their many subjects and to keep trade mobile and legal. Every traveller or caravan had to have a sealed permit describing the number in his band and the route to be followed. A letter from an official named Arshama was written to his manager, Nehtihor, who was on the way to Egypt:

> Do you give him (as) provisions . . . from my estate . . . in your prov-
> inces every day two measures . . . of white meal, three measures of
> inferior meal, two measures of wine or beer, and one sheep, and hay
> according to . . . his horses; and give provisions for two Cilicians (and)
> one craftsmen, all three my servants who are going with him to Egypt
> . . . give them these provisions . . . in accordance with (the stages of) his
> journey from province to province . . . until he reaches Egypt.[117]

The royal roads included postal relays and storehouses. The storehouse
managers were permitted to provide rations to caravans upon receipt of
the correct documents. In addition they were required to submit vouchers.
Records exist of one such, prepared at Hidalu on the Elamite border for a
traveller named Dauna. In 495 BCE, Dauna traversed Sardis to Persepolis and was given an authorization by Irdarpirna (Artaphernes), Satrap of
Sardis and brother of Darius:

> 4.65 BAR of flour. Dauma received. Each of the 23 men received 1.5qa,
> and 1qa for each "boy" . . . Dauma bore a document signed by Ird-
> arpirna. They were traveling from Sardis. They were headed to Perse-
> polis Month 9 of year 27. At Hidalu.[118]

Good roads are the lifeblood of trade. Traffic on the royal roads was
closely monitored by a form of satrapal highway patrol. Those not guilty of
any wrongdoing could journey safely, although armed men usually escorted
caravans. Brigands were severely punished with death and dismember-
ment. Any message without an official seal was confiscated. Nevertheless,
Iranians, Greeks, and others often tried to evade the officials. Harpagus
the Mede once sent a letter to Cyrus inside a *dead rabbit*. The Milesian
Histaieus once placed a message in the scalp of a slave.[119]

Concern for speedy communications traced back to Cyrus himself, one
of history's legendary conquerors whose tomb still exists in Iran. Cyrus
initiated one of history's first postal systems, ingeniously anticipating the
pony express of the later American West. He built a series of 111 post
stations, one day apart, along which men and horses could be speedily
changed and refreshed, providing what Xenophon described as the quickest means of travelling by land yet devised. Persian couriers were fast, but a
primitive from of telegraphy existed via a series of lookout towers stretching from Susa in Elam to Persia. A traveller might take a month to make
the journey, but a series of voices shouting the message from tower to tower
could deliver an early "telegram" in a single day. Signal fires could have the
same effect. The king in Persepolis could know within a day or two what
was happening in Asia Minor.[120]

How much private enterprise was conducted under this comprehensive
and centralized management and infrastructure? Texts from Persepolis seem
to omit mention of merchants and entrepreneurs. Some have concluded

that embryonic capitalism or a free trading network was stifled by the Persian Empire's "socialist" regime. The problem is that the sources are heavily slanted towards war and politics—the Persians were kept busy putting down revolts across their sprawling empire. Nevertheless, overtones emerge of a paternalistic and managed economy, much like some would see in the Canada of the 1950s to the 1970s. Sprawling territorial states with scattered, diverse populations and little in the way of social cohesion are naturally biased towards large-scale publicly funded projects to smooth the way for individual and/or state-sponsored enterprise. On the other hand, it is a reasonable assumption that an empire containing Babylonians, Tyrians, Jews, Greeks, Canaanites, and Indians was bound to possess more than its share of ambitious, experienced merchant classes. The Babylonian archives, discussed in the following, belie the myth of a "socialist" Persian realm, much in the way today's Canada's business community has had to dodge similar accusations from Milton Friedman's disciples in the United States. Pierre Briant, author of the latest and most comprehensive one-volume study of Persia, reassures his readers that "there is every reason to assume that long-distance trade . . . continued in Achaemenid times."[120]

Trade flowed along the excellent royal roads of Persia, as well as by water. Vital timber supplies—ever in demand across the ancient Near East—were shipped along the river systems of Asia Minor and through the Black and Mediterranean Seas. Essential commodities such as grain, wood, stone, and pitch flowed along the extensive canals of Babylonia. Temple capitalism still thrived, although the priests chose to contract shipping to private *tamkāru*. The sailing ships still plying trade at Uruk belonged to both temple overseers and skilled shipowners and boatmen, as they had in the past. A tablet from the Eanna at Uruk during the Chaldean Empire represents a contract of five minas of silver for wood for twenty-two boats required to ship 30,000 measures of asphalt. Asphalt was very valuable, not only for paving roads but as mortar for holding structures together. The labor force included carpenters, builders, smiths, and laborers. Indeed, the most lucrative trade in the Persian Empire was centered around these Babylonian waterways. Collection depots were erected along the major canals for pitch, grain, dates, and asphalt. The huge temple of Marduk in Babylon boasted its own Quay named Bel.[121]

Tablets from Babylonia dating to just before and after the Persian conquest reveal a flourishing of the ancient *tamkārum* capitalism in the old Mesopotamian heartland. In 505 BCE, six merchants pooled their capital, acquired from the wool business, to ship a boatload of barley to Elam. In 499, two more Babylonians were paid to sail with garments to Elam. A pair of tablets from 551 and 550 BCE show large shipments of goods imported from Egypt via the Levant, as shown in Table 6.8.

For the eastern Mediterranean in general, the trading network of the Persian Empire was not very different from that of Nebuchadnezzar's. It encompassed Egypt, Asia Minor, Cyprus, Phoenicia, Syria, Palestine,

Table 6.8   Sample Invoices of Goods Imported From Levant to Babylon

551 BCE:	550 BCE:
Copper from Yamana (Cyprus): 295 minas	Copper from Yamana: 600 minas
Tin: 37 minas	Dye: 81 minas
Lapis Lazuli: 55 minas	Tin: 37 minas
Fibers: 153 minas	Dyed Wool: 16 minas
Alum: 233 minas	Copper from Yamana: 205 minas
Iron from Yamana: 130 minas	Lapis Lazuli: 55 minas
Iron from Lebanon: 257 minas	Fibers: 153 minas
	Alum: 233 minas
	Dye: 32 minas
	Iron from Yamana: 130 minas
	Iron from Lebanon: 257 minas
	Dye: 120 minas
	Spice: 40 minas [123]

Mesopotamia, and the Aegean. Goods were shipped down the Euphrates, producing sales and inventory records from Babylonian import–export traders. An Aramaic document from Egypt dated to 475 BCE offers more evidence that trade and commerce rated as a major activity of the Persian imperium. Persian officials inspected and taxed the omnipresent Greek and Phoenician vessels. Greeks in Ionia were taxed on the value of their goods, and the Tyrians paid a flat rate of 10% on shipments of bronze, iron, wood, tin, textiles, and clay.[124]

CAPITALISM BY ANOTHER NAME

In short, Babylonia under the Persians remained the prosperous commercial core of the Near East that it had been under the Chaldeans. Within twelve days of the fall of Babylon to Cyrus, Babylonian business documents were being issued dated to year one of Cyrus, King of Babylon. The same Babylonian families that dominated business in Mesopotamia under the Chaldeans prospered into the Persian period. It could be admitted that although the Iranians, as a whole, did not seem to possess a panache for business, they proved to be shrewd overseers. Their paternalistic management style encouraged and actively harnessed the acumen of those who were.[125] There are parallels here with the 1920s, when V. I. Lenin, Communist ruler of the new Soviet Union, dealt with a floundering command economy by designating a "New Economic Policy," importing renowned capitalists such as Henry Ford for advice and expertise. Lenin's "New Economic Policy" was, in fact, capitalism. Something similar was in effect under the Persians.

Cyrus wisely preserved the older Chaldean governmental and economic structure. And why not? The rich soil of the Tigris and Euphrates was the traditional breadbasket of Mesopotamia. It continued to produce barley grown on the great temple estates, one growing 50,000 bushels annually. The delectable date palms served as another cash crop affordable by the poorer classes. These were grown in the palm orchards lining the great waterways and canals. As many as 40,000 bushels were recorded growing on one large plantation. Besides having their own serfs, the temples employed hired labor at subsistence wages. Wheat was grown for those who could afford it. Oil and wine, imported from North Syria, were chief luxury items. Coined money was not yet in fashion throughout the Persian Empire, but Babylonia was very much a money economy working to the silver standard. Gold was very rare, and lead and copper went out of use. Records show that the age-old basic unit, the shekel, was worth one *gur*, about five or six bushels of barley.[126]

Temple capitalism was thus the heartbeat of Babylon under the Persians. Priests owned vast flocks of sheep and goats, and leased out oxen and other beasts of burden to contractors. Private farmers continued to prosper, buying oxen at better prices than their ancestors had under Hammurabi. Horses—the key to Persian control and command—were much more expensive. One horse could sell for twenty years' wages. Brick continued to be used for houses and other buildings, as it had in Sumerian times, glued together with cheap asphalt and floated down the Euphrates for sale. The wood used for panels came from the Arameans and Phoenicians in Syria and was much more expensive. Copper and iron came from Cyprus, shipped by skilled Sidonians and Tyrians, transmuting now into an integral part of the Persian trading network. The prices, 3.67 lb. a shekel for copper, and 11.1 for iron, were much lower than in Bronze Age times, thanks to important technological improvements in mining, smelting, and shipping.[127]

Babylonia thus experienced much continuity under the Persians. The *tamkārum* system continued to operate within a vast new market that now extended from Sardis to Samarkand. Several big family concerns flourished in the tradition of Ashur-Imitti. The merchant House of Egibi may even have been of Jewish origin. These experienced importers dealt in wine, honey, wood, lead, dye, dyed wool, lapis lazuli, and alum from Egypt. Their vast network of family concerns, based in Babylon, operated branches as far south as Uruk. The Egibi were among the richest families in both the Chaldean and the Achaemenid empires holding title to rich farmland around Babylon itself, several houses, and many slaves. The Egibi operated throughout Babylonia and into Elam and Persia. They drew up contracts, intended as promissory notes, which were soon to set the standard for most forms of Babylonian commerce.[128]

A typical Neo-Babylonian contract included:

- *The object of the transaction*: a clause such as "for a commercial expedition."
- *The names of the parties involved*: usually from two to five who invested their silver capital, usually in the form of sheets, ingots, or jewelry with an entrepreneur. Babylonians did not use coins until Hellenistic times. Silver was used in financial operations involving real estate and slaves, and sometimes dates, barley, and wool.
- *The terms of the loan or deal*: profits were usually prorated according to the amount invested by each participant, as they had been in Mesopotamia and Phoenicia for centuries. The standard rate of interest was twenty percent.
- *The names of the witnesses.*
- *The place and date of the contract.*[129]

The House of Iddin-Nabu was another prominent trading family in the early Persian period. Iddin-Nabu was not the firstborn, and was adopted by his uncle. Entering into real estate, he soon became independently wealthy through buying and then leasing property. Even the temple on his lands was leased out to a manager who earned a hefty profit for Iddin-Nabu by controlling sacrificial rights and rites. The most extensive Babylonian archives date back six generations into Assyrian times. These show that between 687 (the reign of Sennacherib) and 487 BCE (the reign of Darius I), the merchant House of Ea-Iluta-Bani managed and traded from Borsippa for six generations. Once again, land, slaves, silver, and grain built a family fortune. Date palms for instance could turn a profit of 14%. Most Babylonian families did not have the capital to transact large-scale business dealings, but the great merchant houses would soon become a feature across the ancient world.[130]

The business archives of these Babylonian merchant houses end with the reign of Darius. Possibly they helped finance a nationalist revolt, which Darius suppressed. There are no known records of major Babylonian commercial firms until the rise of the House of Murashu late in the fifth century BCE. Murashu ("Wildcat"), son of Khatin, lived in Nippur. It appears the firm was directed by his sons Enlil-Shum-Iddin (445–421) and Enlil-Khatin (454–437), and in the following generation by Rimut-Ninurta, Enlil-Khatin II, and Murashu II, grandchildren of the patriarch. All employed business agents and worked closely with the *satrap* of Babylonia and other officials of the courts of Artaxerxes I (465–423 BCE) and Darius II (423–405 BCE).[131] One is reminded of the House of Rothschild loaning money to the British government to purchase shares in the Suez Canal (1870s) or the impact of the House of Krupp in Germany.

The Murashu became intimately involved with the management of a Persian Empire that, more and more, gave evidence of slowly collapsing under its own weight. By the fourth century, inflation was becoming a serious problem and the imperial administration began to evolve into a form of cash feudalism. In a manner anticipatory of medieval Europe, the crown under Cyrus had given lands to leading families in return for military service. Feudalism operates in large territories where the central government has limited resources. Darius I systematized Persian feudalism. "Bow land" was given to archers, "horse land" to cavalrymen, "chariot land" to the most powerful. Persia, for all its military muscle, had no large standing army, and the temptation soon arose for vassals to pay grain or dates instead of rendering service. As a result, the fiefs became sources of revenue more than of military power. The value of land in Babylonia by the late fifth century had begun to fall, but the costs of irrigation and upkeep were increasing. Tenants soon found themselves in a tremendous financial squeeze. At this point, the Murashu became the middlemen. The family assets—livestock, money, tools—allowed them to operate the lands and canals and collect taxes for the crown.[132]

In 422 BCE, Year Two of Darius II, one Gadaliama drew up a contract at Nippur with Rimut-Ninurta, the grandson of Murashu, offering to perform military service in his stead:

> Give me a horse with harness and reins, a . . . coat with neckpiece and hood, an iron armor with hood, a quiver, 120 arrows . . . in a sword (?) . . . 2 iron spears, and I will perform the service attached to your share in the tenure land.[133]

The Murashu, themselves, were now contracting the feudal relationships:

> "Rimut-Ninurta agreed and gave him a horse and the military equipment mentioned above, as well as 1 mina of silver for his travel provisions, in order to obey the royal order to go to Uruk in connection with this "horse land."[134]

Under Darius II, many holders of "bow land" declared bankruptcy. By the time of Artaxerxes I (465–423), the Murashu held anywhere from twenty to seventy properties. The norm was five. The Murashu soon held a virtual monopoly over leased crown land, which they rented to small farmers. They colluded with corrupt crown officials, forcing farmers to buy their seed and tools and sink further into debt and slavery. As noted, after 413 BCE the Murashu archives cease. It is likely that Darius II, wisely fearing the enormous concentration of private power at the core of his realm, sought to eliminate a potential threat in the same way that his predecessors had eliminated business dynasties.[135]

The world-conquering Persian Empire seemed to be running out of viable economic alternatives. From state paternalism to an adapted temple capitalism to elite monopolies to a desperate form of feudalism, the Persian Empire began to resemble that of the British on the eve of World War One, a super-state staggering under the too vast orb of its own successful expansion. The Persian realm that had confidently accepted the challenge from the Greek states in the 490s BCE was clearly in trouble as the fourth century dawned. Its fate seemed prefigured by the words of a critic watching that other great amalgam of nations that finally ended in our own times, it also a victim of imperial overstretch "marching to its certain ruin . . . too worn out and flaccid to perform great tasks."[136] Persia's nemesis would once again emerge from the same Grecian territory that had checked its expansion once already. Greek entrepreneurs had been part of the leaven that had leavened the massive economy of the Persian Empire. They would return, revitalized under a conqueror more accomplished even than Cyrus the Great. That story is told in Chapter 8.

7 Publicans and Patriarchs
The Triumph of Roman Family
Enterprise: 146 BCE–14 CE

With the Persian Empire, the balance of power in the ancient Near East shifted away from Mesopotamia for the first time. With the Roman Empire, the balance shifted for good.

In the Western Mediterranean, the seeds planted by the traders of Tyre and the merchants of Euboea germinated two mighty states, either of which, alone, could have dominated the next economy. These were Carthage and Rome. Carthage, chief colony of Phoenicia, inherited the western half of the Tyrian commercial empire. Its princes created an African version of naval capitalism that reached far back into the great continent, pioneered trade in the Atlantic and dreamt of bringing even Europe under its sway. It was not to be. Proud Carthage was supplanted by the citizen-warriors of Rome, whose resolute traders and soldiers successfully adapted the Hellenic market revolution to their own needs. In the process, they built the mightiest empire yet seen, incorporating Asia under its sway and laying the groundwork for the political economy of Western Europe.

AFRICAN CAPITALISM: THE MERCHANT PRINCES OF CARTHAGE

Carthage was settled at the end of the ninth century BCE by seafaring Phoenician merchants in ships with curved prows—a technical innovation that improved vastly upon the concave shaped Nile boats and Assyrian *quinquiremes*. With a rich African hinterland to draw upon—the Sahara being much less formidable a barrier in this period—Carthage got off to a fast start-up as Tyre's granary, shipping wheat to Cyprus and the Levant. The partial conquest of Tyre by Nebuchadnezzar in 574 BCE, the Greek victory at Salamis (480 BCE), and the final humbling of Tyre by Alexander the Greek in 332 BCE greatly weakened Phoenician sea power. Carthage easily assumed leadership of the western half of the vast Canaanite trading network. From 550 BCE onwards, western Phoenician factories, posts, and realms are designated by the name *Punic*,[1] the Roman word for Phoenicia. More and more, the overseas markets originally opened up by Tyre and Sidon—colonies such as Malta, Gozo, Lampedusa, and Pantellaria especially—and the mining and trading investments in North Africa, Sardinia, Sicily, and Spain were directed from Carthage. Carthage extended its mercantile outposts on Sardinia, greatly expanding activity on the island.

The payoffs were immense. Mt. Sirai, deep in the Sardinian interior, for example, became a metal-processing factory. Punic agents spread eastward from Motya in Sicily, founding Maisala and Panormus (Palermo). The silver of Tartessos fattened the Carthaginian treasury and opened up new investment possibilities. Gades and the Iberian mines centered about the Rio Tinto[2] were pivotal to Carthaginian economic expansion. In Spain, the Punic presence would be felt not only in coastal sites such as Abdera, Almuñecar, and Gades (Cadiz), but farther inland as well.[3]

Carthage's "African model" of management directly copied that of Tyre, modified somewhat by the availability of vast tracts of rich farmland in its hinterland. Spreading their estates across Tunisia, Punic potentates prospered as gentry, generals, sailors, managers, shippers, and fervent devotees of Baal-Hammon—sometimes at one and the same time. Intensive agriculture, centered around the manor house, was combined with import–export shipping on a wide scale. Carthage seemed to have the best of both worlds: a surplus in foodstuffs and a tradition of overseas trade—the very dynamic that had eluded Athens. The estate-managers of Carthage often owned their own vessels, triple-decked *triremes*, capable of carrying bulk shipments of commodities on the Great Sea: gold, incense, iron, copper, silver, tin, salt, African animals, and dates. Mines and shipyards were run by a hereditary caste with strong state connections, the business elite and the political elite one and the same.

As at Ugarit and Tyre, long-distance shipments of goods and money between African managers and their resident agents in Sicily, Spain, or Sardinia was internalized, sailing under the same big business house. A mercantilist strategy was fiercely prosecuted.[4]

Combining the writings of Aristotle with archaeology, it is possible to learn more about this African version of palace–temple capitalism. Aristotle praised the Carthaginian constitution and remarked on its stability:

> Many of the institutions at Carthage are certainly good. . . . It is a proof of a well-ordered constitution that Carthage, with her large populace, should steadily keep to the same political system: she has had no civil dissensions worth mentioning, nor any attempt at a tyranny.[5]

Aristotle describes a tightly-knit coterie of princes and traders where membership in a wealthy family was a prerequisite for political power. The Council of A Hundred and Four and the Council of Elders were chosen by both birth and merit. Monarchs were elected, not born. Carthage is admirable, says Aristotle, because "her kings are not . . . always drawn from a single family of no more than ordinary merit . . . [but] from any family which is outstanding at the time, and they are drawn from it by election, and not by seniority."[6] These traits would come to fullest flower in the career of one family, the Barcas, which produced the mighty general Hannibal. A popular assembly played a vital balancing role as well. Appointed boards of merchant-princes served without pay (a forerunner of the British Boards of Trade?) and decided many judicial matters. Carthage had the advantages of social cohesion, the splendid locational advantage of jutting out into the Mediterranean, and a successful mercantile tradition. Ruled by a meritocracy, as well as a progressive oligarchy, her organizing principles were far more preferable to Greek conservatives than the fourth-century Hellenic tyrants. Aristotle did note a few flaws. Generalships and even the crown were for sale, and often one man held more than one office.[7]

AN AFRICAN DIMENSION

Punic enterprise, however, was balanced and diversified, large and small, public and private. Important industries such as mining and munitions were managed by monarchical, priestly, and aristocratic networks. A landed hierarchy managed state and temple property, from which foreigners, freedmen, or slaves were excluded. Carthage produced no Pasions, and far fewer independent, competitive entrepreneurs, than in Greece. Athenians met competition by becoming leaner and perhaps meaner; their Punic rivals retreated into guilds under the tutelage of a patron, *Baal*. The productive potential of the royal mines, arms factories, and shipyards of Carthage was formidable, capable of launching 120 *triremes* in two months. Although the entrepreneurs of Greater Greece toyed with ideas of natural law and inwardly aimed to limit the influence of gods and goddesses over the marketplace, the Carthaginians remained as devout as their Oriental forbearers.

Arms workshops flourished on temple land. Temples were governed by a royal board, with priests directly related to kings or judicial heads of state (this was not unknown in Rome, either). Both Hannibal's father and his grandfather, Abdimelkart, were *suffetes* (consuls) and high priests. Himilkat, a fourth generation *suffete*, installed his daughter, Batbaal, as priestess. The proprietors at the shrines of Melkart, Baal-Hammon, Eshmun, and Reshef were rich enough to own and manage entire communities. Nevertheless, the temple property was "in actual fact in the hands of the Punic aristocracy too."[8] Carthage *was* influenced by the Iron Age and Aegean market revolution in the form of iron technology, coined money, and even, a times, a touch of republican democracy. In essence, Punic maritime capitalism was made-in-Canaan but upgraded for the Middle and Late Iron Age. Carthage adapted the system very well. It remained a political and commercial leviathan until the third century BCE. It took all the élan of the Roman Republic to bring it down. Punic sailors dominated the Mediterranean carrying trade, exporting their own wares and pivoting a rich commercial imperium. Shipbuilding, tool-making, textiles, ceramics, carpentry, and a host of secondary handicrafts flourished alongside agribusiness in Tunisia, destined to become the breadbasket of the Mediterranean.[9]

Thus, rich, robust Carthage added an African dimension to the story of world business. The spectacular amphitheaters, baths, and residences that stretch from Morocco to Libya are impressive monuments to Roman construction, but are often built on Punic originals. Here was a civilization capable of standing with Greece, Egypt, and Mesopotamia as an often ignored pillar in the structure of economic history. For, although civilization began in Mesopotamia, the stone age began in Africa. In economic matters, Africa, the second-largest continent but divisible into five distinct "belts" of terrain and climatic regions, makes any generalization difficult. Through most of the Stone Age, the center of the African continent was in the lead, as the site of such features as the "hand-axe" culture that throve in Kenya and Tanzania.[10] Deep inside Libya, German archaeologist Heinrich Barth, in the 1980s, began to catalogue a "magical" collection of Saharan rock art inscriptions in the area of Akakus from the time when the desert was green. Indeed, Africa's natural fecundity may have inhibited the need to take the next step in economic advance—the development of large cities.

This was not true of the Northeast corner of Africa bordering on Egypt, of course, where interaction with the emerging Delta civilization may well have been decisive and to which anthropologists have given the name "Cushite" or "Meroite." Iron-working may have been invented indigenously south of the Sahara, as well.[11] The French scholar Lebeuf's discovery of the So People around Lake Chad who "lived in towns, worked metals and made fine pottery" points to the possibilities.[12] Bronze Age Africa below the Sahara poured its economic ingenuity into specialized forms of "vegeculture"—perfecting fishing techniques along the sea coasts and river lines. The ultimate attraction for the Carthaginians of North Africa would be the vast mineral deposits that, even today, make the continent the second largest storehouse in the world. The phrase "Gold Coast" done to our own time makes a strong economic point. Punic traders could not long ignore the African interior, as shown in the following. Well might the Romans exclaim, "There is always something new coming out of Africa!" Carthage drew upon this rich and almost obscured African treasure trove.

THE GREEK CHALLENGE

As mentioned in Chapter 6, the Greeks emerged as staunch a rival to Carthage in the west as they had to Tyre and Persia in the east. Hellenic long-distance traders at first flouted the *Eclectic Paradigm* in their overseas transactions, taking their chances with contracts between free individual chieftains guaranteed by law. The Greek challenge developed slowly at first. Neither the Euboeans nor the early Hellenic colonies in Italy and Sicily mounted a serious threat to Tyre or Carthage at first. The turning point came when Colaeus, a trader from Samos, a Greek island just southwest of wealthy Ephesus, landed in Tartessos (Spain) just before 600 BCE. The Iberian king, sensing an opportunity, invited the Greeks to challenge the exclusive Tyrian/Punic monopoly.

It was not the Samians, however, but their Ionian neighbors to the north, the Phocaeans,[13] who posed the bigger threat. Phocaean trading zeal was stimulated by their proximity via the Hermus River to the legendary King Croseus of Lydia. They had been the first to penetrate Sicily and settled Massilia (Marseilles) and other colonies along the French, Italian, and Spanish Riviera, thanks to a technical advantage in sailing ships. The Phoceans put to sea in the early model, small fifty-oared long ships called *pentecolters*. Fast for their day, hard to detect and easy to manoeuver, these vessels were ideal for independent merchants who could dash through the Straits of Messina and along the north coast of the Mediterranean, outrunning their Punic pursuers. Rhodian, Corinthian, Attic, and Ionian pottery in France testifies to this Greek onslaught on the markets of Western Europe.

Soon the rich resources of Spain came into their sights. Greek traders pushed up the Ebro River with their decorative new pottery and iron tools and established the new settlement of Emporion in Catalonia. A second route connected Massilia with the hinterland off Celtic Gaul, a people just beginning to build settlements, forge iron weapons, and till its rich soil. The future wine-growing region of Burgundy was a prime market for Greek expansion, witnessed by the presence of Greek vases in the region of the River Rhône. The majestic Rhone converged with water routes leading to the English Channel and the North. Further east, Phocaean *pentecolters* darted up the Adriatic, founding the settlement of Adria near Venice, trading pottery, jewels, and bronze goods for the amber of the Baltic. The struggle for competitive advantage was clearly joined. The Punic navy sought to monopolize the commerce of the western Mediterranean through bases at Gibraltar and Gades; the Greeks tried to bypass this control to reach new Celtic, Germanic, and Illyrian markets via boat or overland caravan along the valleys of the Rhône, Seine, Elbe, and Danube.

The aggressive Hellenes enticed the northern "barbarians" with their easily reductive coinage and staple items—dates, figs, olive oil in abundance—seeking a share of the very tin, amber, and iron markets that Carthage sought to dominate. By 550 BCE, the founding of Massilia and Ampurias in Catalonia presented the lords of Carthage with the worst incursion yet from Greek entrepreneurs.[14] Greek merchants brought Greek culture, and, of all peoples of antiquity, the Greek sense of play. Of all peoples of antiquity, the Greeks knew to have fun. "Solon, Solon, you Greeks are all children," the Egyptian priests teased the great statesman. Each Greek city worth its salt had to have its gardens, statuary, temples and gymnasium, and, above all, its theatres and odeons where Greek dramatists raised troublesome questions about the cosmos and man's relationship to the gods, and sometimes mocked the gods.

Thus, the more sober Carthaginians worried about an ideological, as well as an economic, challenge from the new western *poleis* arriving in their waters. Hellenic culture posed a long-term philosophic threat, as well as an immediate economic danger to the relatively closed world of Carthage, much as American popular culture today calls into question many of the traditional practices of Asia. "All things flow, nothing abides," said Heraclitus of Ephesus (530–460 BCE). Simonides (556–469 BCE), the first Greek to take money for his poetry, ended up in Syracuse, the gateway to Sicily and largest of all the Greek cities. He wrote, "Strong is the strength of man . . . nothing is everlasting." It is a small step from that to "eat, drink and be merry, for tomorrow we die." A people with such a sceptical worldview would have little regard for the gods of Carthage with their mordant tendency to infant sacrifice and no respect at all for Melqart's alleged blessing on commerce.

Carthage responded by reinforcing naval bases in Sardinia, western Sicily and the Balearics and forging alliances with the Elymians of Sicily. Between 560 and 480 BCE, the kings of Carthage also sought to exploit the resentments Gela and Rhegium harbored against Syracuse, long a base for the Greek transhipment trade. Tradition said that the same day Themistocles faced the Persians at Salamis, the giant Greek colony at Syracuse was facing down the fleet of Carthage (480 BCE). Carthaginian trading partnerships with the Etruscans in Tuscany became military ententes, as well as commercial deals. Numerous Punic artifacts and inscriptions honoring Astarte were unearthed at Etruscan ports documenting an alliance directed mainly against the Phocaean menace. The Phocaean threat came as much from piracy as from direct commercial competition. This intensified after a large portion of the population of Phocaea were driven from their homes by the armies of Cyrus. Many temporarily relocated on the island of Corsica. After 565, Ionian-built corsairs based there and along the Greek Riviera took a heavy toll of Punic commerce in the Tyrrhenian Sea and the northwest Mediterranean. The Greek threat was so strong that it required the combined efforts of the Punic and Tuscan war fleets to defeat it. At the battle of Alalia in 535 BCE, one hundred and twenty Carthaginian and Etrurian ships won a costly victory against half that number of Phocaean vessels. Corsica was now assigned to the Etruscan sphere of influence. The Battle of Alalia—the Trafalgar of its day—helped consolidate Punic control of the western Mediterranean, a control sealed not only by alliance with the Etruscans, but with the rising new Roman Republic.[15]

"TO RULE THE WAVES"

While the Romans were forging a workable Republic and Darius I (522–486 BCE) was consolidating the Persian Empire and Athens ejecting her tyrants, Carthage was enjoying her naval and commercial climacteric.

French scholars J. G. Demerliac and J. Meirat have reconstructed the "vast commercial organization" of Punic naval capitalism, a classic model of the *Eclectic Paradigm* applied in antiquity. The vast distances separating Carthage from the fringes of her empire increased the importance of ports such as Gades and Lixus (on Atlantic Morocco) in managing trading voyages. Unlike independent Greek *poleis*, Punic trading centers were integral parts of a coordinated, centrally-directed system joined together by three important trade routes (see Table 7.1).[16]

Between May and September of every year, commercial flotillas left Carthage bound east, north, and west. Galleys sailed eastward to access the Persian trading sphere that stretched to India. The galleys returned via Egypt and Libya, positioned to oversee trading routes that crossed the Sahara and stretched down into Ghana and Nigeria. Galleys on the northerly route headed via Sardinia for Etruria and outposts south to Sicily. The important westerly route headed to the Balearics and along the Iberian coast to Gibraltar, Gades, and Lixus.[17] Here was another ancient version of the "multinational" organization as described by the *Eclectic Paradigm,* a very location-driven solution for a Carthage whose lifeblood was trade. No ambitious Greek merchant in a fast-moving *penteconter* could finance and carry out trade on such a scale. The annual convoys of Carthage carried large shipments of Spanish silver and copper and British tin, as well as Tunisian wheat and Tyrian silks and other luxuries. It is tempting to argue that only the Carthaginian elite, backed by temple, navy, and state, could afford to put up the capital and assume the risks needed to maintain the trade of such a far-flung consortium.

Market failure, especially for voyages into the Atlantic, was circumvented through internalized bulk trade under the watchful direction of the king's agent-aristocrats living on the spot in Spain and Morocco. Long-distance operations were financed and covered from Carthage. The cost of insuring Mediterranean cargoes alone amounted to a full third of their value. Piracy and sporadic wars raised the costs to two-thirds or even 100%. Only the crown's access to its large estates and temple treasuries could cover such potential losses. The Greek's opening up of overland routes to Europe threatened to undercut the Punic seaborne trade unless piracy and war could be reduced. Piracy, itself, was a very serious menace and another rea-

Table 7.1 Carthaginian Trade Routes: Seasonal Sailing

Easterly Route: May: Carthage-Malta-Sidon/Tyre, links to Persian Empire. September: Return via Egypt to Libya. Overland trading connections to Ghana and Nigeria.

Northerly Route: May: Carthage-Sardinia-Etruria. Connections to Sicily. September: return.

Westerly Route: May: Carthage-Sardinia-Ibiza in Balerics-Iberian coast- Gibraltar-Gades-Lixus. Connections to Iberian network in British Isles. September: return.

---

son for Carthage—like Spain in the 1500s of our era—to move to protect such a vast and complex militarized trading system.[18]

Swarms of Greek, Ligurian, and Albanian pirates lurked in the Tyrrhenian, north Mediterranean, and Ionian Seas. Like vultures, they swarmed in large numbers along Carthaginian trading arteries, calling for a coordinated response. The trading operations of the Punic Silver Fleet were well organized and planned, with a single trading convoy on each major route between May and September. The navy's *triremes* were faster than the merchant ships, with large storage areas to feed crews of one hundred and twenty rowers, as well as the indispensable marines. This tied warships to their bases, so Punic merchant ships themselves carried marines. The Carthaginian navy employed *triremes* for mass sweeps against pirates near Sardinia, the Balearics, Cartagena, Malta, Crete, and the Nile. Cooperation with skilled Etruscan sailors thus made for an alliance of necessity.[19]

Not surprisingly, the tempo of Carthaginian life ebbed and flowed with the annual naval sallies, as much as the rhythm of Roman life was affected by the periodic mobilizations of the army. Every spring in Carthage, busy firms of outfitters, provisioners, warehousers, dockworkers, armorers, and providers of specialty goods acting under royal sponsorship outfitted two hundred *triremes*, each of which carried marines and Libyan, Iberian, Sardinian, and other mercenaries. Once the spring planting was done, 24,000 North African peasants joined them as rowers, planning to return to home base in time for the autumn harvest. One out of every five Carthaginians took part in this carefully calibrated system of naval capitalism. The system worked fine, so long as the need for mobilization was brief. As a result, the merchant aristocracy of Carthage had to win her wars quickly.[20]

Pirates from Greece or Gaul kept the navy occupied, but the Greek Gelonid tyrants of Syracuse foreshadowed the later Roman challenge. Were Syracuse to conquer the independent *poleis* of Gela, Megara, and Himera, it would tilt the balance in Sicily against Carthage. Hence, Gelon the Tyrant attacked Himera in 480, at the same time Xerxes marched on Athens. The Carthaginians were led by Hamilcar of the Magonid family of whom would come Hannibal. Gelon won, and the war raged on throughout the fifth century. Gelonid Sicily challenged both Carthage and Athens as a power in its own right. It joined forces with Sparta and Corinth to hand Athens her decisive defeat before Syracuse in the Peloponnesian War. Carthage, though, fought on with increased savagery, beseeching her *baalim* in prayers laced with an intense and horrific wave of human sacrifice.[21] Himera was recovered. The men of the city were tortured and murdered as blood sacrifices; the women and children were regarded as booty. The multinational Punic army of mercenaries had made Carthage master on land and sea, but only in theory. Her army, ignorant of proper sanitation, was soon decimated by salmonella and typhus.[22] The Sicilian frustration would be a foretaste of her defeat by the Romans.

THE AFRICAN OPTION

In the end, Carthage could not drive the Greeks from Sicily. This led to renewed market development in Africa in the fourth century on both land and sea. Berbers in Tunisia, Algeria, and Morocco were subjugated; feudal estates were erected and wheat production soared. Military posts were erected every twenty or thirty miles along the Maghreb coast, which yields its evidence in Greek artifacts being replaced by Punic.[23] Such a surge of expansion planned with typical Punic forethought had the result that Central Africa was co-opted more fully into the Carthaginian sphere. Caravans braved the Sahara to reach Ghadames, Fezzan, and Garamentes—almost eight hundred miles south and east of Carthage. The attraction was the gold fields and ivory markets of Guinea and Niger. Herodotus, writing in the fifth century BCE, reported that the Garamantes, the Libyan Berber pastoralists living in the region of the Fezzan, were in the habit of raiding the "Ethiopians," that is to say, the Negroes, in four-horse chariots. His report is amply proved by the discovery in recent years of remains of numerous horse-drawn vehicles. These operated in two bands running across the desert towards the great bend of the Niger, one from the Fezzan and the other from southern Morocco. These bands correspond to two of the major caravan routes of later times and help demonstrate that Africa was not the passive recipient of a higher culture. "Chariots would have been used for raiding, not trading, but the one can easily lead to the other," say Oliver and Fage.[24]

In such a way was the Western Sudan brought within reach of these intrepid travelling bands. The attraction here may well have been what it would be a few centuries later—gold and ivory, ostrich feathers, hides, and slaves. A string of trading posts and overland routes stretched eastward into Egypt, well inland from Libyan Cyrenaica.[25] Carthaginian traders based in Lixus reached new African markets via the Atlantic sailing south. One great lure of the inner continent was salt, salt to preserve food and disguise its taste, salt to replace vital fluids lost in those hot semi-tropical climes. Salt later became so important to the Romans that it was used to pay their soldiers. Hence, the word "salary," from the root Latin word "*salus*" for salt. Carthage's economy included the African interior. Nothing seemed beyond her imperial sway. Around 450 BCE, the enigmatic Prince Hanno, of the Magonid house, sent a massive fleet of *triremes* and (supposedly) 30,000 men down the coast of West Africa. The resultant *Periplus of Hanno* was probably doctored to protect valuable market information. The text suggests a possible attempt to plant Punic colonies on the shores of sub-Saharan Africa. The voyage may well have reached as far as the Cameroons. Did Hanno found colonies, or did he turn back, suggesting heavy risks to internalized commerce in markets this far south?[26]

Sailing from Gades (Cadiz) in Spain, Hanno's brother Himlico, headed up the French Atlantic coast to reach the tin mines of Brittany and Cornwall.

Carthage hoped to wrest control over the Iberian tin trade from her branch houses in Gades. This was a move designed to cut out the obnoxious and seemingly ubiquitous Greek-influenced middlemen. Tin from the Celts was paid for with the distinctive Punic horse-head and palm-tree coins, still dug up in Devon and Dorsetshire, although there is no evidence for a permanent Carthaginian establishment. The existence of Celtic import–export centers for tin, furs, and animal skins as far as Britain has excited speculation in recent years of possible Carthaginian-backed voyages to the New World. The notion that the Phoenicians left an inscription on a rock in Brazil is now dismissed as a hoax. Nevertheless, there are hints—but only hints—of a Punic "Westward ho!" Diodorus of Sicily, writing in the first century BCE, reported on African ships blown westward to very large fertile island many days west of Africa. Plutarch (d. 120 AD) discovered a Punic parchment describing lands far to the west. Beyond Britain supposedly lay three groups of islands equally distant from one another. Were these the Orkneys, Shetlands, and Faroes? What of the large island known as *Ogygia*. Was *Ogygia* Iceland? Five thousand *stades* or four hundred and eighty miles west of *Ogygia* was the continent *Epiros*. Was *Epiros* Greenland or even North America? So far, we have only speculative hints. What is surprising are the horse-head coins of Carthaginian type found near navigable rivers across North America. Just how far did the Carthaginian writ run? Some bolder writers have built an elaborate case for royal trading agents in Gades and Morocco enjoying a transatlantic subsidiary mandate. But this needs much more verification at present.[27]

What is beyond doubt is the attempt by Punic admirals based on Gibraltar and Gades to enforce a mercantile monopoly, effectively bottling up their trading competition in the Mediterranean and compelling Greek merchants to exploit, ever harder, the overland river routes into Europe.[28] A few intrepid traders did break the Carthaginian blockade. When the Punic navy once more massed against Sicily in 310 BCE, Pytheas the Greek slipped through Gibraltar and sailed to Cornwall. With his crude sextant, Pytheas discovered that the North Star and Little Dipper were much higher in the sky than in Massilia. Within about fifty years, this discovery hinted to both Greek and Punic mathematicians that the earth was curved, perhaps round.[29] Even early Roman traders, late mariners thought they were, tried their hands at industrial espionage but were less successful than Pytheas. One Roman captain posed as a friend of Carthage and slipped into Gades, where friendly spies told him a Punic vessel was sailing for Cornwall. The Latin skipper followed the Canaanite at a distance until he was spotted. The Punic master scuttled his own vessel on the Spanish shore. The Carthaginian crew made their way overland to Gades to be given a hero's welcome by the princely hierarchy for keeping market data from the intrusive Romans. Ownership advantage is another constant in business history, and the Carthaginians were fanatical practitioners.[30]

The Punic monopoly in the Atlantic would not hold forever. Other rivals were already stirring to challenge proud Carthage.

WAR CAPITALISM: ROUND ONE—THE RISE OF ROME

The intense Greek–Carthaginian export drive accelerated the coming of the Iron Age market revolution across the Italian Peninsula.[31] Latins and Etruscans shared north-central Italy together. Etruscan kings once ruled in Rome. The Etruscan urban centers at Veii, Tarquinia, Populonia, Vulci, and Cerveteri and the Latin centers Lavinium, Ardea, Antium, Satricum, and Rome grew from small Bronze Age settlements. Etruscan gentry soon found a lucrative market in Ischia, an accessible island off Naples, for the iron, copper, and silver mined near Populonia and Vetulonia. Whether the Italians discovered ironworking on their own or learned it from the Euboeans is uncertain. Burials at Veii from 760 BCE show increased use of iron helmets, shields, swords, and chariots. What is certain is that contact with the Greeks could only accelerate the process.[32] By 700 BCE, other Greeks were following the wake of the *penteconters*. Hybrid Etruscan–Greek pottery was made in Campania, and noteworthy works in pottery such as the "Bearded Sphinx Painter" can be discerned in Tarquinia, Caere, and Vulci. By 600 BCE, Etruscan pottery was both more widespread and uniform. Copper and iron were mined by Etruscans and smelted locally as the industry entered its "takeoff" phase. After 650 BCE, the mines on Elba were worked systematically and the ore shipped to more central sites. The Etruscans soon developed the most advanced metalworking techniques in the central and western Mediterranean. Their economy began to specialize, with increasing regionalisation and competition between centers. Tripod and weapons makers concentrated first along the coast, at Tarquinia and Vetulonia, then at Caere and Vulci.[33]

Thus, while Carthage rose to ascendancy, a minor industrial revolution and the potential for trade was growing in Italy. Graeme Barker and Tom Rasmussen document both short and long-distance operations, clearly entrepreneurial in nature, operating within a sophisticated barter economy: "Etruscan maritime trade was in the hands of enterprising individuals and families, rather than being state-directed."[34] Grain consumed in the cities was grown nearby, for roads were poor and there were few large rivers. The growing Greek city–states were Etruria's prime overseas customers. Between 625 and 550 BCE, Hellenic pottery entered Tuscany from Corinth and the Aegean, which showed a robust Greek presence. After 550 BCE, the Etrurian market became increasingly penetrated by Athens. In spite of their newness to long-distance export, merchants in southern Etruscan cities were able to export pottery, bronzes, and amphorae to Spain, France, Corsica, Sardinia, Greece, North Africa, Egypt, and even into the Black Sea.[35]

Etruscan/Latin capitalism bore the marks of a much more cohesive home base. The sloping terrain allowed Italians better overland communication and political unity than their Greek counterparts. The rich volcanic plains of Latium and Campania beckoned as a prize, eagerly grabbed at by extended family groups moving in wholesale with iron weapons and tools. Although there was room for skilled independent enterprise, early business developments tended to be more family-oriented and cohesive. The later story of a small town on the Tiber River eventually running the world makes sense within this context. Indeed, it was two brothers, Romulus and Remus, legend says, who founded Rome. The close-knit family protecting its private claim mattered much more than it did among more diverse Greeks tribes clustered around their acropolis fortresses, only uniting in a crisis. The Greek *polis* was matched by the Latin *comitas,* "community." Roman civilization was thus shaped by geography, like its Greek counterpart, but much differently. The Latin family on the flat plains had not only to defend its precious farmland, but was forced to seek additional land for its surplus population through military expansion. The ideological contours of Roman history were set early: live by the sword or face quick extinction.[36]

Although the Latin tribes were slower to embrace entrepreneurial commerce than their Etruscan neighbors, Rome before 300 BCE was by no means an economic backwater. The city began as a trading center at the strategic junction of the Tiber and the Campania–Etruria roads. A rough equality prevailed—few were rich or poor in the early Latin subsistence economy. Artifacts from the founding eighth century BCE hinted at the business culture to come. The burials at Osteria dell'Osa and Castel di Decima show little class distinction. Only a few ornate spears and swords marked off distinctions in this warrior society. Roman life was even then based upon a powerful *gens* (extended family/clan) and an intricately connected clan or *gens* system.

> "The Romans were like brothers
> In the brave days of old"

sang the poet Macaulay in another age, and there was much truth behind the myth.

Rome's rise was slow but, oh, so steady (see Table 7.2). By 600 BCE, she was an Italian Sparta, armed to the teeth, and the largest fortified city in Latium. Romans borrowed much from the Etruscans and Hellenes in economics, institutions, rituals, and religion, yet still retaining much of their original. Etruscan, Tyrian, and Greek entrepreneurs visited the growing city, bringing the tools and vital farming necessities of the Iron Age. Tombs twenty miles from Rome show evidence of imported Tyrian goods, but seaborne trade up the silted Tiber was still not vital or important. Latins prior to 500 BCE had little to export, save wheat and other primary products from their rich volcanic farmlands. As the Greeks expanded into Gaul and Italy between 600 and 500 BCE, Etruscan cities such as Veii, Tarquinii, and Caere became middlemen between the agrarian interior and the foreign traders of the Tyrrhenian Sea, locus of Elba and Sardinia. Rome slowly attracted more trade though her craftsmen produced but a few gold and copper products to offer in return. Land-based Latin farmers had few means to sell their grain abroad, trading it instead to the local mountain tribes.[37]

In 509 BCE, the Roman landed oligarchy overthrew their monarchy and set up a republic. This form of government better reflected both the warlike and familial character of Roman society. Instead of a single tyrant, Rome was governed by a pair of elected magistrates, or *consuls*, often soldiers, able to veto one another's actions. In a crisis, a consul could assume the office of *dictator*, exercising unlimited power for six months. The Senate represented the powerful landed *patricians*; elected *tribunes* theoretically represented the *plebeian* orders of farmers, laborers, and artisans. A middle stratum or *equites* emerged among the Roman knights, those wealthy enough to own horses and fight on horseback. The Twelve Tables of 450 BCE enshrined the genius of the Roman Republic: a government similar to the Hellenic model, limited in scope, and noticeably unwilling and unable to intervene on behalf of those who might be injured by the market. Individual self-help was to be, nonetheless, mitigated by the all-important *patron* and *familia*.[38]

Roman business centered around the *familia*, or the patriarchal extended family. This included not only the nuclear family, but slaves and other subjects and dependants of the *paterfamilias*—the head of the family. The Roman *familia* was defined not just by "blood relationship" but, according to Professor A. Drummond, "the powers exercised for life by the family head over both the persons and property subject to him."[39] The less fortunate, unable to find protection from the state as in Greece and Persia, sought it via inclusion in the *familia*. The Twelve Tables helped entrench a patriarchal concept of family property and, by implication, family enterprise, in the Roman market economy. This led to a social situation very different from Athens or Phocaea.[40] The patricians of the early Republic, glorying in their oversight of a solid core of hard-working small farmers, saw little reason to cause them to reverse their longstanding prejudice against the market and dirty their hands with trade. On the other hand, Greek, Etruscan, and Oriental traders in Rome were neither excluded, regulated, nor taxed when they sold imported pottery and fabrics from Attica or worked as carpenters, smiths, tanners, dyers, and potters alongside their Roman

Table 7.2 Timeline Rome: Monarchy and Early Republic

Monarchy: 775–509 BCE
Formation of the Republic: 509–343 BCE
Conquest of Italy: 343–265 BCE
Punic Wars: 265–146 BCE

counterparts. Most Roman trade was still small scale. Around 450 BCE, imports and construction, moreover, were virtually halted through much of Italy by a trade depression.[41]

Roman society was thus strongly integrated and tightly knit almost from the beginning. Free markets and family patriarchs were fundamental to the rise of a distinctive Roman form of capitalism. The catalyst that would ignite the mixture would be a crucial "ism"—Roman militarism. During its first one hundred and fifty years, the Roman Republic remained a well-armed local power very much on the defensive, conservative to the core. Around 345 BCE, however, a new phase of intensive and almost constant fighting opened, which lasted for several centuries. Expansion by warfare stimulated both the demand and the market for the rise of a home-grown Roman business and managerial class from the ranks of the knights. Once thrown over to the offensive, Roman warfare was inspired as much by booty as by politics.[42] Each spring, the legions assembled to rout their jealous neighbors. By 350, southern Etruria was a Roman possession and dangerous Celtic invaders had been driven north to the Po. Rome strangled Etruscan commerce by deporting many inhabitants, expropriating farmland, bypassing cities with new roads[43] and planting coastal colonies such as Cosa, future emporium for the powerful Sestii family. This plantation effectively isolated the rich cities of Caere, Tarquinia, Vulci, and Populonia from their markets.

Rome's rise began with the smashing of the Etruscans. From the second century BCE onwards, the west coast of Etruria was transformed by the same villas-and-slaveholding-estate system that had developed in Latium.[44] The juggernaut was rolling. Rome's Latin rivals accepted her hegemony after the Latin War of 340–338 BCE. The peace settlement foreshadowed the later structure of the Late Republic and the Roman Empire. Some states were made Roman territory, others Roman protectorates, and others Roman allies. Citizenship and other rights were granted along with a share of future booty if they fought alongside Rome, who joined the military power of the states she dominated to her own. Italians, Iberians, Africans, Greeks, Macedonians, Anatolians, Syrians, Gauls, Britons, Germans, Illyrians, and others would eventually integrate into this expanding system, still a marvel of imperial expansion.[45]

Rome next vanquished the Samnites, sturdy mountaineers in the southern uplands. This moved them closer to the Greek colonies in southern Italy. Over 45,000 square miles of Italian territory and some three million people were now subject to Roman rule. The Republic could field 60,000 men, twice the size of Alexander the Great's army. Fifteen Roman and Latin colonies were planted between 334 and 263 BCE among the conquered peoples of the peninsula. Land was awarded to 70,000 landless veterans and their families, with much more to come.[46] The economics of plunder—so important in Rome's rise—were perfected in the context of a growing river of tribute extorted from confiscated farmland. The face of the Italian countryside was transformed by the economics of Mars. Faced with growing population, debt slavery, and social unrest, the subsistence economy of Latium was ready for transformation. With many Latin farmers sinking into serfdom, the wars of conquest provided a safety valve for the plebs. Many abandoned their dying farms to settle in a military colony or in Rome itself. The patrician landlords found another source of labor in the thousands of Samnite, Etruscan, and other slaves captured in war.

So it was that Rome became a society vitally dependent upon slaves well before 300 BCE. Family farms gave way to patrician villas operated by slaves. New waves of slaves were integrated into the household economy, being grafted into those family units propped up by the Twelve Tables and later Roman law. War both fed the demand for slaves, and provided slaves to fill the demand. The cycle was dynamic. The reduction of peasant debt and the rise of slave agriculture freed up a large part of the rural population for steady military service.[47] The baleful economics of the perpetual wartime state effected a continuous rotation of populations, with Roman plebeians colonizing Italian lands whose former tenants entered Latium as slaves. One result was that the Italian peninsula, as a whole, became more urban. This, according to Professor T. J. Cornell, was key to enlarging markets for Roman business, which began to thrive:

> The same land was worked by a smaller number of people; since they were slaves they could be worked harder and organized more effectively so as to produce a greater surplus. Increased productivity was stimulated by the development of an urban market in the growing and prosperous city of Rome.[48]

War capitalism was working. Rome's population doubled. It grew from 30,000 in 350 BCE to 60,000 in 300 BCE to a major city of almost 100,000 by 264 BCE. Essential water was supplied through vast new aqueduct systems and wheat entered in small boats via the Tiber. Seaborne trade and a naval establishment became part of Roman life. Specialization accompanied expansion. Exports of black-glaze pottery made in Roman workshops found its way across Italy and Gaul, northeast Spain, Corsica, Sicily, and Carthaginian Africa.[49] The first coins issued by the Republic were circulated in Campania around 326. They were stamped with images of Roman militarism: Mars, winged victory, horses, a laurel-crowned Apollo. Such coinage financed the Appian Way in 312–308 BCE and circulated ever more in the almost inevitable wars against the Greeks of southern Italy. The first coins in Rome itself were struck as early as 269 BCE to pay legionnaires and temple workers. Roman coinage made a political statement: essentially *"In Mars we trust."*

So it was that three centuries before the Caesars, Rome was in the same military ranking as the Hellenistic states of Seleucia and Egypt, and with mighty Carthage. All of these she would soon challenge and ultimately conquer.[50] Already bestriding Italy like a colossus, the stage was set for the next round of Rome's expansion.

WAR CAPITALISM: ROUND II—BUSINESS CULTURE CLASHES

Carthage and Rome were friendly at first. Rome, in the sixth century BCE, was a local peninsular power with little interest in trade. The historian Polybius preserved the Carthage–Rome Treaty of 509 BCE. It showed the managed, strategic nature of Punic trade. Roman traders could work in Carthage, Sardinia, and Sicily but in Africa only north of the Fair Promontory (likely Cape Bon in Tunisia). According to Polybius, the Carthaginians "did not wish them to become acquainted with the coast around Byzacium or the Lesser Syrtes, which they called Emporia because of the great fertility of that region."[51] The more *laissez-faire* Romans allowed Carthaginians to trade anywhere in Italy, so long as they built no forts in Latium, did not interfere with Latin cities or carry weapons on Latin territory. According to Polybius, the treaty showed that the Carthaginians "consider Sardinia and Africa as belonging absolutely to them," and Sicily was only partially under their control. The Romans, on the other hand, only made stipulations concerning Latium, for the rest of Italy was not yet in their hands.[52]

By 260 BCE, Rome was a major rival of Carthage. When the shrewd Greek general Pyrrhus left Sicily for home, he was supposed to have said, 'What a battlefield I am leaving for Rome and Carthage." Two models of economic enterprise, politics and religion, prepared to do battle in a war destined to be even more ferocious than either the Persian Wars or the deadly Greek civil wars of 150 years earlier. Carthage mobilized an extensive network of hierarchically managed organizations centrally directed from the capital itself. Her large enterprises remained in the hands of regal or hereditary princely families with strong mutual connections. Smaller enterprises gathered in guilds dedicated to patron deities. Farming, mining, munitions, shipbuilding, and shipping enterprises actively drew together palace and temple, and the city itself. The business culture of Carthage represented a trading and military strategy along the lines of the *Eclectic Paradigm*. African trade was managed from Libya; Atlantic trade from Spain and Morocco; Mediterranean trade from Sardinia, Sicily, or Carthage itself. The annual trading expeditions of the Silver Fleet, blessed by priests of Baal, still functioned as *de facto* naval campaigns.[53]

On the other side of the Straits of Messina, stood the new business managers of a young and confident citizen-republic running their firms with fierce independence. Many were entrepreneurs, and some were foreigners based in Italy. Some were even slaves for, in Rome, theoretically, a knight, a pauper, or a slave could become a manager. The Roman state was even less interventionist than the Greek *polis*. Private bankers, not temples, lent the money and bore the risks. The gods, borrowed from the Greeks, were fine symbols of patriotism and civic virtue, but not invited to bless or interfere with private markets and private lives. The Roman bent for practicality was in evidence in matters religious. The gods were there, but men must make

Table 7.3   The "Embedded Organization" Perspective of Oriental Enterprise

Variants:
  Mesopotamian: temple capitalism
  Phoenician/Carthaginian naval capitalism
  Egyptian/Minoan: palace capitalism
  Indian: caste-based capitalism
  Chinese: state and family capitalism
  Rome: Publican and family firms in Late Republic and Empire

Networked Relationships:
  Top-down management hierarchies directed from major urban centers
  Interdependence and interlocking of public and private sectors
  Little social mobility permitted

Symbiosis:
  Enterprises co-ordinated for goals defined by hierarchies
  Co-operative
  Royal, feudal and religious relationships cement business alliances
  Positive Sum (win-win): Trust and Reciprocity

Long-term strategic alliances: open, broad, contractual

their own lives. Romans effectively waived the *Eclectic Paradigm* and let the market remain the main arbiter of commerce—at least at this stage. Liquid cash, high interest rates, and trading deals were the only insurance against market failure. The contrasts between the two business models are shown in Table 7.3 and Table 7.4. Table 7.3 sketches the Oriental hierarchical model which Carthage embodied.

Table 7.4 illustrates the Classical entrepreneurial model, operating in its purest form in Greece and compromised yet recognizable in Rome:

Table 7.4   The Western "Discrete Organization" View

Variants:
  Hellenic "household" capitalism
  Roman family and "legionary" (war) capitalism
  Individualism and Independence Versus Networked Relationships:
  Free-standing Greek entrepreneurs
  Enterprise independent of temples and state but with state contracts in Athens and Rome

Competition:
  Business goals set by profit-seeking individuals
  Extensive slave and foreign labor but social mobility permitted
  Business methodology: "all against all" with relationships based heavily on impersonal contracts. More extended Romans *familia* eventually embrace *Eclectic Paradigm*
  Zero Sum (win-lose) with power negotiation

Short-term tactical alliances (limited, contractual, calculative):
  Greek trader's cash deals with banks, partners, and customers
  Roman partnership model: taxation and military contracts with Republic

After Rome interfered in the affairs of a Carthaginian colony on Sicily, she sent her armies to occupy the island. This began the first of the three Punic Wars in 264 BCE. These wars would be the turning point in Roman history, enormously impacting Roman power and Roman life. Rome's "war capitalism" would be tested to the hilt, would endure and then transform the city, bringing vast changes in Roman society. The wars would also provide an enormous market for Roman business as the war machine expanded far beyond its previous size. War, it is said, is the ultimate test of the state. Rome was on its way to world power.

In 264, the odds seemed to favor Carthage, with her vast wealth, professional mercenary armies, tight organization, and the world's leading navy.[54] In the first round, Carthage sent her fleet to cut off the legions in Sicily and land marines in their rear. The Romans quickly moved to play upon their strengths and remedy their weaknesses. One of Rome's greatest unseen advantages was the civic spirit of her soldiers and her entrepreneurial zeal.[55] For example, the Romans soon saw the need for a navy. When a Carthaginian warship was captured intact, Roman innovators set about turning out Roman copies, complete with on-the-spot improvements. The historian Polybius recorded how fast-moving contractors quickly produced one hundred and twenty state-of-the-art warships:

> It was, therefore, because they saw that the war was dragging on that they first applied themselves to building ships. . . . They faced great difficulties because their shipwrights were completely inexperienced . . . since these vessels had never before been employed in Italy.[56]

Polybius saw this as a testimony to the Roman martial spirit, for in this clash between the Elephant and the Whale the Romans originally possessed neither the resources nor the seamanship skills of their powerful enemy:

> But once they had conceived the idea, they embarked on it so boldly that without waiting to gain any experience in naval warfare they immediately engaged the Carthaginians, who had for generations enjoyed an unchallenged supremacy at sea.[57]

Rome, formidable on land, equipped her new warships so as to turn her soldiers into fighting marines. An iron bridge shaped like a crow's beak, called a *corvus*, was designed. It dropped onto Carthaginian decks, letting Roman centurions board the enemy ships and turn the war into a duel of floating armies, and in armies Rome was nearly invincible. By 241 BCE, the naval superiority of Carthage was forever shattered and the war ended with a victorious Roman Republic annexing Sardinia and Sicily.[58] The continuing technical innovations of the Late Iron Age and the headlong but shrewd spirit of patriotism had helped win round one.

With Sicily and Sardinia gone, Carthage turned ever more to Spain and Africa as a source of gold, copper, iron, and silver, as well as corn, oil, wine, salt, and fish. General Hamilcar Barca (237–229 BCE) ruled Iberia with the vice-regal powers typical of Carthage overseas. Loyal to Carthage, the Barcid family governed Spain as their personal fiefdom, a rich estate passed on to the brothers Hasdrubal and Hannibal in 221 BCE. Ruling from Novo Carthago (Cartagena), the Barcids continued the tradition of managed enterprise. Spain turned itself into a vast armory. Revenues from the Rio Tinto mines in the west to the newer mines of Baebelo in the east financed 90,000 infantry, 12,000 cavalry, and fifty warships. With these, Hannibal resumed the war. Many Iberians signed on to fight as mercenaries or personal allies of the Barcids.[59] In one of history's epic campaigns, Hannibal boldly marched his new army over the Alps and deep into Italy, smashing one legion after another, devastating Roman agriculture. Fearful country folk flocked to the protection of the cities. The invasion further concentrated wealth and power in large Italian villas and cities. Rome defeated Hannibal in the end by choking his supplies and brilliantly striking at his base in Africa. It was the Republic's finest hour. Rome took Spain as the spoils of the Second Punic War and ended Carthaginian great-power status at a stroke. One final pre-emptive war of choice was fought in 146 BCE, when Roman armies handily conquered Carthage and razed the city to the ground.[60]

Rome had conquered others. Could she overcome old structures and adapt for the future? The world watched.

THE BUSINESS REVOLUTION: AGE OF THE PUBLICAN

Rome emerged from the Punic Wars an amphibious power, triumphant in the Mediterranean and beginning to expand into the Aegean. Although the Roman economy remained overwhelmingly agrarian and slave-dependent, the centuries of constant and intense warfare had spawned and nourished a full-fledged and thriving Latin commercial establishment. As might be expected, the teeming wealth transformed the simple life on the villas. "Golden plenty from full horn is pouring forth her fruits upon Italy," sang the poet Horace. Pepper and spices from the exotic east entered the city while gourmets preferred peacock, parrot, and flamingo tongue. The sober Roman *paterfamilias* and his matron got a taste of the sweet life and liked it.

Literature of the time provides an interesting insight into how Italy was being remade. Roman business culture was mirrored in the comedies of Titus Maccius Plautus, born around 250 BCE. Plautus found little market for heavy political drama. Romans wanted comedies about everyday life and Plautus gave them "soap-opera" styled characters that satirized the new social norms. These are not unlike 1950s American situation comedies. The *paterfamilias* is feared but often ridiculed as naïve; more Ralph Kramden of *Honeymooner's* fame than J. R. Ewing. His strong but submissive wife often rescues him from himself. In other dramas, a rich playboy falls in love with a girl beneath his station only to find she is really a patrician. In another, a cunning slave tries to "freeload" or "scam" the more productive artisan. In the end, Roman economic values are upheld, not mocked, as everyone returns to their proper role by play's end.[61] In *The Pot of Gold*, a poor man refuses to marry his daughter to a rich lad. To do so would be hitching an ox and an ass. Both asses (the poor) and oxen (the rich) would never tolerate such an arrangement, for "an ass with ox ambitions" ran an unacceptable social risk.[62] Slaves in the comedies are harshly treated. The audience laughs, for slavery is a necessary, natural way of life in which people are seen as investments. Messenio in *The Twin Menaechmi* wins freedom only to live with his former master to find work. Family and slavery had to be upheld at all costs.[63] In *Curculio*, however, Plautus shows that business values are now very much taking over the Roman Way of Life:

> Husbands gambling their fortunes away? Try the Stock Exchange.
> You'll know it by the call-girls waiting outside. You can pick up any-
>   one you want to, at a price . . .
>
> In the lower Forum You'll find the respectable bourgeoisie
> taking their daily stroll. . . . Below the old shops are the moneylenders,
>
> The con-men behind the Temple of Castor, The Tuscan Quarter is
>   the red light district
> Where you can make a living, one way or the other.[64]

While Romans basked in their status as masters of the Western Mediterranean, their experienced battle-hardened legions kept marching—into Macedonia and Greece, then Anatolia, Syria, Mesopotamia, Palestine, Egypt, Gaul, Germany, and Britain. The "perpetual war economy" was a reality. The Republic's chief need was to arm, clothe, and feed its legions and fleets, pay its governors and maintain its roads and public works. This led to a problem. The overstretched Roman state lacked a bureaucracy to guarantee the necessary revenue. The best alternative seemed to contract these functions out to the private sector. The creation of a vast market steadily stretching around the Mediterranean and the profitable contracts of a garrison state permitted the growth of enterprises on a much larger scale than in Greece. Roman businessmen expanded the size of their partnerships. Chief among these were the *publicani,* or publican companies. These became crucial to the development of Roman commerce in the last two centuries of the Republic.[65] This innovation marked an important benchmark in the story of ancient business.

Most business writing in the 1970s and 1980s of our era maintained that terms such as "company" or "corporation" were inappropriate when speaking of ancient business organizations. In 2002, however, Professor Ulrike Malmendier of the University of California at Berkeley argued that Rome's *Societates publicanorum* represented *de facto* corporations. Major legal differences remained between a Roman *societas* and a modern corporation but from an economist's perspective, these new-style Roman corporations outlived their founders and became liable according to the *bona fide* principle. They remained stable, regardless of the departure of individual members. Members could represent and expand public business without incurring personal liability. Finance and management could be separate. Shareholders could buy and shell shares depending upon their confidence in the *publicani*. It is hard to ignore the evidence that these limited liability operations meant that the *societas republicanorum* was the true ancestor of the modern company.[66]

Roman writers documented the rise of the publicans. Roman contractors were older than the Twelve Tables. Even in the days of the kings, it is arguable that the palace delegated some tribute-collection to private individuals. Dionysius of Halicarnassus, in his *Antiquities of Rome* (6.17.2), recorded Consul Postumius Comimus in 493 BCE contracting for the construction of several temples. Over a century later, after the honking geese of Rome alerted the city to an attack from the Gauls, the Republic leased out their perpetual care and feeding to private contractors (Livy 5.47.4; Pliny, *Natural History* 10.26.51). The first documented record of a *societas publicanorum* appeared in Livy's history of the war with Hannibal. Here, in 216 BC/BCE, the Republican government leased the supply of the legions in Spain to three companies of nineteen people (*Ab urbe condita* 23.48.10–49.4). Livy's account points to a great deal of government contracting among the publicans.[67]

Livy gives the impression that government lease-holding was a well-established business. War was expensive and senators could ill afford much in the way of nonmilitary expenses. Nevertheless, the publicans still assembled at the government auctions "in large numbers" and this "encouraged the *censores* to act as they usually did and to sell the contracts as though the treasury were full." In return, none of the contractors "would ask for repayment before the end of the war".[68]

Malmendier described two basic types of publican firms. In the first group were the *opera publica et sarta tecta*, which dealt with legions and public works. In the second were the *opera publica facienda et sarta tecta tuenda locare*, which handled grazing, mining and fishing rights. The larger and better-organized group of *socii* (several great families in alliance) collected the direct and indirect tax revenues of the Republic.[69]

The wealth and power of the publicans continued to expand along with the Roman Republic. The publican operations were constantly reinforced and resupplied by a class of Roman citizens whose emerging power would provide the Late Republic with many of its business managers. Who would run these expanding companies? The plebs lacked the resources, and the patricians were legally barred from doing so . . . at least formally and directly. The famous *lex Claudia* or Claudian Law of 218 BCE had banned senators from lease holding and non-agrarian enterprises. Leadership fell, as previously mentioned, to the equites, the knightly class. These controlled enough wealth to allow them to own and equip a horse for battle and enough discretionary wealth to invest, control, and operate businesses. The Claudian Law foreshadowed the complete consolidation of the knights as a true business class in the Republic.

Although some such firms existed as far back as 500 BCE, this style of business organization came into its own during the Punic Wars. The manufacture and distribution of togas, shields, helmets, swords, and other weapons, plus the all-important provisioning for the far-flung Roman legions, was left in private hands. This made for enormous business opportunities. Publican companies bidding in the open market for military contracts grew enormously as Roman territory expanded. Publican firms also bid for the right to collect Roman taxes, the famous "publicans and sinners" of the Gospels. Professor E. Badian insists that the *publicani* were "an integral part of the *res publica* as far back as we can observe it or trace it."[70] Mars and Mammon; war and capitalism—here was a foreshadowing in many ways of our own "military–industrial complex." The Romans seemed to have squared the circle. But the Republic itself, and its very institutions, were beginning to buckle under the strains of a newly affluent society.

SOCIAL STRAINS OF THE LATE REPUBLIC

The solid, sober Roman society of "Horatius at the Gate," of fighting soldiers, dedicated civil servants and patriotic businessmen was undergoing stresses and dislocation as new wealth poured into the city. The result was typical—deep rifts in social and political life as inequities mounted. Note the outline in Table 7.5.

The Roman conquest of Italy and the Mediterranean world would have been impossible without the development of a superb infrastructure, the construction of roads, temples, and aqueducts under the financial machinations of the *publicani*. Next to agriculture, military contracts were the major business in Rome. Some of these were enormous. It cost one hundred *denarii* (US $5,000) to clothe one centurion, 420,000 *denarii*

Table 7.5   Rome: The Late Republic

The Gracchian Period: 146–121 BCE

Slave Wars and Social Wars: 121–79 BCE

Civil War: 79–31 BCE

to clothe a legion of 4,200. Four legions meant over 1.5 million *denarii,* perhaps $50–75 million. During the Punic Wars, the number of legions grew from four to twenty, returning afterwards to a permanent post-war force of eight or nine. This represented a standing army of 50,000 men at a cost of 3 million *denarii,* or $100–150 million just to clothe them. American society in the 1950s and 1960s seemed to be copying this strange parallel—a form of military Keynesianism where government and business were powerfully linked. In Rome, the sheer volume of these contracts, of which hundreds were let out on an annual basis, ensured market security for the *publicani.*[71]

Many of the managers setting up shop in the Aegean were southern Italians now incorporated into the Roman realm. When Roman legions temporarily destroyed both Corinth and Carthage in 146 BCE, Delos, once seat of the Delian League, the Athenian treasure house, became office site for *publicani* engaged in the twin cornucopias of tax collection and slave-trading. This massive banking and financial headquarters at Delos hired Greek agents and attracted merchants from Syria, Asia, Egypt, and Greece. Delian *publicani* and their agents flocked into Asia Minor in huge numbers. Valerius Maximus stated that Mithridates, king of Pontus, massacred 80,000 Roman citizens "scattered about the cities of Asia for the sake of business." Following this, Roman publicans "went native," representing themselves as Hellenic, rather than Roman, firms and traders. In "going international," they spoke, dressed, and acted as Greeks more than Romans.[72]

Roman Gaul and Spain attracted central and northern Italian publicans. According to the famous orator and writer, Tulius Marius Cicero, these agents dominated commerce in Gaul:

> Gaul is packed with traders, crammed with Roman citizens. No Gaul ever does business independently of a citizen of Rome; not a penny changes hands without the transaction being recorded in the books of Roman citizens. . . . Let one single account be produced in which there is a single hint indicating that money has been given to Fonteius; let them bring forward the evidence of one single trader, colonist, tax-farmer, agriculturist, or grazier out of all the inhabitants; and I will grant that the charge is a true one.[73]

The rise of the publicans was linked to the social and political crisis that would ultimately doom the Roman Republic and transform it from a citizen-state of independent freeholders to a Roman Empire adopting the imperial style and pretensions of the Oriental realms it had digested. Rome may have subjugated a world, but found herself a conquest, at least in terms of government. Debt-burdened farmers continued to be driven off their lands and displaced by vast numbers of slaves imported through Delos. Rural Italy, itself, was becoming depopulated of natives. The city of Rome generated a landless proletariat forced to fend for itself,[74] which would become a hotbed of the unrest William Shakespeare put down to writing in his classic drama *Julius Caesar*. Politics and economics were never more linked.

The ravages of almost indiscriminate booty, imported slaves, war, and debt accelerated the transformation of the Italian countryside from a landscape of independent farmers to one of manorial villas run for profit and manned by imported slaves. Although most of the Senate's patricians tolerated this, a few voices sought to denounce and reverse the more democratically-styled foundations of the old citizen-Republic. In 133 BCE, a century of political turmoil began when Senator Tiberius Gracchus attempted to limit the amount of land one individual could hold. Seeing the very foundation of the monied patrician state challenged, the conservative Senate murdered Tiberius. A decade later, his brother Gaius proposed even more sweeping reforms. The equestrian knights, source of the publican managers, were given formal legal status and political power. Gaius Gracchus hoped to use them as a counterweight to the landed patrician wealth he claimed was strangling the Republic. A reform measure of 133 BCE coincided with Roman expansion into Asia Minor, enormously increasing the power and scope of the publican companies. Vast markets opened as Gaius gave the right to tax the immense wealth of the new Roman province of Asia Minor to the *publicani* who stood ready to reap 45 million *denarii* ($US 22.5 billion) in contracts alone. Gaius, too, however, had made enemies and was murdered at the connivance of the Senate. Rome's own "revolution of rising expectations" fueled the discontent his reforms had unleashed. Politics in Rome became dangerously polarized. Interest-group manipulations replaced the citizen-politicians of the past. Instead of patriotic and self-sacrificing "noble Romans," one found peasantry, proletariat, slaves, freedmen, and other polities divided along class, ethnic, and occupational lines.[75]

The *publicani* reached their zenith at this time. Beginning as large partnerships working in the free-market milieu of Roman Italy, they evolved into modern-style conglomerates or non-specialised mega-firms. An outfitting enterprise might make swords or togas, but specialize in neither. Publican management and work forces were flexible and disposable. Associations of partners came together to carry out a contract and then disbanded—the viritual corporation form management model. Faced with fierce market competition, *publicani* simply could not afford much in the way of permanent staff, which remained lean and flexible, adapting to different markets. What the firms provided instead, according to Professor E. Badian, was "capital and top management, based on general business experience."[76] The small permanent staffs adapted more easily to different branches across an operation facing demands from both public and private contractors. Such companies, says Badian, "can only have functioned . . . by taking over existing substructures and superimposing managing staff."[77] In this heady business climate, organized staffs of skilled miners, tax professionals, arms makers, shipbuilders, bakers, butchers, and candlestick makers offered services to various publican managers as they shifted from contract to contract. The results of all this were that the Roman *publicani* of the second and first centuries BCE were transacting business on a much larger scale than had any private firm in the Near East or Mediterranean before them. Without the aid of bureaucracies or business schools, they were, nevertheless, foreshadowing the first multinational conglomerates and limited liability corporations. Some had a legal existence of their own, as long as the contract their *manceps*, or managers carried out remained binding. Were the *manceps* to die out, the *publicani* could choose another manager to complete the contract. A typical Roman contract included dates of completion and payment, a clause for inspection of work, and an indemnity in case of losses due to war, precursors of our own.[78]

Still, war is always uncertain, and the Roman war economy was an unsettling arena for large publican firms, let alone entrepreneurs. War, and now civil war, was frequent and ferocious. Contracts involved tens of thousands of *denarii*. Terentius Varro Gibba, for example, was a partner in a publican firm who was wiped out in trading and forced to turn to law and other professions to recoup his losses. Internalization within large firms became an essential safeguard to survive in such a high-risk environment. The trend is unmistakeable: Greece and early Rome bypassed the *Eclectic Paradigm* only to return to it as the market economy grew. *Publicani* were associations or partnerships, some combining the capital of a score of partners, or *socii*. The *socii*, operating beneath the *manceps*, represented the shareholders' directors of the firm. Real executive power lay in the hands of the *magistii*. One Sicilian firm was run by the knight Vettius and his *magistii*, Servilius and Antistius, both elected by the *socii*. Beneath this chief executive class lay the company's *decuria*, or divisions, usually headed by other knights. Familial and personal ties among the knights made even competing *publicani* part of a single network, not unlike European business today. A company based in Rome, Campania, or Tarentium operated through its *pro magistro* in Delos, Pergamum, Ephesus, Laodicea, Alexandria, Massilia, Gades, Athens, or Carthage. These officers were not contractors, but salaried branch managers in charge of keeping accounts, collecting taxes, and sending reports to the *magistii* in Rome. One such agent was Terentius Hispo, whose huge firm, with tens of thousands of employees, farmed taxes in Bithynia and Asia. *Pro Magistro* like Hispo also held military, postal, and banking contracts.[79]

The career of the *publicani* was reflected in the life of Cicero, an orator and statesman, but a highly successful businessman in his own right. Cicero held an interest in a publican firm, owned several villas, and defended many publican partners in court. Born into a knightly family near Cassino in 107 BCE, he grew up studying business law under the jurist Quintus Mucius Scaevola. Cicero witnessed the turbulent events rocking the Republic to its foundations. The Consul Gaius Marius saved Rome from Germanic invaders by politicizing the legions—accruing personal loyalty by poising as Rome's defender. Lucius Cornelius Sulla used this tactic to make himself dictator of Rome and slaughter his opponents in the knightly class. Sulla renounced his tyranny, but set the precedent whereby ambitious politicians, backed by newly-politicized legions and publican money, could aspire to permanent dictatorship.[80]

As an eloquent lawyer, administrator in Sicily, public works official, and city magistrate, Cicero defended the knights of the Equestrian Order against the patrician Senate. His goal appeared to be to forge a conservative coalition of the *optimates*, or defenders of property. Cicero saw the common enemy of knights and patricians in the *populares*, whom he saw as Marius and Sulla-like demagogues promising debt relief to the landless masses. This, Cicero felt, would only ruin property rights and undermine social stability. Cicero's writings and speeches are a key source on the *publicani* of the Late Republic, indicating from his allusions that many Roman knights trafficked in the rich trade of Asia. Cicero viewed them as the bulwark of the Republic. Caius Rabirius Postumus and Caraeus Plancius, both *manceps*, were friends of Cicero. Plancius, heir of a long line of knights, was promoter of many Roman firms. His father was the much respected *manceps* of the most influential firm in Asia Minor. Cicero had to defend Caraeus against charges of bribery and corruption. The Plancius firm, meanwhile, wielded considerable political influence on behalf of any office-seeker seeking an alliance.

CARTELS, ROMAN STYLE

The Plancii and other firms in the mid-first century BCE, reached their height when Cicero's ally Cnaeus Pompeius Strabo (Pompey) crushed their enemies, the rulers of Pergamum, and exterminated the pirates along the Eastern Mediterranean. Pompey went on to add both Syria and Judaea to the Roman domain with all the fateful consequences that would ensue for world religious history. The new Roman provincial officials promised to triple revenue for any *publicani* willing and able to invest in these new domains. Although the Consul of Rome awarded tax contracts directly to eastern municipalities, he usually turned to *publicani* such as the Plancii who, alone, had the organized ability and eager staff in place to raise and secure and count the revenue. Stiff competition persuaded the Plancii to join with other *publicani* in Bithynia, Asia, and Cilicia to form a tightly-knit tax cartel. Many reaped windfall fortunes until rampant speculation caused a financial crash in 61 BCE. The *socii* further internalized their operations between 61 and 59 BCE, openly and officially acknowledging the existence of a cartel arrangement. The Bithynian firm of Terentius Hispo formed an arrangement with an Ephesian firm to farm the grazing tax of both Asia and Bithynia. Taxes in Cilicia were probably farmed by another firm, also closely linked to Cicero. The agricultural tithes of Bithynia, meanwhile, were collected by a consortium of companies linked to Pompey himself.

At least in the realm of tax collection, Roman cartelization was grafted onto one of the most prosperous realms of the older Hellenistic economy. According to Tenney Frank:

> the companies had got together, formed a joint company for the exploitation of the chief Bithynian tax, and—as this clearly implies—done away with genuine competition. There had been organization of a sort before, as we have seen; and *publicani* had felt loyalty towards one another as members of the same order. There were at least some who thought that one *publicanus*, in a legal case, should never decode against another.[81]

Frank went on to reveal how this cartelization led to unprecedented internalization advantages for this sector of the Roman economy:

> But there had nevertheless been competition for the contracts; just as, even though manufacturers in a modern state will be closely linked in an association and will defend their joint interests, yet they will normally be in competition with one another where their products overlap. What we find by 51 BCE therefore, was radically different—as different as a cartel is from a manufacturers' organization or a Chamber of Commerce. And, as we saw, the cartel now, after a fashion, must have included the whole upper order of society and of the State, except for a few traditional aristocrats.[82]

Caius Rabirius Postumus, son of Caius Curius Postumus, represented the ideal Roman *manceps*, involved in business across many provinces of the Republic's expanding overseas domain. Caius Rabirius was a philanthropist, as well as a manager. Many of his friends and relatives served as his agents in return for commissions, contracts, and credit. Rabirius lent money to many governments, including Ptolemaic Egypt, an act that resulted in his arrest and trial for extortion and other crimes. Cicero defended his business ally and noted in his defence that Roman managers and partners owned their individual private fleets. Several vessels of Caius Rabirius sailed from Egypt to Puteoli, carrying huge cargoes of papyrus, linen, and glass. Cicero now battled as defender of the knightly order and its business interests. If Rabirius was punished under a dubious law, no *manceps* would be safe from guilt by accusation.[83]

Cicero's writings and court cases hint at the fact that evolving Roman capitalism was, informally at least, integrating knights and patricians. Senators, banned by law from owning ships or firms, nevertheless became silent partners in the major Roman enterprises. Trading for profit was deemed unsuitable for high Roman officials, but profit derived from agriculture or productive land was praiseworthy. Still, Senator L. A. Lepidus erected his own harbor facilities near the mouth of the Tiber to ship the produce of his own villa to Gaul. By Cicero's time, the laws banning patricians from commerce were obsolete as senators traded, owned vessels, and managed business informally through contracts and private arrangements with *socii*. Senators loaned money to publican allies and held company shares. Cicero prosecuted the notorious Vatinius for extorting shares from Julius Caesar and from Roman firms. Senators generally bought unregistered, non-voting shares in companies through which they provided an important part of the operating capital. Many of the senators, moreover, since the time of Sulla were former publican knights who privately continued their profitable associations. By the time Pompey and Julius Caesar clashed for supremacy, all Roman politicians had large investments and decisive influence within Roman firms.[84]

Cicero, himself, reflected the tension of patrician ideals and commercial realities. Denouncing the greed of Carthage and Corinth, he envisioned Rome, a land-based power, as less tainted than its commercial rivals. However, several generations of senators were already heavily invested in shipping and commerce. Cato the Elder, patron saint of modern American libertarians, quietly lent money to agents to form a large firm of fifty partners, owning about four dozen ships among them. Cato's share was held by his former slave, Quintio, to preserve the appearance of propriety. S. Neavius and C. Quinctius ran a small partnership operating a grazing farm in Gaul, with P. Quinctius inheriting his share on the death of his brother. *Publicani* were seen as partnerships, temporarily protected by Roman law, which represented a new sophistication in commercial organization. Managers and partners such as L. Aelius Lamia deployed ships and *negotia* (agents) across the Roman world while they themselves stayed at home, conducting business via a network of dependents, associates, and contacts.[85]

For outward appearance, both the *publicani* and the Roman laws permitting them embodied the remnants of the extended family traditionally protected in Roman society and law. This was, however, the family grown great and swollen to imperial dimensions. In the words of Professor John H. D'Arms:

> the fundamental Roman social unit, the *familia*, enlarged and extended to perform functions far more complex than fulfilment of domestic needs. One such interconnecting web of relationships, among men of varied levels of rank and status, of varying degrees of closeness, and involving various types of expectations and obligations, the Romans knew as *clientela*.[86]

The more patricians such as Cato, Lepidus, Granius, and Lamia took part in business, the more secretive they had to be. The former slaves running firms in Capua, Puteoli, Aquilea, Ostia, and other business centers were often visible agents for hidden patrician managers. Still, the family tie remained central to the operation of large publican operations. The Rupilius family of Praeneste and others were related to senators, and sometimes became senators themselves. The Aufidius family produced a governor of Asia, financiers, and senators. Some knights, such as S. Alfenus, were also bankers. All of these family-based firms kept their residence in Rome, sending members abroad as agents. Knights (and, behind the scenes, patricians) were investing everywhere: Sicily, Africa, Gaul, and, especially, Asia Minor. The *publicani* incorporated the personnel, labor, and capital of the older Oriental business cultures in which they were heavily invested. "Roman" vessels were often of Alexandrian, Tyrian, Sidonian, Cypriot, Anatolian, Rhodian, or Ionian make and manned by Greek or Canaanite crews. Cicero, himself, noted that the Roman *negotiatores* (agents) of Asia employed Greek ships.[87]

The merging of *manceps*, Consuls, and legions hastened the transformation of the Roman Republic into the Roman Empire. To borrow the words of Shakespeare in a commentary on the transformative affect of tightly sequestered money and power in his own country: "This England that was wont to conquer others/Hath made a shameful conquest of itself." The staunch conservative, Cicero, counselled the new gourmands relieving themselves at the vomitorium, "Eat to live, not live to eat." To no avail. The money spigots washed over Rome, flushing away the very values of patriotism and self-sacrifice that had extended the Roman state. Enormous disparities in wealth, class, and economic advantage were stretching the fissures beneath society into a chasm. The Slave Revolt under the famed Spartacus in 73 BCE rocked the seat of the Empire, the worst threat to the capital since Hannibal. The Slave Revolt and the Social War together nurtured the cry for security by both the classes and the masses. The ancient Roman penchant for stability in the state hastened the rise of the first Triumvirate of three Consuls: Marcus Licinius Crassus, Cnaeus Pompeius Strabo (Pompey), and Gaius Julius Caesar.

Crassus, having suppressed the slave revolt of Spartacus, sought to conquer Parthia. He was defeated and slain. Caesar was far more successful in Gaul, from where he mustered his loyal legions, fleet, and publican money to vanquish Pompey in Greece in 49 BCE. Having first championed and then betrayed the *populares*, Caesar's aspirations to a *permanent dictatorship* quickly roused the ire of the Senate, whose agent, M. Junius Brutus, assassinated him. The Ides of March were but prelude to another bitter round of civil war, this time decisive. Caesar's adopted grand-nephew, Octavian, rallied his uncle's supporters to rout first Brutus in 36 BCE and then the Egyptian forces of Mark Antony in 31 BCE.[88]

The Roman world was now under the sole rule of Octavian, who had succeeded where Sulla and Julius Caesar had failed. Octavian, naming himself Augustus Caesar, finally buried the old Republic. His reign inaugurated an era of power and prosperity known as the *Pax Romana*, which would last for two centuries. The Roman Peace would extend the integration of Roman business principles into an economy of near-global dimensions from remote Scotland to remoter Shandong. This time, the momentum of business life would bring even far-off China into its orbit, thanks to the Greek middlemen who had built the first trans-Asian economy. How this early harbinger of a form of globalization had emerged is the story of Chapter 8.

8 The Hellenistic Climax
India, China, Rome 331–100 BCE

The Roman Republic's headlong rush towards empire meant that the city on the Tiber—not just Julius Caesar—bestrode the world like a colossus. In 139 BCE, Attalus II, king of Pergamos, a wealthy kingdom in Asia Minor, willed his realm to the senate and people of Rome, a transaction little-remarked upon by some historians. Yet the implications for the business of empire and the empire's business were monumental.

Such was Rome's growing reputation for political stability, her commitment to *justicia*, law and order, that an Oriental monarch fearful of jealous neighbors pre-emptively surrendered his people's future to the rising power of the Roman Republic.

The action was catalytic, for it now immersed Rome quite legitimately into the life and politics of what historians call the Hellenistic world, as distinct from the Hellenic world of Homer and Solon. The incident points up the immersion of Roman *publicani* and trading firms into the commerce of the east. It also showed how fractious and divided the Greek world had become. Despite world-shaking victories at Marathon (490 BCE) and Salamis (480 BCE), the independent and feuding Greek states continued to live under the shadow of Persian imperialism. Persia's inflated and stagnating economy—groaning under the weight of revolts in Babylon and Egypt—yet stumbled along, its commitment to paternalism preserving a measure of peace and security for smaller ethnic groups. The Greek states remained independent enough to suffer the total disaster of the Peloponnesian War (431–404 BCE), the feud between Athens and Sparta that eventually undid both cities.

Greece was slowly tearing itself apart. Unity of a kind came to the Greek cities under the forceful lordship of Philip, King of Macedonia to the north (359–336 BCE). Philip did not live long to enjoy his victory. Instead, the Greco-Macedonian amalgam was inherited by his brilliant son, Alexander. It is with Alexander that the Hellenistic Age can be said to begin (336–323 BCE). Many historians have minimized its importance when measured by the glory of Classical Greece and the coming grandeur of Rome. Many, as well, have portrayed the Hellenistic period as an extension of Classical Greek civilisation to the Near East. More recent historians, such as Graham Shipley, believe that the Hellenisation of the Near East has been exaggerated: "Few, if any, scholars now suppose that the peoples of the Near East universally adopted Greek language and customs; there is no evidence that this happened."[1] Instead, the Hellenistic Age was one of "coexistence, interaction, and sometimes confrontation between newly settled Greeks and indigenous populations . . . and in a dynamic rather than static social context."[2] Although Greek culture was extended as far as Iran, Central Asia, and even parts of India, three millennia of Near Eastern business organization also survived.

This chapter tells that story. It shows that the Hellenistic Age was a decisive, rather than a merely transitional, epoch in economic history. Greatly stimulated by Alexander's conquests, Greek entrepreneurial ideas interacted ever more fully with the older hierarchical economies of the ancient Near East. The result was an explosion of creativity. "To the conquered land the Greeks brought, first of all, their dynamic approach, their spirit of enterprise and initiative; then, their commercial and banking methods and the plentiful circulation of money," summarized Jean-Phillipe Levy. "Considerable traffic in goods and even foodstuffs was to take place in these areas, often for the first time."[3] The Greek urban economy began to penetrate the Fertile Crescent, symbolized most of all by the impressive new metropolis-seaport at Egypt—Alexandria. The Greek stimulus to the ancient Near East led its merchants and traders to accomplish something not done before. Mainly through considerations of economic advantage, East and West began to come together. Freewheeling Greek ideas encountered hierarchical—yet workable—systems in far-off India and China. By the end of the Hellenistic Age, both the Indian subcontinent and China were slowly and tenuously integrating themselves into a hemispheric-wide trading system. This combine eventually stretched from Scotland to Shandong under the oversight of the Roman Empire, with effects that still shape our world today.

CREATING THE HELLENISTIC WORLD

Alexander, it was said, slept with a copy of Achilles' exploits under his pillow. In many ways, he seemed devoted to restoring the ancient ways venerated by Homer. He seemed committed to sweep away the tired and sordid politics of the *polis*. Alexander, however, was far more than a new Achilles. He entertained visions of a globe-girdling empire, at least as much of the world as was known at that time. In the 330s BCE, he led his Greek and Macedonian phalanxes across the Hellespont and into Asia Minor. In a series of lightning campaigns, he routed the lumbering Persian armies and began to create an empire that stretched from Greece to India. He, himself, crossed into India, seeking glory there, before his weary soldiers urged him to turn back.

Alexander returned to Babylon, his imagined seat of a new universal empire. He took the Near Eastern titles of Shah of Persia and King of Babylon. Alexander now ruled a superstate that had the potential to merge the Greek world with the cultures of Egypt, Babylonia, Syria, Phoenicia, Asia Minor, and Persia, and touched upon India. He had also inherited the colossal gold and silver reserves of Persia—180,000 talents in all, a booty that gave an economic impetus not surpassed until the Spanish looting of the Aztecs in the 1500s of our era. Cities populated with entrepreneurial Greeks and Macedonians were now seeding a world of prosperous merchant princes and guilds. But could it last? Were East and West able to really merge?

At first it seemed unlikely. Alexander's Empire did not survive the sudden death of its founder in 321 BCE. With no heir, the kingdom soon subdivided into four smaller realms, led by Alexander's generals. His general, Seleucus, carved out a Seleucid Empire from the Aramean, Babylonian, and Persian spheres. General Ptolemy ruled as Hellenistic Pharaoh of Egypt, Judea, and Phoenicia. Before his death, Alexander's release of the Persian royal reserves (equivalent to $US 500 billion in 1978 currency) gave an incalculable boost to the money supply. Alexander had given his world the first common currency. Even the Romans adopted silver currency in this period. Greek merchants, mints, and banks brought the innovative business tools of accounting and bookkeeping, cash payments, and interest to the Asian lands as Greek cities began to dot the landscape.[4] The Royal Bank of Egypt funded immense public works such as the Pharos (lighthouse) in Alexandria—soon one of the seven wonders of the world and symbolic of the commitment to seaborne trade. Once more, Egyptian wheat reached India down the Red Sea route. New canals and bridges rose in Mesopotamia and a technological renaissance was launched that came to typify the era.

Greek merchants, bankers, and colonists generally kept to themselves. The merger of Occident and Orient was limited, and yet strategic convergences were a hallmark. Notions of Periclean democracy, out of favor even in Athens, began to fade, as did the optimistic ideology of human progress. Instead, the Oriental concept of semi-divine kingship filtered into the Greek world to be eventually taken over by the Romans under Augustus Caesar. Greek science filtered into the Near East, together with the tradition of philosophical speculation. In a transformation not unlike that of 1970s America, individuals in the period abandoned the idea of a world-conquering civilizing mission—checked in part by the hubris embodied in Alexander, whom the gods took away while still in his thirties. Ideologies stressing narratives of personal salvation took hold. Stoics founded by Zeno (336–264 BCE) retained some of the civic virtues but sought redemption in self-discipline. Epicureans, named after their teacher (342–270 BCE), sought self-fulfilment but also the greatest good for the greatest number. Cynics sought harmony with nature and deflated the hypocrisy of others. Mystery religions flourished.

Yet, curiously and even ironically, scientific discovery and remarkable technological advances leavened an age that had turned inward and despaired of human progress. Hiero of Syracuse built a ship of 4,200 tons. Between 294 and 282, Chares of Lindos began construction on the one-hundred-and-ten-foot Colossus of Rhodes (the Statue of Liberty stands one hundred and fifty-two feet high). The high platform of the temple of Artemis at Ephesus measured four hundred and twenty-five feet long and two hundred and fifty-five feet wide.[5] The fusion of Greek and Babylonian sciences led to engineering approximations to square roots and the all-important *pi*. From Macedonia to India, the Hellenistic states pushed forward the legacy of the Late Iron Age with a flurry of intellectual and engineering break-throughs. Greek thinkers writing and speaking in the all-pervasive Greek language—the language of scholars and common men alike—devised iron plows, pulleys, waterwheels, screw propellers, a workable steam engine, a rudimentary slot machine, and the lateen sail. They computed the size of the earth and determined it was a sphere that orbited the sun. Farmers domesticated peaches, cherries, apricots, and began to rotate crops. All of this helped secure the food supply, the humble and prosaic foundation of any civilization.[6]

Of this Hellenistic economy, historians have elaborated a portrait of an exceedingly mobile, interconnected free market that fused Oriental and Mediterranean worlds. It looked very much like the indispensable forerun-ner for the Pax Romana. Greek entrepreneurialism fertilized older Near Eastern systems. The coinage of Alexander buttressed a mercantile system to which even Roman currency had adopted. Yet, in spite of this "global-ization in embryo," the critics of our own age, led by Sir Moses Finley and his disciples, are not convinced. Strategic investment, they argued, was unheard of, as was investment banking. "Where could one invest in 250 BCE?" they ask. Late Classical and Hellenistic thought, they said, enter-tained only the most rudimentary conception of markets. It did not encour-age the scientific study of productivity. Plato, Isocrates, Aratus, and even Aristotle—or so they claimed—derived honest profit only from farming or natural resources, not from investing money to create more money.[7]

"Hellenic individual private enterprise," wrote German scholar Fritz Heichelheim" . . . became generally embedded into the greatest planned organism of the Ancient world, a contradiction indeed."[8]

The same scholarly debates and issues found in Archaic and Classical Hellenic economic history reappear in the history of the Hellenistic world. Before the 1970s, the "modernizers," such as Heichelheim and Mikhail Rostovtzeff, used industrial era and class-war models to describe supposed economic revolutions.

What these writers would have noted was how much the older models survived. How many Greeks were there in the Egypt of the Ptolemies or in the Syrian–Babylonian–Persian realm of the Seleucids?

Yet when one looks at this Hellenistic world, one is struck by a wide-spread diversity that challenges Finley's assertion considerably. One need look no further than Egypt. The strategic investment in Alexandria and the access it provided to Nile Valley and Egyptian Red Sea ports made possible voyages to and from Arabia, East Africa, and the Indian Ocean, which seriously advances the thesis of an early form of globalization.

PTOLEMAIC "SOCIALISM" MEETS INDIAN CAPITALISM

Despite the Greek cultural conquest, Egypt remained a heavily regimented palace economy. Free trade was rare in an economy that discouraged imports and measured economic growth in terms of royal revenues. Egyptian peasants could drink only Egyptian beer and cook only with Egyptian oil. As in Russia under the Czars and Joseph Stalin, home-grown grain was sold abroad by royal agents and the earnings confiscated by the state, leaving peasant farmers a bare subsistence. Grain, papyrus, and textiles operated as crown monopolies. Other state monopolies imported timber from Anatolia and Lebanon, pitch from Pergamum, copper from the mines of Cyprus, tin from Britain via Carthage, and iron from Anatolia and Etruria. Egypt rejected the Mediterranean's drachma standard in favor of its own currency.[9]

Ptolemaic Egypt constituted "an ancient planned economy . . . no more efficient than its modern counterpart."[10] Ptolemaic policies crushed commerce with oppressive taxation: 50% on olive oil; 25% on bakeries; 16.7% on estates; 24% interest rates on loans; and other duties on herds, slaves, vineyards, sacrifices, business deals, and inheritances. Bureaucrats dictated what was to be grown and where. They extorted funds and permitted wheat to rot. The longsuffering peasants of Egypt sabotaged crops, dikes, and canals in retaliation. This Hellenistic command economy, very much in the Egyptian tradition, resembled modern socialism only superficially. It was designed to extort royal revenue and export grain and papyrus in return for iron, tin, copper, horses, and elephants; and was devoid of any ideology of material progress, equality, and raising the poor man's living standards.[11]

A manual for junior bureaucrats ordered them to inspect canals, sow on schedule, register cattle, supervise grain shipments for Alexandria, keep the largest number of weaving looms in operation, audit all revenues on a village-by-village basis, scrutinise local olive-oil factories, monitor prices, and supervise planting of trees.[12] A directive from 265 BCE shows grain shipped to Alexandria on royal barges: "Give orders for the measurement . . . on the royal barge . . . of the grain . . . and let Killes or the ship-master write you a receipt and seal a sample, and you bring them to me."[13] Royal clerks under Ptolemy II in 259 BCE were to "have authority over all the oil-makers in the district and over the factories and the plant" and were to "seal up the implements during the time when there is no work."[14]

Yet, in spite of this autarchic, regimented tradition, Ptolemaic Egypt served as a key link in the creation of history's first hemispheric economy (see Table 8.1). In spite of the top-heavy orientation of the rulers, much of

Table 8.1   Hellenistic Kingdoms and Asian Connections: 250–31BC/BCE

250–200: Egypt affected by hyper-inflation.	250–200: Parthian revolt in Eastern Iran; economic decline with brief revival under Antiochus III after 223–187. Shihuangdi unifies China: 221.
200–150: Socotra (a set of islands in the Indian Ocean off the coast of the Horn of Africa) entrepot for India and Egypt; Commerce between Iran and NW India extensive.	200–150: Antiochus IV "Epiphanes" fails to Hellenize Judea (175–164); Judeo-Parthian alliance destroys Seleucid power in Near East. Parthia supplants Greeks in Mesopotamia. Zhang Qian of Han Dynasty contacts Parthia on Silk Road (105–115).
150–100: Eudoxus leads Ptolemaic expeditions to India; Indus, Near East merchants trade at Socotra.	150–100: Western Han trade with Near East via Parthian middlemen. Rome supplants Carthage and Corinth and becomes an Asian power. Sima Qian, Han historian foreshadows Adam Smith.
100–31: Ptolemaic officers in charge of Indian Ocean trade until Roman conquest.	100–31: Roman conquest of Syria/Palestine; Han writings under Emperor Wu (141–87) describe Western contact.

the infrastructure and most of the provincial officials and city mayors were Greek. A strategic and tactical flexibility and diversity counterbalanced the old land of the Pharaohs. One-fifth of Alexandria's population may have been of Greek descent. Greek "connectors and fixers" were everywhere, adept at mitigating the sometimes heavy hand of the hierarchy. Egypt was well on its way to becoming the granary of the Roman Empire and a pivotal link between East, West and Africa.

Advances in navigation aided the Greek mariners of Ptolemaic Egypt to continue the tradition of aggressive market-seeking behavior. Sailing down the shores of the Red Sea into the Indian Ocean, they were following in the wake of Hammurabi's flotillas centuries before. The markets of the Indian subcontinent would constitute the first link in an evolving hemisphere-wide economy that Rome would inherit and exploit. A monarch of India would eventually send embassies to Augustus Caesar. The foundations for this complex mega-market were the Greek mercantile incursion into Egypt and the unification of India and the revival of Indian capitalism.

The history of the Indian subcontinent through most of the second millennium BCE and much of the first remains a blank. The Indus Civilization pivoting around the cities of Mohenjo-daro and Harappa gave way to the Vedic, as mentioned in Chapter 3. A Dark Age period ensued, illuminated by only a few religious texts illuminated by scattered artifacts. Even before the Harappan cities vanished, traces of the Sanskrit-speaking Aryan tribes appeared in the Indian countryside. Although a massive invasion cannot be ruled out, the Aryan newcomers seem to have gradually fused with the Harappans. Thus, continuities existed between some elements of the business culture of the Indus Valley and that of the Vedic Period. Even before the first Aryans entered India, a mixed economy and the outlines of the caste system already lay in evidence. Priests dedicated to Shiva pursued ritual purity before 2000 BCE. Eventually, the Aryan tide overran the Punjab and the decaying Harappan cities vanished. In their place arose a warrior society wielding iron swords and spears and manoeuvring fast two-wheeled chariots to totally dominate the remnants of the Harappan population.[15] Historians date the period from 1500–500 BCE as the time of the Aryan Ascendancy.

THE FOUNDATIONS OF INDIA

Unlike the practical, ancestor-oriented civilization of China, the newly syncretistic culture of India preferred the abstract over the concrete. Not unlike the Egyptians, Aryan culture preoccupied itself with the afterlife and a cyclical view of history as embedded in their great literary epics, the *Vedas*. Private enterprise, however, held a much more important role in this society as it moved in to clear the Valley of the Ganges and its often stubborn jungle terrain. A culture-specific Indian model of management developed. Although undated and religious in nature, the Vedic texts provide hints as to how this model must have operated.[16]

Historians date the composition of *The Rigveda* to around 1100 BCE, but its thousand hymns may have been chanted centuries before, back in the Iranian and Indo-European origins of the Aryans. Much of the subject matter glorifies battle. The Aryans, led by their warrior god, Indra; their fire god Agni; and their lawgiver, Varuna, subdued the forts of the dark-skinned ones they called Dasa. The cities latter were torn down and the inhabitants scattered abroad, mainly to the Dravidian regions south in the subcontinent.[17] Plunder was the universal law, the spoils of which were the gifts of Indra: "Bring us the wealth that men require, a manly master of a house, free-handed with the liberal meed."[18] Even their philosophical analogies were military: "Know the Self to be sitting in the chariot, the body to be the chariot, the intellect the charioteer, and the mind the reins."

Aryans also fought Aryans for the richer land of the Punjab. The final book of the epic shows Aryans settling down in the Indus and becoming Indians and farmers.[19] Rivers became sacred. Irrigation began: "They made fair fertile fields, they brought the rivers. Plants spread over the desert, waters filled the hollows."[20] The Iron Age came to India around the same time that it spread through the Aegean and Near East. The use of iron axes enabled Indians to clear the thick tiger-infested rain forests along the Ganges, allowing that sacred river to become the new axis of Indian culture and power. This was in the first millennium BCE. "The deities approached," says *The Rigveda*, "they carried axes; splitting the wood they came with their servants."[21]

Facing enemies human and natural a settled caste system began to crystallize. *The Rigveda* concludes with a speculative, philosophical chapter in which heaven and earth are created from the god Purusha. The priestly Brahman caste comes from his mouth, Kshatriya warriors and kings from his arms, and the toiling Shudras from his feet.[22] The thighs are represented by the Vaishya caste. These were the merchants, artisans, and landowners. As for the workers, only cartmakers appear in the early parts of *The Rigveda*, but gradually carpenters, potters, and smiths appear. In India—unlike the Near Eastern cultures—ancient warriors, kings, and priests were banned from commerce unless needed for survival. Trade, manufacturing, and physical labor were ritually unclean and relegated to the Vaishyas and Shudras. At the bottom were the "outcasts" who either entered the system late or lost their caste status through impurity. These performed such ritually polluting jobs as slaughtering animals and dressing skins. Nevertheless, creativity could not be stifled. The quality Painted Grey Ware—with its circles, spirals, and swastikas—of the early first millennium were probably made by Dravidian Shudras.[23]

Thus, the Indian Market Revolution of the late first millennium would radically differ from the Greek. The caste system effectively proscribed poorer Indians from becoming entrepreneurs. No such distinctions existed in the lands between Assyria and Anatolia or among priests, princes, or merchants. In Tyre, naval warriors became royal merchants. In India, however, commerce and industry was encouraged but strictly delegated to certain castes. Only a hereditary Vaishya could become a merchant. Unless they abandoned Brahmanism/Hinduism and became Buddhists, most Indians could not become Pasions or Phormios.[24] Technical and mercantile skills were generally left to the former Indus people and their descendants, the Dravidians. The Aryans dominated the priesthood and the political/military castes. The Vaishyas and Shudras became the producers. This rather stultifying social system (at least to Western readers), nevertheless, possessed the advantage of stability. Nor did it prove wholly immune to stimulus from outside. The Persian emperor Darius I's conquest of the Indus valley around 513 BCE turned out to be a "fertilizing event introducing new ideas, techniques, and materials." It helped draw India into "the mainstream of sophisticated urban, commercial and political life in the ancient world."[25] What some have called the "Ganges Civilization" adapted its own silver coinage and the Aramaic script and, even more important, learned from the Persians the administrative technique of managing a wide empire.

A UNITED INDIA: THE HELLENISTIC HEMISPHERE

Once Darius had resumed India's contact with the Near East, the benefits became immediately obvious. India became, along with Babylon, the richest source of revenue in the Persian Empire. The medieval Arab word *quttan* gave us the English word *cotton*. The growing of cotton appears earlier on the subcontinent than elsewhere. The shawls of Kashmir and the rugs of India are justly famous, even today. Bleaching, dyeing, tanning, glass-blowing—these arcane arts fascinated Alexander, whose temporary conquest of north-western India permitted the subcontinent to generate its own city named "Alexander." Alexander's Greek incursion helped to provoke the creation of a united India under Chandragupta Maurya.[26]

Here begins a significant epoch in India's history. Originally the ruler of a small state in the Ganges Valley, Chandragupta marched to defeat Alexander's general, Seleucus, in 304 BCE. From his capital Pataliputra, the zealous young ruler applied the lessons of Persian rule with stunning effectiveness—dividing the area into provinces, governors from his own family, and all reported upon by government agents, "the king's eyes and ears." An able bureaucracy kept tabs on taxation and the valuable state mines, granaries, shipyards, and spinning and weaving factories. Chandragupta led his Mauryan Empire (304–180 BCE), stretching from the Punjab to Bengal, into the Hellenistic world of trade and commerce.[27]

Among Chandragupta's advisors was a writer named Kautilya. Kautilya's manual, the *Arthashastra*, contained advice for Indian statecraft but also touched upon economics. The *Arthashastra* was partly a reflection of India's commitment to a mixed economy. It instructed the rajah, or king, to "help his subjects to acquire wealth and do good to them."[28] Espionage was an important tool to this end. Spies could pose as traders, or, more exactly, traders could be employed as spies: "A trader–spy is a merchant in distress but generally trustworthy. This spy should carry on espionage, in addition to his profession."[29] Government was to assume an important role in managing selected public enterprises, as well as helping to stimulate private enterprises:

> He should facilitate mining operations. He should encourage manufacturers. He should help exploitation of forest wealth. He should provide amenities for cattle breeding and commerce. He should construct highways both on land and on water. He should plan markets. He should build dikes [and] . . . should assist with resources and communications those who build reservoirs or construct works of communal comfort and public parks.[30]

Certain enterprises were to be reserved for state ownership: "The ruler should have suzerainty over all fishing, transport and grain trade, reservoirs and bridges."[31] Although much of this sounds like an ancient Indian version of John Maynard Keynes' calls for public oversight, another passage resonates with the supply-side economic thinking that became popular in America in the 1970s and 1980s. The *rajah* must tax the people enough to bring in adequate revenue, yes, but if he taxes the people too much, he will ruin that revenue stream and will deserve to be punished: "He who reduces the revenue consumes state wealth. . . . The officer who doubles the revenue consumes the vitality of the nation. Such an officer should be suitably punished."[32]

Specific duties were laid out, in Chapter 31, for the Director of Trade. He was to estimate both the demand for, as well as the prices of, goods. He must also centralize sources of supply. Unlike the kings of the Near East, the rajahs were to encourage imports, even granting tax exemptions to those "dealing in foreign goods . . . to aid them in making profits."[33] The *Arthashastra* mentioned "corporations and partnerships of local origin." All other foreigners were exempted from lawsuits. What is noticeable is the Mauryan Empire's keen regard for market dynamics, even as it fostered state enterprise. The Director of Trade was instructed to estimate the value of local goods that could be bartered for foreign goods, and then to "estimate the margin of profit" with which to pay foreign taxes and the working expenses for the merchant.[34] If no profit could be made, the director had to find local produce to exchange for the foreign goods. The *Arthashastra* also discussed risk factors, at least as far as minimizing losses. The director "may so arrange as to send one quarter of the valuable merchandise by safe routes to different land-markets," sell merchandise en route to cover costs, or "divert his merchandise to other markets through waterways."[35] Much of the later chapters was devoted to what is now called geo-economics:

"A state should always observe such a policy as will help it strengthen its defensive fortifications and life-lines of communications, build plantations, construct villages, and exploit the mineral and forest wealth of the country, while at the same time preventing fulfilment of similar programmes in the rival state. Whoever estimates that the rate of growth of the state's potential is higher than that of the enemy can afford to ignore such an enemy."[36]

Kautilya shrewdly observed that economic strength is as important as military power, and deeply intertwined with it, a notion axiomatic among Hellenistic princes, both embraced and acted upon:

If a state is weak in treasury or in striking power, attention should be directed to strengthen both through stabilisation of authority. Irrigational projects are a source of agricultural prosperity. Good highways should be constructed to facilitate movements of armed might and merchandise. Mines should be developed, as they supply ammunition. Forests should be conserved, as they supply material for defence, communication and vehicles. Pasture lands are the source of cattle wealth.

Thus, anticipating Machiavelli, Kautilya advises that a state should build up its striking power through development of the exchequer, the army and wise counsellors. Until that time. it is wise to conduct itself as a weak power towards its neighbors. It must seek to evade conflict or the envy of hostile or allied states. If the state is deficient in resources, it should acquire them from related or allied states. "It should attract to itself capable men from corporations, from wild and ferocious tribes, and foreigners, and organise espionage that will damage hostile powers."[37]

The Mauryan Empire was strikingly successful. It unified all but the southern tip of India by 273 BCE. Sri Lankan records show the king of the island sending three kinds of beautiful gems and eight kinds of pearl to the Indian emperor, Asoka. This item shows how rich the subcontinent is and was in precious gems and why mining was so important. Even in our day, Sri Lanka produced the world's largest blue sapphires and star rubies, now in the Smithsonian.[38] Chandragupta's grandson Asoka took over at first as a fierce warrior but soon converted to Buddhism. Although Buddhism condemned craving possessions and acquisitiveness, it also permitted any Buddhist to become a trader. Under Asoka, Buddhist monks voyaged east, west, and south spreading the knowledge of trade routes and merchandise along with the Buddhist creed. The consolidation of the vast subcontinent had opened up new opportunities for the Greek merchant shippers and traders back in Alexandria. Alexandria began to import India's specialized products overland via Arab middlemen or through the Red Sea. Ptolemaic royal merchants moved into cross-border enterprise, monopolizing the trade in Indian, Arabian, and African goods that entered Alexandria, and even many that reached the Levant. The exotic raw materials of India were processed in state workshops.[39]

Later, Hindu and Buddhist literature described the trade routes of classical India. The *Milinda Prasna*, a Buddhist work, described the voyage of a private merchant who paid his port dues in India and then sailed on to China and Southeast Asia. Indian business soon developed Pacific ties. The *Milinda Prasna* also referenced the fast-developing ports that became new markets for Indian traders. "Antakht" represented Antioch, "Roma" was Rome and "Yavanapura," Alexandria. The epic also describes the early growth of Indian exports to Sumatra and Java and through the Red Sea to the territory of the nascent Roman Empire.[40]

The Jain epic *Vasudevahinidi* mentions how a merchant named Charudatta was born into a rich trading family. Indian businesses were family concerns inherited from one Vaisha to another. Charudatta, however, fell into the wrong company and lost all his wealth. To recover it, he set forth on an Indian Ocean voyage. His uncle bought cotton for him, which Charudatta took to the east coast port of Orissa. There, Charudatta bought more cotton and journeyed to Tamralipti in Bengal. Trading in India was a very high-risk business, as was evidenced when Charudatta suffered loss of his goods both by fire and theft. In this picaresque tale, friendship and trust helped reduce risks. Surendratta, a family friend, happened to own a vessel. Thus, Charudatta's voyages eventually turned him into a Pacific-bound trader. He went first to Cambodia and Java, then sailed back west to

Alexandria. The profits were enormous, but once again so were the risks. On his return, Charudatta's ship was wrecked off the west coast of India and he floated ashore, where he was helped by another friend, Rudradatta. He tenaciously continued on to the mouth of the Indus and beyond to Central Asia, trading cloth.[41]

The poetic work *Brihadkatha Sloka-Samgraha* adds more to the story of Charudatta and his tale of incipient globalization. In this account, he is known as Sanudasa. His father was said to hail from the Khmer (Cambodian) kingdom of Champa. After his father's death, Charudatta squandered the family fortune. Unwilling to return home impoverished, the prodigal went on a trading venture to Tamralipti in southern India, where his caravan was dispersed. He then headed for Suvarnadvipa, in Southeast Asia, in search of gold. Charudatta/Sanudasa eventually headed a merchant guild that traded from Bengal to China, and thence out to Malaysia, Cambodia, and Central Asia. Sanudasa was also said to have made voyages to Tanzania and the Bantu regions of South Africa (Azania). The Indian Ocean had been a connector for these economies and cultures for quite some time. The tale mentions Charudatta/Sanudasa trading into the Hellenistic heartland of Yona (Greece) and Paramayona (Asia Minor). It also details a voyage starting in Bengal and proceeding via Malaysia and Cambodia. Another voyage crossed Central Asia through the Vijaya (Jaxartes) and Ishuvega (Oxus). Here Charudatta encountered the Hunas, or Huns. Sri Lanka, Java, and Alexandria also figured.[42] These accounts convey a sense of the reach and clout of Indian-based trading ventures, which would extend the Hellenistic economy into regions few Romans would ever see but to which they were tied by trade and commerce.

Both Hindus and Buddhists operated long-distance trading ventures. Purna Avadana led a merchant guild that financed seven ocean voyages. Avadana then converted to Buddhism and went as far as Burma. Buddhist literature of the late first century BCE describes the risks of long ocean voyages in flimsy Indian vessels. The threats to commerce in the monsoon–tsunami regions of the Indian Ocean were high indeed, and trade guilds were seen as a means of sharing the potential losses of shipwreck and attack.[43]

As in the days of the British *raj*, India's strategic location between Europe and the Near East to her west and China in the Far East would benefit her commercial life tremendously. A second advantage was to accrue in the form of the subcontinent's long-term cultural stability. Brahmanism evolved into Hinduism by embracing the popular polytheism of the Shudras. Buddhism found a way to accommodate itself to an overwhelmingly Hindu culture. Eastern religions, by and large, are very inclusive. The same deity a Hindu might worship as a manifestation of the Brahman might be worshipped as a *bodhisattva* or redeemer in popular Buddhism. Sri Lankan folktales include Vishnu as pat of its pantheon, even though the island is overwhelmingly Buddhist. In India, when the Mauryan Empire finally fragmented, the various *rajahs* or lesser rulers that took its place continued to trade and interact with each other.

CORNUCOPIA INDIA

When northern India fell to invading Scythians, the kingdoms of south-ern India remained independent and soon became the great middlemen of Asia. In the 300's AD/CE, the rajah Samudragupta once again united India. Overseas commerce thrived in this golden age of Classical India. This time not only trade but, eventually, Indian settlement spread to the spice-rich archipelago known in the sacred writings of the *Puranas* as Dvipantara. Today it is called Indonesia.[44] The world was much "flatter" in those quiet South Asian centuries than most Westerners have remotely imagined, as the enduring cultural imprints show. For example, the title "Serendip" (from which we get "serendipity") is the Arab name for Sri Lanka, a word that still endures on that small but strategic island. In Sumatra, "ship cloth" fea-turing fabulous sailing vessels with multiple decks, birds, and animals—an obvious motif for a people connected by sea to the wider world—became symbolic of passing from one spiritual state to the next.[45]

Political unity under the Guptas would later help India assume leader-ship of the hemispheric economy in the fourth and fifth centuries of our era. Pataliputra, along the eastern Ganges, appeared in the writings of the time as a thriving center of horses, elephants, and a wide array of goods—tea, cinnamon, ivory, cloth, silks, peppers, spices, and pharmaceuticals such as opium. A strong banking system flourished, which exercised powerful political influence. Leaders of the financial guild often accompanied the king. Caravan leaders also became influential Vaishyas. Indian records mention Samudradatta, the son of caravan leader Dhanadatta. Indian busi-nesses were largely hereditary, which allowed considerable stability from generation to generation.[46]

India remained a mixed economy down through the Middle Ages. A text dated to 592 AD/CE reveals Vaishyas striving to obtain royal recognition of their rights. Trade practices were to be clarified. There were things the rajah could not do. He could not seize property from a living heir. He could not trump up charges against a Vaishya, his business, or his wife. A Vaishya could not be tried in absentia or charged of a crime without ample evidence.[47] The government, moreover, could not seize his cattle or his carts or his grain. In contrast to China's absolute state, the developing Indian model of business enterprise contained built-in safeguards for property rights and private busi-ness.[48] In other words, forms of free enterprise have had a long tradition on the subcontinent, centuries before the European reconnaissance.

So, althoughe it could be said that the humming ivory workers, bleach-ers, metal-workers, and soap-makers of India had joined the Hellenistic economy late in the second century BCE, it could be argued as easily that Hellenistic world benefited immensely from contact with the Indian sub-continent. Give and take among the nations was more extensive than some today might surmise. The Ptolemies, for example, took advantage of the accumulated maritime experience of the Greek navigators. The energetic

Greeks kept sailing the Eastern Mediterranean even after the decline of Tyre and Sidon and the Roman destruction of Carthage. Some began to sail down the Red Sea to Sheba (Ethiopia and Yemen) and Arabia. The Greeks eagerly sought out the "ivory, apes and peacocks" of the fabled King Solomon's legend, waiting beyond the Red Sea and the vast ocean beyond. Arabs, Persians, and Indians jealously guarded this market knowledge until the year 120 BCE. Then an Indian sailor divulged to the Greek explorer Eudoxus the secret of the great monsoons. The quickest way to and from India was not along the Arabian or Persian shores but across the open sea far to the south. Soon, other Hellenistic mariners were leaving the mouth of the Red Sea to meet the May–September southwest monsoon that brought them to the shores of India, returning with the northeast monsoon that blew in the opposite direction after November. The northeast monsoon also brought sturdy Indian vessels to Egypt. Hellenistic traders set up shop in India, Indian shippers and agents in Alexandria. A new trading regime was born!

Just at this time, the Brahmans of India, temporarily eclipsed by the rise of Buddhism, began to come back into favor. This is reflected in the famous *Laws of Manu*, a manual for Brahmans from which the swirling dynamics of the trade explosion can be deduced. The *Laws of Manu* (c. 100 BCE) set forth the duties of a Vaishya, one of the most important of which was a warning to the sovereign never to tax a Brahaman. After partaking of the sacraments and marriage, a Vaishya must raise cattle or risk committing grave sacrilege. Learning the ways of business became a divine obligation for a Vaishya, who needed to "know the respective value of gems, of pearls, of coral, of metals, of cloth made of thread, of perfumes, and of condiments."[49]

Vaishya had to know how to sow seeds and discern good and bad customers, land and weights. Obtaining market knowledge of the quality of commodities, the trading advantages and disadvantages of different countries and the estimated profit (an early intimation of the awareness of risk!) also qualified as sacred duties.[50] The *Laws of Manu* also mandated the understanding of fair market value and cross-cultural management: "He must be acquainted with the proper wages of servants, with the various languages of men, with the manner of keeping goods, and the rules of purchase and sale."[51]

Moneymaking was encouraged, but only so long as it did not violate Brahmanist teachings and social obligations. A Vaishya had to "exert himself to the utmost in order to increase his property in a righteous manner" and was admonished to zealously feed humans and animals alike.[52]

Brahmanist business codes were a sign of the times—commerce was becoming ever more important and profitable in South Asia. Something new in the world was being birthed—a trans-Asian trading mart pivoting on Ptolemaic Egypt midwived by India. India's strategic position ensured that she would never be bypassed by any power to her west with trading designs into the Pacific. By incorporating India into their system, the Ptolemaic merchants had already taken Step One towards establishing a hemisphere-wide economy that would add China to the mix at last. Step Two would spring from the business operations of the Seleucid rulers controlling Sumer, Babylonia, and Persia.[53]

THE SELEUCIDS: CROSS-CULTURAL
MANAGERS OF THE CHINA ROUTE

That very Seleucus whom Chandragupta routed in 303 BCE had inherited the largest Hellenistic realm from Alexander. The multiethnic Seleucid Kingdom emerged as the territorial successor to Assyria, Babylonia and Persia. Seleucus held sway over Arameans, Babylonians, Assyrians, Iranians, Jews, and many others from the Aegean to the borders of the Iranian Plateau. With a political capital at Damascus and tapping the same Babylonian merchant houses that had been the backbone of the Persian economy, Darius' infrastructure of bureaucracy, highways, and military outposts remained alive and well. Phoenicians, Syrians, Anatolians all fed into this fertile region. Very soon, overland trading caravans would eventually link China to the Mesopotamian market.[54]

In this Seleucid Empire, mixed economies dominated, perpetuating the Mesopotamian tradition of limited free markets operating under and alongside royal monopolies. Greco–Macedonian entrepreneurs moved freely within this structure but the actual process of Hellenization remained thin and superficial. Hellenistic inventions pushed technology toward its highest levels until Galileo's time, but temples and mysticism abounded. The Athenian vision of market and state reinforcing each other was dead even in the Greek homeland. Since earliest times, Hellenic traders rarely intermixed with their host nations, most of whom lived by growing grain and fruit. Much of the non-agrarian sector—construction, metals, textiles, and ceramics—continued as it had before Alexander. Sidon, Tyre, and other cities of the Levant continued the manufacture of glass, purple-dyed garments and vessels as they had done for centuries.[55] The Hellenistic economy, in short, was like other ancient systems—overwhelmingly localized, geared to subsistence with a new technological élan springing up more and more. Greek and Near Eastern models of commerce functioned together, and that very synergy made them greater than the sum of their local parts.[56]

The cities of Tyre and Sidon continued to play an important role into the Hellenistic and even the Roman eras. Both continued an ancient rivalry that had endured for at least seven centuries. By Seleucid times, Tyre was no longer an island but was joined to the mainland by a causeway built by Alexander to conquer it. Now, once again, Tyre was a congested metropolis filled with multistory dwellings, many of which were higher even than the houses of Rome.[57] Strabo the Geographer lived in Asia Minor in the late first century BCE and early first century CE. He described Tyre's rapid resurgence after Alexander's conquest and a terrible earthquake, which all but destroyed the city. Tyre restored itself "by means of the seamanship of its people, in which the Phoenicians in general have been superior to all peoples of all times, and by means of their dye-houses for purple; for the Tyrian purple has proved itself by far the most beautiful of all."[58] Here is a hint that Tyrian sailors and dye merchants maintained a national brand all through the first millennium BCE. The shellfish continued to be caught along the nearby Lebanese coast and the other resources needed for dyeing were also near at hand. According to Strabo, there were many dye works in the city and the smell must have made Tyre unpleasant to live in, but the city continued to prosper through the production of the most skilled textile industry in the Near East/Mediterranean world.[59]

What of Tyre's rival, Sidon? The city–state was far more intellectual than Tyre, seeming to specialize in technology transfer and knowledge production Strabo described the Sidonians as philosophers in astronomy and arithmetic. They began to study practical calculation and night voyages. They applied Egyptian geometry "and at present by far the greatest store of knowledge in every other branch of philosophy is to be had from these cities."[60] According to Strabo, Mochus of Sidon perfected the theory of the atom before or around 1000 BCE. Strabo's own tutor in Aristotelian philosophy was none other than Boethius of Sidon, the brother of the Sidonian philosopher Diodotus. The glass industry also flourished in Sidon. Sand from the beaches between Acre and Tyre was shipped to Sidon and there turned into glass artifacts.[61]

Another important Hellenistic trading center developed on the island of Rhodes. The city's reputation for financial stability was enhanced by Alexander himself, who promoted it and even stored his testament there. Rhodes became a sort of new Athens, though without the intellectual life of the former. When the other Hellenistic kingdoms began to fight among themselves, they each desired the allegiance of Rhodes, which, according to Diodorus of Sicily, "was strong in sea power and was the best governed city of the Greeks . . . a prize eagerly sought after by the dynasts and kings, each of them striving to add her to his alliance."[62] The city became even richer by following a policy of playing its enemies off against one another and receiving gifts from both the Antigonids in Greece and Macedonia and the Ptolemies in Egypt. Rhodes became so powerful that it was able to wage a unilateral on piracy in the Aegean and win it. In spite of a Bismarck-style policy of signing friendship treaties with everyone, Rhodes cultivated a special trading relationship with Ptolemiac Egypt which served as its granary and main source of revenue.[63] Rhodes, however, gained a reputation that permitted it to mediate in maritime trade disputes. When the rulers of the city of Byzantium (it existed long before Constantine) levied duties on exports from the Pontus, cutting into the profits of merchants, "all the traders were aggrieved" and, according to Polybius, "brought their complaint before the Rhodians who were considered the supreme authority in maritime matters."[64]

What of the Phoenicians? The merchant princes of Tyre and Sidon were first under Ptolemaic and then Seleucid rule but, no matter. Creative associations of Levantine traders and shippers continued to function on the basis of the traditional Canaanite model, especially with the excellent new harbors Greek engineers had enlarged and refurbished. With the silver currency in vogue and the Greek *koine* dialect spreading farther and farther, trade was ever more efficient and moving more and more to a cash basis. Tyrian and Sidonian shippers opened offices in Athens and Delos, serving as important links to the Ptolemaic, Attalid, and Seleucid spheres. War, inflation, royal despotism, piracy, and disease, although often triggering market failures, could not stop independent entrepreneurs from expanding, especially in the Aegean. Underneath the thin veneer of Greek culture, the statist and hierarchical traditions going back to Kanesh and Egypt endured. The Hellenistic was thus a period of flux. Noting this and with the advantage of hindsight to foresee the emerging Roman colossus that would prevail after the first century BCE, many historians have bowed to the pressure of historic inevitability. This period has been considered a day of small things. True, the vast Seleucid realms would soon be assimilated by Rome in the west and Parthia in the east, but that was not the whole story by any means. "Trade during the Hellenistic period was truly international," states John P. McKay. "The economic unity of the Hellenistic world, like its cultural bonds, would later prove valuable to Rome."[65]

The eventual fate of the Hellenistic kingdoms, however, has stimulated a fervent debate among economic historians. Ulrich Kahrstedt argued that the technological and scientific progress made under the Hellenistic kingdoms had the potential to trigger an industrial revolution. In the 1930s, Rostovtseff asserted that the bureaucratic bias of fatuous Hellenistic monarchs strangled this potential. The economic historian Heichelheim studied prices, wages, and rents. Before 250 BCE, these showed a healthy economic expansion. After this time, renewed warfare, piracy, and social unrest were seen as the cause of lower economic growth.[66] The debate continues.

If trade in the central Mediterranean had entered a period of stagnation, eastward-looking, the land was bright. Although the lion's share of eastern trade was eventually cornered by Ptolemaic mariners, traders in the Seleucid and Attalid realms built upon the ancient Sumerian–Assyrian–Babylonian trading networks dating from the Bronze Age. Wood, spices, and other luxuries, including Chinese silk, journeyed westward across Persia by caravan from the Mauryan kingdom through the new Seleucid capital near Baghdad, from whence it travelled along the Tigris–Euphrates route to Tyre, Sidon, Antioch, or Ephesus. A second route, that of the ancient Dilmun-boats of Sumerian times, crossed the Arabian Sea and Persian Gulf to Seleucid Babylonia, from whence camels and riverboats journeyed westward.[67]

The eastward orientation of Seleucid trade would help bring about a productive new epoch in hemispheric trade. The rather extensive communications across Seleucid realms originally stretching from Syria to the borders of India would help pivot the growing caravan trade to China. By the second century BCE, Hellenistic merchants would open up a vast new market—the expanding domains of Han China territories along the justly famous Silk Road. Before this could happen, however, all parties would have to reckon with a vast empire standing athwart the overland route to Asia.

THE PARTHIANS: BROKERS OF THE EURASIAN ECONOMY

The historians of Han China wrote of a people they called the Anxi, occupying the flat lands of Iraq and the high Iranian Plateau region after the fall of Persia. In 250 BCE, this territory was still part of the Seleucid realm, but it would not long remain so. A federation of Scythian tribes pouring in from the north known as the Dahae settled north-eastern Iran in 248. In the succeeding decades, the people known as the Parthians began to extend their power westward at the expense of the Seleucids. In 167 BCE, they allied with the Jews in their revolt against the Seleucid Antiochus IV. Between 163 and 150, The Parthian ruler Mithridates I sized control of all of Persia and Media and shot tentacles into Babylonia. The story of the Parthian Empire is an intriguing one, and one long lost to history.

This vast new territorial empire came down to us almost unbeknownst in the term "parting shot," originally "Parthian shot," so named from the battle tactic of these skilful cavalry to ride past enemy formations and fire arrows from horseback at their opponents' rear. The Parthians occupied the space between the Euphrates and the Indus, although the eastern fringes would eventually be ruled by other nomads: the Sakas and Kushanas. Parthia would endure for five hundred years and resist both the Seleucids and the Romans, preventing either of them from duplicating Alexander's feat. Little is known of this vast and mysterious empire. The only written records the Arsacid kings left survive in their coins. Add to this a number of sculptures in the cities they erected in Iraq with the written records of the Greeks, the Romans, and the Chinese, and the evidence is still meagre indeed. Once assembled, however, the facts the story tells are remarkable.[68]

Inheriting the Persian/Hellenistic administrative machine, the Parthians excelled even Darius in cross-cultural management. The Parthians were not Persians. They were much more closely related to the Saka, a Scythian tribe that wandered across Central Asia and the Ukraine. They spoke an Iranian dialect but wrote in Aramaic, although their literature is lost. Parthian religion was more a matter of convenience than conviction. It seems to have been a pre-Zoroastrian form of Iranian religion. Worship of the sun and other deities were common. Magi priests wielded a strong influence. Greek, Babylonian, and Jewish forms of worship were acknowledged and tolerated.

From the beginning, a feudal monarchy governed the Parthian territories. Mounted warrior aristocrats formed one house of the ruling assembly or Megistanes. The more well-known priestly Magi class formed the other. Both houses had the power to choose the king, providing he came from the House of Arsaces. Once in power, the Parthian monarch was absolute, but his position was often insecure.[69]

The victories of Mithridates over the Seleucids signified a major change of control in these regions, but not a social revolution. The nomadic Parthians essentially left the Greeks, Jews, Elamites, Persians, Babylonians, and others alone. From Greek accounts, we know that the vertically-organized Babylonian trading houses and the entrepreneurial Greek merchants provided the Arsacid kings with handsome revenues. From the standpoint of business history it is fortuitous that the Parthians adopted a laissez-faire economic policy. From 115 BCE on, Parthia stood athwart the land bordering the Hellenistic states in the West and an expanding Chinese dynasty in the East. These Parthian middlemen were a key link in the chain that eventually tied China to Rome. The journeys of China's Zhang Qian led to the opening of diplomatic relations between the Chinese and the land they called Anxi. What began with gifts soon developed into an overland exchange. Chinese merchants brought silk and iron westward to the Aramean, Greek, Jewish and Babylonian traders doing eager business in the Parthian realm. Parthian transhippers then moved the wares westward across Iraq on a caravan route that ended in Seleucid Syria. This led to the rise of both Palmyra and Petra to prominence as caravan meccas. In exchange, Syrian textiles and Tyrian glass were shipped across Parthia. Arabian camels also found their way eastward. Most important for the Chinese were the splendid "heavenly horses," which were much bigger and faster than those of China. These were found on the eastern fringes of the Parthian domain.[70]

By 100 BCE, the Silk Road passing across the Parthian realms made possible the conveyance of precious goods back and forth from Syria across Iraq, Iran, Central Asia, Mongolia, Xinjiang, and, finally, deep into Han China. Tenuous as it was, a trans-Asian economy had now come into being. Entrepreneurial Greeks in Egypt and palace-backed Phoenicians in Syria could ship and trade goods across Parthian territory to and from India via the monsoon. Now China would join the system. The "flat world" had reached the Eurasian heartland. Caravans wound along Seleucid-protected routes going across the Iranian plateau. Later, under the Roman sway, this hemisphere-wide economy would include the first European and eventually Euro-African trading market. A people of whom few people have heard, the Parthians had helped bring China into the economy of the Mediterranean world. East and West were linked at last. Even so, one must remember that China had less interest in the wares of the West than vice versa. The two imports that attracted China were horses and jade. Meanwhile, Chinese agents went on to set up a silk bazaar in Rome, the Vicus Tuscus. This was so successful that emperor Tiberius (14–37 CE) found it necessary to prohibit the wearing of silk, so alarmed was he by the drain on the imperial gold reserves. International trade has consequences, then and now.[71]

CHINA LOOKS WEST—MANAGEMENT
THEORY UNDER THE HAN

"The opening of China." It is a phrase that has deep resonances for our day and one that this narrative does well to cover. Even the briefest overview of China is a formidable task, but one that must be attempted in the search for the precursors of globalization.

Although one must be careful about stretching historical analogies, China's development in the Hellenistic Age shows remarkable parallels with the twentieth and twenty-first centuries. In the early 1900's of our era, for example, China was in chaos, subject to feuding warlords and foreign invaders. Final unity was imposed by Mao Zedong and the Communist Party. Mao unified China through extreme measures of totalitarian control. Between 1949 and 1976, China was relatively isolated from the world and subject to radical forms of statist coercion, terror, and intellectual repression. After Mao's death, his successors, led by Deng Xiaoping, relaxed some of the controls and encouraged a mixture of entrepreneurialism and state enterprise. China reached out economically to re-enter a world trading system. Something similar happened in the third and second centuries BCE.

Under the Xia and Shang rulers, China developed in isolation from the Near East and India during the third and second millennia BCE. As mentioned, China entered the Bronze Age over a thousand years after the civilizations to the west (see Table 8.2). During that time, the Chinese economy centred around the valley of the Huang He (Yellow River). Shang China was far more collectivist than either Mesopotamia or India. As in Egypt, everything appeared to be in the hands of the state, even land. The Shang ruled for seven centuries, but was finally overthrown by the chariots of the warlord Wu around 1208 BCE. Eventually, the new dynasty of the Zhou installed itself at the western end of the Huang He corridor. The political ideology of the Zhou contained great import for the future of Chinese business and business culture. From that time, politics in China was subject to the Mandate of Heaven. If a ruler defied that mandate by governing unjustly, as had the last Shang, he was subject to removal by Heaven.[72] Sacrificial victims were no longer required at the death of a ruler.

The Zhou state adopted much of Shang culture and brought it into the Iron Age. Zhou policy would ultimately prove self-destructive. The Zhou rulers delegated power in their huge kingdom to warlords. These warlords were blood relatives, who began to assume more and more power. By 800

Table 8.2   China and Its Early Dynasties

c. 4000 BCE	Farming begins in Yellow River Valley
c. 2500 BCE	Horse is domesticated in China
c. 1500–1050 BCE	Shang Dynasty—first writing in China, massive work in Bronze
c. 1027–256 BCE	Zhou Dynasty, proclamation of the Mandate of Heaven
Confucius 551–479 BCE	
Period of Warring States 403–221 BCE	
Parthia occupies Persia 250–137 BCE	
Ch'in states begin Great Wall 221–206 BCE	
206 BCE–CE 220	Han Dynasty
Great Wall Finished, Silk Road opens	

BCE, China contained some 200 principalities. Thirty years later, another nomadic invasion flooded eastward from the steppes. The Zhou continued to rule from the eastern end of the Yellow River valley. Chinese history entered a period recorded in *The Spring and Autumn Annals*, a narrative once believed to have been written by Confucius himself. The stage was being set for a Chinese market revolution.[73]

Centuries of bureaucratic state control and social collectivism in China had provided an unlikely arena for entrepreneurs. Nevertheless, free thinkers and innovators began to flourish. Because Chinese culture stressed practical rulership in this life—a "this world" ethic—rather than Hindu-style reincarnation in the next, China fathered some of the earliest teachers of what could be called management theory. Such texts in China go back as far as Shang and Early Zhou times. Writings such as *The Great Plan* and *The Officials of Zhou* date from around 1100 BC/BCE, but incorporate material from much earlier times.[74] Passages in *The Great Plan* are older than any, often hard to translate, and thus susceptible to differing interpretations. One passage, though, seems to spell out an ancient Contingency Theory of Leadership:

> The three virtues are rules, firmness, and gentleness. Spell out rules for peaceful people; deal firmly with violent and offensive people; deal gently with amenable and friendly people. Employ firm supervision with those who shirk or lack initiative, gentle supervision with those who are distinguished by their talents and good dispositions.[75]

The same text, translated differently, is much more specific to managers and overseers who are counselled to regard the social context and the subordinates being managed:

The three virtues are correct procedure, strong management, and mild management. Adhere to correct procedure in situations (times) of peace and tranquility; use strong management in situations of violence and disorder; apply mild management in situations of harmony and order. Employ strong supervision with people who lack initiative, mild supervision with the honorable and intelligent.[76]

The Officials of Zhou is a set of instructions about public sector management, but it also shows, say Rindova and Starbuck, "that ancient organizations could be complex, well-defined, and bureaucratic, in contrast to beliefs that complex bureaucracies are a modern phenomenon."[77] The document reveals that "ancient people had interesting and diverse theories about human behavior and management."[78] Some of these theories were very different from the latest hot trends at the Harvard Business School; others anticipate them: "Some managerial philosophies popular today have clear antecedents running back 4,000 years."[79]

For example, the concept of leading by example was set down around 2000 BC. Here is an high official, Kaou-yaou, writing to his ruler, Yu: "If rulers attend carefully to their personal improvement, with concern for the long term, they will be able to show unselfish benevolence and to draw perceptive distinctions among people." If managers followed this wise principle, "all intelligent people will exert themselves to serve their rulers" and the spin-offs in public order and productivity will positively influence even distant subjects. Kaou-yaou argued that success in management came from "knowing people and keeping people satisfied." Already he was light years beyond the ideas of Frederick Taylor. His ruler, Yu, replied that even the wise, legendary King Yao found it hard to do both. Wise rulers who know people can hire the best people for the positions. Satisfied people will cherish their rulers and allow them to be kind. They would have no reason to worry about insubordination or firing people (or worse).[80]

Chinese society possessed a strong cohesion at this time, not too different from the tribal kingdoms of the Bronze Age Aegean. Even the Xia rulers who predated the Shang could not impose their control too far, and some clans had their own armies and could depose anyone who became too despotic.[81] E Yin was prime minister around 1750 BCE. As far back as the early second millennium, he was wisely counselling managers to pay close attention to those underneath them, anticipating the more humane "work involvement" practices of the 1970s of our era:

Do not slight the concerns of the people. Think of their difficulties. Do not yield to a feeling of ease on your throne: Think of its perils. Be careful to think about the end at the beginning. When you hear words against which your mind sets itself, you must inquire whether these words are not right. When you hear words that agree with your own thinking, you must ask whether these words are not wrong.[82]

EARLY CAPITALISM'S DISCONTENTS

This progressive approach embedded in early Chinese writings on the wise management of people arose in an almost totally state-run economy. Private capitalism eventually took root in the Zhou Period, between 1000 and 500 BCE. Records of China's first private, profit-seeking merchants date to the fifth century BCE. Their story has come down to us in *Hou Hanshu*, an official Han Dynasty history complied by the courtier Fan Ye, who died around 445 CE. The *Hou Hanshu*, itself, was based upon the *Shiji (Shi Chih)* by Sima Qian (Ssu'ma Chien) and the *Hanshu* by Ban Gu (P'an Ku). Ban Gu lived from 32–92CE and wrote the first Chinese history, some of which was devoted to the story of China's earliest merchants on record. The *Hanshu* begins with a favorable—even idealized—view of the pre-capitalist Shang and Zhou dynasties. In this era, says this account, everyone, small and great, knew their place. The ancient rulers managed the economy, teaching all to farm and raise animals and live in harmony with the seasons. Everyone was a farmer, a scholar, a craftsman, or a tradesperson, and engaged in the appropriate means of production. According to Ban Gu, markets existed, but their role was quite limited: "There was both an intercommunication of productions of labor and an interchange of men's services by which the people mutually profited." Craftsmen debated with one another on the best application of skill and ingenuity while working on government buildings. Trades people conversed with one another about wealth and profit in the marketplaces.[83] The real market revolution was yet ahead, for the "desires of the people were few; and undertakings were limited. Their wealth was sufficient, and they did not vie with one another."[84]

Under the Xia, and most of the Shang and Zhou, says this reconstruction of China's early past, people esteemed righteous conduct and disesteemed profit, allowing many kings to reign without severity. Then, the *Hanshu* records, the Zhou became decadent and forgot the ancient rites of Yao, China's legendary patriarch. Local feudal lords usurped the power of the king. Conspicuous consumption reigned, as lords decorated their great halls. Agriculture became neglected in favor of quick commercial profits. The inevitable imbalances occurred. Merchandise was plenteous, but there was not enough grain: "Sowers and reapers were few; traders and peddlers many."[85] As the long Zhou Dynasty began to fragment, the central government continued to weaken, especially during the period of the dukes Huan of Qi (685–643) and Wen of Qin (635–628). Warlords began to exert their power. High and low now offended one another as China entered the turbulent "dog-eat-dog" phase of a market revolution linked to political anomie. Tradespeople circulated goods that were hard to obtain, craftsmen made articles of no practical utility, and scholars debated philosophies that were contrary to the natural order, as preached by the Daoists. People turned their backs upon tradition for the pursuit of image and profit.[86]

In short, the *Hanshu* reads as an indictment of an unfettered capitalism in the spirit of Kevin Phillips and George Soros—a capitalism charging along in a land of political strife and a moral vacuum. Qiyuan (Chi Yüan) advised his local Chekiang warlord that wise economic management was akin to sound military management.[87] To achieve hegemony over the others, a ruler needed a rich and powerful kingdom, which necessitated long-term public/private business planning. One needed to make boats in time of drought and wagons in time of flooding: "To anticipate what the future holds and act accordingly is the soundest principle underlying all rules."[88] This was the "business as war" model. It seems that unfettered capitalism, very early, achieved an unsavoury reputation among many Chinese. The reaction was not long in coming, even as free enterprisers continued to do business, some quite ethically.

For example, there was the entrepreneur Fanli. He settled in the strategic trade center of Shandong on the peninsula near Korea. According to his biographer, Panku, he "bought, hoarded, or sold, depending upon the time and the circumstances. He relied on his own judgment and would not blame others whatever the result. Moreover, as a businessman of unusual ability, he knew whom he should entrust with responsibility and at what time he should buy or sell."[89] Here is the true entrepreneur, ready and more than willing to take risks and carry his own "message to Garcia," to borrow a phrase from another business era. Fanli's earned fortune of 300 gold pieces was given to his relatives and friends, and the family business was eventually worth tens of thousands of gold coins in assets.[90]

The merchant Pai Kuei followed commodity prices carefully, buying when others sold and selling when others bought. Pai Kuei lived frugally just as his workers or servants. He didn't, however, conduct business so much as wage it: "If a man is not intelligent enough to change with the circumstances, brave enough to make sudden and drastic decisions, benevolent enough to give whenever it is wise to give, or persevering enough to hold to what he believes to be sound and correct, he should not go into my field, the field of business."[91] One can imagine J. P. Morgan seconding this motion. The struggle for hegemony and the rise of freebooting Chinese capitalism were both characteristics of the bloody and divisive Period of Warring States at the end of the Zhou.

CONFUCIUS SAYS . . .

Thus, the rising mercantile spirit had created many enemies. Both Greek and Roman capitalists had their critics, but these were mild in comparison with the reaction of the sage Kong Qiu (Kung Chiu, 551–479 BCE). Kung Chiu, better known as Confucius, became the foremost thinker to shape Oriental civilization. Born in 551 BCE in north-eastern China, into a family of petty aristocrats, Confucius early became a bureaucrat given charge of grain, flocks, and herds. In essence, Confucius was an idealist trying to solve problems. Seeing warfare and quarrelsome folk all around him, he looked back to the wisdom and ritual ways of China's past. He studied that past to develop his own private curriculum for how a society should run. Through a systematic reflection on how Chinese society worked best, he aimed to restore respect for family, authority, and ethics in a very chaotic time. Confucianism is summarized in *The Analects*, a collection of his maxims:

> Master You said, 'Few indeed are those who are naturally filial towards their parents and dutiful towards their elder brothers but are fond of opposing their superiors; and it never happens that those who do not like opposing their superiors are fond of creating civil disorder. . . . Filial piety and fraternal duty—surely they are the roots of humaneness."[92]

Confucius tutored the warlord of Lu until he was expelled in 501 BC, becoming an itinerant teacher until his death in 479 BC. Confucian doctrine, in its original form, was quite hostile to capitalism. Duty to family, community, and the state was enshrined: "Riches and honours—these are what men desire, but if this is not achieved in accordance with the appropriate principles, one does not cling to them."[93] If a gentleman could not avoid poverty in accord with Confucian principles, then he would have to remain in poverty: "Poverty and obscurity—these are what men hate, but if this is not achieved in accord with the appropriate principles, one does not avoid them."[94] Confucius cited the example of Hui, who lived in a squalid alley with a bowl of rice and a ladle of water.[95]

Self-interest, profit-making, and the acquisition of wealth by individuals was frowned upon, especially if wealth was acquired in an unethical manner: "If one acts with a view to profit, there will be much resentment."[96] Confucius maintained that an ideal gentleman practiced right conduct for its own sake; a petty person acted in a goodly manner because it was merely profitable to do so: "The gentleman is familiar with what is right, just as the small man is familiar with profit."[97] "The gentleman," said Confucius, concerns himself with the Way, "he does not worry about his salary." He reveres the works of the sages, the Mandate of Heaven, and the study of the virtues. He does not worry about poverty even if it comes: "The gentleman understands integrity; the petty person knows about profit."[98] Cultivating friendships with officials and scholars was essential for the aspiring mandarin, but loyalty and responsibility to one's kin held society together at the grassroots, especially obedience to parents. Filial piety lay at the top of the Confucian value system: "In serving father and mother, one remonstrates gently. If one sees they are intent on not following advice, one continues to be respectful and one does not show disobedience; and even if one finds it burdensome, one does not feel resentful."[99] Not only did one need to respect one's parents under any and all circumstances, but one ought not to travel far from them or change from one's father's ways for at least three years.[100]

Confucius preserved many of the ideas set forth by forerunners Kaou-yaou and E Yin. In other words, he recycled much of the ancient Chinese advice on the wise management of people. Managers needed to manage well, set good examples, and exercise loving authority. He went beyond the ancients in asserting that government should actively promote the public good.[101]

Confucius was an activist, calling on people to help make the government work well. Daoism, represented by Laozi (Lao Tzu) and, especially, Zhuangzi (Chuang Tzu), was more in tune with self-interest and the natural order. Zhuangzi, in particular, implied that pure Confucian ideals were impractical. Would a sacred turtle rather "be dead and have its bones left behind and honored?" Would it not rather be "alive and dragging its tail in the mud?"[102] Zhuangzi cynically confronted a warlord who boasted of his virtuous Confucian subjects. What if the warlord were to decree that anyone wearing the Confucian round caps, square shoes, and ornaments not practicing what he preached would be executed. The barb hit home. Only one elderly gentleman dared to wear Confucian garb.[103]

At the end of this golden age of Chinese philosophy and intellectual ferment on how to reorient society, an important book came from the pen of Sun Tzu. This work would become a primer for Chinese, Japanese, Korean, and Vietnamese military strategy, even into modern times. Suntzu lived in the state of Qi and served as its general from 512 to 492 BCE. Winning many battles, he was able to wrest hegemony from the rival state of Jin and was hailed as a military genius. He then wrote a book entitled *Bing Fa* ("Soldier Doctrine"), or, as it is known in English, *The Art of War*. *The Art of War* was destined to shape not only Chinese military strategy, but also Chinese business strategy, for the simple reason that many Chinese and other East Asian rulers view war and business as deeply interconnected. For Chinese managers, even leaders of small family corporations, the marketplace is a battlefield and military strategy can be applied to life-and-death business competition. Suntzu was deeply influenced by the Daoist masters, who taught that all things in the universe are interrelated. He once advised his military superior how to win at the racetrack. The general, he said, should run his fastest horse against his rival's middle horse, his middle horse against his rival's slowest horse, and his slowest horse against his rival's best horse. He would lose one race, but win the other two. The goal was to win the long-term contest, not every race—let your competitor save face and pit only your strong points against the weak points of others.[104]

Both businesses and armies were alike in this Chinese conception. They were to strive for favorable position, defeat competitors, and defend themselves. "Business is war by other means," and both arenas are confrontational activities that need to be well-organized and managed. In both, the leader must employ strategy, tactics, leadership, and gathering of information. This requires high-quality committed people and good company morale. Unlike war, whose purpose is to destroy, the goal of business is the creation of wealth.[105] There is much here that American conservative business "purists" would agree with.

SHIHUANGDI : THE FIRST MAOIST?

This narrative is dedicated, in part, to the proposition that diversity is the way of business history. In the event, neither Confucianism nor Daoism provided an answer to China's disorder, as warlords grew more and more ambitious in the Later Zhou Period. A third and far more severe doctrine would prove the remedy, such as it was. In 221 BCE, a fierce warlord from the state of Ch'in (Qin) unified the country and gave it its name. He proclaimed himself Shihuangdi (First Emperor). Shihuangdi was a disciple of the philosopher Han Feizi, the proponent of Legalism. Legalists taught that a ruler must exercise power with absolute rigidity and absolute control. Shihuangdi proceeded to implement this doctrine in practice. Military roads unified the realm. Weights and measures were standardized. The Great Wall was constructed at a terrible human cost. Qin China was built on terror and blood by slave gangs of hundreds of thousands of political prisoners. The threat of mutilation, slavery, being buried and boiled alive, or being torn apart by chariots kept people in line. In the 1970s, archaeologists uncovered Shihuangdi's ghostly army of 7500 life-size terra cotta soldiers buried near his tomb just east of Xian. Even today, it makes a startling testimony to the monomania it took to unify China.

Shihuangdi could, perhaps, be described as the first Maoist. Mao, himself, took vast inspiration from him. Both rulers were revolutionaries, attempting to destroy the traditions of China's past. Both were totalitarian in their attempt to standardise the thinking of the people, as well as its administration. Shihuangdi attempted the first Chinese Cultural Revolution. Feudal and kinship institutions were replaced by a system of centralised and direct state control. Paradoxically, this most absolute of all ancient Chinese regimes tried to turn many serfs into freehold peasants, foreshadowing the commercialisation of agriculture under the medieval T'ang and Song Dynasties. Not unlike 1960s China, all books glamorising the past were banned, as were those critical of the present. Many were either burned or stored in official libraries. In 212 BCE, almost 500 Confucian and other scholars were executed and laid in a mass grave.

The Qin Dynasty did not survive the death of its founder in 210 BCE. China's new rulers, the Han, strove to preserve unity and economic development while restoring old Confucian values. A Han historian writing in 73 BCE discussed the excesses of the Qin in a manner not unlike the way Chinese writers have recently criticised the excesses of Maoism: "The Ch'in regime. . . . considered men of virtue insignificant while attaching great importance to officials who enforced the law with harshness and cruelty. A man who spoke on behalf of justice was characterized as a slanderer, and any criticism of the government was denounced as the advocacy of heresy. . . . It is no wonder that the Ch'in regime fell in the end."[106]

206 BCE—THE HAN SUCCESSION

If the Qin Empire resembled the totalitarian China of Mao Zedong, that of its Han successors—to stretch an analogy—was perhaps akin to the more open and modernizing China of Deng Xiaoping. Han China created a stable aristocratic society. Still legalist and authoritarian, they nonetheless rehabilitated China's Confucian ideals. The stress on practical rulership and economic growth was a repudiation of the extremes of Shihuangdi. The entrepreneur came into his own. The businessman's greatest champions would be the disciples of Daoism. The Daoist creed operated on the idea of living in harmony with the natural order of life and creation. What could be more natural, argued Sima Qian, than the laws of economic self-interest as manifested in the market. The market, now covering all of China, was a reality of nature. Products flowed back and forth between east and west and from the Yellow to the Yangzi. The mountainous area of Shensi and Shansi in the west produced lumber, bamboo, grain, hemp, flax, and jade, served as grazing for horses, sheep, and oxen, and were covered with hundreds of kilometres of copper and iron mines. Far away to the east, the Shantung coast was a source of fish, salt, lacquer, and silk.

Ah, silk—China's ancient standby. Silk would be the passport to engage the economy of the strange people to the west. To the south, the Yangzi valley produced cedar, gold, silver, lead, and sandstone. The exchange of these products was a fortune waiting to be made, just waiting to be coordinated by a beneficent administration. Sima Qian's *Introduction to Economics* spoke to this natural division of labor that China had been perfecting through all of its political storms:

> All these products the Chinese love dearly. They are the materials for their food and clothing . . . farmers raise crops; the miners bring forth minerals, the artisans fashion into articles what others have produced; and the merchants move raw materials as well as finished products to the market.[107]

Almost 2,000 years before Adam Smith, Sima Qian articulated a primitive form of the *Wealth of Nations*. Not everyone could live up to the statist ideology of the gentleman, he wrote, and it was a good thing they couldn't. Who would grow China's food, make her tools, mine or import gold and silver for her coins, or pearls and jade for her luxuries? Sima Qian touted the inevitability of market forces:

> These activities have gone on and will continue to go on with or without a government, and each person will do his very best to obtain what he desires. . . . Each man . . . seeks profits as water seeks the lowest ground. . . . Wherever profit is, he does not wait for an invitation, and he produces even though nobody has asked him to do so. Does this situation not conform well with the principles of Tao? Is it not a vindication of the soundness of the 'naturalist' theory?[108]

This is as close a parallel to Adam Smith's famed "invisible hand" dictum that the ancient world has given us. In Sima Qian's creed, the producers—the farmers, miners, craftsmen, and merchants—were essential to Chinese life. It was also essential, then, that they be given every incentive to produce and earn a profit, rather than conform to the standards of the mandarin:

> Under the circumstances the best thing to do is to leave people the way they are, and the next best is to channel their materialistic desires through reason. Less desirable is to educate them so that they will reduce or lose such desires, and worse still, to use coercion to achieve the same purpose. Of all the possible courses to take, the worst the government can do is to join the people and compete with them for material gains.[109]

Here is Adam Smith: "The patrimony of a poor man lies in the strength of his hands . . . and to hinder him from employing this strength and dexterity in what manner he thinks proper without injury to his neighbor, is a violation of this most sacred property."[110] By enshrining the first of Smith's three great principles—the benign pursuit of self-interest—Han China was bringing to critical mass ideas that had been percolating for centuries.

CHINA'S INTERNAL DEBATE: INDUSTRY OR AGRICULTURE?

Under the Han, the Confucian establishment debated the proper roles of agriculture, manufacturing, government, and markets. The realities of empire and the perils of still-hostile states persuaded the Emperor Wudi (141–87 BCE) that maintaining a manufacturing establishment constituted a military necessity. The Han manufacturing sector was both hierarchical and monopolistic. The Emperor Wudi nationalized the production of grain, iron, salt, and liquor. The mandarins insisted they acted in the interests of the fair market principle. Like the biblical Joseph, their officials bought grain surpluses and sold them in time of famine. The grain monopolies brought both price stability and imperial revenue as Han emperors began to assert themselves more and more as China's unquestioned rulers by the Mandate of Heaven.

Not everyone approved of these interventionist policies. An unlikely alliance of family entrepreneurs and anti-business Confucians ranged itself against the very concept of public enterprise. In the year 81 BCE, several Confucian scholars sent a written protest to the chief minister in charge of the economy. The arguments of the scholars resembled those of Jeffersonian purists and the savants of the Cato Institute, extolling the free pursuit of agriculture above all. Government enterprise, they said, undermined order and morality. Left unchecked, it would undermine peasant honesty and discourage the virtues associated with farming. Yet if the state encouraged too much economic growth and gain, peasants would swarm into the marketplace. The government needed to stay out of the making and circulating of goods and services.

Rigid Confucians such as these saw economic growth and moral virtue as incompatible. As for the warlike Xiongnu, fierce riders of the steppes, chafing under any form of over-lordship, they believed that if the emperor showed high moral standards and ruled benevolently, he would have no enemies. The sages insisted China must abandon the market and return to the ancient communal ideals. The more rulers that embraced the market, they said, the more their example corrupted the common people. State enterprise drove up taxes and drove down prices. Protests were many as Han China debated taking the plunge into palace-sponsored capitalism, at least in part:

> The government officers busy themselves with gaining control of the market and cornering commodities. With the commodities cornered, prices soar and merchants make private deals and speculate. The officers connive with the cunning merchants who are hoarding commodities against future need. Quick traders and unscrupulous officials buy when goods are cheap in order to make high profits.[111]

Unilateral disarmament and a return to primitive Stone Age communalism did not impress the Han court. The restless semi-barbarian Xiongnu were not impressed by Confucian virtue but by forts and armies. China's sprawling defences needed monetary reserves, and the revenues from public enterprise could provide it. True virtue lay in having a China strong enough to defend its people. To the chief minister, the arguments of the sages bordered upon lunacy. The Han rulers insisted that state enterprise was as old as China itself. The Xia, Shang, and Zhou had encouraged all forms of occupations, including tradesman and merchants. Without them, peasants could grow nothing. Governments created markets from which all would benefit. "Poverty was not beneficial," went their argument, "there was no recommendation in rags and a shortage of merchants perpetuated penury." Such were the reasons the ancient rulers had spread enterprise to all corners of China. The Han would do the same, innovate by looking backwards to national traditions to keep the empire strong. Is this a preview of the policy China is following today?[112] Time will tell.

REACHING WESTWARD

It was under Emperor Wudi that China finally came into fruitful contact with the world far to its west. How did this happen?

Han China faced a terrifying threat from the Mongolian steppes in the form of the Hsiung-Nu or Xiongnu, as discussed previously. Some historians have identified these ferocious Turkish and Mongolian barbarians as the ancestors of the equally terrible Huns, although more recent historians disagree. Cavalry was a deadly weapon on the steppes and the steppes stretched far to China's west. The horses of the Mongolians were bigger and faster than the little ponies ridden by the Chinese. Skilled horsemen could breach even the Great Wall. China needed allies to engage the Xiongnu and needed them quickly. In 139–138 BCE, Wudi sent an expedition led by a military officer named Zhang Qian towards the west. Accompanied by ninety others, Zhang made his way westward through Xinjiang along the southern rim of the Tien Shan mountain range, until he reached the land of the DaXia, or Bactria. They were a fair-skinned people who had once lived on the borders of China and were a showcase of Greek culture. The Xiongnu had driven them westward. Zhang also met with the Parthians and was especially impressed with the people of Ferghana living to the east of the Turkestan bordering the Caspian Sea. He was unable to forge an alliance with them. China was just too far away to render such an alliance feasible.

Zhang returned empty-handed, diplomatically. Economically, it was a different story. In Bactria, Zhang had acquired valuable market knowledge. He learned that the Bactrians were already importing silk fabrics and bamboo from Sichuan. The Parthians minted coins to pay for Chinese silk. Zhang was told that other goods reached these countries from a land called Shengdu: hot, humid, and filled with elephants—*India*. The emperor was elated. China soon annexed Ferghana and thus laid claim to the Silk Trade into the far west. In 126 BCE, the resilient Zhang tried to reach India from China. He got to the mountains of Yunnan but could go no further. The hills and jungles were too formidable. In his third and final voyage, Zhang passed north of the Tienshan and journeyed to the land of the Wu Sun near Lake Balkhash in Central Asia. The Wu Sun were also unwilling to form a Chinese alliance. By the time of his death in 104–103 BCE, Zhang had seemingly failed in his diplomacy but had opened the Han imperial court to the rich trading opportunities that might exist to the west, past the land of the Anxi or Parthia—the Hellenistic states.[113]

With Parthian middlemen and Seleucid trans-shippers plying their skills, it was little wonder that Chinese silk was popular in Rome by the time Julius Caesar died in 44 BCE. A string of territorial empires now bound the great states of antiquity into a hemispheric trading regime that reached from Shandung to Spain. There had been nothing like it before. The ancient world could be seen as being practically flat. The Romans would maximize this splendid inheritance from the Hellenistic Era, certainly no day of small things.

Many goods passed along the Silk Road: pearls from the Persian Gulf or Sri Lanka; coral from the Mediterranean or Red Sea; amber from the Baltic and possibly India; gold, silver, glassware, and horses also went east. China sent silk, iron, lacquer, and bamboo objects and cast metal goods in both iron and bronze.[114]

This was reciprocal trade and it was highly prized by all parties. If the incorporation of China into a trans-Asian economy, linking up with Western Europe through Rome—if this has a modern ring about it, we, perhaps, should not be surprised. Unlike Babylonia, Egypt, Assyria, Ebla, or Hellenic Greece, India and China are the two countries whose history is still being written, whose civilizations are still developing. As of this writing, both countries are modernizing feverishly. Significant numbers of their peoples are caught up in the great rush to integrate into the world economy as part of the metropolitan, rather than as onlookers on the periphery. China's joining the World Trade Organization even sparked a new term that could fit into a fortune cookie—*rushi*, "entering the world." The growth of China, especially, has aroused fears expressed by *The Economist*: "How will this seeming juggernaut change the world"[115]

Now we know. Or at least we have a basis for comparison in the very triumph of ancient business that this book has been documenting. China has joined the world before, and retreated. One of the lessons of this account is a reprise of the old saw that every colossus has feet of clay. The stranding of millions of Chinese commuters over Chinese New Year in January, 2008 is a signal that enormous structural problems still await sorting out in the world's largest country. Other limitations will be addressed in Chapter 9. Thus, a call to cautionary judgments has been part of the trajectory that this book has been describing since the discussion on Uruk in Chapter 1. Professor Ronald Preussen of the University of Toronto was fond of paraphrasing Mark Twain: "Maybe history doesn't repeat itself but it sure rhymes a lot." It seems a good time to incorporate business history into that paradigm.

9 Beyond Globalization
Business and Culture

UNASUR. Lazaro Cardenas. NASCO. APGCI. WHITI.

The very unfamiliarity of these terms and acronyms underlines how glo-balization gets all the media attention, but regionalization is perhaps the major story in the world economy. This is a bold claim, but it bear very mightily on this concluding chapter.

UNASUR stands for the Union of South American Nations, heralded as a reality in Brasilia, Brazil by President Rafael Correa of Ecuador on May 24, 2008. Tucked away in the *Los Angeles Times* on page A4, the UNASUR initiative adopted by twelve nations was hailed as "a regional version of the European Union." Luiz Inacio da Silva, President of Brazil, invited other Latin American and Caribbean nations to join the new trade agreement that also includes the coordination of defence affairs across South America. "Unasur is born, open to all the region," said da Silva, "born under the signs of diversity and pluralism."[1] The days when Secretary of State Henry Kissinger could dismiss the nations to his south as "a strategic pistol aimed at Antarctica" have long since passed. The economic surge of Brazil and the oil wealth of Venezuela and its assertive President would show that to be true. Regional economic integration in South America sheds an indi-rect spotlight on trade and development in North America. This is where Lazaro Cardenas comes into play.

Lazaro Cardenas is the virtually unknown port to the west of Mexico City that hopes to capture much of the container ship trade from Asia pass-ing through the Vancouver–Seattle axis over to Winnipeg, Manitoba and down the North American Super Corridor (NASCO). NASCO is a facet of the virtually unknown APGCIA—the Asia Pacific Gateway and Corridor Initiative.[2] Already under construction, but drawing little media attention apart from environmental groups and worried Teamsters, the proposed NAFTA super highway is, perhaps, the biggest overland transportation project in North America since the Alaska Highway and the 1954 National Highway Act. Four football fields wide, the NAFTA super highway will fork down from Winnipeg through the heart of the United States along Interstate 35 on the way to Mexican ports such as Lazaro Cardenas.

The China and Asian container ship trade is driving the new transportation outlook but it is important to note how the North American trading region is the key to making all this work. Which is to say that the forces of classic globalization—the Asian Pacific trade—is mightily dependent on what happens at the regional level. "The standard map we have in our heads of the post-World War Two trading system is over," says Stephen Blank, a transportation specialist at Arizona State University. "Within ten years we may see ice-free navigation on the Great Lakes," announces Graham Parsons of the Organization for Western Economic Cooperation.[3] A question posed by Dr. Carol Wise of the University of Southern California, a recognized authority on North American Trade, is whether NAFTA can adjust to these new realities. "We are suffering from a lack of continental thinking," adds Professor Stephanie Glob of the City University of New York. "What's needed is double bilateralism like the European Union. People in Canada need to see how their prosperity matters to people in Mexico."[4]

Doubled bilateralism. Continental thinking. Models such as the EU. It seems that regionalism is far from dead; the same is true of the necessity of dealing with diverse populations, policies, and particularism. In its dying days, the administration of President George W. Bush grappled with Congress over the terms of a bilateral trade deal with Colombia. Bilateral tensions in an Age of Globalization. Canadian planners worried about what U.S. security concerns at the border will do for the free flow of trade. What is happening? What is happening is that, in an age of supposed globalization and flattened borders, the issue of culture still looms large. This book has surveyed the history of the major business cultures from the beginnings of civilization down to the Romans. We have emphasized that business models from Uruk to Augustus were quite diverse. Some were organized from the top down, others were very entrepreneurial and still others were a creative blend of the two—sometimes unbeknownst to the powers that controlled them.

THE CULTURAL IMPERATIVE

In true post-modern style, we found that there was no one "right" organizational form. We learned that varied business models reflect the culture it came out of. We have learned that, down through the centuries, if there was any one word or concept that proved the shaping mechanism for business as it evolved along the Euphrates or the Aegean or the Yellow, it was the word *culture*. Cultural patterns affected the direction in which management, labor, and societal organization would flow. The parallels with today were there—patterns we could not have extended out without adding to an already large text. This is why the conclusion of David S. Landes, the former distinguished Coolidge Professor of History and Economics at Harvard University, is so important to our conclusion. Landes supports the thesis that "culture counts." Without being a uni-causationist, Professor Landes reports that, although any story of economic development is complex even involving large elements of chance, "in the final analysis the response to these adventitious events or random events of to the problems caused by geography will be shaped largely by culture." *("Culture Counts: Interview with David S. Landes, Challenge, July-August, 1998)*

There is support for the Landes position in a preface by Wing-Tsit Chan, Adjunct Professor of Chinese Thought at Columbia University, to W. Scott Morton and Charlton M. Lewis' fourth edition of *China: Its History and Culture*. In 2008, what could be called the "Year of China," Chan's words should resonate with readers who have followed our argument throughout. "China is essentially a country of history and culture," says Chan. "Ideologically China turned a complete somersault in 1949, and yet the political structure of provinces and countries is 2,000 years old." True understanding of China, this expert adds, "requires some basic knowledge of Chinese history and culture. . . . It is no exaggeration to say that the Chinese are among the most historically minded people to be found anywhere."[5] The authors are hopeful that this volume has contributed at least somewhat to this understanding.

Culture matters; it matters a lot whether it is the Longshoremen's Union worried about being bypassed by the NAFTA super highway or parents viewing Chinese-made toys at Wal-Mart with a somewhat wary eye. Culture has been a theme throughout, a constant that applies steadying realities on the sometimes utopian-sounding rhapsodies of Globalization's boosters. Culture and diversity. We saw, for example, that Mesopotamian cultures solved their trading problems with a system of merchant princes, as did medieval Germans and their descendants today. Phoenicians and Carthaginians ran their mercantilist trading system as an extension of naval warfare, and so, to a great degree, did medieval Italians, 16th-century Spaniards, 17th-century Dutch, and 20th-century Japanese. The Greek entrepreneurial model was adopted by the British Free Trade School and the militarized entrepreneurialism of Rome recurs in the mass-production, military/industrial economy of America.[6] Some Chinese thinkers saw business as an extension of war by other means, anticipating by centuries some British and American economic thinkers of the purist persuasion. The familial models of Chinese capitalism have endured, and deeper understanding of the medieval Arab and European partnership—although outside our scope—might hold the key to the trust-based business alliances of the post-industrial age. Follow the culture, may be as wise as the modern adage, "Follow the money."

"PROTO-GLOBALIZATION"

A crucial theme developed in this volume is the slow journey of cities, nations, and peoples towards what could be called the proto-global economy. The first economies of the Bronze Age were regional, developing in Mesopotamia, Egypt, India, and China. Keeping in mind that these were the only parts of the world people then knew existed, even the word "globalism" might not be too extreme for such features as the Roman–Han China connection, but we have tried to accept the discipline of our early reviewers. By 1000 BCE, a territorial economy stretched from the Aegean to the Indus. The spread of ironworking—an event very much to compare with our own Industrial Revolution—encouraged its extension into Europe, Africa, and Central Asia. In Hellenistic times (after 330 BCE), a hemisphere-wide economy eventually girdled the latitudes from the Atlantic to the Indian Ocean. China entered this sphere in the late Hellenistic and embraced it more fully in the time of the Roman Republic and Empire. In the Dark Ages, the Muslim caliphate became the heart of a hemispheric Old World economy, which Europe itself began to rejoin after the 1000 CE. This Asian-dominated economy flourished between 1250 and 1350, contracted briefly during the time of the Black Death, but then became undeniably global with the opening of the Americas to European conquest and settlement.

Then the world with which we are familiar today came into being. The insightful Fareed Zakaria, International Editor of *Newsweek*, sees "three tectonic power shifts" creating today's world order. The first was the rise of the Western world, beginning in the fifteenth century with the knowledge explosion unleashed by the Renaissance and the Reformation; the second he sees as the rise of the United States economy in the 1880s. The third great power shift he sees happening now—the rise of the Rest. The United States has watered, mightily, the seeds of globalization perhaps sown first by the British Empire. Nor is the American role finished, argues Zakaria. In spite of the enormous cost overruns of the Iraq War, military spending still amounts to less than 1% of GDP, compared to 1.6% for the Vietnam War (1965–1973).[7] A more Euro-centered view of today's world system might bear harder on how from 1850 on, Europe itself, led by Britain, formed the Second Global Economy of the Industrial Revolution—*"anglobalization,"* in the words of Professor Niall Ferguson. This system was eventually dominated by the United States, a factor of two disastrous World Wars in the heart of Europe, and American innovative genius in applying mass production and the technical application of the internal-combustion engine. With its near-total collapse in the 1930's, a new Third Global Economy, dominated by multinational enterprises, finance capital, global capital shifts, just-in-time delivery, and instant information technology has been steadily rising, consolidating itself in the late 20th century with demonstrable parallels back to medieval times.

An original title for this work was *Globalization 0.5: The Economy from Iraq to Rome.* Our title was inspired by Thomas Friedman's best seller, *The World Is Flat.* Friedman likewise analyzed three eras of Globalization. In his scheme, Globalization 1.0 spans from the time of Columbus to around 1800 CE. Globalization 2.0 stretches from 1800 to 2000 Then Globalization 3.0

Table 9.1   Thomas Friedman's Three Eras

Key Attributes	Globalization 1.0	Globalization 2.0	Globalization 3.0
Time Frame	1492 until around 1800	1800 to 2000	2001 to future
Dynamic Force	How much brawn; how much horse-power, wind power, steam power	Falling transporta-tion costs, later falling telecommu-nications costs—breakthrough in hardware	Software and the global fiber-optic networks that makes us all next-door neighbors
Key Agent for Change	Countries and Gov-ernments	Multinationals	Individuals
Primary Questions	Where does my country fit into global competition and opportuni-ties? How can I go global and collabo-rate with others in my country?	Where does my company fit? How can I go global and collaborate with others in my firm?	Where do I fit into the global competi-tion and opportu-nities of the day and how can I, on my own, collabo-rate with others globally?

Source: Thomas Friedman, *The World Is Flat*, Farrar, Straus and Giroux (2005).

from 2001 on into the future.[8] Table 9.1 captures key issues for each of those eras, and Table 9.2 repeats, in summary form, the key argument of this book: the importance of the ancient precursors of Globalization 3.0.

One not-so-subtle purpose throughout was to offer an antidote to the sometimes blinkered exceptionalism of those who argue that the current system is wholly without precedent. Previous world-system theorists such as Immanuel Wallerstein,[9] Samir Amin,[10] Giovanni Arrighi, and Andre Gunder Frank,[11] have implied as much. Their presentations on the theme of centre and periphery have much to offer. Their application of neo-Marxist thought and the focus on private ownership and the underde-velopment of some countries (and *within* countries, e.g., China) does not invalidate their premises. This is true even if their ideas were rooted too much in the past and seemed oblivious to the way globalization morphs into new and often surprising directions every few years. For that last point, let us cite one anecdote. When one of the authors taught a course on globalization ten years ago, China and India were peripheral subjects. Today, every invited CEO and/or guest speaker, without prompting, talks about both. In the late 1980s and early 1990s, the EU and NAFTA would have been central topics of the day. Now, both have been largely super-seded (although not totally so) to a large degree by Pan-Pacific concerns. The spectre of outsourcing and the fear that the primary competitor for

Table 9.2 An Expanded View of the History of Globalization

Key Attributes	Globalization 1.0	Globalization 2.0	Globalization 3.0	Globalization .5
Time Frame	1492 until around 1800	1800 to 2000	2001 to future	27 BCE to circa 200 AD
Dynamic Force	How much brawn; how much horse-power, wind power, steam power	Falling trans-portation costs, later falling telecommuni-cations costs—breakthrough in hardware	Software and the global fiber-optic networks that makes us all next-door neighbors	Military expan-sion and later pacification in the Roman Empire. Rev-enues needed to support the Empire
Key Agent for Change	Countries and Governments	Multinationals	Individuals	The Empire and the military machine
Primary Questions	Where does my country fit into global com-petition and opportunities? How can I go global and col-laborate with others in my country?	Where does my company fit? How can I go global and col-laborate with others in my firm?	Where do I fit into the global competition and opportuni-ties of the day and how can I, on my own, collaborate with others globally?	What is allowed by my place in society? What empire or what group holds power?

computer jobs now comes from thousands of kilometers away—these anxieties have arisen in the current decade as the source of stress for many planners in North America and Europe and not just perfervid media anchors.

Meanwhile, Roy B. Norton, Minister for Congressional, Public, and Intergovernmental Relations at the Canadian embassy in Washington, wor-ries about the passage of WHTI through the U.S. Congress. WHTI stands for the Western Hemisphere Travel Initiative, to take effect June 1, 2009, requiring passports for ALL land and sea travel into the United States, which could seriously cripple Canadian trade with its best customer.[12] Even United States Trade Representative Kent Tigerton admits how hard it is to get the Americans to the table when discussing crucial border issues with Canada and Mexico. These are regional and bilateral issues looming large in an age of 3.0 Globalization. What will the future hold? Many different perspectives have emerged. Some are alarmist, or at least somewhat pes-simistic,[13] others more hopeful.[14] As of now, an optimistic outlook depends on who you are and where you live.

This summary chapter will try to shed light on these issues.

THE LONG PAST LIVES

The patient reader who has made it thus far might be forgiven for the observation that this book has appeared to be the course in Ancient History that they did not have the luxury to take as an undergraduate. The authors do not apologize for this. We believe that it is beneficial to step outside of our immediate time and place and gain the perspective that only history can offer on some nodal issues that never change.[15] There is encouragement for this thesis in the words of *New York Times* columnist David Brooks. Writing in 2006, Brooks remarked quite insightfully: "The leaders who founded [the United States] were steeped in the classics, Kennedy [Robert Kennedy] found them in crisis, and today's students are lucky if they stumble on them by happenstance."[16] Brooks cites the vivifying hope and renewal that Senator Robert Kennedy found after his brother's 1963 assassination in an overview book on the Greek achievement, entitled *The Greek Way*, by Edith Hamilton. Kennedy was encouraged by the lessons of how the creative, resourceful Greeks confronted their often harsh, fatalistic-seeming, anomic world. Our hope is that these preceding eight chapters have shed some light on what we see around us today, both for the general reader and for the close student of international business.

To business managers and/or or non-academic specialists we must confess: No, we did not find the remains of an IBM or a Wipro in the sands of ancient Iraq. We did, however, find startling precursors of what many might believe are solely modern phenomena. Some of the most pertinent of these were:

- Resource-seeking behavior
- Pockets of capitalism thriving under socialism
- Exploitation of location advantages
- Maritime or naval capitalism
- Common currency arrangements
- Creative deployment of work forces
- Industry specialization
- Beneficial self-interest encouraged

This listing should, at a minimum, imbue modern globalization theorists with a degree of humility. A sense that we are not the superior generation, the culmination of evolution's highest effort, and an awareness that others in similar situation faced not entirely dissimilar challenges—these can strengthen our grip on reality. We noted Pliny the Elder's lament that imports from Arabia, China, and India were costing Rome a huge annual

trade deficit. Pliny's remarks resonate with issues the U.S. has been wres-
tling with recently, at least in the popular media and just as often exaggerated.[17] Just as this book was heading to the publishers, a *New York Times*
article of January 27, 2008 by Para Hanna of the New America Foundation
reiterated points we had raised in our preface. The title? "Waving Goodbye
to Hegemony." Khanna wrote that "U.S. hegemony of the world will soon
be divided by the new 'Big Three:' The E.U., China and itself, while the
'second world' will be the geopolitical marketplace that will decide which
will lead the 21st century."

This may prove an astute commentary. That geopolitical marketplace
now includes such resource-strategic nations as Russia, Canada, Australia,
Venezuela, and Brazil. In early 2008, the signs that Khanna's claim that the
world distribution of power "fundamentally altered" under the steward-
ship of George W. Bush were both readily discernible. One was the influential mass journal *Time* magazine's naming of Russian President Vladimir
Putin as their "Person of the Year" for 2007. The U.S. "unipolar moment"
now seems a temporary feature of the 1990s, a time Khanna referred to
as a "decade adrift." According to this *New York Times* article, today's
Euro-technocrats, strategists, and legislators see themselves as "the global
balancer" between America and China. Both Europeans and Asians are
"insulating themselves from America's economic uncertainties." Khanna
sees a new "non-American world in the offing." What might this mean for
a globalization based on current center-periphery assumptions of Washington's worldwide leadership?

Whether the questions focus on the nature of leadership and corporate
strategy,[18] how to work with foreign partners, why and how organizations and national economies rise and fall,[19] there are lessons that one
can learn from studying the ancient world. They, too, had their "axial
periods," their sudden strategic shifts and surprises. Remember that the
smart bet was Carthage, not Rome, in 264 BCE. We catalogued how
Babylon's day was supposedly over under Persian hegemony, but how the
economic powerhouse on the Euphrates could not be denied. We learned
that the Hellenistic was not at all a "day of small things" sandwiched
between the Persian and Roman apogees, but an exceedingly inventive
and pioneering era, the climax of ancient civilization and the forerunner
of what Khanna calls the "hemispheric pan-regions" of today. It seems
obvious that a survey of the long past and its various epochs sparked
reflection on issues that managers and traders wrestle with today. There
are, undoubtedly, major economic distinctives and challenges in our own
era, but in the final analysis the commonality of situations faced in antiquity can add needed historical perspective, as well as suggest new avenues
of problem-solving.

Consider how important strategic innovation is in today's almost mani-
cally competitive marketplace. There is always the need to make new and
creative connections. With knowledge now doubling every eighteen months,

the ancient past offers us a wider field of data to draw upon than was available to Adam Smith and his generation. The Sixties "r" word, "relevance." applies here with effective force. The problem-solving apparatus employed in the past may possess much more relevance now in an era when innovation is so catalytic to corporate survival. Hong Kong has thrived under Red Chinese control since 1997, much as Greek technology flourished in Ptolemaic Egypt. Innovative exercises? Consider the impact of the introduction of metal currency for the entrepreneurs of the Aegean. On the technical front, the Greek *penteconters* outperformed the lumbering Carthaginian navy at almost every turn. As the biographies of Bill Gates and Steve Jobs and the start-up of Honda in a private garage remind us, innovation may come from the unlikeliest places—a lesson confirmed by a study of the ancient past. Eric von Hipple of MIT has already reminded us that the greatest innovations occur at points of diversity, and a yen for diversity has been a successful mantra since Cyrus sent the Jews back to rebuild Jerusalem.[20]

VIVE LA DIFFERENCE?

One sure lesson from the past is the point we argued in our previous books, *Birth of the Multinational* (1999) and *Foundations of Corporate Empire* (2000).[21] It is this: there is more than one path to success for an economy, a nation, a region, or a firm in a globalizing world. Business today has to make strategic and cultural adjustments "on the fly" in today's hyperkinetic global economy. Hockey great Wayne Gretzky's own contribution to business theory was summarized in his eloquent principle: "Don't skate to where the puck is, skate to where the puck is going to be." The brief time of heady Anglo-American triumphalism—the overblown celebration of the free enterprise system after the fall of Communism in 1991—was neither "the end of history" nor a genuflection to the inevitable rise of free market economics. One book to read here is the impeccably researched *We All Lost the Cold War* (1994) by Richard Lebow and Janice Stein. No less a player than Mikhail Gorbachev told the Washington Post at Ronald Reagan's funeral (June 11, 2004) the same thing. "We each lost $10 trillion," said Gorbachev, "We only won when the Cold War ended." Nevertheless, in the 1990s the Anglo-American model did produce superior results in growth and providing jobs for their citizens. Or so it seemed. The title of the final chapter in our *Foundations of Corporate Empire* was entitled, somewhat provocatively, "Should the World Become American?" Only a few years later, that title seems passé, yesterday's issue. It takes a while for us to discern the mystery of history.[22]

History helps. The recent spate of breast-beating re: the rise of China and India in the Western press is reminiscent on the macro level of the early 1980s, when American managers and corporate leaders were eagerly buying books such as William Ouchi's *Theory Z: How American Business Can*

Meet the Japanese Challenge and *The Art of Japanese Management: Applications for American Executives* by Richard Pascale and Anthony Athos.[23] In the Carter and early Reagan years, an America mired in recession and watching steel mills closing and "rust bowl" spreading, with thousands homeless and Toyota and Nissan pushing Chrysler to the point of bankruptcy—in that era Japan looked like the coming hegemon, just as China looks to some today. American business bidded to emulate the apparent success of a Japanese model that seemed to bring rapid economic growth, high-quality production, job security, high wages, and productivity, workplace harmony, and very low unemployment. Then, in 1989, Japan's economic drive sputtered and the stocks on the Nikkei declined to one-third of their previous value. The Japanese model was no longer the rising sun in the heavens. Thus, when our *Foundations of Corporate Empire* appeared in 2000, we could say, "the free-market Anglo-American model is back in favor."[24] At that time, America was the world's hyper power, with no ready challenger. How quickly times change.

Today, there is much worry of an emerging bipolar rivalry between Washington and Beijing. In 1990, this would have been an astonishing thought. Globalization continually surprised us by morphing in new directions, and yet, was it really globalization or was it not just dynamic, runaway capitalism climbing the steep curve of the business cycle yet one more time? The familiar results of recession and downturn are now threatening Americans as we write in early 2008. For a brief time, the world was a unipolar world with America as the only superpower. It lasted, perhaps, roughly 12 years, not an insubstantial period in our nanosecond culture. This was the period from the fall of the Berlin Wall in 1991 to the beginning of the second Iraq war in 2003. Today, the U.S. is still the dominant power and certainly the world's most desired market, but Beijing seems to have emerged as a competing economic pole. As in the days of Tyre and Athens or Carthage and Rome, rival hegemonies are taking radically different approaches to influencing the world. Once again, the dynamics of culture are not hard to spot. In the 21st century, Washington's approach has been ideologically interventionist under Bush '42. Even a Democratic President may find there is limited leverage to change America's familiar orientation to any significant degree. A renewed emphasis on a more level playing field in word trade and a more positive approach to multilateralism will help but . . . culture rules. American economic and foreign policy reflects America's public culture: the U.S. is not happy for long with being Number Two. American policy towards its trading partners is bound to still have a strong ideological bent. Free traders, beware.[25]

The emerging China–European consensus (if it holds together) looks ideologically agnostic. Above all, it appears to prize peace, development, and trade. But culture works here as well. Han China wanted only horses and jade from its Western partners. Today China seeks commodities and markets, but has traditionally been lacking in the diplomatic skills to skilfully lubricate relations with its new internationalized trading partners. "It cares not a hoot what a country's political or economic model is, so long as oil and raw materials are flowing," offers *International Herald Tribune* columnist, Roger Cohen, a globalist.[26]

In today's nanosecond culture, this, too, may be changing. This has been demonstrated in resource-rich Angola.[27] In Angola, the World Bank and the IMF—both reflecting an American ethos of trimming overhead and reducing the role of government—have pushed Angola for reform in order to bring more democracy and more market style capitalism. The Chinese style of globalization is one of eagerly working with Angola in order to gain access to their significant reserves of oil, a critical need for the giant and growing Chinese economy, without pushing for reform. But it goes beyond just access to oil resources. China's state-owned companies also won huge contracts to strengthen Angola's infrastructure in order to help bring the oil to market. Ah, infrastructure—another word for long-term thinking, not an American strength at present, as such events as Hurricane Katrina dramatically underlined. China's policy in Africa allows for African states to become long-term players and partners in the globalization game, but without having to adopt Western ideas of democracy, cost-cutting, and marketplace reform. This may well be a loss for the average African citizen, but at the moment the option seems appealing to the regimes in power. The phrase "industrialize or perish" may be getting heard again in the geopolitical marketplace, but without all the accoutrements of Western institutions that are, themselves, a facet of—that word again—the culture of the West, especially America.

Business people and business thinkers have to face the question: Are there two or even three or more paths to success in a globalizing world? We have been stepping back to review what we have learned about the business and economic systems of the ancient world. We have chronicled the evidence from history that quite different systems endured, indeed, even prospered, for very long periods of time. Persia's cross-cultural management was able to thrive largely because of a commitment to infrastructure (provinces, roads, and mail systems) and a laissez-faire approach to Babylonian business houses. There is a tempting parallel to Hong Kong's survival under Communist China. The Persian Empire was a coat of many colours, yet its carefully built up investments—deployed with staggering speed by Alexander the Great's opening up of its royal treasury—suggests a parallel with U.S. overseas investment in Western Europe after World War Two. Persia's demise fertilized the spectacular surge of trade in the Hellenistic Period. Culture is culture, but cultures can borrow from each other, sometimes extensively.

Admittedly, in the ancient world change, and even time itself, appeared to move at a much slower pace than today. Nevertheless, it is hard not to be impressed by the length of time that the seven major empires or economic systems we studied lived and prospered. These were not parochial autarkies but, rather, the dominant hegemonies of their world and time. In the case of Egypt and Assyria, both endured periods of eclipse only to rise again. Table 9.3 provides a quick overview review of these seven, how they differed on critical dimensions and the approximate times of imperial sway.

Table 9.3 Business Systems of Antiquity

Empire	Form of Economy	State Involvement	Time of Dominance
Egyptian–African	Palace–Temple	Very High	c. 3100 BCE–476 CE
Assyrian	Temple–Princely	High in Concert with Religion	1808–1050 BCE 966–612 BCE
Phoenician	Temple–Naval–Transcontinental	High in Concert with Religion	1000–334 BCE
Carthaginian–African	Temple–Naval–Transcontinental	Medium in Concert with Religion	810–202 BCE
Greek–Hellenistic	Entrepreneurial	Relatively Low	800–400BCE 331–60 BCE
Persian	Cross-Cultural Management	Medium: State Socialism and Laissez Faire	612–330 BCE
Roman	Legionary Capitalism	Medium to High	202 BCE–476 AD

Today a new world economic order is emerging, but the New World may not be as dominant as in the past. There are the everyday indicators. The perceptive Fareed Zakaria wrote to round out his own best hunches, given in the May–June, 2008 Foreign Affairs. In the February 4, 2008 *Newsweek*, he reported that without infusions of surplus monies from other countries—most notably Kuwait, Saudi Arabia, China, and Singapore—many of America's biggest banks and financial houses would have already gone bankrupt. "The world bails us out," says Zakaria, but at a price. "Power is moving away from the traditional centers of the global economy—the Western nations—to the emerging markets".[28]

This story of emerging power centers is now well known. There is India, Inc., as it has been styled—the land of Chandraguptra is enjoying an exciting surge forward. Sweden is regaining a degree of confidence and Norway is awash in oil money.[29] Both Russia and Japan are enjoying resurgence.[30] Middle powers Canada and Australia are, once again, taking advantage of their huge larders of mineral deposits. This success after decades of troubles—and largely independent of Western financial nostrums, American or European—offers current evidence of the truism of what some might style the "Frank Sinatra school of economics." That is, "I did it my way."

Perhaps the very complexity of the globalized world itself, the cultural anxieties that go along with the market efficiencies of text messaging and cell phones—perhaps this signals that no one system or ideology can embrace all the permutations that are taking place each and every day. Perhaps Marshall McCluhan was right: "The center is everywhere." In the words of a Canadian economist, "the economy is all of us, everywhere and everything." A train derailment in a nearby town can keep customers from their daily round at Starbucks, as well as lengthening the time needed for a factory to get it vital supplies. It was McLuhan, again, who offered in the 1960s that, thanks to modern electronic communications, we are a world without eyelids. Now our 24-hour cable services, scrawl messages creeping below our TV sets, You Tube and My Space, and text-messaging—all of this gives a renewed spin to the theory: "The economy is all of us." This makes even more urgent the need for business leaders to have as wide a view as possible of what is happening around us, plus an awareness of what has both worked and failed in the past. Hong Kong is to China, in some ways, what Babylon was to Persia. Differing economic arrangements for different places call for adjustments all around. A world made safe for diversity.

HISTORY, CULTURE, INSTITUTIONS

History seems to punish monochrome thinking. Which economic system is best? Some thought it was the U.S.S.R. in the 1930s. In the 1950s, America looked unassailable, masters of the business cycle at last! In the 1980s, Japan might have been the favored choice. Others in the 1990s might have plumbed for the Anglo-American model. Today it appears to be a battle royal between the U.S. and Chinese models. We think the answer is more subtle than outward indicators would have us believe. We conclude that three vital factors are central to determining which is the appropriate economic system for a nation. These are history, culture, and existing social institutions, i.e., the way different societies are organized and run. The reality of different business cultures deeply grounded in their history is a vital truism. China's rickety banking structure is a leftover from the days of Mao, yet it seems almost impossible to fix. History affects economics—millions in China remember Japan's "rape of Nanking" as if it were yesterday. Japan will not soon forget "the Nixon shocks" of 1971.

History also creates and shapes particularity. The United States free-market model grew out of American history, seemingly perfected in the "Smokestack America" of the Carnegies and Rockefellers. It generally works, although not for everyone in quite the same way. In the United States, there are political, economic, and social institutions that are quintessentially American, namely a dynamic entrepreneurial but regulated capitalism, balanced by strong traditions of citizenship, government involvement, and charitable voluntarism, along with strong religious roots. Harsh inequalities and relentless individualism are traded for a high degree of freedom and mobility. Short-term thinking and the importance of immediate shareholder returns march hand-in-hand with the willingness to take risks. Just as a fish does not know it is swimming in water, American solutions based on the myth of rugged individualism often appal such close neighbors as Canada, where geography, alone, has necessitated a degree of state intervention that worried Milton Friedman and William F Buckley.

The American model of barnstorming capitalism, mitigated by some form of safety net, may, perhaps, be the way the world works in the world's most powerful economy. It remains our view, however, that any effort to persuade the rest of the world to adopt it in its entirety may be exceedingly short-sighted. The idea that every business transaction is to be conducted in the tenor of the gunfight at the O.K. Corral may be woefully inadequate in the "Stans" that have emerged along the Russian southern borders. At times, American efficiency and problem-solving capacity has not only failed spectacularly (there is still no consensus on the Stock Market crash of 1988, for example), but its lingering "robber baron" mentality has often generated a very unpleasant backlash. A leading British thinker, Will Hutton, makes that point eloquently: "All capitalisms have a different way of reconciling private property, profit and markets to the different concerns and value systems of the wider civic society. The United States represents a particular solution to these dilemmas. But it is this model that is being thrust down the throat of the rest of the world, with huge risks that no part of the American debate seems to recognize."[31]

THE REALITY OF REGIONS

Thus, what many Americans see as a global economy superseding the nation–state—at least outside the United States—is viewed by many Europeans, Asians, and others as just one nation's approach, "capitalism in one country," a turbulent system being imposed on them as a straitjacket. This complaint is now well-known and lies behind the "surprising" support that strongmen such as Hugo Chavez of Venezuela receive from their populaces. But gunboat diplomacy is dead, and the limits of Western intervention in Third World countries may be written in the sands of Iraq in blood, even as we write.[32] Leading academics and policy planners are now discussing the debate about the impact of globalization in new ways. Undoubtedly, the biggest change in thinking is the recognition that the biggest economic activity is taking place in regions. Although almost everyone forgets it, the largest common market in the world is the one between the United States and Canada. Just one Canadian province—Ontario—buys and sells more to its giant neighbor than all of Japan. This, alone, is one reason not to count the United States out as ranking hegemon.

Alan Rugman of Indiana University confirms that not only does the vast bulk of trade take place *within* the trading zones of the EU, NAFTA, or ASEAN, but the lion's share of each nation's foreign direct investment (FDI) also takes place *between and among* these three dominant regional colossi.[33] These facts, alone, suggest to us that the future will continue to see diverse approaches to organizing the marketplace in various regions of the world economy. The NAFTA area will probably continue to be the most homogeneous, as it is dominated by the U.S. economy with the second economy in the region, Canada, a close approximation of the U.S. model. In the ASEAN region, we see greater diversity—from Hong Kong's very laissez-faire approach to China's stunning partial evolution to a more market-driven capitalism. Add to this Japan's Keiretsu system of horizontally-integrated alliances between banks and merchant houses balanced against the more government-guided approach in Singapore. One fact to keep in mind is that, although they share thousands of years of Chinese culture, over the last few hundred years, Hong Kong—a virtual city state—has developed a culture of laissez-faire capitalism, a matching set of social institutions and history of its own, which tell us that Hong Kong is a different business creature from its northern cousins. We should not be surprised—Assyria allowed Tyre to be its window on the Med, just as China has so far wisely allowed Hong Kong its freedom of action. Perhaps economic realities may allow Taiwan the same benefit, especially if the Chinese export drive unaccountably falters.

In the EU regional super-economy, with the potential to become the world's richest, we find enormous differences of culture, history, and institution-building. Especially is this true between the United Kingdom and the continent. The issues that divide the UK and the EU are not petty: should the UK adopt the *euro* currency marker and scrap its tradition of pounds, shillings, and pence? At the heart of the debate is the question of the UK's adopting a more Brussels-flavored continental approach. However, even within continental Europe, there is considerable debate about the best economic strategy. An excellent example of the differences between nations on the continent is found in Marie-Laure Djelic's 1999 book, *Exporting the American Model* (Oxford University Press). Djelic carefully studied the impact of the Marshall Plan on three European economies—France, Germany, and Italy. This extremely statesmanlike measure, a gift of some $16 billion from the U.S. to Europe, made the difference in bringing Western Europe back economically after the carnage of World War Two. Djelic concluded that each country made very considerable adaptations of the American system. Darius I of Persia would have understood perfectly.

Once again the point is made—Anglo-American capitalism in all its Carnegie–Rockefeller glory is only one model of capitalism, one that is firmly and irrevocably rooted in Anglo-American culture. Even to use that term, "Anglo-American," is to raise eyebrows, proving once again that cultural matters matter! T. S. Eliot once defined culture as "all the characteristic activities of a people"—the Royal Family and soccer, The Henley Regatta and a night at the pub. If, as some suggest, we were to take just one system and impose it on other countries, it might fail miserably. Why? Because it goes against human nature—another society's view of the world and how to live. The authors are a Canadian and an American, both of whom have spent extensive periods of time living in Western Europe. We understand the strength of America's underlying Calvinist myth, the belief—and it is a belief—that in this bountiful United States, anyone can succeed; if they don't, it is solely their fault. The very conservative American founding fathers had such respect for orderly society and its distinct institutions that it took the intervention of Benjamin Franklin to edit Thomas Jefferson's noble phrase, "life, liberty, and the pursuit of happiness." The young Virginian had originally inscribed "life, liberty, and property." In Europe, few people own much property in the sense of the wide open spaces that beckoned to Americans pushing from the Atlantic to the Pacific, guided by a vague sense of manifest destiny. This view that "anyone can make it," that the commonwealth is merely a state of nature where the strong will survive—this idea possesses an amazing resilience in the United States. It explains the near-adulation for Gorbachev's old dialogue partner, President Ronald Reagan (1981–89), in many circles. Reagan attempted to balance the budget by slashing the welfare roll (among other things), and lived to tell the tale.

"Sink or swim." "You're on your own." "If you don't work you don't eat." In America, that last has the seeming force of Scripture behind it, as 2 Thessalonians 3:10 makes clear. Such views are simply not accepted in a society such as Finland's or even in Japan, where an individual is seen as part of a group, and the concept of nation trumps that of the state. In those cultures, and to a certain extent also in Canada, if a person becomes an alcoholic, it is seen as a group failure, as well as an individual problem. It goes against social institutions, and there are many societal agencies in place to offer help. The "we're all in this together" *communitarian* ethic affects the way management and workers relate to each other, and even the relationship between universities and business. One of us remembers arriving not so long ago in Gothenburg, Sweden and being driven to the corporate headquarters by a senior manager. He looked troubled. He explained that his company was in the midst of corporate downsizing. What was intriguing was that before the people were dismissed, they had to discuss the list with the union; not something one would usually do in the U.K. or the U.S. But, then again, in Sweden social networking is different, because Sweden's culture is different than what North Americans experienced as part of the growing up process.

Are we arguing that the Japanese, Germans, Swedes,[34] and others are living in Utopia? Not at all! Diversity and respect for culture is our point. We may laugh at some of Michael Moore's wittier barbs, but we are not packing our bags to get back to Europe or Asia anytime soon. We believe that there is much strength to the Globalization thesis, even if its cheerleaders may be describing the workings of globally-linked, turbocharged traditional capitalism. We can see that there are times in a nation's life when it should take a second look and diversify its socialist principles. After all, our text shows that even mighty, hidebound Egypt allowed the entrepreneurial spirit to survive. We sketched the life of the patriarch Joseph, who was the Hebrew Bible's sterling example of the spirit of Horatio Alger or of

Gilbert and Sullivan's self-made ruler of "the Queen's navee." Remember? He began polishing locks and door-handles and

> polished that lock so carefully / That now I am the ruler of the Queen's navee.

American industry pulled out of the 1970s and early 1980s stagflation by becoming, once again, the economic wonder of the world. It dramatically changed course, initiated drastic cost-cutting measures, imposed salary cuts, swiftly remodernized even its rust bowl constituencies, automated, encouraged innovation, cut taxes, and give business a freer hand. In many ways, it worked. American-led globalization does call for reform of inefficiencies and deadwood. It seems reasonable that countries unable to get launched economically should adopt some of these strengths, should continue on their course of reform, of making work pay more than welfare for healthy adults, of putting their banking systems in order, of paying off long-standing government debt, reducing tax burdens that severely penalize innovation, and freeing up an economy for the competitive 21st century.

AGAIN, CULTURE

In conclusion, history has evolved differently in different nations and at different times. History and culture are both symbiotically linked, and a nation's history often reflects deeply-rooted matters of culture. Nations should not wall themselves off behind their tariff walls and skate over what is to be learned from other cultures. Yet, Americans of the 19th century were staunch believers in protecting young and evolving industries, as Hernando de Soto showed in his provocatively titled *The Mystery of Capital: Why Capitalism Triumphs in the West and Fails Everywhere Else* (New York: Basic Books, 2000). The Greeks were not only the great philosophers of antiquity; they were also the great borrowers. They learned from the Phoenicians how to sail the Atlantic and from India how to master the monsoons. National culture is a force, but it is not a law of nature such as gravity. Nations do tend to go in certain directions and not others, and this sometimes limits what can be done. The Chinese experience with building a competitive manufacturing system offers an example here. Their rulers seem to be determined to repeat the mistakes of the polluters and slum landlords of Gilded Age America—already some one million people are said to have died through pollution. Yet China has never had anyone to articulate the commanding vision of "life, liberty, and the pursuit of happiness," and the United States so far remains the only polity committed by decree to securing such benefits for their people.

CULTURE, AGAIN

One last snapshot should help. The Japanese, still in the midst of their painful restructuring, remain determined to do it Japanese-style, even as they launch their own entrepreneurial and high-tech alliances. Japan's public life and economic theorists hover between former PM Junichiro Koizumi pushing for more American style reform and the predictable backlash against too much "Americanization." Against Koizumi's efforts is the phenomenal success of *A Nation's Dignity*, a book that calls upon Japan to shun American-style capitalism and return to more traditional values. Written by Masahiko Fujiwara, a mathematician turned social critic, it has sold more than two million copies.[35] Yet a harsh downsizing proceeds, with estimates of millions of "over-employed" workers on firm payrolls. Some companies, such as Yokogawa Electric, are determined that the system of lifetime work in a firm can survive. They are introducing a merit system of promotion in which workers will compete against one another to improve quality. Unlike many North American CEOs, who believe that job security turns a good employee into a mediocre one, Yokogawa officials argue that, in Japan, it makes them more responsible. Toyota chairman Hiroshi Okuda, who also heads the Nikkeiren, or Japan Federation of Employers' Associations, is also trying to defend the lifetime employment system. Deeming it "suitable for Japanese who highly value stability and teamwork," and expressing doubts about whether the downsizing being attempted at Nissan would work in Japan, the attempt remains to be evaluated.

Job security? It is not the highest of American business values. "They've moved on," became a cliché after the downsizing of the 1990s. Yet it is crucial to remember that the tradition of job security in Japan dates back over two centuries, when children began work as apprentices and were given an allowance when they retired. Again, culture. Close to a majority of companies plan to maintain the lifetime employment system, seeing in it a source of mental health and corporate loyalty. Firms approach American consultants to obtain advice on how to implement early retirement plans instead of lay-offs. According to Kazuhiro Arai, Professor of Economics at Hitotsubashi University, American-style hire-and-fire management is not an option for most Japanese firms, for it runs deeply against the grain of Japanese culture: "The traditional value for Japanese is the spirit of *wa* [harmony]," and the "lifetime employment system pulls out a co-operative attitude and loyalty among Japanese employees who originally have Japanese values."

Arai's view is shared by Hosei University's Professor Masaru Kaneko, who recognizes that many workers have been trained to work only for their companies. Their specialty is loyal service to Toyota or Nissan, not as a mere cog in the wheel or transmission assembly plant. This makes it harder for them to take their skills with them to another firm or—heaven forbid—start their own business, as many would do in America or even Europe. In short, too much American-style job-cutting would be a social disaster in Japan.

Japan's peculiar problems and adjustments point up, again, the theme of this book. It is this: Companies and nations will respond to new challenges in their own ways, conditioned by their own histories and values, much as they did in the ancient past. Mighty Carthage learned that naval capitalism could not sustain a monopoly forever. The old order changed and finally left the Phoenician West in ruins. The Persians, almost conquering themselves along with the weight of their 127 provinces, found that a certain amount of *laissez faire*—expressed very much as letting nations preserve their original cultures—worked very well.

Thus, both the markets of ancient Ebla and today's New Zealand rarely operate in a vacuum. Culture and history and the institutions birthed by that history will continue to affect the economy, and history usually counsels caution. "The economy is all the things that are happening." At this writing, it would seem that the world's trading nations may well have to brace themselves for the entrepreneurial, turbocharged capitalism that comes along with (and perhaps defines) robust globalization. The Japanese experience shows, once again, that markets alone often undermine social stability. "The economy is all of us." It operates in societies where social, religious, and familial ties—the culture—dictate codes of honesty, trust, and cooperation, as well as competition. Such cultures create the very social order, that rule of law, without which markets could not function. In the end, the German social market and the Japanese *keiretsu* may become more like the American model in terms of deregulation and competition, but the German symphony will no doubt play its own distinctive score, and the Japanese garden will prize harmony and inner calm above all, a useful counterpoint to Americans busily at work on constructing a "more level playing field."[36]

If there is wisdom to be learned by our 3,600 year trek through the past, it may well be learning to appreciate the value of the previous paragraph. The architects of globalization—economic planners, CEOs, government officials—have a choice. It is a choice that was articulated in ancient China by the two very different thinkers. We met them in Chapter 8. Sun Tzu counselled, in effect, "Business is war by other means." The alternative vision comes from the pen of E Yin, Prime Minister of China around 1750 BCE. "Do not slight the concerns of the people. Think of their difficulties. . . . Be careful to think about the end at the beginning. . . . When you hear words that agree with your own thinking, you must ask whether these words are not wrong."

The economy; it is all of us. An excellent watchword, whatever the fate of globalization.

Appendix

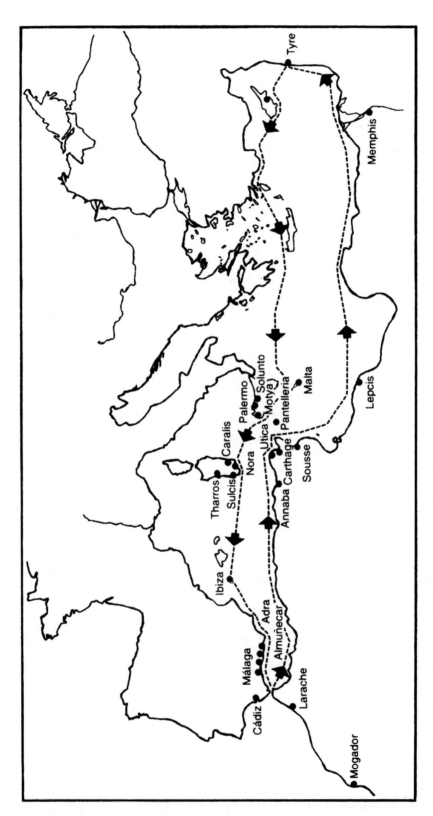

Map A.1 Phoenician settlements and shipping routes in the Mediterranean..

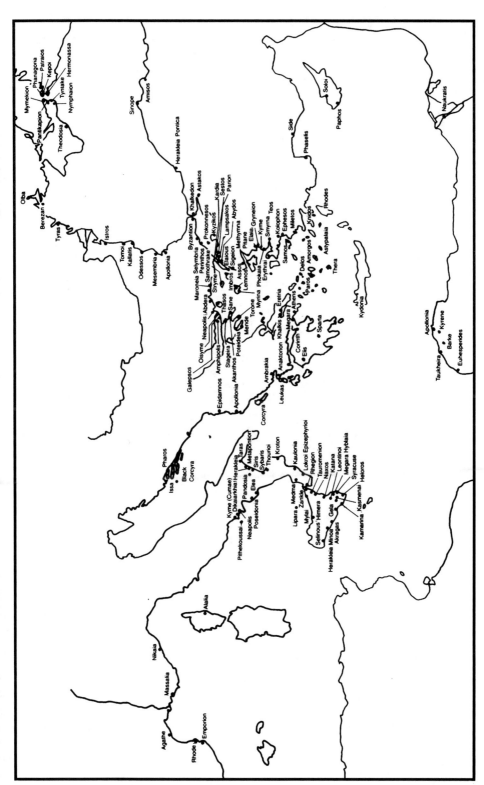

Map A.2   Greek settlements abroad.

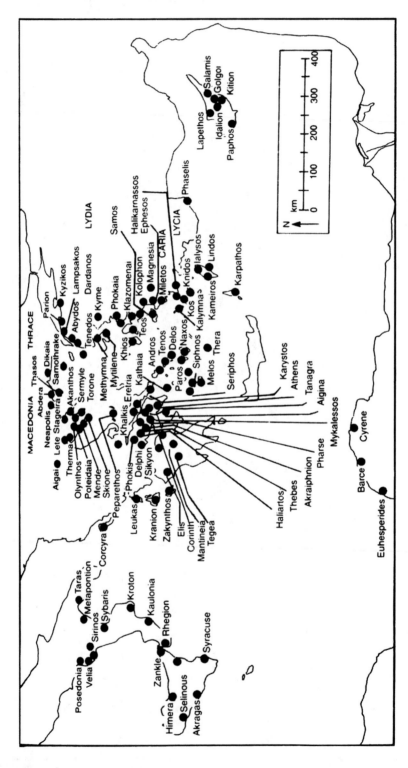

Map A.3   Cities which minted coins before 480 B.C.

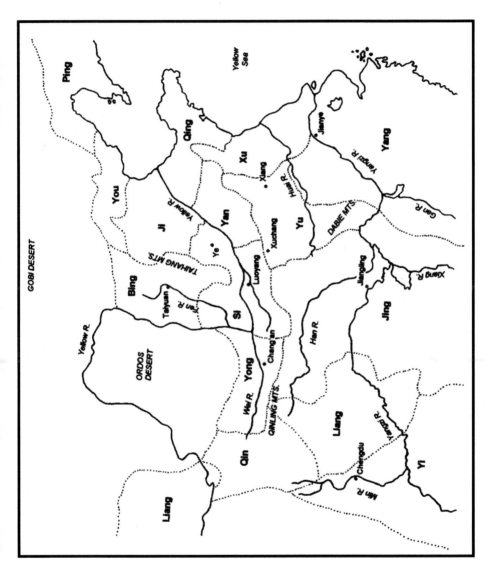

Map A.4 China under the Western Jin dynasty, *ca.* AD 300, showing provinces.

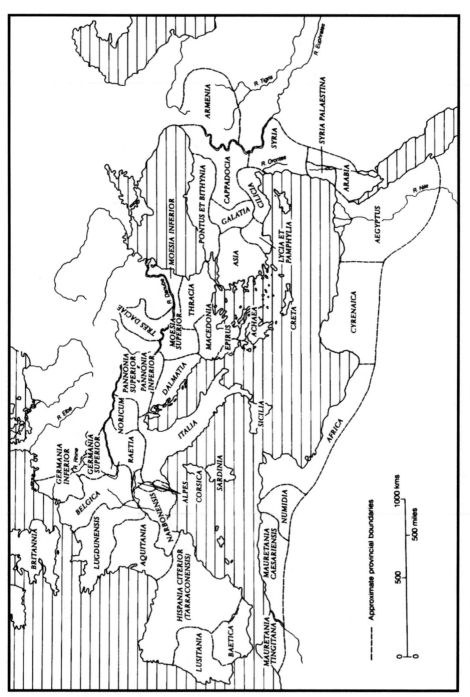

Map A.5 The Roman provinces in the second century AD.

Notes

NOTES TO PREFACE

1. Moore, Karl, and David Lewis. *Birth of the Multinational: 2000 Years of Ancient Business History, from Ashur to Augustus.* Copenhagen: Copenhagen Business School Press, 1999; Ricks, David. "Review of Birth of the Multinational: 2000 Years of Ancient Business History from Ashur to Augustus". *Journal of International Business Studies* 33, no. 2 (2002): 397–98.; Wilkins, Mira. "Review of Birth of the Multinational: 2000 Years of Ancient Business History from Ashur to Augustus". *Journal of Economic Literature* 38, no. 4 (2000): 976–78.

2. See Mallet, Paul. "Was It Common or Was It Single?" *The Times Literary Supplement*, December 15 2000, 26. Dr. Mallet is a fellow at Downing College, Cambridge and an historian of the ancient economy. See also Philip De Souza's comments in De Souza, Philip. "Book Reviews." *Economic History Review* 53, no. 3 (2000): 586–87.

3. Niemeyer, Hans Georg. "Review of Birth of the Multinational: 2000 Years of Ancient Business History from Ashur to Augustus." *Journal of World History* 14, no. 1 (2003): 90–92.

4. Finley, Moses. *The Use and Abuse of History,* London: Penguin Books, 1990, 210.

5. Kanter, Rosabeth Moss. *World Class: Thriving Locally in the Global Economy*: Free Press, 1997, 37.

6. Friedman, Thomas L. *The Lexus and the Olive Tree.* New York: Anchor Books, 2002, 5.

7. Rugman, Alan, and Richard Hodgetts. *International Business.* 3rd ed. London: Prentice Hall, 2003.

8. Bordo, Michael D. "Globalization in historical perspective: Our era is not as unique as we might think, and current trends are not irreversible." *Business Economics* (2002): 20.

9. Giddens, Anthony. *The Consequences of Modernity.* Cambridge: Polity Press, 1990.

10. Robertson, Roland. "Globality, Global Culture, and Images of World Order." In *Social Change and Modernity*, edited by H. Haferkamp and N. Smelser. Berkley: University of California Press, 1992, 395–411.

11. Scholte, Jan Aart. *Globalization: A Critical Introduction.* London: Palgrave, 2000, 15–17.

12. Friedman, *The Lexus*; and Friedman, Thomas L. *The World Is Flat: A Brief History of the Twenty-First Century.* 2nd ed. New York: Farrar, Straus and Giroux, 2006. The second edition of *The World Is Flat*, published a bare

six month after the first edition, includes 100 pages not in the first edition, a testament to the speed of change inherent in the discussion of globalization.

13. Engardio, Pete, Aaron Bernstein, and Manjeet Kripalani. "The New Global Job Shift." *Business Week*, February 3 (2003); Dehoff, Kevin, and Vikas Sehgal. "Innovators without Borders." *Strategy + Business*, August (2006); Couto, Vinay, and Ashok Divakaran. "How to Be an Outsourcing Virtuoso." *Strategy + Business*, August (2006). Then there are the numerous stories in the Wall Street Journal, such as "Novartis to Set up Drug R&D Center in China." In *Wall Street Journal*. Hong Kong: XFN-Asia, 2006.

14. We use the EU May 2003 definition, which the EU adopted on January 1, 2005 for defining micro, small, and medium size enterprises. A "micro" enterprise, a new category in the EU definition, is less than 10 employees; "small" means anything under 50 and "medium" means 250 or less. See the *SME definition: User Guide and Model Declaration*, published by Enterprise and Industry Publications arm of the European Union.

15. Karl pulled down from his shelf the international business textbook currently in use at McGill University for the undergraduate International Business course: Hill, Charles W. L. *International Business: Competing in the Global Marketplace*. 6th ed. Boston: McGraw-Hill/Irwin, 2007. He was quite surprised by the number of topics that he would be covering in the winter term and that had surfaced during the writing of this book.

NOTES TO CHAPTER 1

1. Any list of prominent researchers and writers would include names such as Porter, Levitt, Dunning, Drucker, Thurow, Yip, Rugman, Casson, Buckley, Ohmae, and other executives writing in annual reports and interviews.

2. Hobsbawm, Eric. *The Age of Extremes: A History of the World, 1914–1991* New York Vintage Books, 1994, 3.

3. Greenspan, A. "Market capitalism: The role of free markets," *Vital Speeches of the Day*, (May 1998): 14, 64, 418–421. See also Wessel, David. "Greenspan Sees Asian Crisis Speeding World-Wide Move to Market Capitalism," *The Wall Street Journal*, April 3 1998, A2.

4. In the Nordic countries and much of Europe, a key measure is not having "too" large a gap between rich and poor, the wealthiest and the poorest elements of society. In the Anglo-American model, greater relative emphasis falls on the freedom of individuals to succeed or, indeed, fail. In ancient Assyria, as shown in Chapter 4, appeasing the gods was the *sine qua non*. However strange to our postmodern ears, it appeared perfectly legitimate to the multinational managers of Ashur.

5. Ferguson, Niall. Empire: *The Rise and Demise of the British World Order and the Lessons for Global Power*. London: Penguin Books, 2002, xxv.

6. Rostow, W. *The World Economy: History and Prospect*. Austin: University of Austin Press, 1978. See also North, D. *Structure and Change in Economic History*. New York: W. W. Norton, 1981; Chandler, A. *Scale and Scope: The Dynamics of Industrial Capitalism*. Cambridge: Harvard University Press, 1990; Powelson, J. *Centuries of Economic Endeavor: Parallel Paths in Japan and Europe and Their Contrast with the Third World*. Ann Arbour: University of Michigan Press, 1994.

7. Orlin, L. *Assyrian Colonies in Cappadocia*. The Hague: Mouton, 1970; Larsen, M. T. *The Old Assyrian City–State and Its Colonies*. Copenhagen: Akademisk Forlag, 1976; Aubet, M. E. *The Phoenicians and the West: Politics, Colonies and Trade*. Cambridge: Cambridge University Press, 1987.

8. Dunning, John H. *Multinational Enterprises and the Global Economy.* Wokingham: Addison-Wesley, 1993, 96.

9. Karl's work has been published in leading business journals, including: *Strategic Management Journal, Journal of International Business Studies, Human Relations, Management International Review, Business History, World Business, Across the Board, Leader to Leader, Strategy + Business, The Academy of Management Executive, Journal of Applied Behavioural Science, Policy Options, Marketing Research,* and *the Journal of Brand Management.*

10. David's work has been published in a number of journals, including: *Florilegiun, Management International Review,* and *Business History.*

11. Kemp, B. *Ancient Egypt, Anatomy of a Civilization.* London: Routledge, 1989, 233.

12. Kemp, *Ancient Egypt,* 233.

13. Kemp, *Ancient Egypt,* 233.

14. See, for example, for Fourth Quarter 1994, Chandy, P. R., and Thomas G. E. Williams. "The Impact of Journals and Authors on International Business Research: A Citational Analysis of Jibs Articles," *Journal of International Business Studies* 25, no. 4 (1994): 715–28. The authors found Dunning the most cited author in this key international business journal. An earlier article from the First Quarter 1991, Morrison, Allen J., and Andrew C. Inkpen. "An Analysis of Significant Contributions to the International Business Literature," *Journal of International Business Studies* 22, no. 1 (1991): 143–53. This report ranked International Business scholars by their publications and citations and suggested that Professor Dunning was one of the top 10 international business scholars in the world.

15. There are competing theories on why a firm "goes international." Two other important theories that seek to explain foreign activities of firms are the internationalization theory of the MNE. See Buckley, P. and M. . Casson. *The Future of the Multinational Enterprise.* New York: Holmes & Meier, 1976; Hennart, J. F. *A Theory of Multinational Enterprise.* Ann Arbor: University of Michigan Press, 1982. The second is the macro-economics theory of foreign direct investment. See Kojima, K. "Reorganization of North-South Trade: Japan's Foreign Economic Policy of the 1970's," *Hitotsubashi Journal of Economics* 23 (1973): 630–40; Kojima, K. *Japanese Direct Investment Abroad.* Monograph series 1 vols, Social Science Research Institute. Tokyo: International Christian University, 1990.

16. Dunning, 3.

17. The term "strategic competencies" comes from Bartlett, C., and S. Ghoshal. "Changing the Role of Top Management: Beyond Structure to Processes," *Harvard Business Review* January–February (1995): 86–96; J. Kay uses the term "distinctive capabilities" in Kay, J. *Foundations of Corporate Success.* Oxford: Oxford University Press, 1995.

18. Dunning, *Multinational Enterprises*; Buckley and Casson, *The Future of Multinational Enterprise.*

19. In Anglo-American economies, growth is the mantra and managers who do not deliver "results" are often threatened with removal by shareholders. Investors look for a return from firms higher than those from safer investments, such as banks or government bonds. This justifies the risks they take in corporate investment. Returns required from new small firms by "Business Angels" (see Coveney, Patrick, and Karl Moore. *Business Angels: Securing Start up Finance.* Chichester: John Wiley, 1998.), or wealthy private investors, can reach levels of over 40% a year, compared to the 4% or 5% earned from a British savings account in the local high street bank. Investors on the continent

and in Japan have traditionally been more patient, but that seems to be breaking down under the pressure of global investors who are willing to quickly move their investments to other countries in the race for high returns.

20. They can also turn to using their Firm Specific Advantages (FSAs) in allied markets, what might be called horizontal extension. An example is Virgin expanding in its home market of the U.K. by buying a rail line, although such moves add to the risk, e.g., can McDonald's really make a good salad?

21. This based on Fortune magazine's "Fortune Global 500." *Fortune* (2005).

22. Wal-Mart has struggled overseas. It has enjoyed success in Canada and the United States but has announced its withdrawal from South Korea in May, 2006. Germany soon followed in July, 2006.

23. Fulford, B. "Proxy War in Japan." *Forbes* (2002). http://www.forbes.com/global/2002/0930/024.html (access June 16, 2008)

24. See his best seller, Porter, M. *The Competitive Advantage of Nations*. Boston: The Free Press, 1990.

25. Aerospace giant Bombardier announced that it would be making parts for its' regional jet fleet in Mexico. See "Bombardier to Build Mexican Facility," *Globe and Mail*, October 27, 2006, B7.

26. Piggott, C. "Why Europeans Wait Longer to Be Free," *The European* (April 1998).

27. Naik, G. "China's Spending for Research Outpaces the U.S., R&D," *Wall Street Journal* (2006), A2. It went on to report that "spending in China has been growing at an annual rate of about 17%, and is far higher than the 4% to 5% annual growth rates reported for the U.S., Japan and the European Union over the past dozen years." Earlier in 2006, a *Wall Street Journal* article, July 19, 2006, by Megha Rajagopalan reported that, "India and China, long considered cost-saving havens for corporate call centers and back-office staff, are attracting the research labs of the world's biggest companies . . . One survey of 186 top companies found more than three-quarters of research and development sites planned through 2007 are slated for India and China (page B4)." Is this globalization or capitalism by another name?

28. Buckley, P. "The Role of Management in Internalization Theory," *Management International Review*, 33, 3, (1993): 197–207.

29. We use the term "foreign subsidiaries" here very broadly to include forms short of subsidiaries such as a sales office.

30. Saggs, H. W. F. *The Might That Was Assyria*. London: Sidgwick and Jackson, 1984, 289–90.

31. Saggs, *The Might*, 294–6; Wiseman, D. J. *The Expansion of Assyrian Studies*—An Inaugral Lecture Delivered on 29 February 1962. London: Oxford University Press, 1962, 4–5; Budge, E. A. W. *The Rise and Progress of Assyrian Antiquities*. London: Martin Hopkinson and Co. Ltd., 1925, 11–22.

32. Budge, *The Rise*, 64–67; Saggs, *The Might*, 294–97; James, P., I. J. Thorpe, N. Kokkinow, R. Morkot, and J. Frankish. *Centuries of Darkness: A Challenge to the Conventional Chronology of Old World Archaeology*. Brunswick, NJ: Rutgers University Press, 1993, 261–64.

33. Budge, *The Rise*, 111–14; Saggs *The Might*, 297–98; James et al, Centuries, 261–64.

34. Budge, *The Rise*, 47–52, 68–73, 80–84.

35. James et al., *Centuries*, 261–4; Wiseman, *The Expansion*, 5–6.

NOTES TO CHAPTER 2

1. Barber, Benjamin. *Jihad Vs. Mcworld*. New York: Ballantine Books, 1995, 23.

2. In Otazo, Karen. "On Trust and Culture." *Strategy + Business*, Autumn (2006), Otazo reviews five excellent books on the topic of social networks.
3. *Worlds of History: A Comparative Reader*, Volume Two: Since 1400, edited by Kevin Reilly. Vol. 2. New York: Bedford/St. Martin's, 2007, 506.
4. Van de Mieroop, Marc. *A History of the Ancient near East, Ca. 3000–323 B.C.* Malden: Blackwell Publishing, 2004, 15–16.
5. A trail of pottery from the late Stone Age indicates two streams of migration from the mountains of Iran to the Iraqi plains. The northerly flow settled in northern Iraq and gave rise to the Halaf culture. The southerly branch founded the Ubaid culture, progenitor of the Sumerian civilization. From Rohl, D. M. *A Test of Time, Legend: The Genesis of Civilisation.* Vol. 2. London: Century Publishing Co., 1998, 136–37. "This is consistent," says Rohl, "with the Genesis tradition which relates that the ancestors of the Hebrew patriarchs left Eden and eventually ended up in the 'Land of Shinar'—ancient Sumer" (Rohl, *Test*, 131).
6. Ecology shapes history. Today's concern with global warming and its impact on our climate and our economy is reflected in the worldwide attention paid to an 2006 report by the former and Senior Vice-President of the World Bank. Anciently, medium-term climate change allowed for the development of a more sophisticated civilization, however experts appear to be believe that global warming doesn't bode as well for our time.
7. Pollock, Susan. *Ancient Mesopotamia: The Eden That Never Was.* Cambridge: Cambridge University Press, 1999, 78–79.
8. Pollock, *Ancient*, 186–87.
9. Jay, Peter. *The Wealth of Man.* 1st ed. New York: Public Affairs, 2000, 15–16.
10. Pollock, *Ancient*, 86–87; Pollock, *Ancient*, 94–96.
11. Pollock, *Ancient*, 86–92.
12. Algaze, Guillermo. *The Uruk World System: The Dynamics of Expansion of Early Mesopotamian Civilization.* Chicago: University of Chicago Press, 1993, 61–73, 110–11.
13. Algaze, *Uruk*, 96.
14. Algaze, *Uruk*, 61–73; Algaze, Uruk, 110–11.
15. Algaze, *Uruk*, 104.
16. Kurht, Amélie. *The Ancient near East, C. 3000–330 Bc.* 2 vols. Vol. 1. London: Routledge, 1995, 21; "The Tradition of Empire in Mesopotamia." In *Power and Propaganda: A Symposium on Ancient Empires*, edited by Mogens Trolle Larsen. Copenhagen Akademisk Forlag, 1979, 47, 77.
17. Algaze, *Uruk*, 105.
18. Larsen, *Power*, 46–47.
19. Pollock, *Ancient*, 93.
20. Pollock, *Ancient*, 95–96.
21. Pollock, *Ancient*, 104–106.
22. Yale archaeologists William J. Hallo and William Kelly Simpson see memories of these events in the Genesis account of Cain and his progeny: Enoch, Irad, Mehujael, Methushael, Lamech, and Tubal Cain. Tubal Cain's listing may recall early Sumerian coppersmiths, (Gen 4:17–23, Biblical references from New International Version here and throughout). See Hallo, W. J., and W. K. Simpson. *The Ancient Near East, a History.* New York: Harcourt Brace Jovanovich, 1971, 27–33.
23. Pettinato, Giovanni. *The Archives of Ebla: An Empire Inscribed in Clay.* Garden City, NY: Doubleday, 1981, 174.
24. Hallo and Simpson, *Ancient Near*, 27–33; Nissen, H. J. *The Early History of the Ancient near East: 9000–2000 B.C.* Chicago: University of Chicago

Press, 1983, 39–64; Pettinato, *The Archives*, 174; Childe, V. G. *New Light on the Most Ancient East.* New York: Frederick A. Praeger, 1953, 129.
25. Hallo and Simpson, *Ancient Near*, 31–34.
26. Kuhrt, *Ancient Near East*, 28.
27. Kuhrt, *Ancient Near East*, 43.
28. National Geographic Book Service. *Everyday Life in Bible Times*, edited by James Pritchard. Washington: National Geographic Society, 1967, 43.
29. National Geographic, *Everyday*, 28–29; Jay, *Wealth*, 19–20; Pollock, *Ancient*, 17.
30. Jay, *Wealth*, 21.
31. Jay, *Wealth*, 28–29; Jay, *Wealth*, 19–20; Pollock, *Ancient*, 17.
32. Pollock, *Ancient*, 119–20.
33. Pollock, *Ancient*, 122.
34. Pollock, *Ancient*, 122.
35. Pollock, *Ancient*, 123.
36. Pollock, *Ancient*, 123–4; Archaeology, The Joukowsky Institute of. "The Archaeology of Mesopotamia: Early Dynastic Period (Early Bronze Age) in the Diyala River Basin." http://proteus.brown.edu/mesopotamianarchaeology/799, May 25, 2008.
37. Pollock, *Ancient*, 186.
38. Hallo and Simpson, *Ancient Near*, 34.
39. Kuhrt, *Ancient Near East*, 25; Kuhrt, *Ancient Near East*, 31–32.
40. "Enmerkar and the lord (or Land, conflict with text?) of Aratta," Electronic Text Corpus of Sumerian Literature from Oxford University's Faculty of Oriental Studies.
41. Enmerkar.
42. Enmerkar.
43. Enmerkar.
44. Hallo and Simpson, *Ancient Near*, 33–49; Kramer, Samuel Noah. *The Sumerians: Their History, Culture, and Character.* Chicago: University of Chicago Press, 1963, 73–4.
45. Sandars, N. K. *The Epic of Gilgamesh: An English Version With an Introduction.* London: Penguin Books, 1972, 68.
46. Sandars, *Gilgamesh*, 68.
47. Sandars, *Gilgamesh*, 104–5.
48. Pettinato, *Archives*, 95.
49. TM 75.G.2136, in Pettinato, *Archives*, 107; TM.75.G.2420, lower edge II 3'–18', in Pettinato, *Archives*, 105.
50. TM 75.G.1682, Pettinato, *Archives*, 259.
51. Pettinato, *Archives*,156.
52. Pettinato, *Archives*,156–63.
53. TM 75.G.2070, Pettinato, *Archives*, 201.
54. Pettinato, *Archives*, 166.
55. Pettinato, *Archives*, 180.
56. Pettinato, *Archives*, 180.
57. Pettinato, *Archives*, 184.
58. TM 75.G.1980, obverse vi.1–3, Pettinato, *Archives*, 185.
59. TM 75.G.1390, obverse ii,1–3, Pettinato, *Archives*, 187.
60. Pettinato, *Archives*, 201.
61. Johnson, Paul. *Civilization of Ancient Egypt.* New York: Harper Collins, 1999, 18.
62. Hallo and Simpson, *Ancient Near*, 229.
63. Hallo and Simpson, *Ancient Near*, 18–42.
64. Hallo and Simpson, *Ancient Near*, 43.

65. Saggs, H. W. F. *Civilization Before Greece and Rome.* New Haven: Yale University Press, 1989, 134–36.
66. Kemp, *Ancient Egypt*, 232.
67. Kemp, *Ancient Egypt*, 233–35.
68. Kemp, *Ancient Egypt*, 235–36.
69. Kemp, *Ancient Egypt*, 237–38.
70. Kemp, *Ancient Egypt*, 245.
71. Kuhrt, *Ancient Near East*, 41–3; Kramer, *The Sumerians*, 53–56.
72. Larsen, *Power*, 76 says "South Mesopotamia has no source of metals, no trees that produce suitable timber for larger constructions and only insignificant amounts of stone. The focus of much documented commercial and imperial activity is the acquisition of these items" [Kuhrt, *Ancient Near East*, 21].
73. Larsen, *Power*, 77–79.
74. Van de Mieroop, *A History*, 63.
75. Kramer, *The Sumerians*, 276–84; Forster, B.R. "Commercial Activities in Sargonic Mesopotamia." *Iraq* 39, Part 1 (1977): 38–39.
76. Pettinato, *Archives* 182.
77. Enki and Ninhursag, translated in Kramer, *The Sumerians*, 279.
78. Enki and the World Order, Kramer, *The Sumerians*, 176. We have altered the formatting of the quote and removed some brackets for clarity's sake.
79. Mellnik. "An Akkadian Illustration of a Campaign in Cilicia?" *Anatolia* 7 (1963): 101–02, 10–11.
80. Forster, "Commercial", 35–36.
81. Forster, "Commercial", 37.
82. Forster, "Commercial", 32–33; Forster, "Commercial", 36–37.
83. See Hodell, D. A., J. H. Curtis, and M. Brenner. "Possible Role of Climate in the Collapse of Classic Maya Civilization." *Nature* 375 (1995): 391–94; also Sandweiss, D. H., K. A. Maasch, and D. G. Anderson. "Transitions in the Mid-Holocene." *Science* 283 (1999): 499–500.
84. Niroma, Timo. "The Climax of a Turbulent Millennium: Evidence for Major Impact Events in the Late Third Millennium Bce." (2001), http://personal.eunet.fi/pp/tilmari/tilmari2.htm.
85. Niroma, "The Climax".
86. A widely cited article on this topic is Cullen, H. M., P. B. deMeocal, S. Hemming, G. Hemming, F. Brown, T. Guilderson, and F. Sirocko. "Climate Change and the Collapse of the Akkadian Empire: Evidence from the Deep Sea." *Geology* 28, no. 4 (2000): 379–82.
87. See remarks by Professor Harvey Weiss, quoted in Niroma, "The Climax".

NOTES TO CHAPTER 3

1. Durant, Will. Our Oriental Heritage. Vol. 1, *The Story of Civilization.* New York: Simon and Schuster, 1942, 1–2.
2. Van de Mieroop, *A History*, 72.
3. Hallo and Simpson, *The Ancient near East*, 86–87.
4. Hallo and Simpson, *The Ancient near East*, 82.
5. Curtis, John Briggs, and William W. Hallo. *Money and Merchants in Ur Iii.* Cincinnati: Jewish Institute of Religion, 1959, 105–12.
6. Jay, *The Wealth*, 22.
7. Postgate, J. N. *Early Mesopotamia: Society and Economy at the Dawn of History.* London: Routledge, 1992, 220–1.
8. Postgate, *Early Mesopotamia*, 220–1.

9. Garelli, Paul. *Les Assyriens En Cappadoce*. Paris: Librarie Adrien Maissoneuve, 1963, 171–72; Postgate, *Early Mesopotamia*, 220–1.
10. Goetzmann, William N. "Financing Civilization." New Haven, 2001. <http://viking.som.Yale.edu/will/finciv/chapter1.htm>.
11. Goetzmann, "Financing."
12. Goetzmann, "Financing."
13. Goetzmann, "Financing."
14. Leeman, W. F. "Uet V 367." In *Foreign Trade in the Old Babylonian Period, as Revealed in Texts from Southern Mesopotamia*, 36–37. Leiden: J. N. Brill, 1960, 36–37.
15. Goetzmann, "Financing."
16. Goetzmann, "Financing."
17. Empire, page 14.
18. Lal, B. B. "The Chronological Horizon of the Mature Indus Civilization." In *From Sumer to Meluhha: Contributions to the Archaeology of South and West Asia* in Memory of George F. Dales, Jr., edited by Jonathan Mark Kenoyer, 15–25. Madison: Prehistory Press, 1994.
19. Basham, A. L. *The Wonder That Was India*. New York: Grove Press, 1959, 15.
20. Basham, *The Wonder*, 16.
21. Blood, Peter R. *Pakistan: A Country Study*. 6th ed. Washington: Library of Congress, 1995, 5.
22. Kenoyer, Johnathan Mark. "The Harappan State, Was It or Wasn't It?" In *From Sumer to Meluhha: Contributions to the Archaeology of South and West Asia* in Memory of George F. Dales, Jr., edited by Jonathan Mark Kenoyer, 71–80. Madison: Prehistory Press, 1994.
23. Chert is fine-grained silica rich sedimentary rock. According to "Chert." Wikipedia (2008), http://en.wikipedia.org/wiki/Chert, "In prehistoric times, chert was often used as a source material for stone tools."
24. Kenoyer, "The Harappan," 74.
25. Kenoyer, "The Harappan," 75.
26. Kenoyer, "The Harappan," 76–77.
27. Schulberg, Lucille. *Historic India*. New York: Time-Life Books, 1968.
28. Schulberg, *Historic*, 20.
29. Ratnagar, Shereen. *Encounters: The Westerly Trade of the Harappa Civilization*. Delhi: Oxford University Press, 1981, 156–66.
30. Excavations of the city are described at http://www.harappa.com
31. Wolpert, Stanley. *A New History of India* 6th ed. Oxford: Oxford University Press, 2000, 14–15.
32. Schulberg, *Historic*, 33.
33. Wolpert, *A New History*, 16–17.
34. Wolpert, *A New History*, 18.
35. Wolpert, *A New History*, 18–19.
36. Wolpert, *A New History*, 19.
37. Durant, *Our Oriental*, 395.
38. Wolpert, *A New History*, 19–20.
39. For more on the importance of winds and trade in India, a useful article may be Tripati, Sila, and L. N. Raut. "Monsoon Wind and Maritime Trade: A Case Study of Historical Evidence from Orissa, India." *Current Science* 90, no. 6 (2006): 864–71. See also Casson, Lionel. "Rome's Trade With the East: The Sea Voyage to Africa and India." *Tapa* 110 (1980): 21–36.
40. Ratnagar, Shereen. *Encounters*, 166–68.
41. Ratnagar, *Encounters*, 168–72.
42. Ratnagar, *Encounters*, 172.
43. Ratnagar, *Encounters*, 172–78.

44. McKay, John P., Bennett D. Hill, John Buckler, and Patricia Buckley Ebrey. *A History of World Societies: From Antiquity to 1500*. Vol. A. Boston: Houghton Mifflin Company, 2000, 63.
45. Ratnagar, *Encounters*, 178–82.
46. Ratnagar, *Encounters*, 188.
47. Ratnagar, *Encounters*, 192.
48. Ratnagar, *Encounters*, 198.
49. McKay, et al., 63.
50. Ratnagar, *Encounters*, 222.
51. Ratnagar, *Encounters*, 198.
52. Ratnagar, *Encounters*, 222.
53. Ratnagar, *Encounters*, 222.
54. Ratnagar, *Encounters*, 225.
55. McKay et al., *History of World*, 64.

NOTES TO CHAPTER 4

1. Saggs, H. F. W. *The Might That Was Assyria* London: Sidgwick and Jackson, 1984, 264–68.
2. Older views still prevail. In a recent biography of King Hammurabi (Van de Mieroop, Marc. *King Hammurabi of Babylon: A Biography, Blackwell Ancient Lives*. Oxford Blackwell Publishing, 2005, 171.), Marc Van De Mieroop of Columbia University sets forth his subject as "probably the only king of Mesopotamia whose fame is not based on his destructive powers and conquests, but on the positive benefits he brought to his people, and to humanity in general."
3. Marc Van De Mieroop, *A History of the Ancient Near East ca. 3000–323 BC*, Blackwell History of the Ancient World, 1, paperback, Oxford: Blackwell, 2003, 89–90
4. Lewy, Hildegard. "Assyria: C. 2600–1816 B.C." *In Early History of the Middle East*. Cambridge: Cambridge University Press, 1971, 752.
5. Lewy, "Assyria," 752.
6. Lewy, "Assyria," 752; Saggs, *The Might*, 5.
7. Læssøe, Jorgen. *People of Ancient Assyria, Their Inscriptions and Correspondence*. Translated by Danish by F. S. Leigh-Browne. New York: Barnes & Noble, 1963, 37–39.
8. Lewy, "Assyria," 752–62.
9. Orlin, Louis Lawrence. *Assyrian Colonies in Cappadocia*. The Hagne: Mouton, 1970, 58–59.
10. Lewy, "Assyria," 758–59.
11. Veenhof, K. R. "Some Social Effects of Old Assyrian Trade." *Iraq* 39, Part 1 (1977): 115–16.
12. Postgate, *Early Mesopotamia*, 212–13.
13. Hallo and Simpson, 63; Gurney, O.R. *The Hittites*. London: Penguin Books, 1952, 82; Orlin, *Assyrian* (The Hague), 7–8; Orlin, *Assyrian* (The Hagne), 23–25.
14. Orlin, *Assyrian*, 7; Orlin, *Assyrian*, 199–200.
15. Orlin, *Assyrian*, 200.
16. Postgate, *Early Mesopotamia*, 216.
17. Finegan, Jack. *Archaeological History of the Ancient Middle East*. New York: Dorset Press, 1986, 99–121; Saggs, *The Might*, 23–121.
18. Dates based upon Kurht, *Ancient Near East*, 81, 85–6; Lewy, "Assyria," 756–58.

19. Özgüç, Tahsin. "Early Anatolian Archaeology in the Light of Recent Research." *Anatolia* VII (1963): 2–3, 6; Özgüç, Tahsin. "The Art and Architecture of Ancient Kanesh." *Anatolia* VIII (1964): 28–37; Emre, Yunus. "The Art and Architecture of Ancient Kaneshthe Pottery of the Assyrian Colony Period According to the Building Levels of the Kanis Karûm." *Anatolia* VII (1963): 87–91.
20. Ozguc, "The Art," 31–37; Özgüç, Tahsin, Nimet Özgüç, Emin Bilgiç, U. Bahadir Alkim, Kenan T. Erim, R. Naumann, George Bass, J. Birmingham, D. C. Biernoff, and D. H. French. "Recent Archaeological Research in Turkey." *Anatolian Studies* 14 (1964): 24–25.
21. Özgüç, et al, "Recent Archaeological," 37–39; Özgüç, et al., "Recent Archaeological," 24–25.
22. Dates based upon Kurht, *Ancient Near East*, 81; Kurht, *Ancient Near East*, 85–86; Kurht, *Ancient Near East*, 90–91; Lewy, "Assyria," 756–58; Hallo and Simpson, *The Ancient*, 27–54; Mallowan, M. E. L. *Early Mesopotamia and Iran*. New York Mc Graw Hill, 1971, 12; Finegan, *Archaeological History*, 50; Finegan, *Archaeological History*, 58; Finegan, *Archaeological History*, 60; Özgüç, "Early Anatolian," 2–3, 6; Ozguc, "The Art," 28, 31–37; Emre, "The Art," 87–91.
23. Larsen, *The Old Assyrian*, 235–41.
24. Larsen, *The Old Assyrian*, 235–41.
25. Orlin, *Assyrian*, 51–52.
26. Veenhof, "Some Social Effects," 110.
27. Orlin, *Assyrian*, 27–28.
28. Veenhof, "Some Social Effects," 115.
29. Veenhof, "Some Social Effects," 115.
30. Veenhof, "Some Social Effects," 111–12; Larsen, Mogens Trolle. "Partnerships in the Old Assyrian Trade." *Iraq* Part 1 (1977): 119–20.
31. It is difficult to accurately date events in this time period according to The Cambridge Ancient History. 3rd ed. London: Cambridge University Press, 1970, 193: "The chronology in ancient western Asia bristles with problems." The chronology given is the most accepted among historians.
32. Puzur-Ishtar: "As soon as the country recovers [retrouver] his order, act in accord with your father's instructions, arise and come here. Your father will not have to worry. You will especially need to be on good terms with your brother and not argue" (TC III, 112, Ichisar, Metin. Les Archives Cappadociennes Du Marchand Imdi Lum Paris: Editions A.D.P.F., 1981, 12). Another letter she wrote to Puzur-Ishtar says, "Viens vite ici, je vais partir avec toi. Dans Kanes, jevais prendre soin dela maison de ton pere et de la tiene afin que personne ne paroise mettre en difficulte la la maison devotre pere" [Ichisar, Les Archives, 12]
33. CCT IV 27a; 47a; KTS 18, Ichisar, *Les Archives*, 35–37.
34. Saggs, *The Might*, 30–33; Orlin, *Assyrian*, 52–58; Larsen, "Partnerships," 119–20.
35. Saggs, *The Might*, 30–33: Orlin, *Assyrian*, 52–58; Larsen, "Partnerships," 119–20.
36. CCT IV 18a, Ichisar, *Les Archives*, 190.
37. CCT IV 47a, Ichisar, *Les Archives*, 191.
38. Ichisar, *Les Archives*, 191–92.
39. Ichisar, *Les Archives*, 191–92.
40. Pettinato, *Archives of Ebla*, 86.
41. CCT 8, 9, 10, Ichisar, *Les Archives*, 224.
42. CCT IV 22b, Ichisar, *Les Archives*, 228.
43. TTC 27, Ichisar, *Les Archives*, 199–200.

44. ATHE 27, Ichisar, *Les Archives*, 203–204.
45. ICK 92, Ichisar, *Les Archives*, 192–3; TC III 54, Ichisar, *Les Archives*, 198.
46. CC II 7, Ichisar, *Les Archives*, 218–9.
47. Orlin, *Assyrian*, 24.
48. Gen. 12.6, 16; 13.2; 14; 18.22–33; 19.1, King James Version.
49. Gen. 23.6, King James Version.
50. Kurht, *Ancient near East*, 111.
51. Kurht, *Ancient near East*, 111.
52. See again the excellent biography of Hammurabi: Van de Mieroop, *King Hammurabi*. This presents the first biography written in English of the famous Babylonian lawgiver. It draws on the extensive writings of his time, including those by Hammurabi himself.
53. James, et al., *Centuries of Darkness*, 338.
54. "Laws of Hammurabi." In Roth, Martha T., ed. *Law Collections from Mesopotamia and Asia Minor*. 2nd ed. Atlanta: Scholars Press, 1997, 99.
55. "Paragraph 100." In *Law Collections from Mesopotamia and Asia Minor*, edited by Martha T. Roth. Atlanta: Scholars Press, 1997, 99.
56. "Paragraph 100." In *Law Collections from Mesopotamia and Asia Minor*, edited by Martha T. Roth. Atlanta: Scholars Press, 1997, 100.
57. From "Marduk." Wikipedia (2008), http://en.wikipedia.org/wiki/Marduk, we learn that Marduk ("solar calf"; Biblical: *Merodach*) was the Babylonian name of a late generation god from ancient Mesopotamia and patron deity of the city of Babylon When Babylon permanently became the political center of the Euphrates valley in the time of Hammurabi (18th century BC), Marduk started to slowly rise to the position of the head of the Babylonian pantheon, a niche he fully acquired by the second half of the second millennium BC.
58. "Paragraph 103–107." In *Law Collections from Mesopotamia and Asia Minor*, edited by Martha T. Roth. Atlanta: Scholars Press, 1997, 100–101.
59. James, et al., *Centuries*, 338.
60. For more on Mentuhotep II and the Middle Kingdom see Grajetzki, Wolfram. *The Middle Kingdom of Ancient Egypt: History, Archaeology and Society* (Duckworth Egyptology). London: Gerald Duckworth & Co Ltd, 2006.
61. Trump, D. H. *The Prehistory of the Mediterranean*. New Haven: Yale University Press, 1980, 156–7.
62. A translation in English can be found in Lichtheim, Miriam. *The Old and Middle Kingdoms*. Vol. 1, Ancient Egyptian Literature Berkeley: University of California Press, 1973.
63. Genesis 37:25–36.
64. Genesis 39: 1–8, 22–3; 41: 40–4, 47–9, 56–7; 47: 13–26.
65. An excellent history of Crete can be found in Willett, R. F. *The Civilization of Ancient Crete*, London: Phoenix Press, 2004.
66. Willett devotes a chapter to the critical role of the palace in his The Civilization of Ancient Crete. Ellen Adam has an article entitled "Power Relations in Minoan Palatial Towns: An Analysis of Neopalatial Knossos and Malia." *Journal of Mediterranean Archaeology* 17, no. 2 (2004): 191–222.
67. More on findings from recent excavations in Crete can be found in Shaw, Joseph. *Kommos: A Minoan Harbor Town and Greek Sanctuary in Southern Crete*. Athens: American School of Classic Studies at Athens, 2006.
68. Martin, Thomas R. *Ancient Greece, from Prehistoric to Hellenistic Times*. New Haven: Yale University Press, 1996.
69. Heinrich Schliemann was a quite astonishing amateur archaeologist, whose field techniques left much to be desired by today's much exacting standards; nevertheless few believed in the existence of a real Troy. The importance of this talented amateur is suggested by the chapter that the late Daniel J.

Boorstin, a Pulitzer Prize-winning author and social historian who was the librarian of Congress, devoted to him in his 1983 book, *The Discovers*. New York: Random Huose, 1983.

70. Sinaranu was reputed to have sent a ship from Ugarit to Crete in the middle of the 13th century BC. See Wachsmann, Shelley. *Seagoing Ships and Seamanship in the Bronze Age Levant*. College Station, Texas: A&M University Press, 1998.

71. Martin, *Ancient Greece*, 25–28

72. Martin, *Ancient Greece*, 29; Thucydides' account of the Greek past, penned many centuries later, contained a great deal of guesswork: "The dwellers on the sea-coast now began to acquire property more than before and to become more settled in their homes and some, seeing that they were growing richer than before, began also to put walls around their cities. Their more settled life was due to their desire for gain, actuated by this, the weaker citizens were willing to submit to dependence on the stranger, and the more peaceful men, with their enlarged resources, were able to make the lesser cities their subjects and later on, when they had at length more completely reached this condition of affairs, they made the expedition against Troy." Thucydides. *History of the Peloponnesian War*, Books I and Ii. Translated by Charles Forster Smith. Cambridge: Harvard University Press, 1969, viii; 1–4.

73. Shaw suggests strong evidence of lengthy trade with Italy in Shaw, Kommos.

74. Martin, *Ancient Greece*, 32; Ridgway, David. *The First Western Greeks*. Cambridge: Cambridge University Press, 1992, 3–6.

75. Chinese names are transliterated into English by either the traditional spellings or the new pinyin, which is now adopted in China itself. Under pinyin, which is used in this book, Fukien, for example, is rendered as Fujian, Sung as Song, Ch'in as Qin, Cheng Ho as Zheng He, Yangtze as Yangzi, Kwangtung as Guangdong, Chou as Zhu, etc.

76. Kwang Chih-Chang held the John Hudson Chair of Archaeology at Harvard, his book, *Shang Civilization*, New York: Yale University Press, 1980, is a classic in the field. He died in 2001.

77. Barnes, Gina L. *The Rise of Civilization in East Asia: The Archaeology of China, Korea and Japan* London: Thames and Hudson, Ltd., 1999, 108–17.

78. Kwang Chih-Chang. *Shang Civilization*. New York: Yale University Press, 1980, 223.

79. McKay, et al., *History of World Societies*, 86–87.

80. Gasciogne, Bamber. *The Treasures and Dynasties of China*. London: Jihnathan Capre Limited, 1973, 26–29.

81. Cheng-lang, Chang. "P'u-Tz'u P'ou T'ien Chi Ch'i Hsiang-Kuan Chu Wen-Ti." *K'ao-ku Hsüeh-pao* 1 (1973): 93–118; Kwang , *Shang Civilization*, 226–27.

82. McKay, 88

83. Kwang, 226.

84. Gasciogne, 20

85. Hallo and Simpson, *Ancient Near East*, 117.

86. An interesting article on climate change as a reason for the disappearance of the Indus Valley civilization is authored by Staubwasser, M., F. Sirocko, P.M. Grotes, and M. Segl. "Climate Change at the 4.2 Ka Pb Termination of the Indus Valley Civilization and Holocene South Asian Monsoon Variability." *Geophysical Research Letters* 30 no. 8 (2003): 7.1–7.4. See also Weiss, H. "Beyond the Younger Dryas: Collapse as Adaptation to Abrupt Climate Change in Ancient West Asia and the Eastern Mediterranean." In *Confronting Natural Disaster: Engaging the Past to Understand the Future*, edited by G. Bawden and R. Reycraft, 75–98. Albuquerque: University of New Mexico Press, 2000.

NOTES TO CHAPTER 5

1. The Kassites were a little known people of unknown origin who ruled southern Mesopotamia for some four centuries (1595–1158 BCE). See Hoyland, Robert. *Arabia and the Arabs: From the Bronze Age to the Coming of Islam.* London: Routledge, 2001.The winners sometime write history. Otherwise, we might know more about these rulers of Babylonia for over four hundred years, the longest-lasting dynasty in its history.
2. "Hittite Laws," paragraph 5, Roth, *Law Collections*, 217.
3. Roth, *Law Collections*, 225–26.
4. Roth, *Law Collections*, 226.
5. Roth, *Law Collections*, 226–34.
6. Roth, *Law Collections*, 232.
7. Roth, *Law Collections*, 233.
8. Roth, *Law Collections*, 235.
9. Roth, *Law Collections*, 177–78.
10. Roth, *Law Collections*, 177–78.
11. Colello, Thomas (ed.). "Syria, a Country Study." Washington: U. S. Government, Supt. Of Docs., U.S.G.P.O., 1988, 4.
12. Bondi, Sandro Philippo. *The Origins in the East*, edited by Sabatino Moscati, The Phoenicians. New York: Rizzoli, 1999, 23–9, 23–5.
13. Pettinato, *Archives of Ebla*, 226.
14. Wilson, John A. "The Admonitions of Ipu-Wer." In *Ancient near Eastern Texts Relating to the Old Testament*, edited by James B. Pritchard, 441–2. Princeton, NJ: Princeton University Press, 1969, 441–2. The text has been cleaned up of italics and parentheses for clarity by ourselves.
15. "The Story of Sinuhe." In *Ancient near Eastern Texts Relating to the Old Testament*, edited by James B. Pritchard, 18–22. Princeton: Princeton University Press, 1969. The quote is from page 19, lines 29–31. The text has been cleaned up of italics and parentheses for clarity by ourselves.
16. "A Trip to the Lebanon for Cedar." In *Ancient near Eastern Texts Relating to the Old Testament*, edited by James B. Pritchard, 243. Princeton: Princeton University Press, 1969.
17. Markoe, Glenn. *The Phoenicians*. Berkeley: University of California Press, 2000, 16.
18. Markoe, *Phoenicians*, 16–18.
19. Markoe, *Phoenicians*, 16–18.
20. Markoe, *Phoenicians*, 16–21.
21. Aubet, Maria Eugenia. *The Phoenicians and the West: Politics, Colonies, and Trade*. Translated by Mary Turton. 2nd ed. Cambridge: Cambridge University Press, 2001, 114–19.
22. "The Jounrey of Wen-Amon to Phoenicia", in Aubet, 2001, 356–362, 358.
23. Aubet, "The Journey," 358–59.
24. Aubet, "The Journey," 360–62.
25. Kuhrt, *The Ancient Near East*, 300–301.
26. Moscati, Sabatino. *The World of Phoenicians*. London: Weidenfeld and Nicholson, 1968, 8–9; Harden, Donald B. *The Phoenicians*. 2nd ed. New York: Praeger, 1962, 83.
27. Moscati, *The World of Phoenicians*, 8–9; Harden, *The Phoenicians*, 83.
28. Rib-Hadda King of Byblos to Akhenaten, EA 89; Kuhrt, *The Ancient Near East*, 300.
29. Kuhrt, *The Ancient Near East*, 301–02; Linder, Elisha. "Ugarit, a Canaanite Thalassocracy." In *Ugarit in Retrospect: 50 Years of Ugarit and Ugaritic*, edited by Gordon D. Young, 38. Winona Lake: Eisenbrauns, 1981.

30. Linder, "Ugarit," 38; Kuhrt, *The Ancient Near East*, 302.
31. As discussed earlier, see Porter, Competitive Advantage of Nations.
32. PRU IV, 17.424C in Heltzer, Michael. "Sinaranu, Son of Siginu, and the Trade Relations between Ugarit and Crete." *Minos* 23 (1988): 7–13. We have edited the text for clarity.
33. PRU, VI, 30, Ras Shamra 18.500, Heltzer, Michael. *Goods, Prices, and the Organization of Trade in Ugarit: Marketing and Transportation in the Eastern Mediterranean in the Second Half of the Ii Millennium B.C.E.* Wiesbaden Dr. Ludwig Reichert Verlag, 1978, 124.
34. Heltzer, *Goods*, 129.
35. Tammuz, Oded. "Mare Clausum? Sailing Seasons in the Mediterranean in Early Antiquity." *Mediterranean Historical Review* 20, no. 2 (2005): 145–62 discusses the issue of whether navigation in antiquity came to a almost complete standstill in the winter, in the course of his article he discusses some of the trade that took place in thirteenth, eleventh, and fifth centuries BCE between Egypt, Phoenicia, Greece and others.
36. Heltzer, Michael. *The Economy of Ugarit*, edited by Wilfred G.E. Watson and Nicolas Wyatt, Handbook of Ugaritic Studies. Leiden: Brill, 1999, 423–54.
37. Heltzer, *The Economy of Ugarit*, 440–41.
38. Letter of Hattusilis in Heltzer, *Goods*, 127.
39. Heltzer, *The Economy of Ugarit*, 441–43.
40. PRU [Royal Palace of Ugarit], III, 15.138 in Heltzer, Michael. "Sinaranu," 9.
41. Heltzer, "Sinaranu," 7–13.
42. Heltzer, *Goods*, 136; Linder, "Ugarit," 35.
43. Rainey, A. F. "Business Agents at Ugarit." *Israel Exploration Journal* 13 (1963): 316–17; Heltzer, *Goods*, 136; Linder, "Ugarit," 35.
44. Heltzer, "Sinaranu," 11.
45. PRU III 16.238, Heltzer, "Sinaranu," 12–13. Text edited for clarity.
46. Heltzer, *Goods*, 140–42.
47. Heltzer, *Goods*, 142–43; Heltzer, *Goods*, 147.
48. Linder, "Ugarit," 35.
49. Linder, "Ugarit," 32.
50. Linder, "Ugarit," 33.
51. Heltzer, *The Economy of Ugarit*, 444.
52. Heltzer, *The Economy of Ugarit*, 446.
53. Heltzer, *Goods*, 4–7.
54. Heltzer, *The Economy of Ugarit*, 453.
55. Heltzer, *Goods*, 135–37.
56. A note on European parallels is in order. The arsenal of Venice in the 1300's and 1400's was state-run, although shipbuilding remained in private hands. The rulers of Venice, Genoa, and even France contracted with these private ship-makers. Ships on long voyages sailed in convoys. The Venetian Senate and Admiralty directed and managed armadas of both public and private vessels to minimize risk. In the 1500s, Portuguese vessels trading with India and the Spice Islands sailed under a crown monopoly. The boundaries between Portugal's navies and her merchant marine were fluid, as Lisbon sought to wrench the Indian Ocean and Western Pacific middleman trade from established Asian rivals. The Dutch displaced the Portuguese in the 1600s. Dutch naval capitalism joined well-organized farming magnates to a strong fleet to protect overseas trade. See Chapter 12 of Moore, Karl, and David Lewis. *Foundations of Corporate Empire: Is History Repeating Itself?* London: Financial Times/Prentice-Hall, 2000.
57. Herman, Arthur. *To Rule the Waves: How the British Navy Shaped the Modern World*. New York: HarperCollins, 2004, xix.

58. One thinks of modern Japan where samurai-style administrators "built a web of enterprises and institutions tied to the 'political merchants' who joined forces with the government while letting the state take many of the social risks" (McMillan, Charles. *The Japanese Industrial System*. 3rd ed. New York: Walter De Gruyter, 1996, 58). The samurai tradition has often meant donning business suits and bringing warrior codes into the market-place. The boundaries between public and private sector in Japan are porous. According to Professor Charles McMillan, "the absence of a strong anti-business ideology among government officials or anti-government sentiment among business leaders" means that Japanese rulers and businessmen, instead, reflected "a considerable degree of non-ideological or pragmatic adjustment to circumstances" (McMillan, *The Japanese*, 56–57). Bronze Age economies were, by and large, temple- and palace-based with some private trading. Michael Heltzer feels it inaccurate to speak of "companies" operating in Ugarit, Byblos, Sidon, or Tyre. Most of the foreign trade was in luxuries. Comparing the hierarchical structure of Phoenician business to that of contemporary Japan is a useful exercise, provided one does not draw the parallel too closely, given the profound differences between the modern Japanese state with its large professional public sector. Many functions once performed by tamkāru are now done by salaried civil servants in Japan. Japanese businessmen today are not in the direct employ of the Emperor Akihito, (Author's personal correspondence with Professor Emeritus Michael Heltzer, from Haifa, January 8, 2001).
59. Heltzer, Goods, 131; *Linder*, "Ugarit," 35; Rainey, "Business Agents," 318–19.
60. Linder, "Ugarit," 40–41.
61. Rainey, "Business Agents," 314.
62. Rainey, "Business Agents," 315.
63. Ferguson, *Empire*, xix.
64. Stieglitz, R. R. "The Geopolitics of the Phoenician Littoral in the Early Iron Age." *Bulletin of the American Schools of Oriental Research*, no. 279 (1990): 11; Aubet, *The Phoenicians*, 27; Aubet, *The Phoenicians*, 29–32; Aubet, *The Phoenicians*, 35.
65. Cross, F. M. "Phoenicians in Sardinia: The Epigraphical Evidence." In *Studies in Sardinian Archaeology*, edited by M. S. Balmuth and R. J. Rowland, 57. Ann Arbour: University of Michigan Press, 1987.
66. Aubet, *The Phoenicians*, 43–46; Stern, Ephraim. "New Evidence from Dor for the First Appearance of the Phoenicians Along the Northern Coast of Israel." *Bulletin of the American Schools of Oriental Research*, no. 279 (August, 1990): 29–30; Gal. "Hurbat Rosh Zayit and the Early Phoenician Pottery." *Levant* XXIV (1992): 173–85.
67. Aubet cites several classical sources to prove Tyre struggled with an overpopulation problem: Justinus, Epitome 18.3, 50; Curcius Rufus 6.4.20, Tertullian, De Anima 30; Sallust, Jugurtha 19.1–2. Aubet, The Phoenicians, 76.
68. I Kings 5:6–11.
69. Aubet, *The Phoenicians*, 44–45; Elat, M. *The Monarchy and the Development of Trade in Ancient Israel*, State and Temple Economy in the Ancient near East, Proceedings of the International Conference Organized by the Katholieke Universiteit Leuven from the 10th to the 14th of April, 1978. Louvain, Belgium: Catholic University of Leuven, 1979, 526.
70. Deuteronomy 2:27
71. Conventional dating schemes place the Iron Age of Phoenician influence before 1200 BCE. Some of the new lowered chronologies would place the early Iron Age in Solomon's and Ahab's time. James, et al., *Centuries of Darkness*, 159. There are Biblical references to the Phoenician presence: I Kings 10:18, 22:39; Ezek. 27:6; Amos 3: 15, 6:14.

72. Archaeologist Ephraim Stern spoke of "internal movement of goods between the Phoenicians in Dor and those in Cyprus, where intensive Phoenician settlements should have begun?" Stern, "New Evidence," 32; Stern, "New Evidence,".

73. "Poems About Baal and Anath." In *Ancient near Eastern Texts*, edited by James B. Pritchard, 132, 1969. The text has been cleaned up of italics and parentheses for clarity by ourselves .

74. Pritchard, "Poems about Baal and Anath," 138. The text has been cleaned up of italics and parentheses for clarity by ourselves .

75. Silver, Morris. *Economic Structures of Antiquity Westport*: Greenwood Press 1995, 6.

76. Silver, *Economic Structures*, 7.

77. Silver, *Economic Structures*, 18–19; Silver, *Economic Structures*, 25–27.

78. Silver, *Economic Structures*, 19.

79. Silver, *Economic Structures*, 8.

80. Silver, *Economic Structures*, 10.

81. Clifford, Richard J. "Phoenician Religion." *Bulletin of the American Schools of Oriental Research* 279 (1990): 55–66.

82. Silver, *Economic Structures*, 32.

83. Silver, *Economic Structures*, 33.

84. Childe, Gordon. *What Happened in History*. Harmondworth: Penguin Books, 1964, 145.

85. Aubet, *The Phoenicians*, 50.

86. Clifford, "Phoenician Religion," 55–66; Aubet, *The Phoenicians*, 54–55.

87. "Text of Ashurnasirpal Ii Expedition to Lebanon." In *Ancient Near Eastern Texts*, edited by James B. Pritchard, 276, 1969.

88. "Text of Shalmaneser Iii Inscription." In *Ancient Near Eastern Texts*, edited by James B. Pritchard, 281, 1969.

89. One thinks of modern Japanese- and Korean-style subcontracting. Under this arrangement, trading companies in Kition, directed by harbormasters and temple officials, would have permanent and perhaps even hereditary partnerships with guilds of metal casters who would turn the copper they were supplied into finished goods. Aubet, *The Phoenicians*, 51–54; Moscati, *The World*, 98; Heltzer, *Goods*, 119–23.

90. Harden, *The Phoenicians*, 52–53; Harden, *The Phoenicians*, 63–67; Aubet, The Phoenicians, 214–18.

91. Tuza, Vincenzo. "Sicily." In *The World of Phoenicians*, edited by Sabatino Moscati, 231–53. London: Phoenix Giant, 1999; Ciasca, Antonio. "Malta." In *The World of Phoenicians*, edited by Sabatino Moscati, 254–58. London: Phoenix Giant, 1999; Acquaro, Enrico. "Sardinia." In *The World of Phoenicians*, edited by Sabatino Moscati, 254–58. London: Phoenix Giant, 1999. Sardinia was more thickly settled by the Tyrians than Sicily. Tyrian activity centered on the small harbor-island of Sulcis, located off the southwestern shore, during most of the eighth century B.C. True to type, the temple and the marketplace were the first institutions to be erected not only in Sulcis but in her daughter colonies. Civil functions were assumed by the shrine of Melqart. A Phoenician inscription deciphered from Nora not only dated the first merchants to the reign of Pygmalion, but illuminated the key role of the army in winning Tyre her trading rights amid hostility. The inscription records the victory of Milkaton, son of Shebna, general of King Pummay who fought with the Sardinians, drove them out and established peace with the defeated natives. Barreca, F. *The Phoenician and Punic Civilization in Sardinia*, Studies in Sardinian Archaeology, Volume Ii, Sardinia in the Mediterranean. Ann Arbor: University of Michigan Press, 1989, 152–3; Cross, "Phoenicians," 55–56.

92. The portrait of Phoenician traders in Homer's Odyssey is one of utter dis-
honesty. They act out of total self-interest, cheat their clients, lie to them, and
even sell them into slavery. See Homer. "Books 13, 14, 15." In *The Odyssey*, translated by A. T. Murray. Cambridge: Harvard University Press, 1995,
270–484. One needs to keep in mind, as we will see in the next chapter, that
Homer disliked trade and commerce and idealized the noble, the farmer, and
the warrior.
93. Jones, Horace Leonard. "Strabo 3.5.5." In *The Geography of Strabo*, 135.
Cambridge: Harvard University Press, 1949.
94. Aubet shows how the temple of Melqart in Gades was crucial for supervising
the entire venture, just like Phoenician branch-temples in Sulcis and Moyta.
"The first Tyrian colonies in the west . . . started . . . as sanctuaries administered by a priestly group directly linked to the interests of Tyre." Aubet, *The
Phoenicians*, 278. The massive Gades shrine copied Melqart's temple in Tyre
architecturally and decoratively. A huge administrative complex housed the
Melqart priesthood controlled by a handful of aristocratic families. Melqart
worship, including his role as the supernatural King of Tyre, allowed priests
active control over Ibero–Phoenician business. Aubet, *The Phoenicians*,
273–79; Silver, *Economic Structures*, 6–10. The Gades temple became the
key link with Tyre, both as guarantor of honest exchange and source of
finance capital: "In distant places where he [Melqart] possessed a temple, his
function was a very concrete one: to ensure the tutelage of the temple of Tyre
and the monarchy over the commercial enterprise, thus converting the colony
into an extension of Tyre, and also to guarantee the right of asylum and hospitality which, in distant lands, was equivalent to endorsing contracts and
commercial exchanges" (Aubet, *The Phoenicians*, 177).
95. Aubet, *The Phoenicians*, 92; Finegan, *Archaeological History*, 105; Oded,
Bustenay. "The Phoenician Cities and the Assyrian Empire in the Time of
Tiglath-Pileser Iii." *Zeitschrift des Deutschen Palästina-Vereins* 90 (1974):
39, 46–48.
96. Aubet, *The Phoenicians*, 92. The presence of private merchant princes in the
Tyrian economy is supported by Isaiah's denunciations: "The burden of Tyre.
Howl, ye ships of Tarshish; for it is laid waste, so that there is no house, no
entering in. . . . Be still, ye inhabitants of the isle; thou whom the merchants
of Zidon, that pass over the sea, have replenished. And by great waters the
seed of Sihor, the harvest of the river, is her revenue; and she is a mart of
nations. . . . As at the report concerning Egypt, so shall they be sorely pained
at the report of Tyre. Pass ye over to Tarshish; howl, ye inhabitants of the
isle. Is this your joyous city, whose antiquity is of ancient days? Her own feet
shall carry her afar off to sojourn. Who hath taken this counsel against Tyre,
the crowning city, whose merchants are princes, whose traffickers are the
honourable of the earth?" (Isaiah 23:6–8).
97. Aubet, *The Phoenicians*, 54–59.
98. Dunning, *Multinational Enterprises and the Global Economy*, 75–86.
99. Aubet, *The Phoenicians*, 95–96.
100. Moscati, Sabatino. "Colonization of the Mediterranean." In *The World of
Phoenicians*. London: Phoenix Giant, 1999, 47–56; Tuza, "Sicily," 231–53;
Ciasca, "Malta," 254–58; Acquaro, "Sardinia," 259–278; Harden, *The
Phoenicians*, 63.
101. "The structure of the Phoenician settlements was linked with the homeland mercantile 'companies,' in a family based organization. . . . Some of
these 'companies' possessed large numbers of ships . . . [that] would provide the capital for their trading activity . . . as sponsoring and protective
private institutions. It was indeed a private enterprise, owned by traders,
who organized their workforce, ships and voyages. The traders seem to

have had a high status and an equally high political rank, based on a kin-ship organization. . . . Moscati also mentions the textile industry developed at Carthage, which apparently was based on 'family lines.'" Gamitó, T. Judice. *Social Complexity in Southwest Iberia: 800–300 B.C: The Case of Tartessos*, B.A.R. International Series, 439. Oxford: B.A.R., 1988, 54.

102. "The pattern of Phoenician trade was linked to specialist production cen-ters, connecting different areas and political systems which otherwise would not have been drawn together, and establishing a rate of exchange much to their own advantage. They could do this fairly easily since they had a monopoly on both the specialized manufactures that were widely desired, and the marine transport, so they could stimulate demand where they chose to do so. A virgin market was the ideal since it could be scoured hard for huge profits; this accounts for their interest in Spain, especially in the silver mines behind Huelva in the Rio Tinto, and near Cástulo in the Sierra Morena. The Phoenicians were able to locate new metal sources, and unlock the wealth from them, unhindered, for a century and a half. The traders worked through a system of Phoenician family firms, who had representatives in their home town in the eastern Mediterranean as well as in their new markets and factories; they owned their own ships, too, and were prepared to take risks which their overlords could not well calculate, or were unwilling to do, and so profited greatly." Harrison, Richard J. *Spain at the Dawn of History: Iberians, Phoenicians and Greeks* (Ancient Peoples and Places). London: Thames & Hudson, 1988, 42.

103. Jones, Horace Leonard. "Strabo 3.5.3–4" In *The Geography of Strabo*. Cambridge: Harvard University Press, 1949, 131–35; Tsirkin, *Economy of the Phoenician*, 548–51; Tsirkin, *Economy of the Phoenician*, 554; Tsirkin, *Economy of the Phoenician*, 557; Tsirkin, *Economy of the Phoenician*, 563; Harrison, *Spain at the Dawn of History*, 43–44.

104. Harrison, *Spain at the Dawn of History*, 47.

105. Gras, Michel, Pierre Rouillard, and Javier Teixidor. "The Phoenicians and Death." *Berytus, Archaeological Studies* XXXIX (1991): 145.

106. Tsirkin, *Economy*, 557.

107. Barreca, *The Phoenician*, 152; Gras, et al., "The Phoenicians," 145.

108. Tsirkin, *Economy*, 559; Greek vessels and Cypriot artifacts were found in both Malta and in Iberian and Ibero–Phoenician tombs before 700. Tsirkin, *Economy*, 559–60.

109. Isa.23:1.

110. The treaty's text, preserved in Assyrian royal correspondence, reveals, more than any other document, the managed nature of trade in the Phoenician world: "These are the ports of trade and the trade roads which Esarhaddon king of Assyria [granted] to his servant, Baal: (to wit): toward Akko, Dor, in the entire district of the Philistines, and in all the cities within Assyrian terri-tory, on the seacoast, and in Byblos, (across) the Lebanon, all the cities in the mountains, all the cities . . . which Esarhaddon gave [to] Baal [. . .] [to] the people of Tyre, . . . in their ships or all those who cross over, in the towns of [Baal], his towns, his manors, his wharves, which [. . .] to [. . .] as many as did lie in the outlying regions, as in the past . . . nobody should harm their ships." (Pritchard, *Ancient Near Eastern Texts*, 534).

111. E. Lipinski. *Les Phéniciens Á Ninivé Au Temps Des Sargonide: Ahonasti, Ortier En Chef*, Atti Del I Congresso Internazionale Di Studi Fenici E Punici, Roma, Vol. 1. 5–10 Novembre, 1979. Rome: Consiglio Nazionale della Ric-erche, 1983, 12434.

112. A. L. Oppenheim. "Essay in Overland Trade in the First Millennium B.C." *Journal of Cuneiform Studies* 21 (1967): 253.

113. Oppenheim, "Essay in Overland," 253.
114. I. M. Diakonoff. "The Naval Power and Trade of Tyre." *Israel Exploration Journal* 42, no. 3–4 (1992): 170–77.
115. Ezek. 27:12, 25, 33.
116. Ezekiel echoes an earlier narrative poem—the story of Jonah. Jonah, a fierce anti-Assyrian nationalist, paid the fair on a ship going to Tarshish. When a storm threatened the ship, the Tyrian sailors threw all their wares overboard. Jonah 1:3–5. Both Jonah and Ezekiel document regular voyages between eastern Tyrian settlements and Iberia. Ships carried heavy bulk wares and multinational crews worshipping a number of deities.
117. Diakonoff, "The Naval Power," 182; Diakonoff, "The Naval Power," 193.
118. Wright, Christopher J. H. *The Message of Ezekiel*. Downer's Grove: Inter-Varsity Press, 2001, 242; 265–66.

NOTES TO CHAPTER 6

1. Jaspers, Karl, and Paul Keegan. *The Origin and Goal of History*. London: Routledge, 1953, passim.
2. See Finley, Moses I. *The Ancient Economy*. Berkeley: University of California Press, 1999; Viljoen, Stephen. *Economic Systems in World History* London: Longman Group Limited, 1974, 44–47; Mattingly, David J., and John Salmon, eds. *Economies Beyond Agriculture in the Classical World*. Vol. 9, Leicester-Nottingham Studies in Ancient Society. London: Routledge, 2001.
3. Viljoen, *Economic Systems*, 44–47.
4. Martin, *Ancient Greece*.
5. Thomas, Carol G., and Craig Conant. *Citadel to City–State: The Transformation of Greece, 1200–700 B.C.E.* Bloomington: Indiana University Press, 1999, 8–9.
6. Martin, *Ancient Greece*, 25–28; Thomas and Conant, *Citadel*, 10–16.
7. Martin, *Ancient Greece*, 29; Thucydides account of the Greek past, penned many centuries later, contained a great deal of guesswork: "the dwellers on the sea-coast now began to acquire property more than before and to become more settled in their homes and . . . growing richer than before, began also to put walls around their cities. Their more settled life was due to their desire for gain, actuated by this, the weaker citizens were willing to submit to dependence on the stranger, and the more peaceful men, with their enlarged resources, were able to make the lesser cities their subjects and later on, when they had at length more completely reached this condition of affairs, they made the expedition against Troy." Thucydides. *History of the Peloponnesian War*, 1–4; 8.
8. Martin, *Ancient Greece*, 32; Ridgway, *First Western Greeks*, 3–6. The subject of piracy is a rich and intriguing one. The best book is de Souza, Philip. *Piracy in the Graeco–Roman World* New York: Cambridge University Press, 1999.
9. Martin, *Ancient Greece*, 32. The 300 year Dark Age (1200–900 BCE) matches developments across the Near East. Peter James and his colleagues have questioned the Dark Age theory seeing no break between the Helladic/Mycenean Bronze and Homeric Iron Ages. See James, et al. *Centuries of Darkness*, 68–94; Henry, Roger. *Synchronized Chronology: Rethinking Middle East Antiquity*. New York Algora Publishing, 2003 offers an even more radical tack, insisting that the Dark Ages are a "fiction" traced to misreading records of Egypt; Robert Sallares thinks this is going too far, in that recent Greek finds stress "the completeness of the break at the end of the

250   *Notes*

Mycenean period." See Sallares, Robert. *The Ecology of the Ancient Greek World.* Ithaca: Cornell University Press, 1991, 64.

10. Redfield, James M. "The Development of the Market in Ancient Greece." In *The Market in History*, edited by B. L. Anderson and A. J. H. Latham. London: Croom Helm, 1986, 29–32.

11. Tandy, David W. *Warriors into Traders: The Power of the Market in Early Greece.* Berkeley: University of California Press, 1997, 106–111; Redfield, "The Development," 32–33. In *The Odyssey*, Telemachus told the suitors occupying his home that "it would be far better for you to eat away my treasures and eat my cattle." Homer. *The Odyssey of Homer.* Translated by Richard Lattimore. New York: Harper Perennial, 1991, 2.74–75. Odysseus (Ulysses) had his royal storeroom, filled with gold, bronze, garments, olive oil, and wine [2.334–41]. When Odysseus fails to return to his wife, Penelope, Telemachus becomes acting patriarch and advises Penelope to attend to "the loom and the distaff, and see to it that your handmaidens ply their work also" [1.356–60].

12. Redfield, "The Development," 32; Homer, *The Odyssey*, 2. 287–95.

13. Homer references, Homer, *The Odyssey*, 2.270–72; 7.108–109; 8.159–164; 2.276–77.

14. Biers, William R. *The Archaeology of Greece: An Introduction.* Ithaca: Cornell University Press, 1986, 105–125; Homer, *The Odyssey*, 2.193–95.

15. According to Heichelheim, the "planning economy of the Ancient Orient and . . . tribal collectivism of earlier times were . . . reactionary," being replaced by a new age "in which free individualism and its creations had a fundamentally decisive role to play for millennia." Heichelheim, Fritz M. *An Ancient Economic History from the Palaeolithic Age to the Migrations of the Germanic, Slavic and Arabic Nations* Translated by Joyce Stevens. Vol. I. Leyden: A.W. Sithoff, 1965, 196–197.

16. "The extensive overseas contacts of Cyprus . . . explain the diffusion of this discovery both eastward and westward" argues Snodgrass in Snodgrass, Anthony M. "Iron and Early Metallurgy in the Mediterranean." In *The Coming of the Age of Iron*, edited by Theodore A. Wertime and James D. Muhly. New Haven: Yale University Press, 1980, 338–39, 341. Peter James' revised chronology would lower the date of the Cypriot chronology to match the evidence from Phoenicia and the Near East, which "would in turn push down by some 150 years the absolute date for the end of the Late Bronze Age in Cyprus, currently set at c. 1050 B.C." The lowered dates suggested previously, would, however, place the beginning of the Cypriot Iron Age around 1050 instead of 1200 B.C. and the full Cypriot Iron Age in Hiram's and Itobaal's time around 900 B.C. at the very end of the Greek Dark Age [James, et al., Centuries of Darkness, 161]. According to Snodgrass, "developments . . . follow those in Cyprus with a fidelity which argues a close dependence on Cypriot technological secrets and perhaps even a reliance on importing Cypriot artifacts ready-made" [Snodgrass, "Iron," 345].

17. Thomas and Conant, *Citadel*, 82.

18. Thomas and Conant, *Citadel*, 70–71.

19. Osborne, Robin. *Greece in the Making, 1200–479 BCE* London: Routledge, 1996, 27–28. The unusually heavy preponderance (some 80%) of iron artifacts in the Athenian finds suggests that a shortage of tin needed to make bronze in the Greek world provided an enormous incentive for the early development of iron-working. See Osborne, *Greece*, 27; Snodgrass, "Iron," 348–52. Homer describes "a Phoenician man, well skilled in beguilements, a gnawer at others' goods" offering Odysseus a trading opportunity in North Africa. His real goal is to sell the hero into slavery. Homer, *The Odyssey*,

14.285–97. The site of Lefkandi in Euboea, itself, was excavated between 1964 and 1966. The findings at Xeropolis Hill and some two hundred graves and funeral pyres showed that Lefkandi may not only have escaped the destruction at the end of the Bronze Age, but was a flourishing center during the Hellenic Dark Age, however long or short it may have been: "When much of Greece was depopulated, Lefkandi was an active center." Sackett, L. H, and M. R. Popham. "Lefkandi: A Euboean Town of the Bronze Age and Early Iron Age (2100–700 B.C.)." *Archaeology* 25, no. 1 (1972): 13. Already thriving at the end of the tenth century BC (conventional chronology), the settlement saw its richest period of burials at the end of the ninth. These burials showed a number of links with Cyprus and Syria [Sackett and Popham, "Lefkandi," 16–18]. See Ridgway, *First Western Greeks*, 12–15, 24; Hawkes, Christopher. "Commentary I: The Greek Venture and Archaeology." In *Archaeology into History I: Greeks, Celts and Romans, Studies in Venture and Resistance*, edited by Christopher Hawkes and Sonia Hawkes, 1–2. London: Dent and Sons, Ltd., 1973, 1–2.

20. Ridgway, David. "The First Western Greeks: Campanian Coasts and Southern Etruria" In *Archaeology into History I: Greeks, Celts and Romans, Studies in Venture and Resistance*, edited by Christopher Hawkes and Sonia Hawkes. London: Dent and Sons, Ltd., 1973, 5, 8.

21. Tandy, *Warriors into Traders*, 62–63.

22. Papadopoulos, John K. "Phantom Euboeans" *Journal of Mediterranean Archaeology* 10, no. 2 (1997): 193–96, 200. Most of the pottery at Al Mina was not even Euboean, but Phoenician, Attic, Samian, Rhodian, Corinthian, Chian, and Milesian. [Papadopoulos, "Phantom Euboeans," 200–202]. Most of what the Greeks sent east was in the form of open drinking cups called skyphoi; other types of vessels came from Cyprus and the Levant, indicating "a very specific and co-ordinated market strategy that does not clearly point to the Greeks as the instigators" [Papadopoulos, "Phantom Euboeans," 202].

23. Professor Redfield describes Hellenic commerce as "informal [and] entrepreneurial in a world which provided security neither of contracts nor possession, and bringing an erratic and unpredictable return." He adds that "it is perhaps not extravagant to think that the trade route fueled the whole Greek economic takeoff in the mid-eighth century BCE" (Redfield, "The Development of the Market," 43).

24. Tandy, *Warriors*, 64–66.

25. Thomas and Conant, *Citadel*, 111–13.

26. Papadopoulos, "Phantom Euboeans," 202.

27. Papadopoulos, "Phantom Euboeans," 202; Tandy, *Warriors*, 66–69.

28. Ridgway, "The First Western Greeks," 13–18; Buchner, Giorgio. "Pithekoussai, Oldest Greek Colony in the West." *Expedition* (Bulletin of the University Museum of the University of Pennsylvania) 8, no. 4 (1966): 12.

29. Ridgway, "The First Western Greeks," 26.

30. Ridgway, "The First Western Greeks," 26.

31. "The establishment of a permanent Euboean "home base" abroad—with all that such an operation inevitably required in the way of investment of men and resources—would surely not have been contemplated without a preliminary period of elementary market research; and it surely would never have undertaken at all unless the cause had been seen to take effect, with the mechanics of supply and demand arranged" (Ridgway, "The First Western Greeks," 27–28).

32. One amulet mentioned Pharaoh Bocchoris, reigning around 720 B.C., establishing a date for the Geometric and Protocorinthian pottery of the Euboean network; Buchner, "Pithekoussai," 7.

33. Redfield, "The Development of the Market," 41.
34. Homer, *The Odyssey*, iv.80–85.
35. Thomas and Conant, *Citadel*, 83–93; Thomas and Conant, *Citadel*, 101–103.
36. Tandy, *Warriors*, 19–42.
37. Thucydides, *History of the Peloponnesian War*, 7.
38. Osborne, *Greece*, 70; Comparisons of the graves of children with adults suggest the rise was gradual and not an explosion. Osborne claimed "slow and steady population growth, continuously from the tenth century BCE on, not a sudden explosion in the eight;" Osborne, *Greece*, 79–80.
39. Osborne, *Greece*, 125; Osborne, *Greece*; 128–29.
40. The economic growth of ancient Greece is almost impossible to quantify with statistics, but no more so than late medieval and early modern Europe, where actual documentation is equally scarce. See Starr, Chester G. *The Economic and Social Growth of Early Greece, 800–500 B.C.* New York: Oxford University Press, 1977, 13–15.
41. Redfield, "The Development of the Market," 44–45.
42. Biers, *The Archaeology*, 126; Tandy, *Warriors into Traders*, 135–38; Thomas and Conant, *Citadel*, 104.
43. Osborne, *Greece*, 175–76.
44. Osborne, *Greece*, 176.
45. Childe, *What Happened in History*. Harmondworth: Penguin Books, 1964, 190.
46. Hanson, Victor. *The Other Greeks: The Family Farm and the Agrarian Roots of Western Civilization*. New York: The Free Press, 1995, 292–303.
47. T. Walter Wallbank, Alastair M. Taylor, Nels M. Bailkey, *Civilization Past and Present*, Chicago: Scott, Foresman and Company, 1962, page 32.
48. Childe, pages 201–202.
49. Ridgway, "The First Western Greeks," 19–20.
50. Pindar. *The Odes of Pindar, Including the Principal Fragments*. Translated and edited by Sir John Sandys. New York: G.P. Putnam's Sons, 1924, 133.
51. Thucydides. *The Complete Writings of Thucydides: The Peloponnesian War*. Translated by Crawley. New York: Modern Library, 1951, 1–6; Michell, H. *The Economics of Ancient Greece*. New York: The Macmillan Company, 1940, 236–37.
52. Starr, *The Economic*, 28; Starr, *The Economic*, 31.
53. Green, Peter. *A Concise History of Ancient Greece to the Close of the Classical Era*. London: Thames and Hudson Ltd., 1979, 60–63.
54. Green, *A Concise History*, 33–34.
55. Green, *A Concise History*, 33–34.
56. Down through the centuries, the word "tyrant" has become a synonym for oppressive one-man rule. Aristotle saw tyranny as a perversion of royalty. Whether they were hereditary rulers or individuals that seized power by force, tyrants, according to Aristotle's definition, were out for themselves. Aristotle. "Politica." In *The Works of Aristotle Translated into English*, edited by W.D. Ross, Vol 10, Book III, §1279b. Oxford: Oxford University Press, 1961.
57. Aristotle viewed the majority of the tyrants in the Greek world quite unfavorably. He defined tyranny as the unchecked power of a single ruler who was accountable and responsible to no one but himself. Although aristocrats and oligarchs ruled to benefit the rich, to the detriment of the poor, and democrats vice versa, tyrants, in Aristotle's view, ruled to the detriment of rich and poor alike. Naturally, neither the tyrants nor their supporters would view it that way. Aristotle, "Politica," 1295 a–b.

58. Pheidon defeated Sparta around 669 BCE and likely unified the Argos region. Pausanias commented: "Here are common graves of the Argives who conquered the Lacedaemonians (Spartans) in battle at Hysiae." Pausanias, 2.24.7. "Tyrants: Classics 371/History 391." Reed College http://homer. reed.edu?GkHist/Tyrants.html.
59. Thucydides, *The Complete Writings*, 1.13; Pausanias, 2.24.7. "Tyrants: Classics 371/History 391." Reed College http://homer.reed.edu?GkHist/Tyrants. html.
60. Pausanias, 2.24.7. "Tyrants: Classics 371/History 391." Reed College http:// homer.reed.edu?GkHist/Tyrants.html.
61. Ure, P. N. "The Tyrant as Capitalist." In *Problems in Ancient History, Volume One, the Ancient near East and Greece*, edited by Donald Kagan. New York: Macmillan, 1966, 215, 222.
62. Ure, "The Tyrant," 223–25.
63. Hesiod. *The Works and the Days*, Translated by Richard Lattimore. Ann Arbor: University of Michigan Press, 1962, 15–118, 53–67.
64. Hesiod, *The Works*, 20–21.
65. Hesiod, *The Works*, 20–21.
66. Hesiod, *The Works*, 20–21.
67. Hesiod, *The Works*, 95–101
68. Hesiod, *The Works*, 99–101.
69. Hesiod, *The Works*, 99–101.
70. Hesiod, *The Works*, 35.
71. Hesiod, *The Works*, 39.
72. Hesiod, *The Works*, 38–47.
73. Tandy, *Warriors*, 135–38; Tandy, *Warriors*, 194–217; Thomas and Conant, *Citadel*, 108–109.
74. Thomas and Conant, *Citadel*, 108–111.
75. Buchner, "Pithekoussai," 8.
76. These craftsmen were "peculiarly open to economic pressures and incentives," Murray, Oswyn. *Early Greece*. 2nd ed. London: Fontana Press, 1993, 223.
77. Murray, Oswyn. *Early Greece*. Sussex: Harvester Press, 1980, 223.
78. Osborne, Robin. *Archaic and Classical Greek Art* Oxford: Oxford University Press, 1998, 87.
79. Osborne, *Archaic*, 90–91.
80. Osborne, *Archaic*, 90.
81. Osborne, *Archaic*, 207.
82. Osborne, *Archaic*, 95.
83. Osborne, *Greece*, 243.
84. Childe, ibid., 207. Athens proper in 500 was not much larger than Argos, with 15,000, or Corinth; Meier, Christian. *Athens: A Portrait of the City in Its Golden Age*. Translated by Robert and Rita Kimber. New York: Henry Holt and Co., 1998, 35–38; Meier, *Athens*, 57–60; Cohen, Edward E. *The Athenian Nation*. Princeton: Princeton University Press, 2000, 10–23.
85. Plutarch. *The Lives of the Noble Grecian and Romans*, Translated by John Dryden, Modern Library Series, Vol. 1. New York: Modern Library, 1979, 97–117, 99.
86. Plutarch, *The Lives*, 104; Beginning in 2000 with his Politics of Rich and Poor. New York: HarperCollins, 1990, the former Republican strategist, Kevin Phillips, intensified his warning against an emerging American plutocracy of wealth disparity.
87. Plutarch, *The Lives*, 104.
88. Plutarch, *The Lives*, 104.

89. Plutarch, *The Lives*, 106.
90. Plutarch, *The Lives*, 110.
91. Plutarch, *The Lives*, 112–116.
92. Lattimore, Richard. "Solon" In *The Norton Book of Classical Literature* edited by Bernard Knox, 240. New York: W.W. Norton and Company, 1993, 240.
93. Lattimore, "Solon," 240.
94. Lattimore, "Solon," 242.
95. Roebuck, Carl. *Ionian Trade and Colonization*. Chicago Ares Publications, 1994, 87–90.
96. Roebuck, *Ionian Trade*, 87–90.
97. Heichelheim, *An Ancient Economic History*, 215–17.
98. Osborne, *Greece*, 250–58.
99. Heichelheim, *An Ancient Economic History*, 218.
100. Von Reden, Sitta. "Money, Law and Exchange: Coinage in the Greek Polis." *The Journal of Hellenic Studies* 117 (1997): 154–76.
101. Silver, *Economic Structures*, 19–21.
102. Plato, himself, would eventually denounce the proliferation of private cults in Greece and the ownership of many of these cults by private families. The Eteoboutadai family of Athens operated the shrines of Poseidon and Athena on the Acropolis. The shrine of Zeus was owned by the Praxiergidai; the famous Eleusinian Mysteries were operated by the Eumolpidai and Kerykes. Religious entrepreneurs founded sanctuaries, hired priests, and charged revenues, theology itself being somewhat influenced by the market revolution. Euripides and other playwrights, moreover, were not slow to accuse these "religious entrepreneurs" of less than sincere devotion to their gods and goddesses. The ruler Pentheus of Thebes in Euripides' "Bacchae" accused the prophet Teiresias of making a financial killing in the handsome fees he was charging for divining the will of his new deities. Professor Morris Silver recognized that in Greece, "entrepreneurs also played a central role in cultic innovation" Silver, *Economic Structures*, 30.
103. Olmstead, A. T. *History of the Persian Empire* Chicago: University of Chicago Press, 1959, s208–212.
104. Barnstone, Willis. "Xenophanes." In *The Norton Book of Classical Literature* edited by Bernard Knox. New York: W.W. Norton and Company, 1993, 233, 240. Even as early as Homer's time, at least a few well-to-do Greeks had begun to question the old moral order along with the old economy. Telemachus symbolised those who, in the eighth century, had already abandoned the faith of their parents: "I believe no messages any more, even should there be one, nor pay attention to any prophecy, those times my mother calls some diviïer into the house and asks him questions." Homer, *Odyssey*, 4. 414–16.
105. Green, *Concise History*, 99.
106. Green, *Concise History*, 96–106. Persian toleration always had its limits. Their style of cross-cultural management (see the following) was often modified, although not rescinded. Economics and religion were linked here, also. Babylon revolted early in Darius's reign and Babylonian national feeling, centered around worship of Marduk, was brutally suppressed. Samaritan and Arabian hostility to the Jewish restoration in Palestine forced a temporary halt to the rebuilding of the temple in Jerusalem. Commerce continued in Judea under Persian-appointed governors, who were forced to take action against fraudulent practices. Debt-ridden Jewish peasants were forced to mortgage homes, fields, and even children to the landed aristocracy and public officials to purchase grain. Officials charged exorbitant interest rates to their

countrymen. The Persian appointee, Nehemiah, summoned the priesthood and forced the Jewish elite to cease these practices. The book of Nehemiah highlights practices widespread in the Persian Empire, notably the onerous tax system. The levy on wealth real or assumed, instead of actual earnings, drove many into destitution. "There were also those that said, 'We have borrowed money for the king's tribute, and that upon our lands and vineyards'" (Nehemiah 5:4). Darius reorganized and standardized his domain into 157 satrapies stretching from Egypt and Asia Minor to the borders of India. More and more Iranians were inserted into the local administration. He also reformed the tax system. Subjects would be taxed upon earnings at a flat rate of 20%, not assumed wealth. Herodotus and other ancient sources show the amount of tax paid by each satrapy in the empire. India was the richest, followed by Babylonia, Egypt, and Media. India paid about three hundred and sixty talents or 330,000 pounds of gold dust. Babylonia paid around 1,000 silver talents, Egypt seven hundred, and Media four hundred and fifty.

107. Herodotus. *The Histories*, Translated by Aubrey De Sélincourt. London: Penguin Books, Ltd., 1996, 61–62. Herodotus remarked: "This was intended as a criticism of the Greeks generally, because they have markets for buying and selling, unlike the Persians who never buy in open market, and indeed have not a single market-place in the whole country" (Herodotus, *The Histories*, 75, 1.153).
108. Herodotus, *The Histories*, 74–75, 1.188–191; Van De Mieroop, *A History*, 267–271.
109. Snell, Daniel C. *Life in the Ancient near East, 3100–332 Bcee*. New Haven: Yale University Press, 1997, 99.
110. Ezra 1.1, KJV.
111. Ezra 1.1–11; 6.1–5, KJV.
112. Ezra 6.7–12.
113. Olmstead, *History*, 102–103.
114. Nehemiah 5:4, NKJV; for a careful summary of the Jews under Persia see Miller, J. Maxwell, and John H. Hayes. *A History of Ancient Israel and Judah* Philadelphia: Westminster Press, 1986, 450–473.
115. Herodotus, *The Histories*, 191–193, 3.90–95.
116. Olmstead, *History*, 144–45.
117. Briant, Pierre. *Cyrus to Alexander: A History of the Persian Empire*, Translated by Peter T. Daniels. Winona Lake: Eisenbrauns, 2002, 361.
118. Briant, *Cyrus*, 361–364.
119. Grelot, P. "Letter from Arshama to His Steward Nehtihor." *Documents araméens d'Egypte*, no. 67 (1972); Driver, G.R. "Aramaic Documents of the Fifth Century Bce, No. 6." In *Cyrus to Alexander: A History of the Persian Empire*. Translated by Peter T. Daniels, edited by Pierre Briant. Winona Lake: Eisenbrauns, 2002, 364.
120. Briant, Pierre. "Persepolis Fortification Tablets, 1404." In *Cyrus to Alexander: A History of the Persian Empire*, Translated by Peter T. Daniels, 365. Winona Lake: Eisenbrauns, 2002.
121. Briant, *Cyrus to Alexander*, 368–370.
122. Briant, *Cyrus to Alexander*, 370–371. There are allusions to this unprecedented equine activity in the biblical Book of Zechariah with its differently colored horses forming the stuff of prophetic visions but accurately recalling the Persian intelligence networks—"the King's eyes and ears" (Zechariah 1–6).
123. Briant, *Cyrus to Alexander*, 377.
124. Briant, *Cyrus to Alexander*, 378–380.

125. Textes cunéiformes, musée de Louvre, no.12.84, 551 BCE; Yale Oriental Services Babylonian Texts, no.6.168, 550 BCE, both in Briant, *Cyrus to Alexander*, 385–386.

126. Briant, *Cyrus to Alexander*, 385.

127. Olmstead, *History*, 77.

128. Olmstead, *History*, 77–79.

129. Olmstead, *History*, 79–81.

130. Olmstead, *History*, 83–84.

131. Joannès, Francis. "Private Commerce and Banking in Achaemenid Babylon." In *Civilizations of the Ancient near East*, Volumes Three and Four, edited by Jack M. Sasson, 1475–85. New York: Scribner 1995.

132. Joannès, "Private Commerce," 1476–1479.

133. Joannès, "Private Commerce," 1481.

134. Joannès, "Private Commerce," 1481.

135. Contract between Gadaliama and Rimut-Ninurta of Murashu at Nippur, 422 BCE in Joannes, "Private Commerce," 1481.

136. Joannès, "Private Commerce," 1481.

137. Snell, *Life in the Ancient*, 104–105; Joannès, "Private Commerce," 1475–1485.

138. Max Nordau quoted in Tuchman, Barbara. *The Proud Tower: A Portrait of the World before the War, 1890–1914* New York: The MacMillan Company, 1962, 33.

NOTES TO CHAPTER 7

1. Hadas, Moses. *Imperial Rome*. New York: Time-Life, 1965, 37. "Punic" is derived from the Roman term for "Phoenician," but applied mostly to the Greco–Roman era culture and dialect of , as distinct from the .

2. One of the largest mining firms in the world is still the London-headquartered, Rio Tinto, plc. According to the company website, The Rio Tinto Company was formed in 1873 to mine the ancient copper workings at Rio Tinto in Spain.

3. Tlatli, Salah-Eddine. *La Carthage Punique: Étude Urbaine: La Ville, Ses Functions, Son Rayonnement*. Paris: Librairie d'amerique et d'Orient, 1978, 234–35. Colonies that once considered Carthage second-rate "were soon obligated to recognise her hegemony and submit to her orders" (Tlatli, La Carthage, 247). The start of a distinctively Punic, as opposed to a Phoenician, culture could be detected even before 600 BCE when statues in the Balerics, Sardinia, and Sicily show new elements of western Mediterranean origin in the form of exaggerated sexual organs. Lancel, Serge. *Carthage: A History*. Oxford: Blackwell, 1995, 82; Lancel, *Carthage*, 82–83; Tlatli, *La Carthage*, 236–241.

4. See the character of Hanno of Calidun in Plautus's comedy "Poenicus:" "Carthaginian tradesmen were apparently shipowners at the same time." Tsirkin, Yuri B. *The Economy of Carthage*. Edited by E. Lipinski, Studia Phoenicia Vi Carthago, Acta Colloqui Bruxellensis Habiti Diebus 2 or 3 Mensis Maii Anni 1986. Louvain: Uit giverij Peeters, 1988, 131. The economic elite "was the same time a political elite." Tsirkin, *The Economy*, 132. "The trade policies of aristocratic Carthage tellingly reflected the ambitions of most of the ruling oligarchy for active foreign commerce. As shown earlier, sometimes the Carthaginian State sought to secure an exclusive zone for the home traders, but in other cases, when it deemed it profitable, it allowed a free unrestricted commerce with their trade partners. . . . It is almost certain that the nobility

of Carthage had in its ownership some mines, too. Pliny (NH XXXIII 96) reports that the pit of Baebelo in Spain brought Hannibal 300 pounds of silver every day. The daily income bespeaks the fact that Hannibal was the master landowner of this pit. The silver was his daily income, not a tax resultant from the subordination of Spain to Carthage" (Tsirkin, *The Economy*, 131).

5. Aristotle. *The Politics of Aristotle*, Translated and Edited by Ernest Barker. Oxford: Oxford University Press, 1982, 84.
6. Aristotle, *The Politics*, 84.
7. Aristotle, *The Politics of Aristotle*, 2.11.1–15, 1272a 21–1273a32, 83–87.
8. Tsirkin, *The Economy*, 133; Tsirkin, *The Economy*, 132–134.
9. Tsirkin, *The Economy*, 128–134.
10. Oliver, Roland, and J. D. Fage. *A Short History of Africa*, Harmondsworth: Penguin Books, 1978, 1984, 14
11. Murray, Jocelyn (ed.). *Cultural Atlas of Africa*, New York: Facts on File Publication, 1982, 47
12. Shinnie, Margaret. *Ancient African Kingdoms*, London: Edward Arnold (Publishers) Ltd, 1965, 67
13. Phocaea was an ancient city on the western coast of , not to be confused with the Phoenicians.
14. "The whole north of the western [Mediterranean] basin fell, for all practical purposes, under their control, as well as the tin traffic . . . across the valley of the Rhône . . . of Cornwall. The maritime and commercial power of Carthage was . . . placed in jeopardy by this new rival and by the whole encirclement strategy of Greek imperialism." Glotz. G. *Ancient Greece at Work*. New York: W.W. Norton and Company, 1967, 123.
15. Tlatli, *La Carthage*, 252–254; That there was "a real alliance between Carthage and the principality of southern Etruria" is shown by the very name of the Etruscan port of Punicum, which, according to French archaeologist Serge Lancel, "gives assurance of the reality of the commercial [and perhaps also demographic] presence of Carthaginians" (Lancel, *Carthage*, 85). Recent excavations in the nearby cemetery of Byrsa proved Etruria was exporting and importing goods to and from Carthage at the end of the sixth century BCE. An ivory plaque written in Etruscan boasted that the engraver was Punic and from Carthage (Lancel, *Carthage*, 85–86).
16. Demerliac, J. G., and J. Meirat. *Hannon Et L'empire Punique*. Paris: Les Belles Lettres, 1983, 186–90.
17. Demerliac and Meirat, *Hannon*, 186–190, state that "only Carthage was rich enough to finance such enterprises" (Demerliac and Meirat, *Hannon*, 190). Demerliac and Meirat regard it as certain that Gades and Lixus "obtained the necessary financial delegations from the capital and also played an important banking role in the economic system" Demerliac and Meirat, *Hannon*, 190–191.
18. Demerliac and Meirat, *Hannon*, 192.
19. This made for a case study in long-range thinking that would earn the admiration of World War Two strategists of the Battle of the Atlantic. Each May, the Punic navy reconnoitered the Greek ports in Italy, shifting patrols to Sardinia, Corsica, and Spain down to Gibraltar until the galleys cleared the Pillars of Hercules. Replenishing in June in North Africa, the triremes patrolled the regions near Malta to cover the mercantile fleet from Tyre in July, sometimes assisted by Corinthian or even Syracusean vessels if a pro-Carthaginian party were in power. Demerliac and Meirat, *Hannon*, 194–198.
20. Demerliac and Meirat, *Hannon*, 202–205; "as with any organisation, this system had its advantages and its inconveniences . . . thanks to it the Punic metropolis was able to mobilise, in a very brief time, in case of war, a force

that was powerful and maintained in a very high degree of training and cohesion" (Demerliac and Meirat, *Hannon*, 205).

21. "The leadership of the various Phoenician settlements of the west now fell more and more to Carthage, but there was one huge obstacle constantly blocking all hope of peaceful trade: the Sicilian Greeks. The battle for Sicily would become a constant and tragic theme, a leitmotif of the Punic period lasting all the way down to 241 BCE. Carthage's prime adversary was the city–state of Syracuse and it allies. Syracuse had to be stopped—but how?" (Soren, David, Aicha Ben Abed Ben Khader, and Hedi Slim. *Carthage: Uncovering the Mysteries and Splendors of Ancient Tunisia* New York: Simon and Schuster, 1990, 51–53); Re: infant sacrifice: "For a Carthaginian general each campaign was a holy war. A loss was an impiety, and a failed leader might be expected to sacrifice himself on a pyre or starve himself to death. The general-king was expected to solicit the good favor of the gods every day through sacrifice and consultation of the omens" (Soren, et al., *Carthage*, 59–60).

22. Soren, et al., *Carthage*, 60–61; "Carthage was at last a true superpower, standing on the threshold of controlling the trade and manipulating the politics of the entire western Mediterranean. It was a watershed moment, one that had taken centuries to create, and Hannibal was determined to make the most of it" (Soren et al., *Carthage*, 60).

23. Lancel, *Carthage*, 96–98.

24. Oliver and Fage, 1984, 61.

25. Lancel, *Carthage*, 91–95; Tlatli, *La Carthage*, 241–45.

26. The overland Libyan route may have been more profitable after all. See Soren et al., *Carthage*, 68–72; Hanno "may simply have overreached his capabilities. To establish a far-flung network of colonies required a powerful support system, which he couldn't deliver" (Soren et al., *Carthage*, 72).

27. Fell, Barry. *Saga America*. New York: Quadrangle, 1980, 64–73. See Guzzo, Maria Giulia Amadasi. "Did the Phoenicians Land in America?" In *The Phoenicians*, edited by Sabatino Moscati, 657–60. New York: Rizzoli International Publications, Inc., 1999, 657–660 on the Phoenician hoax. The existence of Punic regional trading mandates covering the Atlantic suggests an even more tantalising possibility, but one dismissed by most historians; Soren et al., *Carthage*, 73–74. The hints of rather extensive economic ties between Carthage and America is an idea considered too far-fetched by David Soren and most orthodox archaeologists studying both Carthage and ancient America. Fell went so far as to see this hypothetical New World trade as the foundation of Punic world power, with the timber and precious metals needed to sustain that power in the face of Greece and Rome coming from American shores. He argues an export trade of Cypro-Phoenician mass-produced bronze art replicas in Carthaginian ships visiting America. Substantial gold was acquired in return, but insufficient to provide adequate ballast. "To meet this need, the Carthaginian ships picked up shipments of large pine logs from the Algonquian tribes of northeastern North America, to whom they traded adequate stocks of iron-cutting tools, axes, and other desirable items, including occasional bronze art replicas . . . and also low-value Carthaginian coins of attractive appearance, glass beads, and the like. Such trade, profitable alike to the Amerindian and the Carthaginian, would result in a steady input of gold and lumber on the home markets in Carthage, would yield the timbers needed to build ships, and provide them with straight masts and oars, and in addition would yield the Carthaginian state the gold ingots required to produce the coinage that apparently financed the military and naval operations of the Sicilian War, and later of the First Punic War" (Fell, *Saga America*, 86).

28. Soren et al., *Carthage*, 73–74; Himlico's voyage was intended to "establish major trading connections with remote centers producing valued raw materials" (Soren et al., Carthage, 72); "The Punic sources themselves are silent of any mention of voyages to Britain. Excavations in Cornwall show the mines being worked by the Britons themselves even in Roman times. More recent digs qualify this picture by confirming that Punic traders did in fact visit the island of Britain. Glass beads and other Carthaginian artifacts have been unearthed at locations like Castle Dore in Cornwall" (Fell, Saga America, 52–53). Dr. Fell's work, and that of the Epigraphic Society he founded, is unorthodox and quite controversial. Most of the academic establishment still rejects his assertions that Germans, Celts, and Canaanites journeyed to the New World. "Diffusionism," the belief in migrations of peoples and cultures from continent to continent in the Bronze and Iron Ages, has been severely attacked since the 1970s. Nonetheless, some of Fell's evidence is intriguing.
29. "Never before had any Western navigator been able to sail so far north; Carthaginian commercial interests would not permit it" (Fell, *Saga America*, 60).
30. Fell, *Saga America*, 51.
31. MIT's Peter Temin argues that "the economy of the early Roman Empire was primarily a market economy. The parts of this economy located far from each other were not tied together as tightly as markets often are today, but they still functioned as part of a comprehensive Mediterranean market." From his paper Temin, Peter. "A Market Economy in the Early Roman Empire." MIT Dept. of Economics Working Paper, no. 01–08 (2001).
32. Freeman, Charles. *Egypt, Greece and Rome, Civilizations of the Ancient Merditerranean.* Oxford: Oxford University Press, 1998, 301–302.
33. Barker, Graeme, and Tom Rasmussen. *The Etruscans.* Oxford Blackwell Publishers, 1998, 203–207. Similarity between Etruscan pottery and vessels "suggests a close rapport between different workshops in the same center, though whether this took the form of collaboration or competition we cannot tell" (Barker and Rasmussen, *The Etruscans*, 207). There are, as yet, many unanswered questions about the organization and management of Etruscan industries (Barker and Rasmussen, *The Etruscans*, 208–210).
34. Barker and Rasmussen, *The Etruscans*, 215.
35. Barker and Rasmussen, *The Etruscans*, 210–214. Even though much of the mining was done in northern sites such as Elba, the main export centers lay in southern Etruria "suggesting that the southern cities controlled the sea trade" (Barker and Rasmussen, *The Etruscans*, 214).
36. Although the spiky mountains of Greece almost totally prevented overland communication and conquest, the mountainous geography of Italy encouraged her peoples to turn inward, not outward. Italy had few good natural harbors and a somewhat larger supply of good farmland, especially around the area known early as Latium. These factors encouraged the Romans to expand overland instead of overseas before the third century BCE (Freeman, 307).
37. Cornell, T. J. *The Beginnings of Rome: Italy and Rome from the Bronze Age to the Punic Wars C.1000–264 BCE.* London: Routledge, 1995, 48–57. The early Latins named themselves, not after their polis like the Greeks (e.g., Plato of Athens), but after their gens, that is their clan or group of families followed by their personal praenomen, or first name (Freeman, 302). The thirty communities of the Latium plain were more inclusive than the rather xenophobic Greek states. Sharing a common Latin culture they early permitted sharing rights of marriage, citizenship and trade with members of any other Latin clan (Freeman, 308–309); Barker and Rasmussen, *The Etruscans*, 201–215.

Frank, Tenney. *An Economic History of Rome*. 2nd ed. New York: Cooper Square Publishers, 1962, 18–23; 31–33.

38. Drummond, A. "Rome in the Fifth Century, I: The Social and Economic Framework." In *The Cambridge Ancient History, the Rise of Rome to 220 B.C.*, edited by F. W. Walbank, A. E. Astin, M. W. Frederiksen, R. M. Ogilvie, and A. Drummond. Cambridge: Cambridge University Press, 1990, 144–45.

39. Drummond, "Rome," 147.

40. "The power of the family head is notorious, extending even to the right to kill those subject to him. This presumably reflects a strong collective emphasis on the need for vigorous discipline in the component elements of the community, not least to regulate the relations between families since the heads of households were responsible to each other for the private actions of those subject to them" (Drummond, "Rome," 147–48).

41. Drummond, "Rome," 125–30.

42. Rich, John. "Fear, Greed and Glory: The Causes of Roman War-Making in the Middle Republic." In *War and Society in the Roman World*, edited by John Shipley and Graham Shipley. London: Routledge 1995, 44–46. "The habit of constant war was as old as the Republic" (Rich, "Fear", 45).

43. One of the most famous expressions about Rome was, "All roads lead to Rome." It may be more accurately rendered "all roads lead from Rome." A central reason to build these roads was to move the Roman army more quickly ("celeritas") and quell rebellion in the provinces. Although built for an overriding military purpose, the roads also allowed business to be more easily transacted.

44. Cosa, a smaller version of Rome itself, was a paradigmatic colony designed to control the coastal plains, wrest good farmland from the Etruscans, deprive them of their ports, and dampen their desire to remain a seafaring power with an independent foreign policy. Etruria, after 400 BCE, was a spent force. Veii was destroyed in 396 BCE, Volsinii in 264 BCE, and Falerii in 241 BCE. Populations were resettled at the point of the sword. The Etruscan cities of the north would last longer and fare better temporarily. No Roman settlements were planted between Vulci and the River Arno before 100 BCE. Treaties were concluded between Rome and the northern city–states. After the civil wars of the 80s BCE, however, many of them were punished for supporting the losing side. With the exception of a few, like Arezzo, most of the southern Etruscan centers would be abandoned well before the collapse of the Roman Empire (Cornell, *Beginnings of Rome*, 262–275).

45. Cornell, *Beginnings of Rome*, 348–49.

46. Cornell, *Beginnings of Rome*, 380.

47. Cornell, *Beginnings of Rome*, 333; Cornell, *Beginnings of Rome*, 394–95.

48. Cornell, *Beginnings of Rome*, 394.

49. Cornell, *Beginnings of Rome*, 385–88.

50. Cornell, *Beginnings of Rome*, 394–98.

51. Polybius. "The Histories." In *The Rise of Roman Empire*, translated by Ian Scott-Kilvert, edited by F.W. Walbank, 3.22, 200. London: Penguin Books, 1979.

52. Polybius, "The Histories," iii.23, 200–201. The text quoted by Polybius read: "There shall be friendship between the Romans and their allies and the Carthaginians and theirs on these conditions: The Romans and their allies shall not sail beyond the Far Promontory unless compelled to do so by storm or by enemy action. If any one of them is carried beyond it by force, he shall not buy or carry away anything more than is required for the repair of his ship or for sacrifice, and he shall depart within five days. Those who come to trade shall not conclude any business except in the presence of a herald

or town-clerk. The price of whatever is sold in the presence of these officials shall be secured to the vendor by the state, if the sale takes place in Africa or Sardinia" (Polybius, "The Histories," iii.22, 199–200).

53. Carthage, now a "great common-market trading community extended from Egypt across North Africa to Spain . . . under the control of the wealthy financiers who also comprised the Council of One Hundred" (Fell, *Saga America*, 74–75).
54. One could think of the difference between imperial Britain facing a series of colonial wars overseas and then fighting two World Wars in Europe as a comparison. Rome may well have lost at least some 50,000 citizens between 218 and 215 BCE, about 17% of her young men and 5% of her whole population (Rich, "Fear," 44–48).
55. Polybius records "so long as the Carthaginians held unchallenged control of the sea, the issue of the war still hung in the balance" and that "while the Italian coasts were repeatedly raided and devastated those of Africa suffered no damage" (Polybius, "The Histories," i.20, 62).
56. Polybius, "The Histories," 62.
57. Polybius, "The Histories," 62.
58. Lazenby, J. F. *The First Punic War: A Military History*. Stanford: Stanford University Press, 1996, 61–80. This details the story of the Roman triumph at sea.
59. Scullard, H. H. "The Carthaginians in Spain." In *Rome and the Mediterranean to 133 B.C.*, edited by A. E. Astin, F. W. Walbank, M. W. Frederiksen, and R. M. Ogilvie. Cambridge: Cambridge University Press, 1989, 20–43.
60. Lazenby, J. F. *Hannibal's War: A Military History of the Second Punic War*. Norman: University of Oklahoma Press, 1998, 49–86. Lazenby tells the story of Hannibal's devastation of Roman Italy and details the destruction of Carthage on pages 243–46. See also Polybius, "The Histories," 20–118; Polybius, "The Histories," 97–176.
61. Arnott, Peter. *The Romans and Their World*. New York: St. Martin's Press, 1970, 69–96.
62. Plautus. "The Pot of Gold." In *The Romans and Their World*, edited by Peter Arnott. New York: St. Martin's Press, 1970, 81.
63. Arnott, *The Romans*, 88–92.
64. Plautus, "The Pot of Gold," 78. The "Stock Exchange" is Arnett's free translation of "the basilica" (Arnott, The Romans, fn .4, 96).
65. Badian, E. "Publicans and Sinners." In *Private Enterprise in the Service of the Roman Republic*, 16. Ithaca: Cornell University Press, 1983.
66. Malmendier, Ulrike. *Societas Republicanorum*. Cologne: Böhlan Verlag, 2002, 1–5, 15–20.
67. Malmendier, *Societas Republicanorum*, 34, 59.
68. Badian, "Publicans and Sinners," 16.
69. Badian, "Publicans and Sinners," 16.
70. Badian, "Publicans and Sinners," 16.
71. Badian, "Publicans and Sinners," 16–25. The annual pay of a Roman soldier was 900 sestertii a year in Augustan times, or 225 denarii. Greene, Kevin. *The Archaeology of the Roman Economy*. Berkeley: University of California Press, 1990, 48, 59. The denarius was equivalent to a day's pay by the time of Jesus.
72. Valerius Maximus, ix. 1. 3, quoted in Frank, Tenney. "Rome and Italy of the Empire." In *An Economic Survey of Ancient Rome*. Baltimore Johns Hopkins Press, 1940. According to Frank's dated but exhaustive and valuable study of Roman economics, "not very many actual citizens were in Asia, but . . . the publicans had non-citizen agents there who worked along side other 'independent business men'" (Frank, "Rome and Italy," 278).

73. Cicero, "For Fontiero," §11–12, quoted in Frank, "Rome and Italy," 1940, 281.
74. Roman Italy's depopulation traced to the heavy casualties borne by the urban poor and peasantry in the wars fought in Spain and Gaul. Then came terrible civil conflicts waged within Italy herself at the onset of the first century BCE. The Social War, alone, would cost 100,000 casualties on each side. Frank, "Rome and Italy," 283; Frank, "Rome and Italy," 291.
75. Badian, "Publicans and Sinners," 52–66
76. Badian, "Publicans and Sinners," 37
77. Badian, "Publicans and Sinners," 37
78. Badian, "Publicans and Sinners," 67–72.
79. Badian, "Publicans and Sinners,", 67–72. According to Badian, "the ties among all the companies were particularly close, so as to constitute a cartel" (Badian, "Publicans and Sinners," 74). Roman companies varied greatly in size as well as profitability, the firm of Hispo being one of the largest. Sadly, historians still have very few hard statistics on trade and production for the Roman world (Badian, "Publicans and Sinners", 75–77).
80. Arnott, *The Romans*, 138–47; Everitt, Anthony. *Cicero: The Life and Times of Rome's Greatest Politician.* New York: Random House, 2001.
81. Frank, "Rome and Italy," 107; Badian comments on "companies getting together into a cartel . . . and it seems to have been done quite openly and officially" (Badian, "Publicans and Sinners," 106; Frank, "Rome and Italy," 344–346). Taxes on grazing and port trade in Sicily were collected not by the publicans, but by smaller firms operating as "branches of a larger company of publicans" (Frank, "Rome and Italy," 345). The publicans would make their presence felt in the dying Republic by lending indebted municipalities money to pay each new Roman exaction. Many cities defaulted on their astronomical new debts between 84 and 70 BCE and became indebted to the firms. After 70 BCE, Lucullus was forced to take numerous measures to alleviate these debts, including a twenty-five per cent tax on crops (Frank, "Rome and Italy," 32–33).
82. Frank, "Rome and Italy," 107.
83. "The Speech of M.I. Cicero in Defence of Caius Rabirius Postumus," Yonge, C. D. (ed. and Trans.) *The Orations of Marcus Tullius Cicero*, Volume III, London: G. Bell and Sons, ltd, 1913, 438–56.
84. Livy, 21 63. 4 and Polybius, 6.56.1–3, in D'Arms, John H. *Commerce and Social Standing in Ancient Rome.* Cambridge: Harvard University Press, 1981, 20; D'Arms, Commerce, 36–37; Badian, "Publicans and Sinners," 48–53. In his cross-examination of Vatinius, in a scene reminiscent on any prime-time TV courtroom, Cicero demanded of him "Did you extort shares, which were at their dearest at the time, partly from Cæsar, partly from the publicani?"[Against Vatinius, 29, quoted in Badian, 102].
85. Badian, "Publicans and Sinners," 38–41; "L. Aelius Lamia . . . supported the publicani of Syria, and . . . may have had negotia in Bithynia, furthered his negotia in Africa through procuratores, liberti, familia, and was helped as well by his friendships, in this case by Cicero's direct intervention on his behalf with the governor of Africa, Vetus" (Badian, "Publicans and Sinners," 42).
86. D'Arms, Commerce, 36–37.
87. Badian, "Publicans and Sinners," 42–44; Badian, "Publicans and Sinners," 48–53; Badian, "Publicans and Sinners," 94–96. "The laws designed to bar aristocrats from trade had the long-term effect of encouraging forms of business organization which permitted patricians to become hidden partners in an extended form of family enterprise" (Badian, "Publicans and Sinners," 45–46; Cicero, *Letters to Atticus*, 2.16.4, referred to in Frank, 1940, 356–57).
88. Casson, L. *The Ancient Mariners: Seafarers and Sea Fighters of the Mediterranean in Ancient Times.* New York: Macmillan, 1964, 206–208.

NOTES TO CHAPTER 8

1. Shipley, Graham. *The Greek World After Alexander*, 323–30 BC. London: Routledge, 2000, 1.
2. Shipley, *The Greek World After Alexander*, 1.
3. Levy, Jean-Phillipe. *The Economic Life of the Ancient World*. Chicago: The University of Chicago Press, 1967, 34.
4. Green, Peter. *Alexander to Actium, the Historical Evolution of the Hellenistic Age*. Berkeley: University of California Press, 1990, 362; Freeman, Charles. *Egypt, Greece and Rome: Civilizations of the Ancient Mediterranean*. Oxford: Oxford University Press, 1996, 270–78.
5. Clayton, Peter, and Martin Price (eds.). *The Seven Wonders of the Ancient World*. New York: Barnes and Noble Books, 1993, 80; 130.
6. Green, *Alexander to Actium*, 362–68.
7. Green, *Alexander to Actium*, 362–68.
8. Heichelheim, *An Ancient Economic History*, 9.
9. Casson, *The Ancient Mariners*, 175–76.
10. Green, *Alexander to Actium*, 368.
11. Green, *Alexander to Actium*, 366–99 says "As in the comparable modern case of Soviet Russia, what really surprises is that agricultural production did not seize up altogether." Green, *Alexander to Actium*, 369; Demetrios, head of the royal mint in Alexandria, directed his agent, Apollonios, in 258 B.C. to "the foreigners who come here by sea and the merchants and middlemen and others" who "bring . . . their local money" to convert their coinage "into new money . . . in accordance with the decree which orders us to receive and remint." See "Letter to Apollonios About Reminting Coins, #84." In *Greek Historical Documents: The Hellenistic Period*, edited by Roger S. Bagnall and Peter Derow. Papyrus: Scholars Press, 1981, 133–4.
12. "Instructions of the Dioiketes to an Oikonomos, #85." In *Greek Historical Documents: The Hellenistic Period*, edited by Roger S. Bagnall and Peter Derow. Papyrus: Scholars Press, 1981, 134–37.
13. "Order for Delivery of Grain, #92." In *Greek Historical Documents: The Hellenistic Period*, edited by Roger S. Bagnall and Peter Derow. Papyrus: Scholars Press, 1981, 144–45. A papyrus from 251 B.C. recorded that the shipmaster Dionysios embarked with a large shipment of barley with Necthemebes the agent of the royal scribe for transport to the royal granary at Alexandria. "Receipt for Embarkation of Grain, #93." In *Greek Historical Documents: The Hellenistic Period*, edited by Roger S. Bagnall and Peter Derow. Papyrus: Scholars Press, 1981, 251.
14. When there was work, they were to compel the oil-makers to work every day and stay beside them to make sure they did so, "Revenue Laws of Ptolemy Philadelphos, #95." In *Greek Historical Documents: The Hellenistic Period*, edited by Roger S. Bagnall and Peter Derow. Papyrus: Scholars Press, 1981, 156.
15. Kulke, Hermann, and Dietmar Rothermund. *History of India*. 3rd ed. London: Routledge, 1998; Sedlar, Jean W. *India and the Greek World: A Study in the Transmission of Culture*. Totowa Rowman and Littlefield, 1980; Nigam, Shyamsundar. *Economic Organisation in Ancient India (200 BC–200 AD)*. New Delhi: Munshiram Manoharlal Publishers PVT. Ltd., 1975; Nakamura, Hajime, and Philip P. Wiener. *Ways of Thinking of Eastern Peoples: India–China–Tibet–Japan*. Honolulu: East-West Center Press, 1966.
16. Indian culture is deeply influenced by religious philosophy. Science and mathematics in India developed on heavily Brahmanist and otherworldly foundations, and has a very strong religious orientation. See Nakamura and Wiener, *Ways of Thinking*, 160–161.
17. Rigveda 6. 26, 47; 7. 5–6, Kulke and Rothermund, *History of India*, 35.

18. Rigveda, 6. 53, Kulke and Rothermund, *History of India*, 36.
19. Rigveda, 6. 25, 28, 46, Kulke and Rothermund, *History of India*, 37.
20. Rigveda, 4.33, Kulke and Rothermund, *History of India*, 37.
21. Rigveda, 10.28, Kulke and Rothermund, *History of India*, 38. According to Kulke and Rothermund, excavations have not yet found evidence of systematic clearing of the jungle (Kulke and Rothermund, *History of India*, 38).
22. Rigveda, 10.90, Kulke and Rothermund, *History of India*, 39.
23. Kulke and Rothermund, *History of India*, 40–41.
24. The Laws of Manu, 10.81–3, 98. The citations, originally from Buehler, Georg. *The Sacred Books of the East*. Vol. 25. Oxford: Clarendon Press, 1886 and reappear in McNeill, William H., and Jean W. Sedlar (eds.). *Classical India*. London: Oxford University Press, 1969, 153–55.
25. McKay, John. *A History of World Societies: From Antiquity to 1500*. Vol. A. Boston: Houghton Mifflin, 2007, 75.
26. India was the Twentieth Satrapy of Darius' realm. The annual revenue of the empire was 14,560 Euboean talents, of which Indian gold accounted for 4,680. Herodotus, *The Histories*, 192–93.
27. McKay, *A History of World Societies*, 75–76.
28. "Chapter 6." In *Essentials of Indian Statecraft*. Kautilya's Arthashastra for Contemporary Readers, edited by T. M. Ramaswamy. Bombay: Asia Publishing House, 1962, 19.
29. "Kautilya, Arthashastra, Chapter 10." In *Classical India*, edited by William H. McNeill and Jean W. Sedlar. London: Oxford University Press, 1969, 21.
30. "Kautilya, Arthashastra, Chapter 21." In *Classical India*, edited by William H. McNeill and Jean W. Sedlar. London: Oxford University Press, 1969, 26.
31. "Kautilya, Arthashastra, Chapter 21." In *Classical India*, edited by William H. McNeill and Jean W. Sedlar. London: Oxford University Press, 1969, 26.
32. "Kautilya, Arthashastra, Chapter 29." In *Classical India*, edited by William H. McNeill and Jean W. Sedlar. London: Oxford University Press, 1969, 29.
33. "Kautilya, Arthashastra, Chapter 29." In *Classical India*, edited by William H. McNeill and Jean W. Sedlar. London: Oxford University Press, 1969, 30.
34. "Kautilya, Arthashastra, Chapter 29." In *Classical India*, edited by William H. McNeill and Jean W. Sedlar. London: Oxford University Press, 1969, 30.
35. "Kautilya, Arthashastra, Chapter 29." In *Classical India*, edited by William H. McNeill and Jean W. Sedlar. London: Oxford University Press, 1969, 30.
36. "Kautilya, Arthashastra, Chapter 41." In *Classical India*, edited by William H. McNeill and Jean W. Sedlar. London: Oxford University Press, 1969, 33.
37. "Kautilya, Arthashastra, Chapter 54." In *Classical India*, edited by William H. McNeill and Jean W. Sedlar. London: Oxford University Press, 1969, 36.
38. Fernando, P. R. K. "Literature Evidences of Gem-Industry in Ancient Sri Lanka." In *Gemtalk: Voice of the Gem Industry in Sri Lanka*, edited by Ajith Perara. Church Road: Pririte Enterprises (Pvt) Ltd., April–June, 2008, 7.
39. Casson, *The Ancient Mariners*, 179; Casson, *The Ancient Mariners*, 185–87.
40. Chandra, Moti. *Trade and Trade Routes in Ancient India*. New Delhi: Abhinav Publications, 1977, 129–30.
41. Chandra, *Trade and Trade Routes in Ancient India*, 130–31.
42. Chandra, *Trade and Trade Routes in Ancient India*, 141–42.
43. Chandra, *Trade and Trade Routes in Ancient India*, 141–44.
44. Chandra, *Trade and Trade Routes in Ancient India*, 169–71.
45. McKay, John. *A History of World Societies: From 800 to 1815*. 6th ed. Vol. B. Boston : Houghton Mifflin College Div, 2004, 506.
46. Chandra, *Trade and Trade Routes in Ancient India*, 169–75.
47. Chandra, *Trade and Trade Routes in Ancient India*, 169–75.
48. Chandra, *Trade and Trade Routes in Ancient India*, 169–75.

49. "Manu, 9.329." In *Classical India*, edited by William H. McNeill and Jean W. Sedlar. London: Oxford University Press, 1969, 149–151.
50. "Manu, 9.331." In *Classical India*, edited by William H. McNeill and Jean W. Sedlar. London: Oxford University Press, 1969, 151–55.
51. "Manu, 9.332." In *Classical India*, edited by William H. McNeill and Jean W. Sedlar. London: Oxford University Press, 1969, 151–55.
52. "Manu, 9.333." In *Classical India*, edited by William H. McNeill and Jean W. Sedlar. London: Oxford University Press, 1969, 151–55.
53. Casson, *The Ancient Mariners*, 179; Casson, *The Ancient Mariners*, 185–7.
54. Shipley, Graham. *The Greek World after Alexander*, 271; 275–77.
55. Shipley, Graham. *The Greek World after Alexander*, 295–301.
56. Shipley, Graham. *The Greek World after Alexander*, 295–301.
57. Strabo. *The Geography of Strabo*. Translated by Horace Leonard Jones. Vol. VII. Cambridge: Harvard University Press, 1954, 267–69.
58. Strabo, *The Geography of Strabo*, 269.
59. Strabo, *The Geography of Strabo*, 269.
60. Strabo, *The Geography of Strabo*, 269–71.
61. Strabo, *The Geography of Strabo*, 271–73.
62. Diodorus, Siculus. *Diodorus of Sicily*. Translated by Russell M. Geer. Vol. X. Cambridge: Harvard University Press, 1954, 356–57.
63. Diodorus, *Diodorus of Sicily*, 356–57.
64. Polybius. *The Histories*. Translated by W. R. Paton. Vol. II. Cambridge: Harvard University Press, 1960, 415.
65. McKay, *A History of World Societies* Vol. B, 135–36.
66. Heichelheim, *An Ancient Economic History*, 28–35.
67. Strabo, *The Geography of Strabo*, 269; Musti, D. "Syria and the East." In *The Hellenistic World*, edited by F. W. Walbank, A. E. Astin, M. W. Frederiksen and R. M. Ogilvie. Cambridge: Cambridge University Press, 1984, 197–203; Casson, *The Ancient Mariners*, 178–79.
68. Rawlinson, George. *The Sixth Great Oriental Monarchy, or the Geography, History and Antiquities of Parthia*. Chestnut Hill: Elibron Classics, 2002, 84–95.
69. Tarn, W. W. "Parthia." In *The Roman Republic, 133–44 B.C.*, edited by S. A. Cook, F. E. Adcock, and M. P. Charlesworth. London: Cambridge University Press, 1977, 574–613; 588–602.
70. Tarn, "Parthia," 598–99; Boulnois, Luce. *Silk Road: Monks, Warriors and Merchants on the Silk Road*. Translated by Helen Loveday. New York: W. W. Norton and Company, 2005, 75–85.
71. Gascoigne, *The Treasures and Dynasties of China*, 82–83.
72. Barnes, *The Rise of Civilization*, 134; Hucker, Arthur O. *China's Imperial Past, an Introduction to Chinese History and Culture*. Stanford: Stanford University Press, 1975, 22–35.
73. Hucker, *China's Imperial Past*, 30–35; Barnes, *The Rise of Civilization*, 134.
74. Hucker, *China's Imperial Past*, 30–35; Barnes, *The Rise of Civilization*, 134; Rindova, Violina P., and William H. Starbuck. "Ancient Chinese Theories of Control." *Journal of Management Inquiry* 6 (1997): 144–59.
75. Karlgren, B. *The Book of Documents*. Stockholm: Museum of Far Eastern Antiquities, 1970 cited in Rindova and Starbuck, "Ancient Chinese Theories", 149.
76. Chan, W. T. *Source Book in Chinese Philosophy*. Princeton: Princeton University Press, 1963; Legge, J. *The Chinese Classics*. New York: Oxford University Press, 1865; Karlgren, *The Book of Documents*, all cited in Rindova and Starbuck, "Ancient Chinese Theories," 149.
77. Rindova and Starbuck, "Ancient Chinese Theories," 146.

78. Rindova and Starbuck, "Ancient Chinese Theories," 146.
79. Rindova and Starbuck, "Ancient Chinese Theories," 146.
80. Rindova and Starbuck, "Ancient Chinese Theories," 149–50.
81. Rindova and Starbuck, "Ancient Chinese Theories," 150.
82. Wu, K. C. *Ancient Chinese Political Theories*. Shanghai: The Commercial Press, Limited, 1928; Legge, *The Chinese Classics*; both cited in Rindova and Starbuck, "Ancient Chinese Theories," 150–51.
83. "Hanshu 91.1–2." In *Food and Money in Ancient China: The Earliest Economic History of China to A.D. 25, Han Shu 24, with Related Texts Han Shu 91 and Shih–Chi 129*, edited by Gu Ban, Qian Sima and Nancy Lee Swann, 414–16. Princeton: Princeton University Press, 1950.
84. "Hanshu 91.2." In *Food and Money in Ancient China: The Earliest Economic History of China to A.D. 25, Han Shu 24, with Related Texts Han Shu 91 and Shih-Chi 129*, edited by Gu Ban, Qian Sima, and Nancy Lee Swann, 417. Princeton: Princeton University Press, 1950.
85. "Hanshu 91.3." In *Food and Money in Ancient China: The Earliest Economic History of China to A.D. 25, Han Shu 24, with Related Texts Han Shu 91 and Shih-Chi 129*, edited by Gu Ban, Qian Sima, and Nancy Lee Swann, 418. Princeton: Princeton University Press, 1950.
86. Ban et al., "Hanshu 91.3", 418.
87. See the biography of Pan Ku in "Hanshu, Book 91, §133." Li, Dun J., ed. *The Essence of Chinese Civilization*. Princeton: D. Van Nostrand Co., Inc., 1967, 317.
88. "Pan Ku, Hanshu, Book 91, §133." Li, *The Essence of Chinese Civilization*, 317.
89. "Pan Ku, Hanshu, Book 91, §133." Li, *The Essence of Chinese Civilization*, 317.
90. "Pan Ku, Hanshu, Book 91, §133." Li, *The Essence of Chinese Civilization*, 317.
91. "Pan Ku, Hanshu, Book 91, §133." Li, *The Essence of Chinese Civilization*, 317.
92. Confucius. "Analects 1:2." In *The Analects*. Oxford: Oxford University Press 1993, 3.
93. Confucius, "Analects 4:2," 13.
94. Confucius, "Analects 4:2," 13.
95. Confucius, "Analects 6:11," 21.
96. Confucius, "Analects 4:2," 14.
97. Confucius, "Analects 4:2," 14.
98. Confucius, "Analects 4:2," 14.
99. Confucius, "Analects 4:2," 14.
100. Confucius, "Analects 4:2," 14–15.
101. Rindova and Starbuck, "Ancient Chinese Theories," 151.
102. Zhuangzi (Chuang Tzu), translated by Burton Watson, Document 6 in Buckley, Patricia, ed. *Chinese Civilization and Society: A Sourcebook* New York: Free Press, 1981, 17.
103. Zhuangzi (Chuang Tzu), translated by Burton Watson, Document 6, pages 17–20 in Buckley, *Chinese Civilization and Society*, 18.
104. Chen, *Asian Management Systems*, 40–42.
105. Chen, *Asian Management Systems*, 41.
106. Wen-shu, Lu. "On the Severity of Punishments." In *The Essence of Chinese Civilization*, edited by Dun J. Li, 187–88. Princeton: D. Van Nostrand Co., 1967, 187.

107. Chien, Ssu-ma. "An Introduction to Economics." In *The Essence of Chinese Civilization*, edited by Dun J. Li, 314–16. Princeton: D. Van Nostrand Co., Inc., 1967.
108. Chien, "An Introduction to Economics," 314–16.
109. Chien, "An Introduction to Economics," 314.
110. Smith, Adam. *An Inquiry into the Nature and Causes of the Wealth of Nations*. Edited by Edwin Cannan. New York: Modern Library, 1937, 140.
111. "The Debate on Salt and Iron," Document 7 in Buckley, Patricia, ed. *Chinese Civilization and Society: A Sourcebook* New York: Free Press, 1981, 26.
112. "The Debate on Salt and Iron," Document 7 in Buckley, Patricia, ed. *Chinese Civilization and Society: A Sourcebook* New York: Free Press, 1981, 24.
113. Boulnois, *Silk Road*, 59–74.
114. Boulnois, *Silk Road*, 95–96.
115. Franklin, Daniel. *The World in 2006*. London: The Economist, 2005, 34.

NOTES TO CHAPTER 9

1. Sibaja, Marco. "South American union is created," *Los Angeles Times* (May 25, 2008, A4; Feng Tao (ed.) "Unasur to boost financial self-sufficiency in S. America."
2. Bras, Stephen. "Guadalajara to Winnipeg: The Progress of the Mid-Continent Trade Corridor," and Parsons, Graham. "Pacific Crossroads: Canada's Gateways and Corridors," from The Association for Canadian Studies in the United States (ACSUS) 19th Biennial Conference, Toronto, Ontario, Canada (November 17, 2007). Bras works with the International Affairs and Trade Department, Kansas City; Parsons is with The Organization for Western Economic Cooperation.
3. Blank and Parsons, 19th ACSUS Biennial Conference (Toronto, Ontario, Canada), November 17, 2007.
4. Professors Wise and Glob, personal interviews by Neil Earle, who helped with the editing of this book, November 16, 2007.
5. Wing-Tsit Chan in Morton, W. Scott and Charlton M. Lewis' *China: Its History and Culture* (New York: McGraw-Hill, Inc., 1995), xiii–xiv.
6. Although some might dissent, the U.S. economy has benefited from robust strong military spending since WWII ("military Keynesianism"). The U.S and Canada, almost alone of the major economies, emerged from WWII stronger than in 1939. Later, the Korean War, Vietnam, the Cold War, Star Wars, and Desert Storm all provided considerable boosts to the U.S. economy. In addition, military R&D spending was a key factor in America dominating the high tech era. There are resonances here with Rome's Legionary Capitalism.
7. Zakaria, Fareed. "Is America in Decline: Why the United States Will Survive the Rise of the Rest," *Foreign Affairs* (May–June 2008), 42–43.
8. Others have offered up different definitions of eras of globalization, the most popular seems to be two eras. Michael Bordo, economics professor at Rutgers, suggests: "The record reveals two ages of pervasive globalization: from the mid-nineteenth century until 1914 and since the early 1970's" in his article, "Globalization in historical perspective: Our era is not as unique as we might think, and current trends are not irreversible," *Business Economics*, January 2002, pp. 20–29. Others sharing this view include Barry Eichengreen and Harold James, of the University of California, Berkeley, and Princeton University, respectively in their paper, "Monetary and Financial Reform in Two Eras of Globalization," a revised version of a

paper prepared for the NBER Conference on the History of Globalization, Santa Barbara, 4–6 May 2001. NBER is the National Bureau of Economic Research.

9. See Wallerstein, Immanuel Maurice. *The Capitalist World-Economy*. Cambridge University Press, 1979 for an influential collection of Wallerstein's essays on the working of capitalism as a world system over historical time. The 1970s offer a focus on his key themes of conflicts between core and periphery and bourgeois and proletarian.

10. Arrighi is an Egyptian born Neo-Marxist author of more than 30 books. Among his best known books are *The Dynamics of Global Crisis*, with Andre Gunder Frank and Immanuel Wallerstein, London: Macmillan, 1982 and *La question paysanne et le capitalisme* with Kostas Vergopoulos, Paris: Editions Anthropos-Edep, 1974.

11. See Andre Gunder Frank and Barry Gills seminal study of systems-theory *The World System: Five Hundred Years or Five Thousand?* London: Rutledge, 1993. The editors argue for the interconnectedness of historical patterns over five millennia, rather than just since the rise of modernity. It includes a forward by William H. McNeill and contributions by Immanuel Wallerstein and Samir Amin.

12. Roy B. Norton, personal interview with Neil Earle, copyeditor of this book, at an academic conference, November 16, 2007.

13. See Mark Steyn's *American Alone: The End of the World as We Know It*, Washington: Regnery, 2006, which paints quite a frightening picture of demographics and their impact on the West.

14. Zakaria, Fareed. "The Rise of the Rest," *Newsweek* (May 12, 2008), 24–31. This excerpts the author's 2008 bestseller *The Post-American World*, which argues that the U.S. is still in a powerful position to shape the multi-polar world that gas emerged.

15. This point was in part inspired by an opinion piece in the *New York Times*, November 26, 2006, "The Education of Robert Kennedy," by David Brooks, a leading columnist for the *New York Times*.

16. Brooks, "The Education of Robert Kennedy."

17. In the U.S., there has been relentless criticism of the second Bush Administration on this score.

18. On strategy and leadership, see former McKinsey consultant Partha Bose's *Alexander the Great's Art of Strategy*, New York: Gotham Books, 2004.

19. See Diamond, Jared. *Collapse: How Societies Choose to Fail or Succeed*, New York: Viking, 2004.

20. Gary Hamel, an insightful writer on business strategy, has discussed how allowing new voices into the process of innovation development is one of the most important ways forward for those corporations looking for greater innovation. One of the greats in the field of innovation, Eric von Hippel of MIT, in his classic book on the subject, Sources of Innovation, has identified end-user innovation as, by far, the most important and critical source of new ideas. In our experience, end-users are voices that are often overlooked when corporations think about new products and other innovations. In *Medici Effect: What Elephants and Epidemics Can Teach Us About Innovation* (Harvard Business School Press, 2006) thinker Frans Johansson points us back to the time of the Medici family of Renaissance Italy and how their patronage helped develop European arts and culture. As the Roman leap into naval power showed in their death struggle with Carthage, great innovations often occur along unfamiliar lines of difference.

21. Moore, Karl and David Lewis. *Birth of the Multinational: 2000 Years of Ancient Business History.* Copenhagen Business School Press, 1999, and Moore and Lewis, Foundations of Corporate Empire.

22. In "Globalization for Whom?" Dani Rorik, writing in Harvard magazine (July–August, 2002) made the salient point of how following fully evolved strategies from the "have" nations—exemplified in the WTO and the IMF—can gave a deleterious affect on smaller, struggling economies (29–31). A more strident similar point was made by Kishore Mahbubani's "The Case Against the West: America and Europe in the Asian Century." See *Foreign Affairs* (May–June 2008), 111–124.

23. Ouchi, William. *Theory Z: How American Businesses Can Meet the Japanese Challenge.* Reading, MA: Addison-Wesley, 1981; Pascale, Richard and Anthony Athos, *The Art of Japanese Management: Applications for American Executives.* New York: Simon and Schuster, 1981.

24. Portions of this paragraph are adapted from our previous book, *Foundations of Corporate Empire.* This quote is from page 287.

25. At least, that is view at the time of writing this book. For example, see the *Wall Street Journal Asia* article by Greg Hitt and Neil King, Jr., "U.S. vote tests free trade—Democrats' majority in Congress imperils some pending deals," 13 November 2006, page 11. The authors say "Democrats' stances against free trade helped build the party's success at the polls and could tip the balance on trade matters. The new dynamic could put a definitive end to the already troubled effort to reach a global agreement to reduce tariffs and open markets, known as the Doha round."

26. Cohen, Roger. "The new bipolar world China vs. America Globalist," *International Herald Tribune,* 22 November 2006.

27. Traub, James. "China's African Adventure," *Sunday New York Times Magazine,* November 19, 2006, 74–82.

28. Fareed Zakaria, 'The World bails Us Out,' *Newsweek,* Feb 4/08, page 44

29. Sweden in later 2006 elected a more conservative government, nevertheless one that pledged to retain much of the famed Swedish welfare system. See Sherwood, Joel and Terence Roth. "Sweden faces overhaul—Ruling party's loss opens door for sales of state-held assets", *Wall Street Journal Europe,* 19 September 2006, 12. All this "despite an economy growing at its fastest pace in six years and strong state finances." Sweden has changed yet is still considerably different from the Anglo-American model.

30. The Economics Editor of the *Times of London* in an October 30, 2006 article, entitled, "After dawns, a Truly Rising Sun has Come at Last," reported that, "Japan is back. After a 'lost decade' mired in the economic trap of deflation, protracted bouts of recession, and repeated failures to secure a sustained recovery, the world's second-largest economy at last seems to have embarked on a fully fledged resurgence. Japan is set to record a fourth consecutive year of continuing growth at or above its long-term 'trend' rate. GDP should expand this year by about 2.7 per cent, on the heels of a 2.6 per cent gain last year." Times' Gary Duncan concludes, "After false dawns, a truly rising sun has come at last," in "Japan: The Renaissance", page 43.

31. Hutton, Will. "America's Global Hand." *The American Prospect,* Vol. 11. No. 2, December 6, 1999. This insight may now be dated.

32. Janice Gross Stein and Eugene Lang, *The Unexpected War: Canada in Khandahar,* Toronto: Viking Canada, 2007, 301–302.

33. Rugman, Alan. *The End of Globalization,* New York: American Management Association, 2001; Moore, Karl and Alan Rugman, "Think Regional, Act Local, Forget Global," *Strategy + Business,* Summer, 2004.

34. In March 2007, Swedish Prime Minster Fredrik Reinfeldt announced in an op-ed piece that the four parties in his center–right coalition had agreed to abolish the country's 60-year-old tax on the net personal wealth in the forthcoming budget. The result of this tax had been that some of Sweden's brightest lights, like Bjorn Bork, Ikea founder Ingvar Kamprad, and ABBA's Bjorn Ulvaeus had fled their homeland to be tax exiles. Welcomed by conservative newspaper around the world, was a bold change to Sweden's traditional approach.
35. From, Pilling, David. "Relations With the US: Backlash against 'reckless' drift," *Financial Times.com*, November 6, 2006.
36. This last paragraph draws on Martin Gannon's book on national cultures, *Understanding Global Cultures: Metaphorical Journeys Through 28 Nations, Clusters of Nations, and Continents*, 3rd edition. Sage, 2003.

Index